Exploring Wines & Spirits

Also published by the Wine & Spirit Education Trust

Behind the Label

EXPLORING WINES & SPIRITS

CHRISTOPHER FIELDEN
in association with
THE WINE & SPIRIT EDUCATION TRUST

with a Foreword by
HUGH JOHNSON

Erratum

An error has appeared in the Champagne maturation paragraph of Exploring Wines & Spirits.

The fourth sentence of paragraph five on page 289 of Exploring Wines & Spirits should be amended to read:

For non-vintage Champagne, it has to be a minimum of fifteen months and for vintage Champagne at least three **years**.

PUBLISHED BY
THE WINE & SPIRIT EDUCATION TRUST

Wine & Spirit Education Trust,
1 Queen Street Place, London EC4R 1QS

Registered Charity Number 313766

First Published 1994

Reprinted 1994, 1995, 1997

© Wine & Spirit Education Trust 1994

ISBN 0 9517936 4 0

British Library Cataloguing-in-Publication Data.
A catalogue record for this book is available from the British Library.

Designed by Colin Hall and Partners, London WC2H 9PA

Typeset in Palatino by Discript, London WC2N 4BL

Printed in Hong Kong by Mandarin Offset

Cover illustration by Caroline Church

To

David Burroughs

and

Francis Montague Jones

FOREWORD

Why is London still called the world's wine capital? Why does Britain have a taste for wine as catholic and demanding as any nation's?

The reasons go far back into history. But they are renewed with each new generation.

For centuries we have traded with what we still tend to regard as the more fortunate lands of the south, where wine is a staple. For three medieval centuries we put down deep roots in western France, united under one crown with our own island. From France, when the tie was broken, we turned to Spain and Portugal, going so far as to remodel their more promising (and more accessible) wines into the Sherry and Port which are essentially British developments, if not inventions.

Not just in London, but in every considerable coastal town we have nurtured a tradition of wine-merchants, from the 8th century winefleet setting out from York to fetch Rhenish from the Rhine, to Chaucer's 'shipman' rolling home from Andalucia to Hull, or Bristol, or Southampton. Chaucer's father was a London vintner, and so, six centuries later, was Ruskin's: also in the Sherry trade.

Empire, of course, made it all easier. The deep pockets of the English 'milord' were as persuasive in Italy as they were in Spain, South Africa – everywhere he went – in conjuring out the best of the crop. Byron put it in a characteristic nutshell:

> 'If England mourns her bleakness we can tell her
> The very best of vineyards is the cellar.'

Perhaps, indeed, it became too easy to carry on comfortable and profitable traditions. Certainly, when the charismatic young Frenchman André Simon arrived in England at the beginning of this century to represent Pommery Champagne, he found the senior members of the London wine trade, with very few exceptions, in a state of 'apathy and ignorance' that 'puzzled and irritated' him. Although young members of the trade were willing and keen to taste and learn, not one of their employers was prepared to take on the role of teacher. Thus in 1908, when the newly-founded Wine Trade Club announced a series of lectures and tastings for its members, only one volunteer appeared; the irrepressible André Simon himself. Later he put down to the need to prepare lectures on every major wine region, in a series that lasted until the outbreak of the first world war, his own remarkably deep and wide-ranging knowledge. It could be said that with his compilation of these pioneering lectures he drafted the curriculum for the 20th century wine trade. Certainly he anticipated the foundation of the Institute of Masters of Wine by 45 years, and the Wine & Spirit Education Trust by 61.

How different the high-tech wine world of the end of the 20th century. Today's curriculum is both spectacularly wider and infinitely deeper in scope. The average well-informed consumer today knows as much as a professional did, not eighty, but only perhaps forty, years ago. To be a professional in the wine trade today is more exacting by far than it has ever been – and correspondingly, of course, that much more rewarding.

Hence the need for this new textbook of the modern wine world, which I have every pleasure in commending. It sets out crisply and clearly, but always with humour and humanity, the ground-rules by which a modern wine-merchant must operate – both legally and commercially.

The Higher Certificate Candidates, not only from these shores but from more and more countries, who in the course of their studies will get to know this book backwards, will be thoroughly grateful for such a lucid, precise and pithy textbook.

Hugh Johnson

CONTENTS

ACKNOWLEDGEMENTS

The authors would like to acknowledge the invaluable assistance given by all those who have been involved in the production of this book.

Particular thanks are due to the late Francis Montague Jones for his guidance and editorial work on the early versions of the manuscript and to Cornelia Bauer for her detailed research and to Jan Wrigley for her welcome guidance. Thanks are also due to David Bird MW for his advice on the technical chapters and to John Boodle of the Wine Standards Board of the Vintners Company for his careful checking of the labelling information.

We are grateful to the various wine promotional bodies and commercial offices who have always been willing to help, in particular the Australian Wine Bureau, the Champagne Bureau, Food & Wine From France, the German Wine Information Service, the Greek Wine Bureau, the Italian Institute for Foreign Trade, the New Zealand Wine Guild, the Portuguese Government Trade Office, the Sherry Institute, Wines of South Africa, Wines From Spain and the Wine Institute of California.

A debt of gratitude is owed to Colin Hall and Partners for their efforts in converting the raw manuscript into its present form, and particularly Andy Sumner for his design work.

The authors also acknowledge the assistance given by Caxton Tower Wines in granting access to their tasting room for the photograph on page 50; Denbies Vineyard in granting permission to photograph their annual pruning; Château Loudenne for the use of the *Courbes de Fermentation*; Waverley Vintners, Bulgarian Vintners and La Gerla Estate for the use of examples of their labels.

Photographic Credits:
20, 22, 37, G. Spence private collection; 47, Pall Process; 89, 94, 96, Sopexa/Food & Wine From France; 134, 137, 140, Mick Rock/Cephas; 150, D. Wrigley, private collection; 163, G. Spence private collection; 257, Richard Bamfield/Brown Brothers; 264, Kevin Judd/New Zealand Wine Guild; 291, CIVC; 305, The Sherry Institute of Spain; 321, 322, 325, 348, G. Spence private collection. All other photographs are from the Wine & Spirit Education Trust picture library and were taken by members of the Trust staff.

INTRODUCTION

Since it was founded almost twenty-five years ago, with the motto *Gustibus mens dat incrementum* (Knowledge enhances sensory perception) the Wine & Spirit Education Trust has been the principal source of product knowledge for those employed in the Drinks Industry in the United Kingdom. In that time over 100,000 candidates have sat examinations at one of three progressive levels: Certificate, Higher Certificate and Diploma. The Trust is dedicated to the highest standards, not only those it sets for the candidates coming forward for its examinations, but also in the support it gives to course tutors and students.

In this latter context, the provision of sound, cost-effective study materials is an important priority. At the Certificate and Higher Certificate levels, the cornerstone of the students' Study Pack is the course textbook. In 1989, the Trust took the opportunity to publish a new textbook for the Certificate course, *Introducing Wines and Spirits and associated beverages*, since relaunched as *Behind the Label*, which has received wide acclaim as an approachable introduction to a large subject. The next logical step was to adopt the same approach when the Higher Certificate textbook was due for renewal. The result is before you.

This book's predecessor, *Wine Regions of the World*, by David Burroughs and Norman Bezzant, has had a remarkably good run, going through two editions and eight reprints. At each stage the chance was seized to keep it up to date. Eventually, and especially in such a fast changing environment as the international wine and spirit industry, a fresh start was called for. *Exploring Wines & Spirits* is therefore a totally new book, with fresh text, maps, colour illustrations and a sequence of chapters that closely follows the Higher Certificate syllabus.

There is a wealth of information in this book, partly as a result of frequent comments made by employers concerning the gap between Higher Certificate and Diploma. *Exploring Wines & Spirits* aims to cover the Higher Certificate syllabus thoroughly, and to act as a "springboard" for those students progressing towards Diploma. Those readers whose immediate concern is success in the Higher Certificate Examination should therefore take note of the frequent inclusion of "Key Lists" throughout the text, which will remind students of the priority knowledge required in each area.

A book such as this cannot be the sole source of information and guidance for a candidate preparing for the Higher Certificate award. Use of the other elements of the Higher Certificate Study Pack, especially the syllabus, the extra maps and the self-test questions and answers will assist, but students should still read around the subject as far as possible, if only to ensure that they keep up to date.

And there is one thing that this book cannot do. It cannot reproduce the myriad hues, aromas and sensations available in the wines that emanate from the millions of vineyards spread across the globe; it cannot replicate the simple pleasure of a glass of wine. But in seeking to explore the reasons why the wide variety of wines in the world all taste as they do, I hope it will enhance your perceptions of the wines you come across, be you interested amateur or trade professional.

Peter Hasslacher
Chairman of Trustees
Wine and Spirit Education Trust

CHAPTER 1

VITICULTURE

The making of wine falls into two parts, the growing of the grapes, or viticulture, and the turning of those grapes into wine, vinification. Grapes are grown for a number of purposes other than for the making of wine (table-grapes, dried fruit and jams are just three) but they do not concern us here.

TIIE VINE

The grape is the fruit of the vine, a member of the Ampelidaceae family. The *Vitis* genus of that family is split into a number of species and of these, just one, the *Vitis vinifera*, literally the wine vine, most concerns us, for more than 99% of all wines consumed in the world are made from this species. All the familiar grape names like Chardonnay and Cabernet Sauvignon, are varieties of *V. vinifera*.

The origins of *V. vinifera* are confused. It would appear that it has evolved over many thousands of years from wild vines growing in Central Asia. Over this time something over one thousand recognisably distinct varieties of wine-producing grape have developed; each of these will have its own idiosyncrasies that enable it to play its part in wine-production in some corner of the world's vineyards.

Other members of the *Vitis* genus do have minor walk-on parts to play in the world of wine, however: *V. labrusca* grapes are used for wine-making in New York State, Madeira and Russia, *V. riparia* and *V. rupestris* often provide the rootstock on to which *V. vinifera* scions are grafted (see below). These species are of American origin, having been imported to Europe initially in the 19th century. Wine produced from their fruit has an unpleasant flavour, described as "foxy".

Vine Development
The crucial factor in the development of modern viticulture came with the wholesale destruction of European vineyards by the phylloxera aphid (see page 15) in the second half of the nineteenth century. As *V. vinifera* vines were killed off by the louse, growers rapidly had to find alternative vines to produce the necessary grapes. They first turned to the American *V. labrusca* vines, which were known to be tolerant of

phylloxera, but the inherent flavours in the grapes for the most part proved unacceptable.

Hybrids
The next stage was to try breeding in the American vines' tolerance by crossing *V. vinifera* and American species. Vines are mostly self-pollinating but to produce a crossing, the vine-breeder has to take pollen from one variety or species, pollinate a second and plant out the resulting seeds. Such vines have been found to have individual merits, for example, the large yields of the Noah, or the ability to ripen in cool climates of the Seyval Blanc. The result of such a crossing, involving two species, is known as a hybrid or interspecific crossing. Unfortunately it has been found that, with only a few exceptions, such as the Seyval Blanc, the foxy taste is not eradicated. Because of this no quality wine may be made from hybrid varieties within the EC, but there is no doubt that certain hybrids have a major role to play in the global wine picture, particularly where winemaking may be difficult, and they are capable of producing excellent wines.

Eventually it was discovered that the European *V. vinifera* could be grafted on to American rootstocks, and would thereby be protected.

Clones
A more recent extension of vine knowledge has been the emphasis on clonal selection. In this process, plants of a particular variety are selected from existing vines for certain individual characteristics (which might be finesse, high yields, good colour, early ripening, disease resistance and so on). Individual vines that show the desired characteristics are used to take cuttings which are then grafted, planted out and further assessed. This selection process may cover several generations. Commercial propagation is then carried out by cuttings to maintain fidelity.

Crossings
In parallel with clonal selection, there has been much work on developing new varieties of *V. vinifera* by crossing. The Germans have been in the forefront of this, and crossings such as Müller-Thurgau and Scheurebe are now widely planted. The Davis campus of the University of California has also developed varieties such as Centurion and Emerald Riesling to meet local needs. The German crossings have generally been for cool climates, and the Californian for hot. To save confusion, a crossing of two varieties of *V. vinifera* is simply referred to as a crossing, not a hybrid.

Grafting
Though there are considerable areas in Chile, California, Hungary and

TYPES OF GRAFT

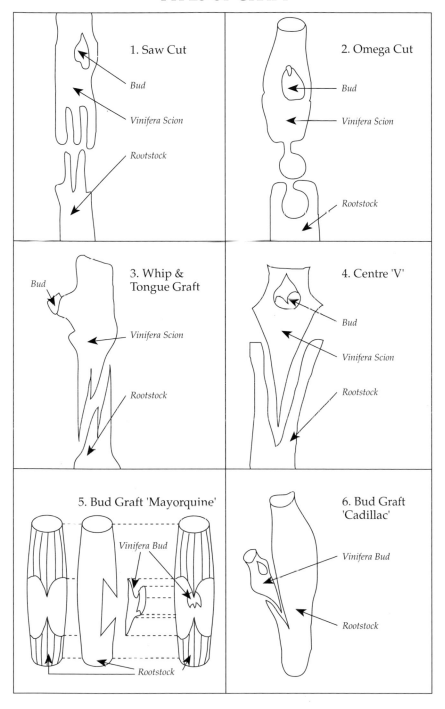

South Australia, for example, where grafting is not essential, most vineyards are now planted with grafted vines because of phylloxera. As a result, each vine consists of two parts: the rootstock of an American species and the scion of the desired *V. vinifera* variety. Most grafting is now carried out by a machine such as the "Omega", in a vine nursery. This and other grafting styles are illustrated on page 3. The choice of the rootstock is just as important as the scion, for it has to be adapted to the soil and the climate of the vineyard and to the *V. vinifera* variety. Each region will have its preferred rootstocks. Major vineyards will have their own nurseries where the vine propagation is carried out.

Selection of Grape Variety
There are more than a thousand varieties of grapes used for making wine throughout the world but many of these have little more than local relevance. There are, however, a number which have a global reputation, either because they are grown throughout the world, or because they are a major constituent in a classic wine. Amongst these, the most important are listed at the end of this chapter.

In most of the more traditional wine-producing regions of western Europe, the choice of grape variety will be governed by tradition and by law. This can lead to some great wines, which have been made from varieties not traditional to the region, only having the most basic status in the wine hierarchy. This has been particularly the case in Tuscany, for example, where the introduction of Cabernet Sauvignon, by certain growers, led to a number of very expensive *vini da tavola* being created. In some cases wine laws are revised to accommodate these "new" wines.

The selection of grapes for a particular site has often been based on the characteristics of the vines themselves. The annual cycle of a vine's growth will vary slightly from one variety to another. Certain varieties will bud later than most, some will ripen earlier or later than others. Different vine varieties are, therefore, suited to different sites. For example, in the frost-prone Marne valley in the Champagne region, the Pinot Meunier variety is preferred as it buds a few days later than Pinot Noir, making it less susceptible to spring frosts. In Germany Riesling produces the best wines but sometimes ripens so late that the crop is spoiled by bad autumn weather; in order to guarantee a harvest many growers have planted the earlier ripening Müller-Thurgau.

In those countries where wine legislation is less stringent there is much more flexibility as to the selection of varieties. In California, for example, it is not strange to see grapes native to a number of different regions, soils and climates in France, growing side by side.

CLIMATE

Historically vines were cultivated near to the market for the wines they produced. For example, Paris was surrounded by vineyards which no longer exist. These made wines for those who could not afford the fine wines of Burgundy and Champagne, whose prices were often inflated by transport costs. Similarly, in medieval times, many monasteries in Britain would have their own vineyard to provide communion wine. Now, with the coming of railways, fast shipping services and good road networks, vineyards have been planted with more thought to their suitability for viticulture rather than ease of access. One of the factors taken into account is the climate of the region.

For grapes to ripen satisfactorily, a minimum of 1500 hours sunshine is normally required. To ripen fully, red grapes need more heat and sunshine than white. This is why most marginal vineyard areas, those close to the limits of vine cultivation such as Germany and England, are planted more with white varieties and those reds that are grown are usually early-ripening varieties.

For a vine to grow satisfactorily, it also needs to absorb considerable amounts of water over the year, normally at least 700 mm of rain, although some cooler regions exist on less. In drier regions outside the EC this is often replaced through irrigation, which is forbidden within the EC except for young vines and experimental vineyards.

Although wild vines grow widely throughout the world, commercial vineyard areas are concentrated in two broad bands in the northern and southern hemispheres, roughly between 30 and 50° latitude. It is here the correct balance between warmth and coldness, sunshine and rainfall, can be found to create the ideal growing conditions for the vine and ripening conditions for its fruit. North and south of these bands it is too cold to ripen grapes, and between them there is no cold season to give the vines a chance to rest. Factors other than latitude also affect the climate, allowing vineyards to be planted in the UK at latitudes of 51 °N or in sub-tropical parts of South America.

Climatic conditions can be classified in a number of ways, two of which are used in viticulture. European Community vineyard regions are zoned, with, for example, the cooler, northern vineyards in Britain and most of Germany being in Zone A and those in the south of Europe being classed as Zone C IIIb. Permitted must treatments (see chapter 2) vary according to the zone. For example, in Zone A the alcoholic content of a wine may, in poor years, be increased by up to 4.5% by chaptalisation, and the wines can be de-acidified; whereas in southern Italy (Zone CIII b) tartaric acid may be added but de-acidification and chaptalisation are forbidden. Zones A and B are not sub-divided; Zone C is divided into

THE WORLD WINE PRODUCING AREAS

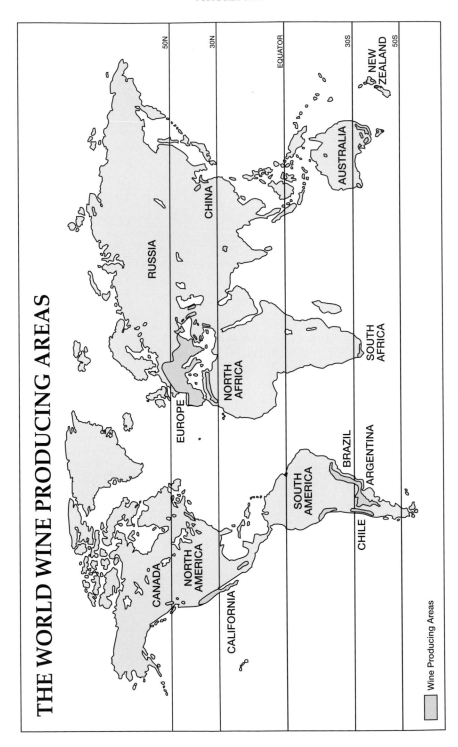

50N

30N

EQUATOR

30S

50S

CANADA

NORTH AMERICA

CALIFORNIA

RUSSIA

CHINA

EUROPE

NORTH AFRICA

AUSTRALIA

NEW ZEALAND

SOUTH AFRICA

SOUTH AMERICA

BRAZIL

ARGENTINA

CHILE

Wine Producing Areas

five, designated C Ia, C Ib, C II, CIIIa and C IIIb, allowing finer definition of the rules.

In many New World regions the climate is classified using the degree-day system, originated by the University of California, Davis. The system works on the principle of heat summation, whereby the average daily temperature is multiplied by the number of days in the growing season (April to October in the northern hemisphere), giving a figure that allows different regions to be compared. As the vine does not grow when the temperature is less than 10 °C only the temperatures above this value are considered.

Both systems have their uses in comparing one region with another but neither can totally define the climate as they do not take all the climatic factors into consideration.

Proximity to large bodies of water will moderate the climate, so, for example, the vineyards of Bordeaux, close to the Atlantic, have a maritime climate of warm summers and cool winters, less extreme than the harsh continental climate, of extreme summer heat yet cold winters, experienced by the landlocked vineyards of La Mancha in central Spain.

In winter and spring rivers help to reduce the damage caused by frost as the movement of water keeps the surrounding air moving. Water will increase the humidity and thereby can help create the ideal conditions for noble rot, the essential factor in the production of the finest sweet light wines.

Topography and altitude will also affect the climate. Mountains can be the source of cold winds, such as the Mistral that blows through the northern Rhône, whilst temperature drops with increasing altitude, so vineyards planted at high altitude will be cooler than the latitude might indicate.

A region will have an overall climate but individual vineyard sites have their own climatic conditions, often differing from one vineyard to the next. These microclimates might better suit a particular vineyard for the production of higher quality wine than its neighbour.

In more marginal vineyard areas it is essential that the vine receives the maximum amount of sunshine during the growing period. In this, the individual contours of a slope can have a considerable effect by increasing the vines' exposure to the sun. In areas at the extreme northern boundary of vine cultivation the aspect of a vineyard can increase the exposure and thereby significantly improve the ripeness of the resulting grapes. An example of this is the Mosel valley where the best vineyards are planted on very steep south-facing slopes.

Prevailing winds also may play an important role, either favourable or unfavourable. Many fine vineyard areas would not exist if they were not protected from them by mountain ranges or forests.

SOIL

The question of the role that soil composition plays in the quality of a wine is one that is becoming more widely discussed. As a broad generalisation, it can be said that certain grapes seem to be suited to certain soils. The most important factor, however, is that the soil drains well. Poor wine comes from vines with "damp feet".

The best wines are often those that come from stressed vines, those which have to fight for their existence. If the soil is poor the vine will send its roots deep down into the subsoil to find water and nutrients, collecting trace elements and minerals as it does so and thereby improving the quality of the fruit. On rich soil the roots tend to grow laterally, finding fewer minerals. There is a tendency for the vine to overcrop in richer soils, diluting the quality of fruit. Vineyards are often planted on soil so poor that it would not support other crops.

Classic wines are often produced as the result of a happy three-way marriage of soil, climate and grape variety, a combination the French call *terroir*. For example, gravel, temperate maritime conditions and the Cabernet Sauvignon grape combine to produce the great wines of the Médoc, whereas Gamay is associated with a warm climate and granite in Beaujolais, and Riesling with slate in the cool vineyards of the Mosel. Many New World viticulturists believe that the soil is of less importance than their European counterparts think, their theory being that, provided the soil is well drained, its composition does not affect the style of the wine.

VINEYARD OPERATIONS

Planting
A grower may plant a vine for two reasons: either to establish a new vineyard, though with overproduction in the Community this is unlikely in Europe, or to replace old vines which have been grubbed up.

The life of a vine can be long; there are century-old vines still in production in California, Australia and the Muscadet region. Generally speaking, the older the vine is, the finer the wine it produces. However, there is a price to pay as the older the vine is, the lower its yield. The main aim of any grower is to produce a profit, so a balance has to be reached between quantity and quality. Each grower has to decide the optimum age for his or her vines, when he will grub them up. Generally, this will happen when they are between 35 and 50 years old. Normally he will rotate his replanting programme so as to have most of his domain still in production. Often the land will be left fallow for three years or so, and this too has to be taken into consideration.

Once again, in western Europe, tradition and legislation have a large part to play in how a vineyard is planted, though there are a number of local factors that might have to be taken into consideration. These might include the steepness of the plot on which the vines are being planted, the form of pruning that is to be used, whether the vineyard is to be cultivated mechanically or not and whether the grapes are to be picked by hand or machine.

Before the young vines are planted, the soil has to be prepared to a fine tilth. The young vines might be protected against weeds by covering the ground around the vine with black plastic sheeting or from animals by individual guards on each vine. The first yield normally comes in the third year from planting and in many areas the first fruit is forbidden for the making of wine.

The density of the planting might vary from three thousand vines per hectare, up to ten thousand or more. Apart from the factors listed above, this decision will be based on how much stress the grower wants to place upon the vines; the theory being the more vines per hectare, the greater the stress, the better the wine that is produced. Low density planting is cheaper initially as fewer vines have to be bought and planted.

Once established the vine's shape will be governed by the way in which the vine grower prunes and trains it, but every vine has certain distinct parts:

Roots
Trunk
Cane/spur
Shoots
Flowers/fruit
Leaves

The *V. vinifera* scion which, in time, forms the vine's trunk, is the visible part of the vine, with the graft usually just above ground level. Shoots, bearing tendrils and leaves, grow from the scion. These shoots will mature and become orange-brown over the course of the following winter, at which point they are called canes. Buds will form where the previous season's leaves joined the cane, and these are the source of the new shoots. A cane will have between eight and fifteen buds, each of which will form a shoot. The vine's flowers, and therefore fruit, will develop on shoots formed in the spring of the same year. If a cane is pruned short, to only two or three buds, it is referred to as a spur. By the end of the next year the canes and spurs are old wood and are often removed at pruning, with new replacement canes or spurs having been allowed to grow.

When a vineyard is replanted there is a long period of disruption, during which grapes cannot be produced. To reduce the financial burden of this, head-grafting is becoming more popular in New World vineyards. This is when the variety of a vine can be changed by re-grafting on to mature vines in the vineyards. This makes it easier for the producer to react quickly to the demands of the market.

Pruning

An integral part of the legislation for most quality wine areas in Europe is the way in which the vine will be pruned and trained. The object of the main, winter, pruning is generally twofold: to position the buds that will form shoots for the production of fruit in this particular harvest, and to prepare the vine for fruiting in future harvests. Pruning will also be used to restrict or optimize the final yield by controlling the number of buds, and therefore the potential quantity, and therefore quality, of fruit produced. Further roles of pruning throughout the growing season might be:

the restriction of vegetation, to concentrate the vigour of the vine into production of fruit;

to control the leaf canopy so that the bunches of grapes have the optimum exposure to (or shade from) the sun, and aeration to limit potential fungal infection;

to keep the vineyard tidy to ease work throughout the growing season and vintage.

Most quality wine regions will have maximum yield figures as part of their legislation. For example, in Alsace, the base figure for Pinot Noir is 80 hectolitres of wine per hectare (hl/ha), whilst in Romanée-Conti in Burgundy, the equivalent figure is 35 hl/ha. The difference in yields will

Guyot pruning, before and after, showing the amount of wood removed.

be reflected in the fruit concentration, and therefore relative quality, of the two wines. By leaving fewer buds on the canes the Burgundian grower will restrict the number of shoots and therefore the number of bunches of grapes produced.

There are two basic types of pruning: spur, in which a number of short, two to three bud spurs are left on the vine, and cane, where one or two longer canes, each of eight to twelve buds are left (see illustration).

Training

Once the vine has been pruned, any remaining canes will then be trained. The training system used will relate to the type of pruning employed. In some areas, the vines will be free-standing, and in others, they will be trained along wires. With the advent of machine picking, wire training is becoming more common, as is wider spacing between the rows of vines.

BUSH (SPUR) PRUNING

Vine pruned where shown to leave sufficient 2-3 bud spurs to maintain the number of fruiting shoots.

GUYOT TRAINING SEQUENCE

A mature double Guyot vine before pruning

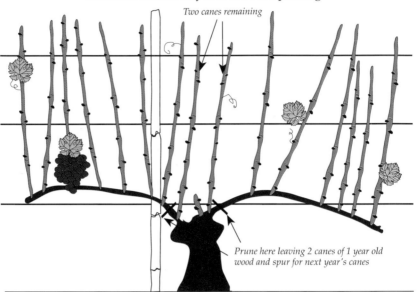

Two canes remaining

Prune here leaving 2 canes of 1 year old wood and spur for next year's canes

The same vine after pruning, double Guyot trained

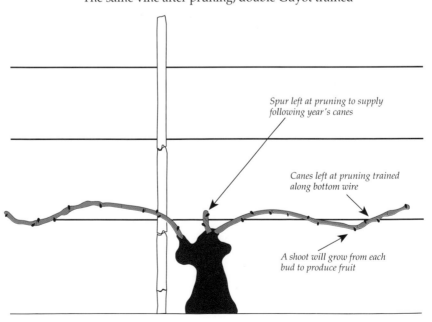

Spur left at pruning to supply following year's canes

Canes left at pruning trained along bottom wire

A shoot will grow from each bud to produce fruit

HIGH CORDON TRAINING

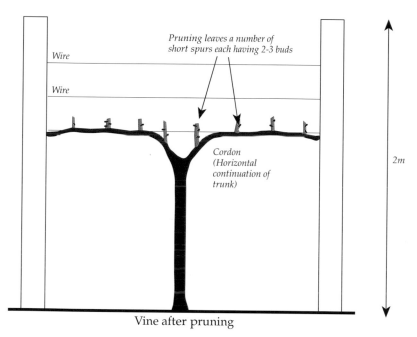

Pruning leaves a number of short spurs each having 2-3 buds

Wire

Wire

Cordon
(Horizontal
continuation of
trunk)

2m

Vine after pruning

Shoots develop from each bud

Fruit
zone

2m

The same vine, fully grown

The training of the vine, too, varies greatly according to such factors as the climate, the vineyard and the yield required. Vines may be trained low to benefit from reflected heat or to avoid wind-damage. They may be grown high, away from reflected heat from the ground. This also has the advantage of increasing the air circulation and minimising rot in humid conditions.

There are three main systems for training vines:

1. _The bush system, with its common variation the gobelet._ This spur-pruned system is used in warmer vineyard regions such as those of Beaujolais, the Rhône Valley, the South of France and Spain. As air circulation is poor, this is not suitable for damp vineyard regions, where rot may be a problem, nor is it advisable for areas which suffer from spring frosts as the vines are close to the ground. The vines are free-standing and there are normally four to five spurs left around the head of the vine trunk. In the gobelet system, the shoots are tied together at their tips.

2. _The replacement cane system, which includes the Guyot, as practised in Burgundy and Bordeaux._ Here canes are trained along lateral wires, with new producing canes being used each year: one in the case of Guyot simple, two in the case of Guyot double.

3. _The cordon spur system is most often used in vineyards fully adapted for mechanisation._ The trunk of the vine is developed horizontally, with a number of spurs left along its length. This may be a low cordon, as in the Cordon de Royat system in Champagne, or high, as in the Geneva Double Curtain system.

PROBLEMS FOR THE VINE

As with any other agricultural product the vine is susceptible to a variety of hazards. These can be grouped under four headings: soil, weather conditions, pests and disease.

Soil

It is essential that the best grape variety and the ideal rootstock are chosen for the soil in the vineyard. Whilst, for example, Chardonnay produces its finest wines on chalky soil, that soil can make the vine susceptible to chlorosis, a malady of the vine caused by a lack of free iron, particularly prevalent in lime-rich soils. The vine's leaves yellow and yields drop as photosynthesis is reduced. Careful selection of suitable rootstock is the best solution, but in an established vineyard the soil can be treated with ferrous sulphate.

Mineral deficiencies in soil can be minimised by judicious fertiliser application.

Weather Conditions

Frost

Frosts can be a hazard in both winter and spring. Winter frosts only cause damage if very severe, but can kill the vines; the simplest protection against this is earthing up. Spring frosts are a particular hazard in the more temperate vineyard regions, when damage occurs to the young and delicate buds. Traditionally protection was by lighting smudge-pots, which generated smoke and kept frost at bay, now replaced by heaters, when frosts are forecast. In parts of California, wind-machines are common.

Alternatively, many vineyards now employ the aspersion system of frost protection. Sprinkling-systems are installed in the vineyards and, when spring frosts are forecast, the vines are sprayed with water so that the shoots will be protected by an insulating coat of ice.

Drought

Within the European Community irrigation is forbidden except under abnormal circumstances. In the New World it is common and might take one of a number of forms; overhead sprinklers, ground-level drip-irrigation or, as happens in Chile and Argentina, the diversion of streams through the vineyards.

Hail

Summer hail can be very destructive and damaged berries can, in due course, impart a distinctive off-taste to the wine. The best protection is insurance; or sending a plane up to seed the potential storm-clouds with chemicals, so that rain falls rather than hail.

Coulure and millerandage

The vine is a self-pollinating plant but needs warm, dry and breezy weather for the flowers to set and to pollinate successfully. *Coulure* is the term used when the flower does not set, *millerandage* when the fruit fails to set, usually as a result of poor pollination. There are certain grape varieties that are more prone to this problem than others but it is most frequently caused by cold, rainy weather at the crucial relevant development stage.

Pests

Phylloxera vastatrix

This insect, which is a native of the east coast of North America, first reached Europe in 1860. It lives almost exclusively on the vine. Phylloxera has a complicated life cycle, involving winged adults and burrowing larvae. It is the larvae which cause the most damage as they feed on the roots of the vine and, in the case of *V. vinifera*, the sap will drain out through the roots and the vine will die. Native American vines have developed tolerance to phylloxera by forming calluses over the wound to prevent this bleeding. It can also form galls on the underside of the vine's leaves. These galls, which affect American vines more than *V. vinifera*, are not particularly injurious to the vines themselves, but they contain the eggs which become the next generation.

Phylloxera is now endemic throughout most of the world's vineyards. All new plantings will, therefore, be European scions grafted on to American rootstock. Sadly, the aphid has now adapted its lifestyle, and certain rootstocks believed to be phylloxera-resistant and widely planted in California have since not lived up to their expectations, causing serious problems for growers there (see page 270).

Grape moths (Cochylis, Pyralis and Eudemis)
Their caterpillars attack the buds in the spring and the grapes themselves later in the year. Treatment is by spraying the vines with insecticides.

Red spider mite and yellow spider mite
These are most prevalent in hot, dry weather. They have become increasingly common recently because insecticides have killed off their natural predators. They infest the leaves and thus lessen the vegetative growth. They are normally combated with specialist sprays, except in organic vineyards where their predators have been encouraged.

Nematodes
These are microscopic worms that attack the roots of vines. Treatment is very difficult, so prevention is the best measure. This involves totally sanitising the soil before plantation and selecting resistant rootstocks.

Birds and animals
In some countries birds can be very destructive. Often they soon learn to ignore automatic alarms. Netting seems to be the best solution but is expensive. When necessary, vineyards should be fenced as a protection against such animals as badgers, deer and wild boar, which will feed upon ripe grapes.

Disease
In order to minimise vineyard disease, regular sprayings will take place during the growing season. Generally, these will be done by tractors driving through the vineyards, but occasionally, where the vineyards are on steep slopes, or when very rapid action needs to be taken, it will be done by helicopter or plane. Otherwise it will be done on foot.

In most temperate vineyard areas, where there is rainfall during the growing season, something between eight and twelve sprayings will be necessary each year. In more generous climates, with rain-free summers and autumns, much fewer will be needed.

Oidium (powdery mildew)

This fungal disease develops on the leaves of the vine as a white powdery growth of spores and eventually will cause the berries to split. The solution is to spray with sulphur.

Peronospera (downy mildew)

Another fungal disease, affecting the leaves with a downy growth of fungus, and reducing their effectiveness. Originally the only treatment was copper sulphate and lime in solution (Bordeaux mixture), now systemic fungicides

Oidium causes the grapes to split.

are also used and the disease has become less widespread as a result.

Botrytis cinerea (grey rot or noble rot)

Depending on circumstances, it is either welcomed or dreaded by the grower. A fungal disease that is often spread by damp, humid conditions, it presents a bigger problem for black grapes than white as it causes loss of colour in the wine and because of maceration on skins, can lead to off-flavours. As grey rot it tends to affect mostly immature berries. Early treatment by spraying is advised though this has to be completed before the grapes begin to ripen. It can seriously affect both yield and quality.

In the right conditions, essentially damp mornings and dry afternoons, this is the *pourriture noble* or *edelfäule* that is essential for the production of the great sweet white wines of Bordeaux, Germany and elsewhere. In its benevolent form the botrytis will affect ripe grapes, consuming water from the berry by way of microscopic filaments through the pores of the grape-skin. This concentrates the sugars, reducing the grape to a shrivelled raisin. The fact that it is never uniform in its development means that several pickings may be needed to complete the harvest.

Black rot

Yet another fungus, brought on by heavy rain and affecting both the leaves and the grapes. Treatment is by spraying with Bordeaux mixture.

Eutypiose ("Dead-arm" or Eutypa)
This is a fungal infection which appeared for the first time in the vineyards of Burgundy in 1988. This attacks the vine-wood through pruning cuts. No successful treatment has yet been discovered.

Anthracnose
A fungal disease most common in hybrid vines planted in damp soil. It is recognised by stains appearing on the leaves, which eventually become holes. Treatment is as for downy mildew, spraying with Bordeaux mixture.

Court-noué
This is a contagious, viral disease which stunts the growth of the vine and leads to very low yields from ill-formed bunches of grapes. There is no known cure. Infected vines have to be dug up and the land sanitised. It is recommended that it should not be replanted. However, in more expensive vineyard regions this may prove impracticable.

THE VINEYARD CALENDAR

The year for the grower starts immediately after the harvest. When this takes place varies considerably. In France, for example, it will begin in the Midi towards the end of August and will finish in Alsace in November or, occasionally, even later. In the southern hemisphere, the picking may begin in February, with the year's work developing from then.

Each picture of a grower's life must therefore vary, and even within each region it changes rapidly with the arrival of new techniques and more sophisticated modern machinery.

As just one example, therefore, here is what the vineyard year of a grower using the single Guyot training method in northern France might look like.

October:
After the vintage, apart from work in the cellar, the main priority is to clear those vineyards that are going to be replanted, or land that is to be planted for the first time. Also, any unproductive vines within the rows should be uprooted and the soil prepared for their replacement.

The vines' leaves change colour and begin to fall with the first frosts.

November:
Autumn ploughing to break up the soil.

Autumn pruning. The year's producing branch is cut off as are any non-productive canes. The dead shoots are then burnt in portable braziers.

The bases of the vines are earthed up to protect them against winter frosts (*Buttage*).

Any soil that has been washed down the slopes during the previous season has to be carried up again.

The sap falls and the vine is dormant from now until the spring. Shoots lignify to form canes, with embryonic buds at the points where leaves and tendrils grew.

December:
Continuation of November's work.

January:
The beginning of the main pruning. By tradition, in many parts of France, this does not start before the feast-day of the vignerons' patron saint, St Vincent, January 22nd.

Pruning is the most specialised work in the vineyard, for each individual vine has to be treated in its own way – and will be known to the grower. In many ways it is like the education of a child.

February:
Continuation of pruning.

March:
End of pruning.
Spreading of fertiliser.
Grafting of new vines.

The vine sap begins to rise and the first signs of growth will be seen.

April:
The earth is taken away from the bases of the vines (*Debuttage*).

Hoeing, again to break up the soil around the vines.

Tying down of the year's productive cane to the lower wire.

Planting of young vines from the nursery, which were grafted the previous year. These will either be new plantings, or individual replacement vines in the rows.

Spreading of herbicide.

The new season's buds burst, later to become shoots. These buds are easily damaged by frost so various protective measures must be taken in frost-prone areas.

May:
Distinct growth of shoots, first leaves form on the vine, and the cane matures further to form old wood.

Planting of the newly-grafted vine-stock in the nursery.

First spraying against insects and fungal diseases.

Suckers must be removed.

The spreading shoots are brought in within the horizontal wires. This is done for two reasons: it enables the sunlight to reach the nascent bunches better, and it clears the rows for the tractors to pass (*Relevage*).

Copious growth of shoots.

June:
Relevage continued.

The branches are tied to the horizontal wires (*Accolage*).

Spraying.

Sanitising of land cleared for planting.

The vine will normally flower in June in the northern hemisphere.

The vine flowers (*floraison*), and fruit then sets on the shoots. This takes place quite rapidly in ideal conditions, often only taking about a week; but in poor weather can take as long as three weeks, with a knock-on effect on the harvest. As a generalisation, the vintage will take place 100 days from flowering.

July:
Accolage.

Trimming of the vine shoot-tips to see that the maximum amount of nutrient is diverted to the grape-bunches.

Spraying.

Once pollinated the grapes begin to form. These are embryonic Müller-Thurgau grapes.

If the fruit set has been overabundant, the grower may remove surplus bunches to restrict production and increase quality. This may become essential if the maximum yield figure is under pressure.

Vigorous growth of vegetation; berries still small.

August:
Trimming.

Preparation for the vintage: cleaning of press-house and all equipment.

This is the quietest month, as spraying should not be continued in the four weeks up to picking. It is during this month that much basic repair work is done.

SUGAR vs ACID DURING RIPENING

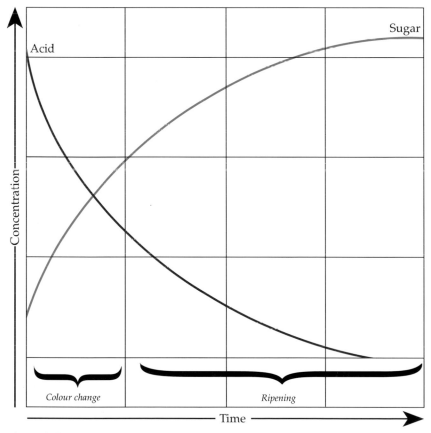

The graph shows the increase in sugar and the decrease in acidity in the last eight weeks of ripening.

About one hundred days from the flowering the grapes are ripe and ready for harvesting.

Early in the month, the grapes take on colour (until this moment, black grapes have been green). Berries swell as they reach maturity (*Veraison*).

September:
Final preparations for vintage continue, the winery equipment will be cleaned and serviced.

Grapes will be tested regularly for sugar content, usually carried out in the vineyard with a refractometer.

Harvesting.

The Vintage
As grapes ripen the sugar content increases as the acidity decreases. Thus, the grower can pick early to maintain acidity in hot years, or delay picking to optimise sugar levels, but with reduced acidity.

The vintage will take place when the grapes reach a desirable level of maturity, though impending unfavourable weather conditions may have to be taken into consideration.

Harvesting can be either by hand or machine, the choice being decided by the type of wine to be made, financial considerations and topography. Machine harvesting requires considerable investment, which can be a problem for smaller producers, unless a group of growers share the harvester, but has the benefit of speed and flexibility, including night harvesting when necessary. Machine harvesters work by shaking the vine and collecting the ripe berries which fall off, leaving the stalks behind. It is, therefore, not selective, taking all the ripe berries from the vines, whether healthy or not, and is only feasible on flat or gently sloping dry land. Manual harvesting is slower, labour intensive and inflexible. It does, however, allow a great deal of selection of the grapes: unripe or rotten grapes can be left on the vine, or conversely, only botrytized fruit selected for dessert wines. Less damage occurs to the grapes as the bunches are harvested whole, complete with the stalks, so it is essential for wines like Lambrusco bianco and Champagne where colour from the skins is unwanted. Hand picking can be done in all terrains; indeed, steep vineyards, such as the Northern Rhône, the Mosel and the Douro, can only be harvested by hand.

From now, the work moves from the vineyard to the cellar.

MAJOR GRAPE VARIETIES

White Grapes

Aligoté
This is an early-ripening variety mainly grown in Burgundy where it produces the Bourgogne Aligoté. The wine is generally high in acidity and for early drinking. The yields are normally high. It is also widely planted in Bulgaria.

Chardonnay (Beaunois [Chablis])
This grape has been described by Jancis Robinson as the happiest of all combinations and has expanded widely from its Burgundian roots, being now planted virtually world-wide. It is at its best on chalky soils, but is liable to suffer from chlorosis and powdery mildew. The yields are moderate and the wine can lose its character when these are pushed too far. It gives wines that normally age well in wood, which gives it a round, buttery flavour.

Chasselas (Dorin, Fendant, Perlan [Switzerland])
Mainly cultivated as a table grape in France, it is used for making lesser wines in Alsace, Pouilly-sur-Loire and Savoie (Crépy). In Switzerland, however, it is a major variety under a selection of regional names. It gives a high yield of light wines.

Chenin Blanc (Pineau de la Loire [Loire], Steen, [South Africa])
This interesting grape is capable of producing a broad range of wines from the bone-dry to the great sweet Loire wines of Bonnezeaux and Quarts de Chaume. It is also widely planted in South Africa and California. As might be gathered, it is liable to botrytis.

Gewürztraminer
A native of northern Italy this grape is at its best in Alsace, where it gives distinctive spicy wines with hints of exotic fruit (lychees particularly). It is now widely grown in Australia (where it is generally blended with Riesling), New Zealand and California. It is also found in eastern Europe. It can give superb botrytized wines.

Müller-Thurgau
A cross whose parentage is in doubt; certainly one parent is the Riesling, the other could be either another clone of Riesling or possibly Silvaner. This is now the most widely planted grape variety in Germany. It gives very high yields of generally undistinguished wines. This has led to its being widely uprooted in New Zealand in a search for higher quality.

Muscadet (Melon de Bourgogne)
Originally a Burgundian variety, it is now almost solely grown for producing the dry, white Loire wine of the same name, a rather neutral flavoured, crisp wine. Apparently, much of the Pinot Blanc grown in California is in fact Muscadet.

Muscat
There are a number of different Muscats grown around the world, but they have one thing in common; they give wines, often fortified or sparkling, with an intensely grapey taste. The best come from the Muscat Blanc à Petits Grains, but this is particularly sensitive to mildew and gives low yields. Of its poorer relatives, the best known is probably the Muscat of Alexandria.

Palomino (Listan [France])
The major grape for Sherry production, at its best on chalky albariza soils. The grapes are high in sugar and low in acidity. The variety is also widely planted in South Africa.

Pedro Ximenez
A sensitive vine, susceptible to disease, that gives exceptionally high yields of grapes with high sugar levels. It is the major variety in Montilla and widely planted in Argentina. In sherry production the grapes are dried, so that the sugars are concentrated and the resultant wine is used for sweetening purposes.

Pinot Blanc (Clevner [Alsace], Weissburgunder [Austria], Weisser Burgunder [Germany], Pinot Bianco [Italy])
Long confused with the Chardonnay, this vine is still grown in small pockets on the Cote d'Or. It is more common in Alsace, where plantings have increased for the production of Crémant. It is also found in Italy. It gives a good yield of fresh, fruity, simple wines.

Pinot Gris (Pinot Beurot [Burgundy], Tokay-Pinot Gris [Alsace], Ruländer [Germany], Pinot Grigio [Italy])
This grape tends to give flavourful, almost oily wines rather high in alcohol and slightly low in acidity. Probably at its best in Alsace, where the bunches, in the best years, are left to be affected by botrytis. In Italy, particularly Friuli, the wines tend to be more neutral in character.

Riesling: (Rhine Riesling, Johannisberg Riesling [New World], Weisser Riesling [South Africa])
A major variety, widely planted around the world. It produces the classic wines of Germany, particularly in the Rheingau and Mosel vineyards. The best wines have high acidity with a minerally, peachy or petrolly

aroma; however, the vine's hardiness makes it ideal for late-harvest wines. In Germany it produces relatively low yields of about 65 hl/ha. Its name has been widely adopted, particularly in newer vineyard areas, for varieties that have little to do with the true Riesling, e.g. Laski Rizling, Hunter Valley Riesling, Cape Riesling.

Sauvignon Blanc (Fumé Blanc)
A classic grape variety planted widely in Bordeaux, the Loire Valley (Sancerre and Pouilly-Fumé) and the New World. It should be planted on poorer soils and it is prone to rot. It is generally used to produce dry wines with marked acidity, either with or without oak ageing, but is also an important constituent of Sauternes, where it is used to add acidity to the blend. It tends to have a distinctive herbaceous, green, vegetal taste.

Sémillon
This grape often shows at its best in a blend, archetypically in Bordeaux with the Sauvignon Blanc. It is planted around the world and, because it is susceptible to botrytis, is often responsible for great sweet wines.

Silvaner (Sylvaner [Alsace])
Once Germany's most widely planted variety, the popularity of the Silvaner is now in decline. On exceptional sites it is capable of making great wine, but more often it gives something of which the main characteristic is acidity. It is widely planted in Alsace and the South Tirol, and is capable of big yields, but is susceptible to frost damage.

Trebbiano (Ugni Blanc, Saint-Emilion)
The most common white wine variety in both Italy and France, where it produces dull wines, some of which, due to their acidity, are ideal for distillation. It also is widely found in Australia. Thick skins make it resistant to rot, though it is susceptible to downy mildew.

Welschriesling (Riesling Italico, Laski Rizling, Olasz Rizling)
No relation of the true Riesling. It is widely planted in central Europe and Northern Italy, where it appears to adapt to all manner of soils and gives big yields of easy-to-drink wine.

Black Grapes

Barbera
The most common red wine variety in Italy. It is at its best in Piedmont. It has also been widely planted in California. It ripens late and thrives on poor chalky soils. It gives a big yield of wines which are generally fresh and acidic and should be drunk young.

Cabernet Franc

Mainly a subsidiary grape in Bordeaux, it is also responsible for Chinon and Bourgueil, and the less fashionable Cabernet Rosé d'Anjou, in the Loire Valley. It is also planted in Eastern Europe. There are some plantings in California. It accepts wetter soil than the Cabernet Sauvignon, and gives higher yields. Unblended, the wine has a stalky, redcurrant flavour.

Cabernet Sauvignon

The grape with perhaps the widest reputation for the production of red wines. It is the great vine of the Médoc in Bordeaux and is widely planted throughout the world including Chile, Australia, California and Bulgaria. It buds late, lessening the danger of damage from spring frosts, the grape-bunches are loosely formed, and the grapes are thick-skinned, have a high skin to pulp ratio and are resistant to rot and insects. It has a low yield. Because of the nature of the grape the resultant wine is full-bodied and tannic, with a blackcurrant taste, and ages well.

Carignan (Cariñena, Mazuelo, Carignane [California])

Though originally coming from Spain, this is now the most widely planted variety in France. It is susceptible to fungal diseases and is capable of giving very high yields of poor wine on the plain. On slopes, the yields are smaller and quality proportionately higher.

Gamay

A Burgundian grape that was historically widely planted on the Côte d'Or and condemned for its high yields and poor quality. Now its heartland is Beaujolais, where it produces its finest wines on granite soils. It is also grown in Touraine and the Ardèche. The wine should be drunk young, It will have a fruity (cherry, raspberry) flavour and purplish tinge.

Grenache (Garnacha [Spain], Cannonau [Sardinia])

The most widely planted red wine grape in Spain, from where it originates. It is the main grape in Navarra and is a constituent of Rioja. It is also widely planted in the Southern Rhône Valley and the South of France, and is found in California and Australia, particularly the McLaren Vale region. By itself, or as the major constituent, it is responsible for many great rosé wines and is used in the blends of such great red wines as Châteauneuf-du-Pape and Rioja. In this guise it benefits from oak-ageing. Grenache wines have a tendency to oxidise early and can be highly alcoholic. The grapes are susceptible to mildew.

Merlot (Médoc Noir [Hungary])

The second great black grape variety of Bordeaux and the dominant one in Saint Emilion and Pomerol. It has recently become very fashionable in the United States and, as a result, there have been widespread plantings in California – and the South of France. It also succeeds in New Zealand. Probably at its best blended with Cabernet Sauvignon. It suffers from downy mildew and grey rot but is resistant to oidium. As a wine, it has a round, rather soft fruitiness and low tannin. It matures relatively quickly.

Nebbiolo (Spanna)
The classic red Italian grape from the chalky soils of Piedmont, where it produces the great wines of Barolo and Barbaresco. It gives wines high in tannin and acidity, at their best after long ageing in cask. The taste has been described as "tar and roses".

Pinot Noir (Spätburgunder [Germany], Pinot Nero [Italy])
No grape can have created such a great reputation from just one region as the Pinot Noir has from Burgundy. Whilst it is planted widely round the world, nowhere else, with the possible exception of parts of California, does it create its perfect wines. There is a broad range of clones of this variety, and the best have to be selected to produce the finest wines. The Pinot's yields are small; it demands well-drained soil and is liable to both mildew and rot. Perhaps these factors present too much of a problem for all but the most exacting grower. At its best it gives wine whose flavour is a "summer pudding" selection of soft red fruits. When old, the wine can take on a peculiar aroma of rotting vegetation.

Sangiovese (Brunello)
Widely grown in Italy, this variety is one where clonal selection shows its true merits. At its best its rich fruit is responsible for the finest Chianti and Brunello di Montalcino; at its worst, for many of the truly sad wines that one can find in Italy. It is now being blended with Cabernet Sauvignon to produce some of the "super-Tuscan" wines.

Syrah (Shiraz [Australia])
One of the great grapes of the world when grown on poor soil. Responsible for the great reds of the Northern Rhône it is also being grown throughout the South of France to improve blends. Widely planted in Australia, where it is frequently blended with Cabernet Sauvignon. It gives full, heavy, deeply fruited wines with a hint of blackberry.

Tempranillo (Ull de Liebre, Cencibel, Tinto del Pais [Spain], Tinta Roriz [Portugal])
This grape is widely planted throughout the northern half of Spain and is the dominant grape in quality Riojas. It is also planted in Portugal and

Argentina. It ripens early and likes chalky soil. It has a nose of Morocco leather, and tastes of overripe strawberries.

Zinfandel
California's distinctive grape variety, whose origins are now thought to be in Italy (the Primitivo?). It is capable of giving a broad variety of styles of wine from the ubiquitous White Zinfandel to late-picked Californian "Ports".

CHAPTER 2

VINIFICATION

Once the grapes are harvested, the next stage in the creation of wine is vinification, the conversion of those grapes into wine. Viticulture and vinification are complementary; neither is more important than the other. It is the job of the grower to produce the best grapes from his vineyards, that of the winemaker to make the best wine from those grapes. (In such a situation, the word best could be interpreted to mean "the most commercially desirable".) In many cases, the two roles of grower and winemaker will be carried out by the same person. The intrinsic quality of any wine comes from the vineyard: good wine cannot be made from poor grapes. However, it is quite possible to make poor wine from good grapes.

The date of the vintage having been decided by the optimum ripeness of the grapes in relation to the wine that will be made from them, picking will commence. In those areas where a number of varieties are grown, or where a property consists of a number of different parcels of vines, there may well be a broad spread of dates when the grapes achieve this optimum ripeness.

Large wineries that buy in grapes from a number of growers, and co-operative wineries, will also have to take the organisation of the grape reception into consideration. Growers may be instructed to bring in certain grapes on certain days in order to spread the workload.

The ripeness of the grapes is assessed by measuring the density of the juice: here a refractometer is being used in the vineyard.

CONSTITUENTS OF THE GRAPE

Winemaking is the transformation of the juice of the grape, the sugar in it being converted into alcohol. The juice will also include acids, flavours and small amounts of natural compounds such as pectin. Water is of

Chardonnay grapes arriving at the winery. From the reception hopper they will be transferred directly to the press.

course the major constituent. The skins and, in some cases, stalks, also have their roles to play.

The ripeness of the harvest is judged by the amount of sugar in the grapes. As the grapes ripen the density of the juice increases with the increase in sugar so a rough idea of the potential alcohol content can be arrived at by measuring the juice's density, or "must-weight". A number of scales have been devised but those most often used are Beaumé and Oechsle. For comparison, the following table shows the Beaumé and Oechsle scales alongside the potential alcohol.

Oechsle	Beaumé	Potential Alc. (% vol.)
65	8.8	8.1
70	9.4	8.8
75	10.1	9.4
80	10.7	10.0
85	11.3	10.6
90	11.9	11.3
95	12.5	11.9
100	13.1	12.5
105	13.7	13.1
110	14.3	13.8
115	14.9	14.4

Must-weight is affected by other compounds within the grape, not just

CROSS-SECTION OF A GRAPE BERRY

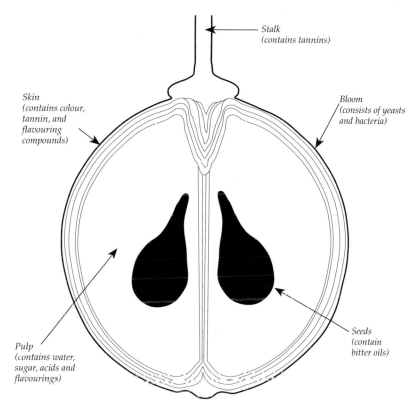

Stalk
(contains tannins)

Skin
(contains colour,
tannin, and
flavouring
compounds)

Bloom
(consists of yeasts
and bacteria)

Pulp
(contains water,
sugar, acids and
flavourings)

Seeds
(contain
bitter oils)

sugar, so theoretical potential alcohol may differ from that achieved by the winemaker. Furthermore, the winemaking processes used will affect the final alcohol. For example, some alcohol will be lost during the manufacture of red wine fermented at a high temperature. In general, 17 grams per litre of sugar will produce 1% alcohol by volume in white wines, but 19 g/l are needed for red.

With a few rare exceptions the juice of a grape, contained in the pulp, is colourless. This can easily be seen if you peel a black grape. All the colouring material is in the skin, along with some flavouring constituents and tannins. The waxy bloom on the outside of the grape skin contains the yeasts needed to start the fermentation, and bacteria. There are two groups of yeasts; wine yeasts (Saccharomyces cerevisiae), which are anaerobic, that is they can operate without oxygen, and wild yeasts, which need air (i.e. they are aerobic). The latter will produce off-flavours in the final wine. The most important bacteria present is acetobacter, which will, in the presence of oxygen, turn the wine into vinegar. If uncontrolled, the wild yeasts would start fermentation, but die off at about 4% vol., when the wine yeasts would take over, converting the remaining sugar to alcohol, which would then be destroyed by the acetobacter. Many of the functions of winemaking are concerned with controlling this natural progression.

The role played by the stalks is less than in the past. The stalks are generally removed before the grapes are pressed, though in certain regions some growers will leave a proportion in, to add tannin to their red wine. Removing the stalks will damage the structure of the grape berry, so where white wine is being made from red grapes the bunches will be left intact.

Pips impart an unpleasant astringency to the wine if crushed. Modern techniques make for a more gentle pressing of the grapes, so this is now generally avoided.

PRESSING

At some stage in the making of every wine, complete separation of the liquid and solid constituents of the fruit is achieved by pressing. This may be prior to the start of fermentation in the case of white wines, or after a period of contact between juice and skins, in the case of rosé and red wines.

PNEUMATIC PRESS

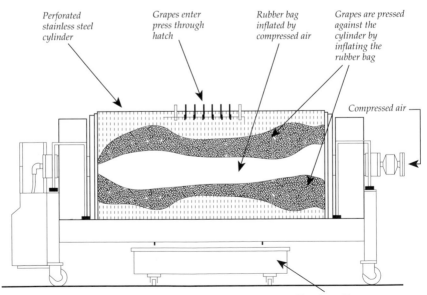

Pneumatic presses use compressed air to achieve a gentle pressing of the grapes.

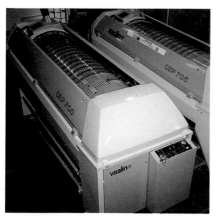

Early presses were vertical but most regions now use horizontal presses, which are more controllable.

The development of the wine press

Traditionally, all wine presses were vertical, with the pressure on the grapes coming from above through a screw. More recently there has been a move to horizontal presses. With models such as Vaslin, the pressure comes from the ends, again applied by way of a screw, but can be controlled more exactly than in the vertical press. The latest presses (Willmes and Bucher) consist of an inflatable rubber tube, within a perforated, horizontal, stainless steel cylinder. Here the pressure is gentle and gradual. A more delicate wine requires gentler pressing of the grapes and may, indeed, be made from just free-run juice.

The volume of juice extracted from the grapes will vary from one variety to another and from one region to another. As a general rule, however, one kilogram of grapes will yield one bottle (75 cl) of wine.

TREATMENTS

Fermentation is a natural process, but will not naturally produce good wine. There are a number of adjustments available to the winemaker, both before and during fermentation, either to improve the must, or to control the winemaking process and maximise the quality of the wine.

Chaptalisation

In cooler climates, it can happen that there is insufficient natural sugar in the grapes for the wine to reach a satisfactory degree of alcohol. In such circumstances chaptalisation (sometimes called must-enrichment) may be carried out. This is the addition of sugar to the must, either before or during fermentation, to increase the alcohol content to the required level. This process is forbidden in many parts of the world, and is strictly controlled where it is permitted. If judiciously carried out, chaptalisation can improve wines, but if abused it can ruin them.

Sulphur

Sulphur, or more specifically sulphur dioxide (SO_2), is almost indispensable in the winery. It acts as an antiseptic and an anti-oxidant. It is now widespread practice to kill off the wild yeasts and bacteria present on the grape with SO_2 before fermentation starts to avoid the off-flavours they would cause.

Traditionally winemakers would cleanse their casks by lighting a sulphur candle in each one, which would give off SO_2 gas as it burnt.

Sulphur dioxide is also useful after fermentation. Bulk wines will have SO_2 added to avoid oxidation and to kill any bacteria or yeasts present which would cause spoilage.

Sulphur can be added in the form of a metabisulphite compound, as present in Camden tablets used in home brewing, or in gas form from pressurised cylinders.

Care must be taken not to use excessive amounts as this will result in an unpleasant smell and taste in the wine. Because of this the European Community has set strict limits on the amounts permitted in various types of wine, ranging from 160 milligrams per litre for dry red wines to 260 mg/l for sweet whites.

Yeasts
Yeasts are present by the million on the grape skins and around the winery so, once the grapes are crushed, fermentation will start naturally. However, it is becoming more common, particularly in New World wineries, for the winemaker to select particular cultivated yeasts that are most suitable for the wine to be made. Cultured yeasts, normally added in the form of dried powder, reduce the need to add SO_2 and may be selected to give a particular character to the wine. Specially cultivated yeasts are essential in the production of certain wines. For example, the second fermentation in Champagne needs yeasts capable of operating at high pressure.

Other Adjustments
There are a number of other treatments which may, or may not, be permitted in a particular region. These include acidification of those wines lacking acidity, or de-acidification of those wines with too much. Acidification is normally carried out by the addition of tartaric acid in powder form, although citric acid is sometimes used. In Europe, the process is limited to the warmer regions, but is common in many New World wineries. De-acidification is carried out by neutralizing excess acidity by the addition of potassium bicarbonate. It is most common in cool climates. If there is insufficient tannin, this too may be added in the form of powder, or by including some of the stalks in the vat, although this is less common in modern wineries than it was once. Legal controls exist for all of these treatments.

FERMENTATION

Fermentation is the conversion of sugar, by the interaction of yeasts, into alcohol with a by-product of CO_2 gas. The chemical formula for this conversion, in its simplest form is:

$$C_6H_{12}O_6 \longrightarrow 2CH_3CH_2OH + 2CO_2 + \text{heat energy}$$

Thus, in theory, the higher the sugar content of the grape, the higher the ultimate alcohol content of the wine. However, the winemaker may seek to stop the fermentation before total conversion of the sugar has been achieved in order to produce a medium-dry or even sweet wine. Any unfermented sugar remaining in the wine is called residual sugar. Even dry wines will have a small quantity of sugar which cannot be fermented, but not sufficient to be detected on the tongue.

When discussing the alcoholic content of any wine, the amount of ethanol in the wine is measured as a percentage by volume and is called the "actual alcohol". The residual sugar present is referred to as the "potential alcohol" and the sum of the two is the "total alcohol".

Yeasts generally die when there is about 15% alcohol in the wine, even if unfermented sugar remains. At the end of the fermentation, the yeasts die and fall to the bottom of the fermenting vessel, forming a sediment in the vat called lees.

Heat is also generated during fermentation, and this will need to be controlled, especially for white wines. During the fermentation, the temperature of the must in each vat will be monitored and recorded on a graph. If necessary the vat will be cooled by the use of a water-jacket or by pumping the wine through a heat exchanger. The density of the must is recorded at the same time on the same graph, as illustrated. The reduction in density shows the decrease in the sugar content and the increase in alcohol content.

This temperature control during fermentation is one of the most important advances in modern winemaking. From the moment that the grapes are brought in to the press-house temperatures will be controlled as the character of a wine can vary considerably depending on the temperature at which it has been fermented.

In hotter climates more and more frequently grape-picking is done at night so that the grapes arrive at the press-house cool. In more marginal climates, however, such as Burgundy, the ambient temperature may be so low that fermentation will not start naturally. In such a case the must has to be heated gently, often by passing warm water through a metal coil, either within the fermentation tank,or round its exterior.

COURBES DE FERMENTATION

Red

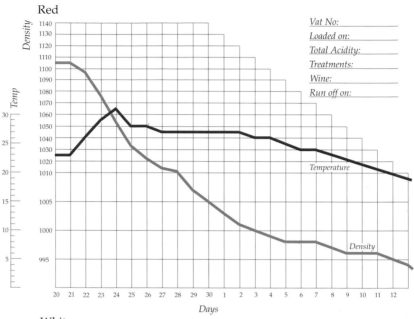

White

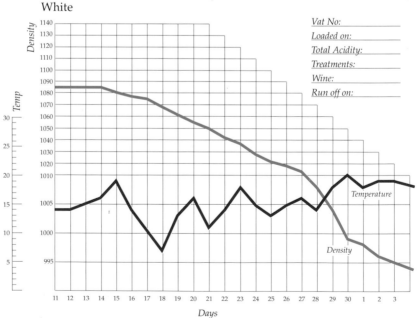

Courbes de Fermentation for red and white Bordeaux. These graphs show the decrease of density and variation of temperature of the must over time. The peaks on the temperature trace for the white wine vat indicate the points at which the winemaker chilled the must. The density of the red must falls more rapidly than that of the white as the fermentation temperature is higher.

Red, rosé and white wines are vinified in different ways, each using similar equipment but in a different sequence.

Red and Rosé Wine Vinification

Red and rosé wines are generally made solely from black grapes. It is particularly important that these are picked in perfect condition and that they are not affected by rot, as this will lighten the colour of the wine.

The classic treatment is for them to be destalked and crushed. The resultant mass is put into a vat where it is allowed to ferment.

Red Wine

With red wines, the fermentation should begin at about 20 °C, but will cease to function if the temperature reaches about 35 °C. It is essential therefore that the temperature of the fermenting mass is controlled. The ideal temperature may well vary from region to region and from grape variety to grape variety. For the Pinot Noir in Burgundy somewhere between 30 °C and 32 °C is perceived to be ideal. The temperature is higher for reds than whites to aid the extraction of colour.

If left to itself, a fermenting vat of red wine will soon have a thick mass of pulp and skins on the surface. If nothing is done about this, the juice will take on very little colour. It is essential therefore, that as much colouring matter be extracted from this mass as possible. There are various ways of achieving this, they include:

Pumping over (remontage) – Most red wine is now produced by pumping over. This involves drawing wine off from the bottom of the vat and pumping it on to the top, thus breaking up the crust. This is normally done twice a day.

Heating – If the grapes are heated at the start of fermentation, the skins release their colouring matter more freely, resulting in a very deeply coloured wine. The danger of this thermovinification process is that it can give the wine a "soupy" taste.

Breaking up (foulage or pigeage) – In this the crust is broken up from above. Traditionally this meant men getting into the vat and

Red wine is fermented with skin contact. Remontage, or pumping over, ensures good colour and tannin extraction.

THE WINE MAKING PROCESS

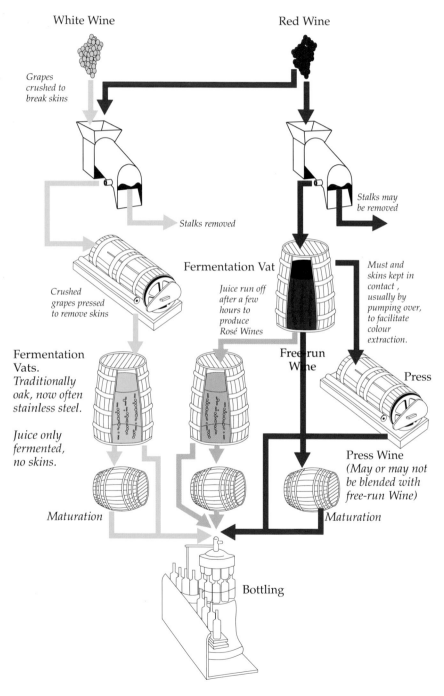

White Wine

Red Wine

Grapes crushed to break skins

Stalks removed

Stalks may be removed

Fermentation Vat

Crushed grapes pressed to remove skins

Juice run off after a few hours to produce Rosé Wines

Must and skins kept in contact , usually by pumping over, to facilitate colour extraction.

Fermentation Vats. *Traditionally oak, now often stainless steel.*

Juice only fermented, no skins.

Free-run Wine

Press

Press Wine *(May or may not be blended with free-run Wine)*

Maturation

Maturation

Bottling

trampling the crust down. This was a dangerous operation as there was always a likelihood that they might be overcome by the CO_2 being given off. Now, the same effect is achieved with paddles or rakes.

Rotary fermenters – This is a modern technique where red wines are fermented in horizontal tanks which can rotate to bring the skins back in contact with the juice.

To concentrate the colour and tannin in a wine it is possible to draw off some of the fermenting juice, thus increasing the proportion of solids to juice in the vat. This also leaves the producer with a quantity of rosé wine. This is now becoming more common in Burgundy, but was particularly used in California when there was a movement to produce the gutsiest of all wines, particularly Zinfandels.

Ideas about the length of vatting required have changed. It used to be thought that the longer the wine and skins were left together (maceration), the more colour, tannin and flavour would be extracted. Colour extraction occurs rapidly at the beginning of maceration, slowing up slightly as the fermentation continues; tannin is slower initially so longer maceration is required for wines destined for long maturation. Current thinking suggests that there is no reason why skin contact should be continued once all the sugar has been converted into alcohol.

Typical maceration times might be six days for a wine with good colour and moderate tannin, but twelve or more for a tannic wine requiring ageing. If the maceration time is limited to two days and the wine drawn off to ferment without the skins, a rosé wine, with very low tannin will result.

The length of time required to complete the fermentation varies from area to area and grower to grower, lasting anything from one to three weeks. The objective with virtually all red wines is to convert all the sugar in the juice to alcohol.

Carbonic maceration
Aside from the traditional method of fermenting red wines, there are a number of other techniques. Of these, one of the most widely practised is carbonic maceration. In this, complete bunches of uncrushed grapes, together with their stalks, are placed in vats under a blanket of carbon dioxide. The fermentation begins within the grapes themselves, they ultimately burst and a more normal fermentation then takes place. This extracts colour but not tannin, and the resultant wines are soft and full of fruit. They generally do not age well. The Beaujolais region in the south of Burgundy uses a semi-carbonic maceration for the bulk of its wines.

There are half-way houses between the traditional and carbonic maceration methods, and often wines made in the two ways are blended together before bottling.

Whichever vinification method is used, when the vatting has finished the free run wine *(vin de goutte)* is drawn off. What remains, the grape skins gorged with juice, is then pressed. This gives the press wine *(vin de presse)*, most of which will be blended in with the rest and then either put into barrels, or back into the vat, to undergo the secondary, or malo-lactic fermentation, and ageing. The final pressing of the skins often yields wines which are too tannic and coarse to be used for blending and these will be distilled.

Rosé wine
There are essentially three ways of vinifying rosé wines. In the first the grapes are pressed directly and the juice is then fermented, as in white wines. Technically this produces a vin gris. Most traditional rosés produced in the European Community are made by an abbreviated red wine vinification, with crushed grapes being macerated for one to three days before the pale coloured juice is run off to continue its fermentation without the skins. The third method, the saignée method, requires the grapes to be destalked, but not crushed, and vatted for 12 to 24 hours – the lesser the contact, the paler the colour. The juice is then run off and fermented without skin contact. Rosé wines are usually fermented in tank rather than cask and bottled young.

In the European Community, with the exception of Champagne, it is forbidden to make rosé wines by blending together red and white.

White Wine Vinification
White wines have to be treated with more care than reds as the danger of oxidation of the grapes is more real. The grapes are pressed on arrival at the press-house as colour and tannin are not required, though there may be two or three hours contact with the skins at low temperature to impart more flavour and fruit. The juice is drawn off from the press, either into vats, or into casks where it is allowed to ferment.

Normally, fermentation will take place at a lower temperature (usually between 15 and 20 °C, sometimes even as low as 9 °C) and over a longer period than red wine. This is to concentrate the fruit flavours of the wine and to avoid loss of freshness. Given that the fermentation reaction itself creates heat, this may well mean that the must will need cooling. In a modern winery, this is a straightforward process, for each vat will normally have its own individual refrigeration/heating system.

If the wine is fermented in barrel the lees are often stirred up, to impart even more flavour to the wine. A number of winemakers are producing white wines fermented in new oak. Once the fermentation is over the

PUMPING OVER

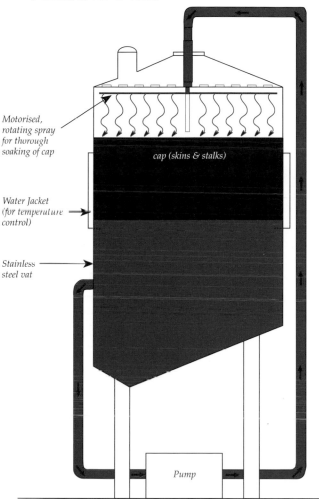

Motorised, rotating spray for thorough soaking of cap

cap (skins & stalks)

Water Jacket (for temperature control)

Stainless steel vat

Pump

wine will be racked (transferred into clean casks) to avoid spoilage caused by over-long contact with the lees.

Sweet wine
A sweet white wine can be created in a variety of ways:

The best wines are made from grapes that are so rich in sugar, often as a result of concentration by botrytis, that the fermentation stops naturally when the yeasts have converted as much sugar into alcohol as they can. This happens both in wines such as Sauternes and Tokaji, which have an actual alcohol content of 13–14% vol., and for wines such as Trockenbeerenauslese which can be as low as 7% vol.

If a fermenting must is filtered using a membrane filter, which is so fine that it removes all the yeasts, before the sugar has been consumed, a sweet wine will result. As not all the sugar has been fermented the wine will also be light in alcohol.

For lesser quality wines the yeasts can be killed before they have finished their work by the addition of SO_2.

In some countries, particularly Germany, medium-sweet wines are made by the addition of unfermented grape must or *süssreserve*. This is a sterile product made by membrane-filtering must before fermentation starts, or by dosing it with SO_2. *Süssreserve* is added to dry wine after fermentation to sweeten it and, in many cases, to balance the acidity.

A cheaper method, also carried out once the fermentation has been finished, is the addition of concentrated must. This is not used for high quality wines as the concentrated must tends to give the wines a "varnishy" character.

The yeasts can also be killed off by the addition of alcohol, as in the production of Port, Vins Doux Naturels of France and other similar wines. This is covered in more detail in chapter 18.

Malo-lactic Fermentation

During malo-lactic fermentation, lactic bacteria convert the tart malic acids (as in apples) into the softer lactic acids (as in milk). For red wines this fermentation is considered to be necessary and may be encouraged by keeping the temperature high and SO_2 levels low.

With many white wines, the malo-lactic fermentation is not permitted to take place, refreshing acidity being welcomed in most white wines. It is discouraged by the use of higher levels of SO_2.

MATURATION

Most wines, of all colours, are made for early drinking, requiring the minimum of maturation. Many finer wines, however, will benefit from some period of ageing, whether in bottle or cask. This particularly applies to red wines. Some wines have a minimum ageing period included in the regulations governing their manufacture.

To survive medium or long term ageing the wines will need high levels of tannin, acidity or alcohol, but more importantly must have a high level of fruit.

The question of cask ageing is one for the winemaker to decide. Generally, the better the wine the greater the need for barrels – and for new oak. They will add tannin to a wine and also soften out some of the other characteristics by means of a very slow oxidation. Factors that might well be taken into consideration when selecting new barrels are the source of the oak, the way it has been cut, aged and whether it has been "toasted" or not. Small casks have a more marked effect on the wine than large ones as a result of the greater ratio of wood surface to wine. The standard small cask is the barrique, which contains 225 litres, the equivalent of 300 bottles, or 25 cases. It has now been adopted by wineries in most parts of the world.

New oak adds an aroma and flavour of oak to the wine, usually identified by a vanilla or smoky character, and adds wood tannins. This effect diminishes as the cask gets older, so a one year old cask gives less flavour than a new one and by the time the cask is four years old very little flavour or tannin is added.

A declining scale of the contribution that the vessel used for ageing makes to a wine might read something like:

Small new oak barrels
Second-hand oak barrels (one or two years old)
Large old oak casks
Neutral vats: stainless steel, epoxy, glass-lined

Normally, a cask-aged red wine will spend a maximum of eighteen months to two years in cask before bottling. During this time, the casks will be topped up (ouillage) regularly and racked every six months or so. Before the final racking, the wine will usually be fined (see below), to settle any suspension present.

Whilst most white wines will have been fermented in vat, some will then be aged in cask for a short period of time. This is because of the extra flavours that the wood imparts to the wine. Sadly, there are now many short-cuts, such as addition of oak flavour, which can achieve the same effect. Most white wine is simply bottled young for early consumption.

FINING

Throughout its life, wine is likely to precipitate certain deposits. We will see in the chapter on tasting that white wines in bottle may throw a tartrate deposit. Red wines also, in time, throw deposits, and this may be a reason for decanting.

During the life of a wine in bulk too, a number of heavy particles will naturally fall to the bottom of the vat or cask. Wine will also contain a certain amount of lighter matter which would naturally remain in suspension. In order to clear this there are certain agents which, when mixed with wine, will coagulate the suspension and cause it to fall to the bottom. Amongst such substances are albumen (egg white), diatomaceous earth (bentonite), isinglass and ox blood, as well as many proprietary products. These agents combine with the suspension, forming heavier clusters of matter which will settle under the effect of gravity. This process is known as fining, and may take place on one or several occasions during a wine's life in bulk.

STABILISATION

One of the winemaker's roles is to ensure that the finished wine remains stable during its intended life span. Instability can take a number of forms, but is of one of two basic types: chemical or microbiological.

Chemical instability

Tartrates
The most common chemical instability leads to the formation of calcium- or potassium-tartrate crystals, which look like sugar. White wines are particularly prone, with cold weather often the cause. This is natural and in no way affects the quality of the wine. However, because certain markets, particularly the United States and Japan, insist on wines remaining star-bright, many wines will be chilled in bulk when they are young in order that the tartrates are precipitated before bottling.

Casse
Casse is a term used to describe a number of chemical faults in a wine that give rise to haziness or a deposit, usually with off smells and flavours. Technically, oxidation is a form of casse. Oxidation, or oxidic casse, is identified by an orange-brown colour in the wine. It may be prevented with the use of SO_2, possibly with ascorbic acid, or by physically preventing contact between the wine and oxygen. It is very difficult to cure.

It is possible that the proteins in a wine may be unstable and give rise to a casse, in this case a grey haze in the wine, but there is usually no associated off smell or taste. Fining with bentonite should prevent this, and may cure it.

Other casses result from over high levels of metals, particularly iron and copper, though better cellar hygiene and equipment means these are less of a problem now. Iron produces a grey deposit and a smell of bad eggs; copper produces an orange-brown colour and a musty smell. The most common cure for both iron and copper casse is what is known as "blue fining", using potassium ferrocyanide. As this is potentially dangerous the treatment must be carried out by a qualified chemist.

Microbiological instability

Micro-organisms – yeasts, and especially bacteria – are responsible for a number of problems as well as desirable reactions in wines. Sometimes it is simply a question of timing, as in the case of a further alcoholic fermentation after a wine has been bottled. Other potential problems include acetic spoilage, caused by aerobic acetobacter converting the ethanol in the wine to vinegar. This can spread from one cask to another so needs to be prevented by the addition of suitable doses of SO_2 which combines with oxygen and renders the acetobacter inoperative.

Wines may also suffer from rod bacteria, although this is now rare due to improved cellar hygiene. There are four forms of rod bacteria infection: *tourne*, giving a dull appearance and a mousy smell, *graisse* making the wine viscous and oily, *amertume*, causing bitterness and loss of colour, and *lactic taint*, again showing as a mousy smell and a turbid wine. All of these are prevented by the use of SO_2 and sterile bottling.

One way of preventing such unwanted problems is by killing the micro-organisms, using SO_2 or heat. Pasteurisation, used mainly for red wines, is an example of the latter. This is generally achieved by a "flash" system, which heats the wine to a temperature of 95 °C for 1 to 2 seconds only. This is widely used amongst the larger producers in areas such as Beaujolais, where large volumes of wines of consistent quality are needed.

A more gentle method of eliminating unwanted micro-organisms, and certainly one that does less harm to a wine, is physical removal by filtration to create a "sterile" wine. This can be done at normal temperatures, and will usually be part of the bottling process.

FILTRATION

In order to prepare the wine for bottling, the last positive action that a winemaker takes in the life of a wine, he will do his best to ensure that it is perfectly bright. Modern technology enables the winemaker to remove even the finest invisible matter from wine. There is, however, the danger that, as filters are not selective, some of the character of the wine might disappear with the unwanted particles. As a rule of thumb, the finer the quality of the wine, the more gentle the filtration will be as long as stability can be assured. Indeed, there are some winemakers who feel that it is better to bottle their naturally stable wines unfiltered. If the wine is other than dry it will not be stable and will have to go through some form of stabilisation, either heat-treatment or filtration.

Most wine will be filtered through a plate filter which will remove any unwanted particles from the wine. Those which are light in alcohol, or have some residual sugar, are more prone to spoilage and often will be sterile filtered using a membrane, or cartridge, filter which acts as a sieve that is so fine as to be able to remove both yeasts and bacteria. As the cartridges are easily blocked, the wine will previously have been plate-

PLATE FILTER

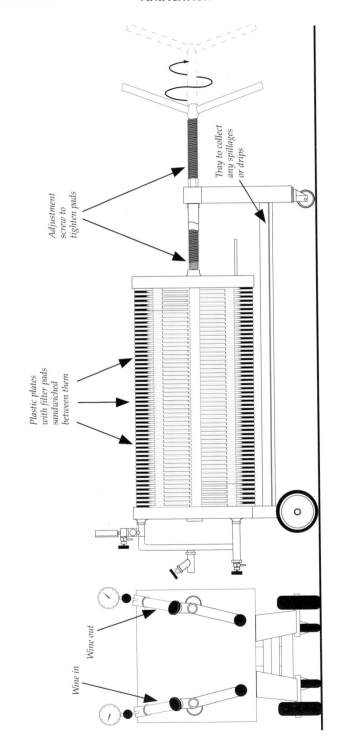

Adjustment
screw to
tighten pads

Tray to collect
any spillages
or drips

Plastic plates
with filter pads
sandwiched
between them

Wine out

Wine in

The plate filter consists of a number of plastic plates interspersed with filter pads, which are available in various grades. The pipe-work is arranged so that wine will pass through one filter pad only, so, increasing the number of pads will increase the maximum throughput of wine.

The housing for a membrane filter, used in the winery to ensure sterility of wine at bottling. This casing will contain cartridges of filter medium.

filtered to remove larger particles. Sterilising grade membrane filters give a wine that is totally free of any micro-organisms, so it is important to avoid later contamination by ensuring complete sterility of the bottling lines, bottles and corks.

BOTTLING

White wines tend to be bottled much earlier than reds, often just four months or so after the vintage. These are wines which are often specifically made for drinking young. They will have spent all their life up to bottling in a temperature-controlled stainless steel vat.

Wines that are potentially unstable because they are either low in alcohol, or have some residual sugar, or both, should undergo cold sterile bottling. This involves the complete sterilisation, not only of the wine as already discussed, but also of all filling equipment, bottles and closures. Cold in this case means normal winery temperature. By contrast, certain cheaper wines may be "hot" bottled: this is the poor man's form of pasteurisation.

As this is the last stage in the active treatment of a wine, it is essential that all the efforts that have been taken so far should not be wasted at the last moment.

Bottle Ageing
For a period of time after a wine has been bottled, it can suffer from what is known as "bottle sickness". This can lead to it showing badly.

The majority of wines are bottled for immediate consumption. However, there are many which will then improve after many months or years further ageing in bottle: for example, Vintage Port may not reach its peak until 30 years after bottling. It is essential that this ageing time should be spent undisturbed in a dark cool place with a constant temperature (preferably about 13 °C). The bottles should be stored lying on their side, so that the corks remain moist to provide the optimum seal.

A technical glossary appears at the end of this book.

CHAPTER 3

TASTING TECHNIQUE

Tasting has a very important role to play within the wine trade for it is by regular tasting that the individual can build up a memory bank of wines that will enable him or her to make qualitative judgements in the future. With demands from the consumer being angled more and more towards value for money, and there being ever broader sources of wines available to the buyer, it is logical that the public will have to rely on the wine trade professionals either to pre-select, or to advise on, purchases.

It is an important skill at a number of stages in both winemaking and marketing. A winemaker will taste wine during the production process to monitor progress, while blending, and as part of the final quality control checks prior to release. A buyer for, say, a chain of wine merchants or a supermarket will taste a range of similar wines when selecting a new wine to list

The ability to do this can only be gained from experience, and there should be a systematic approach to all tasting.

PREPARATION FOR TASTING

In tasting, three senses have a primary role to play:

sight (to analyse the appearance of the wine)
smell (to analyse the nose) and
taste (to analyse the palate)

The sense of touch has a secondary role.

It is imperative that each of these senses should be permitted to operate to maximum effect, thus it is essential that all tasting takes place in as neutral an environment as possible.

It is essential that the location of the tasting is not influenced by outside smells and that the light is suitable. Ideally this should be natural daylight, but daylight fluorescent strip-lighting is the next best thing. The taster should have a white background against which to look at the wine:

The ideal tasting room, with plenty of natural light, neutral colour scheme and white surfaces. Spittoons and sinks are available for tasters to use.

either the surface of the tasting-bench or, alternatively, a sheet of plain white paper.

The taster, too, must be as neutral as possible. Obviously the palate must be clean; any after effects of food, smoking or even drinking can easily alter one's perceptions of a wine. It can often be helpful to chew a piece of plain bread or take a mouthful of plain water in order to clean the palate.

The smell of tobacco lingers long in clothes and can be all-pervading. Similarly, perfume, hair-lacquer and aftershave will affect the taste of the wines, probably more so for others than the wearer.

For those who suffer from hayfever, there can only be sympathy; tasting without one of the senses working effectively is that much more difficult.

Finally, it is important that there is no smell in the tasting-glass. Detergent, glass cloths and storage boxes can all leave traces; glasses should be clean, both to the eye and the nose, before tasting.

Equipment
What is the ideal tasting-glass? It should be large enough to hold a tasting measure of wine with plenty of space above it. The sides should slope in, in a tulip shape, so that the wine can be swirled around to release the smell and to concentrate it at the top, to be nosed. There should also be a

stem so that the glass can be held without the temperature of the wine being affected, and so that the colour can be assessed. All of these features have been incorporated in the ISO (International Standards Organisation) glass illustrated.

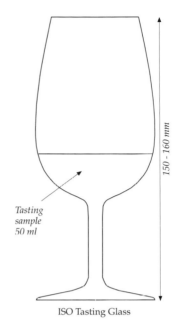

150 - 160 mm

Tasting sample 50 ml

ISO Tasting Glass

For serious tasting there should be a glass available for each wine to be tasted. This makes comparisons more simple and it also allows the taster to leave the wine in the glass and to keep coming back to it, to see how it develops in contact with the air.

The taster should also be equipped with paper on which to make notes. Tasting is very personal, so, of necessity, the notes will be also, but a systematic approach will aid future comparison. Notes should be retained and collated, so that comparisons can be made later, either with other wines, or with the same wine at different stages in its life-cycle. Much can be kept in the memory, but it is often easier and safer to consign thoughts to paper.

The Wines

The preparation of wines for tasting is also important. To be appreciated at its best each wine has its ideal temperature. White wines should be served cool, but not cold. Red wines should be served at room temperature. Wines may be decanted prior to being tasted, for one of two reasons: either to separate the wine from any deposit in the bottle, or to enable it to breathe. For blind tastings, there is another reason: to put it into a neutral bottle.

The order in which wines are tasted is also of great importance, for the palate should not be overwhelmed by what has passed before. For white wines, dry should come before sweet. With red wines it is rather more difficult. Some people feel that older wines should be tasted before young ones, because they are likely to be more delicate. There are others who will always start with the young wines, and work backwards in age. As white wines are generally lighter in flavour than reds, they are usually tasted first.

It is also worth remembering, in the context of a serious analytical tasting, that most wines are made to be consumed with food. Thus, many

Spanish and Italian red wines, for example, may appear harsh when tasted in isolation. On the other hand, they may marry well with the local cuisine, heavily dependent on olive oil.

THE STAGES OF TASTING

Appearance
There is a distinct order in which the senses should be brought into play when tasting wine. Quite naturally, sight is the first to play a role, and a wine's appearance is the aspect that most people find easiest to describe.

Clarity
Clarity is of vital importance in a wine. Cloudiness is the first indication a taster has that there may be something wrong. It may be caused by one of two things. If the wine is undergoing a re-fermentation in the bottle, or is suffering from bacterial problems, these will be confirmed both on the nose and the palate. The alternative, if it is an old wine, is that it may not have been decanted well, though in certain very old wines it is often difficult to decant them star-bright.

Intensity and colour
The colour of a wine and the intensity of that colour are basic features and much can be told from them. To get the true colour of a wine, the glass should be held at an angle of 45 degrees away from the taster, against a plain white background. This will often reveal two distinct colours; the first is in the body, or core, of the wine, the second on its rim.

Red wines get paler in colour as they get older – and the first sign of this age will be on the rim, which will change from purple through ruby to a russet colour and then, with great age, one which is distinctly brown. Whilst it is possible to obtain greater or lesser colour extraction from red grapes, by varying the method of vinification, each grape variety has its own intensity of colour. Indeed, there are certain grapes which are grown solely for adding colour to a wine.

White wines will have a broad, watery edge and can have a greenish tinge when young but will deepen with age, becoming deep yellow-gold with a greater graduation of colour towards the rim. The use of casks, too, can have an effect on the colour of a white wine. Often quite young wines can have a golden tint because they have been put into new oak.

When describing the colour of a wine, it is essential not to use the simple colour like red or yellow. These should be qualified as much as possible. Red, for example, might be anything from tawny, through garnet, brick red and ruby to purple. Yellow could be pale straw, lemon or gold. Each of them has a distinctive image.

RIM vs CORE

Rim Edge (Always watery)

Rim extends from the edge to the main body of the wine. The rim may be only a few millimetres wide in a young concentrated wine, or a centimetre or more in a mature wine.

The main body of colour

Other observations

There are other things to observe in the appearance of a wine. "Legs" or "tears" are the traces that are left on the sides of the glass, when swirled round. They usually indicate high alcoholic content or a high level of residual sugar.

In white wines one sometimes comes across a deposit of crystals, looking rather like sugar. These come about as the result of tartrates precipitating in cold weather; in no way do they affect the quality of the wine.

Sometimes small bubbles may be apparent in what is supposed to be a still, not sparkling, wine. This can indicate one of two things. Either there has been an unwanted secondary fermentation in the bottle or, and this is quite common with young white wines, such as Muscadet sur lie, some residual CO_2 has been deliberately left in the bottle to maintain the wine's freshness. In the first case the wine will smell of apples and yeast, is unstable and should be rejected. In the second it is an attribute.

Nose
It is possible to begin to make a qualitative judgement of a wine by just looking at it, but sight is no more than the first step in the progression towards decision making. The second step is smell.

Condition
Often it is possible to tell the quality of the wine by its nose. The first thing to consider is the condition of the wine. Is the wine clean, or unclean? Experienced tasters will exercise caution when first nosing a wine, giving each wine a gentle sniff first and only afterwards, if all is well, swilling the wine round the glass and taking a deep sniff. This is because some wine faults can adversely affect the sense of smell for some considerable time. The most common faults that can be picked up at this stage are:

Corkiness – This can be recognised by a distinctly musty smell, imparted to the wine by a tainted cork. In faint cases this can be confirmed by tasting. It has nothing to do with any particles of cork which might be found in the first glass of wine when it is poured. These should in no way affect the taste; either that glass should be rejected – or the granules can be picked out!

Sulphur dioxide – The smell that is perhaps the most aggressive of all, and is common in cheaper white wines, is sulphur. This is used as a preservative and to prevent secondary fermentation in sweeter wines but, used to excess, will give an acrid smell of burnt matches. It can literally get right up your nose and make you wheeze.

Acetic – This is the smell of vinegar, caused by the presence of vinegar bacteria and oxygen together, usually as a result of very poor practice in the winery.

Oxidation – A wine suffering from this is sometimes described as "maderised", i.e. smelling burnt like the wines of Madeira. It can also be recognised visually, the wine having taken on a brownish colour.

Intensity
Assuming the wine's condition to be sound, the next step is to decide on the intensity of the aroma, for this can give a hint as to the quality of the wine. A weak smell may indicate a weak, insipid wine; fine wines will normally have a more intense nose, though can sometimes appear "closed" or "dumb", particularly when young. A healthy, pronounced nose is always a good sign. The nose can become insensitive to aromas so tasters devote most concentration to the first deep sniff. The nose can be encouraged by swirling the wine about in the glass to expose more

surface area to the air and liberate the aromas or bouquet. Should this not be sufficient then cupping the glass in the palm of one, or even both hands to warm the wine slightly may help.

Development
Wines change over time, and their state of development can be assessed on the nose. A youthful wine smells of the primary aromas of the grape(s) used in its production. With ageing, they tend to soften and harmonise better, thus a wine which is more subtle and complex on the nose, is likely to be both more mature, and of higher quality. There is a profound difference between age and maturity, a five-year-old cru classé claret from an outstanding vintage will be immature, whereas a Beaujolais Nouveau of the same age will probably be well over the hill. Eventually, the nose is likely to become tired, or even oxidised or acetic.

In the technical vocabulary of tasting, aromas are generally perceived to apply to young wines, and are derived from the fruit itself, and the term bouquet applies to the smells which develop as a result of ageing, in particular bottle ageing.

Fruit character
There is little that is more individual than one's perception of odours or flavours. Each person has in his, or her, memory a limited number of tastes and smells. These can be built up with experience – and then they can be related to the wines of each grape variety, or region.

Smells and tastes can be classified in a number of ways; these are only some suggestions, with some possible examples:

Fruity – the grapey aroma of young Muscat wines, the blackcurrant taste of a young Cabernet Sauvignon, the tropical fruit of many late-harvest wines.

Floral – the flowery aroma of young Müller-Thurgau based German wines.

Vegetal – the rotten leaves of some old Burgundies, the grassiness of young Sauvignon Blanc.

Spicy – a Gewurztraminer from Alsace, the vanilla of many oak-treated Australian Chardonnays.

Other smells that may be found include honey, old leather, smoke and farmyards. The important factor is the retention of these smells in the memory bank, together with the wine to which they are attached.

Although many sweet wines have a distinctive nose, sugar is not volatile, and therefore cannot be detected by the sense of smell. There are wines, such as some *trocken* wines from Germany, which smell "sweet" and yet are in fact dry.

Taste
Of the major senses used in tasting, the final one is taste. Ideally, this should help confirm impressions already made and add the final important details.

In order to liberate the full flavours of a wine a taster will purse his, or her, lips and draw air into the mouth, over the wine while tilting the head slightly forward. It is surprising to what extent a wine will open up in this way as the volatile components are released.

A number of elements in a wine are detected by physiological reactions in the mouth, involving the sense of touch as well as taste. Different facets of the wine's palate are detected by different parts of the tongue and gums, so it is important to expose all parts of the mouth to the wine.

Sweetness
When the wine is placed in the mouth, the tip of the tongue will react if it is sweet; this explains why sweetness is often the first thing to become apparent.

Acidity
The sides of the tongue, towards the back, detect acid so this is normally noticed just after the sweetness, although acidity may continue to show through to the finish. Strong acidity makes the mouth water; wines lacking acidity will be flabby and unappealing. If it is salty (rather rare in a wine), the sides of the tongue, towards the front will take note and if it is bitter, the middle of the tongue towards the back.

Tannin
Tannin, which is an important constituent if a wine is to age well, has a drying effect on the gums and tongue, in contrast to the salivating effect of acid. It is most pronounced in young red wines destined for long cellarage. A similar sensation, can sometimes be had from fine red wines that are just past their peak, when they begin to "dry out".

Body
Body, sometimes called "mouthfeel", is the impression of a wine's weight in the mouth. Some wines feel light, and are referred to as light-bodied; others feel heavy, and are called full-bodied.

Alcohol
Finally the alcohol in a wine, which is difficult to detect unless unusually high or very light, can give a warming sensation at the back of the mouth.

SENSITIVE AREAS OF THE TONGUE

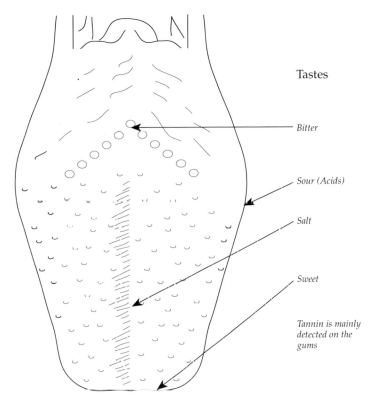

Tastes

Bitter

Sour (Acids)

Salt

Sweet

Tannin is mainly detected on the gums

As "low alcohol" has a specific legal meaning it is safer to refer to wines with little alcohol as being light, rather than low, in alcohol.

Alcohol is an essential ingredient in wine, generally representing about 12% of the total volume. The essential taste of a wine comes from the grapes that have been used and the way they have been treated. Alcohol holds these flavours together, and rounds them off. It is part of the body in a wine, but not the body itself. It is important for the level of alcohol in any wine to be in balance with the level of flavour; thus a full-flavoured wine such as Châteauneuf-du-Pape can support a higher level of alcohol than a delicate Mosel Riesling Kabinett wine.

Fruit character, intensity and length
The fruit characters on the palate should confirm those previously found on the nose, though they may be more or less distinct. However, they can be more complex, for there should be three distinct stages in the taste of a wine. The first might be called the immediate impression and this may last for only a short time, then comes the middle ground when one

obtains the full flavour of a wine in the mouth. Finally, there is the finish or length, the period of time the wine's flavour lingers on the palate after the wine is spat out. This can last for some time, another pointer to quality.

Conclusions
The tasting of any wine must lead to conclusions. These will almost certainly include the level of quality and state of maturity. As many wines, when tasted, are not necessarily ready for drinking, the potential development of the wine may also need to be considered. In the case of a blind tasting, the vintage and origins, both geographical and varietal, may be required. These should lead to an overall estimation of the wine in commercial terms. When tasting a wine of which the identity is known, it is important to consider whether or not the observations match the wine. A young Muscadet should not, for example, have a deep golden colour.

Whenever possible, one should always taste against a price. If the price is not stated, an estimate of the selling price should be arrived at. Tasting, in isolation, is only of limited value. The exercise becomes much more valuable, when inherent value and cost are both considered.

Finally, whilst we all have our own likes and dislikes, the professional taster should aim to be as objective as possible in the evaluation of any wine.

TASTING NOTES

In order to assist students in their tasting and note taking the Wine & Spirit Education Trust has developed progressive guides to tasting at each of the three course levels. A copy of the Higher Certificate approach to tasting is shown, along with a sample tasting note.

The left-hand column lists those aspects which should be considered for every wine tasted. The right-hand column offers a number of examples of terms which may be used, but is not intended to be an exclusive list.

AN APPROACH TO TASTING

APPEARANCE

Clarity   : clear–dull
Intensity   : pale–deep
Colour   : white   : lemon–gold
                                 : rose   : pink–orange
                                 : red   : purple–ruby–tawny
Rim vs Core   : compare colour and intensity

Nose

Condition   : clean–unclean
Intensity   : weak–pronounced
Development   : youthful–mature
Fruit character   : e.g. fruity–floral–vegetal–spicy

Palate

Sweetness   : dry–medium–sweet
Acidity   : low–medium–high
Tannin   : low–medium–high
Body   : light–medium–full
Fruit intensity   : weak–pronounced
Fruit character   : e.g. fruity–floral–vegetal–spicy
Alcohol   : light–medium–high
Length   : short–medium–long

Conclusions

Quality   : poor–acceptable–good
Maturity   : immature–ready to drink

Details of wine

COUNTRY:	*FRANCE*	**PRODUCER:**	*CAVE CO-OP DE CLOCHE MERLE*
REGION:	*BURGUNDY*	**SUPPLIER:**	*A WINEMAKER*
NAME OF WINE:	*BEAUJOLAIS NOUVEAU*	**TASTING DATE:**	*1/12/9X*
QUALITY STATUS:	*A.C.*	**PRICE:**	*£ XYZ*
VINTAGE:	*199X*	**OTHER DETAILS:**	—

Appearance
(CLARITY, INTENSITY, COLOUR, RIM vs CORE)

Clear, medium intensity core of ruby red, with a pale purple rim.

Nose
(CONDITION, INTENSITY, DEVELOPMENT, FRUIT CHARACTER)

Clear, medium pronounced, very fruity, youthful aroma of tinned strawberries / cherries.

Palate
(SWEETNESS, ACIDITY, TANNIN, BODY, FRUIT INTENSITY, FRUIT CHARACTER, ALCOHOL, LENGTH)

Dry, high acidity, very low tannin, light bodied, very fruity, similar to the nose - cherries, strawberries, medium alcohol with a medium length.

Conclusions
(QUALITY, MATURITY)

Good quality, fully mature, drinking now.

A good tasting note of a young Beaujolais following the Systematic Approach to Tasting written in a Wine & Spirit Education Trust tasting notes booklet.

CHAPTER 4

THE LABEL

From the earliest of times wines have been known by their origins. In the Bible, specific wines are mentioned by name and the classical Greeks and Romans created hierarchies for wines based upon their quality. In Shakespearean times, casks would be branded to show what they contained. Early wine labels showed the minimum of detail – perhaps no more than the name of the village from which the wine came.

In this century there have been two distinct moves which have led to more detail appearing on the label. The steady growth in wine consumption, especially in countries without a long wine tradition, has led to the consumer wanting to know more and more about what he or she is drinking. In the United States, for example, this has led to a small essay often appearing on the back label with a full description of the wine, its vintaging, its ageing and bottling, frequently going into quite technical details.

In parallel with this, the increasing complexity of the trade has led to moves towards protection both of the consumer and the producer. In the world of wine, this has meant that the label on a bottle of wine now gives certain guarantees. It is, if you like, a birth certificate, an identity card, and a travel document as well as a letter of introduction.

This chapter is concerned with the legal aspects of labelling. As far as the UK is concerned, both national and supra-national (European Community) legislation applies.

European Community law exists in many forms. The provisions governing labelling are mostly contained in EC Regulations, which are translated into all the principal EC languages and published in EC Official Journals. The Regulations are legally binding and supplant any national laws covering the same areas. European Community law will ultimately apply to all alcoholic beverages but where it has yet to be promulgated English law remains in force.

Whilst there are separate legal systems in England and Wales, Scotland, Northern Ireland and the Isle of Man, as far as labelling is concerned what pertains in England may be taken as the norm.

Until European Community regulations are brought into force for all alcoholic drinks, the bodies of law controlling the various categories are as follows:

Still light wines – EC laws totally

Sparkling wines – EC laws totally

Semi-sparkling wines – EC principle, English detail

Liqueur wines – EC principle, English detail

Aromatized wines – EC principle, English detail

Spirits – EC principle, English detail

Other alcoholic beverages – English law

European Community regulations covering both spirits and liqueur wines have been published but at present these only outline the general principles. Until the detail has been published in the form of regulations, English law applies but it has been altered in order to comply with current EC directives.

Liqueur wine is the legally correct term for those wines to which extra alcohol in the form of grape spirit has been added, either during or after fermentation. Before joining the EC, Britain, along with the rest of the English-speaking world invariably referred to these wines as fortified wines, a term still used in many books and magazine articles.

Enforcement
There are separate controlling bodies for the different levels of the wine trade in Britain. At the wholesale level, inspection of those products covered by EC regulations is in the hands of the Wine Standards Board (WSB), a body funded by the Worshipful Company of Vintners and run by them in conjunction with the Ministry of Agriculture, Fisheries and Food (MAFF). Their network of inspectors covers the whole of the United Kingdom. The WSB's main role is as an enforcing body but they are also very happy to advise importers and potential importers on labelling matters. They cannot, however, advise on matters of English law.

At the retail level, control is exercised by the Trading Standards Officer, an employee of the Local Authority.

The Wine & Spirit Association of Great Britain and Northern Ireland publish guidelines for labelling, and will answer technical questions on labelling, but their services are only available to fully paid-up members.

ENGLISH LAW

First things first: every prepackaged drink must have a label; the only place where unlabelled packaged drinks are permitted is the producer's, or bottler's cellars. In the case of, say, old Vintage Ports, which traditionally do not bear labels, a luggage label must be attached to the neck. Labels are normally paper, affixed to the bottle, but screen printing directly on to the glass is also permissible.

In contrast to European Community law, the fundamental premise of English labelling law is that anything which is not specifically forbidden by the rules is permitted.

On the label, there are six pieces of information that have to appear:

1. A description of what the product is – a brand name alone does not suffice, even though the consumer may well know what the nature of the product is without being told. For example, "Cutty Sark Scotch Whisky" rather than just "Cutty Sark".

2. The country of origin has to be shown separately; so even if, for example, the label says "Italian Lager Beer", it must also state: "Produce of Italy". Wine labelling, which is covered by EC law, is less strict on this so, for example, "French Table Wine" would suffice.

3. The name and address of an entity prepared to take responsibility for the goods within the EC. This might be the producer of, say, a beer; a supermarket group selling under its own label; or an importer for goods which have come from outside the EC. If a product is bottled by one company under contract, all liabilities lie with the company for which the bottling is carried out, rather than the bottler. In the case of own label products, liability rests with the company whose name and address appears on the label, whether or not they manufactured the product.

4. The contents of the package expressed in metric terms. A label may bear an "e" mark by the contents, which makes export to other EC countries easier as it is a sign that those contents are guaranteed by the competent authorities in the producing country within the European Community, and have been bottled in accordance with the EC Liquids Directive. Packages so marked cannot be challenged by authorities in an importing European Community country. Packages not bearing the "e" mark may be destructively tested on importation to another EC country. The "e" mark has no legal status when applied to goods packaged outside the EC.

5. For goods packaged since May 1st 1988, the alcoholic strength must be shown, expressed as a percentage by volume (% vol.) to the nearest 0.5%, measured on the internationally standard Organisation Internationale de

Métrologie Légale (OIML) scale. Those goods bottled before that date need not show the alcohol content.

6. For such packaging or products as may necessitate it, a "best before" or "sell by" date must be included. A great many alcoholic drinks are excepted: for instance, products of more than 10% vol., or with a shelf life of more than 18 months, and all bottled wines. Beers, on the other hand, need one; wines packed in tetrapack or bag-in-box may well need one too. Special conditions of use, for example, "Refrigerate after opening and consume within three days," which are obligatory for many foodstuffs, are considered unnecessary for most alcoholic drinks.

Beverages with Low Levels of Alcohol
Over the past few years, a demand for wine or beer-style products with a lower alcohol content has been created. The description of these has been tightly laid down, with both the upper and lower limits in each category strictly controlled:

Strength:
0 – 0.05% vol.   = Alcohol free
0.05 – 0.5% vol. = De-alcoholized
0.5 – 1.2% vol. = Low alcohol
1.2 – 5.5% vol. = Reduced alcohol

As the definition of wine in the EC requires it to have at least 8.5% alcohol by volume (6.5% in Germany) the term "alcohol free wine" is forbidden. "De-alcoholized wine" is permitted if the product is obtained from base wine which itself conforms to the EC definition of wine.

It is important to distinguish between the various categories; a customer requesting an alcohol-free drink should not be offered a low-alcohol one, for instance. Similarly it is wrong for a shop to display a reduced alcohol beverage in a display headed "Low Alcohol Drinks."

WINE LABELLING REGULATIONS IN THE EUROPEAN COMMUNITY

Still Wines
All still wines offered for sale in the European Community must, by law, be labelled in accordance with EC regulations, even if produced outside the EC. The precept behind the controls is that anything that is not specifically permitted is forbidden. Implicit in those regulations are five different categories for still wines:

1. Quality Wine Produced in a Specified Region (QWPSR)
This is a category for wine made from grapes grown within a specified region in the European Community, and cannot, therefore, apply to

wines from outside the Community. The region concerned must be registered with the EC, and legislation in each member country will implement the EC criteria for the category. Such legislation will cover:

grape varieties authorised or recommended;
viticultural practices, especially pruning systems used;
maximum vineyard yields;
controls on winemaking, acidification, enrichment, ageing requirements, etc;
minimum (and in some cases maximum) alcoholic content and analysis of the finished wine, including, in many cases, organoleptic analysis (tasting).

Many European countries have two categories of QWPSR. France has Appellation Contrôlée (AC) and the lesser, and smaller, category of Vin

QWPSR LABEL

QWPSR region, as registered with EC. Grapes will have been grown within the region and wine made according to the rules set for the wine.

Registered Trade Mark

QWPSR category in Italian wine law.

Vintage 1987

Name and address of producer and bottler.

Alcohol content (OIML)

Volume contents and 'e' mark

Country of origin

Délimité de Qualité Supérieure (VDQS). Italian Quality Wine is divided into Denominazione de Origine Controllata (DOC) wines and those in the higher quality Denominazione di Origine Controllata e Garantita (DOCG); whereas Germany uses the terms Qualitätswein bestimmter Anbaugebiete (QbA) for most of its QWPSRs and Qualitätswein mit Prädikat for the top wines. Details of these wines and the other countries' QWPSRs are covered in the following chapters.

Some producers will, in addition to AC, DOC etc, use the local equivalent of QWPSR on the label, either in full or abbreviated: VQPRD in France and Italy, VCPRD in the Iberian countries.

Once registered, significant protection is afforded to regional names and any attempt at passing off may be brought to court.

All other wine fit for human consumption produced in the EC is referred to as Table Wine. Two categories exist: Table Wine with geographical description and Table Wine.

2. Table Wine with Geographical Description
This is a wine, other than a quality wine, from a European Community country, which mentions a specific source within, and is produced under the laws of, that country. No confusion should exist between the geographical description of a table wine and any QWPSR region. Examples of table wine with geographical description include:

Spain: Vino de la Tierra
France: Vin de Pays
Germany: Landwein, Deutscher Tafelwein Rhein

This wine may have a vintage and up to two grape varieties mentioned on the main label.

3. Table Wine
The term table wine can be expressed on the label in any of the principal European languages, e.g. vin de table, vino da tavola, vino de mesa, tafelwein. It can only be applied to wine produced within the European Community, so the term Californian Table Wine, for example, is not permitted within the EC. Wines from different EC countries can be blended together, but this must be stated on the label in the language of the consuming nation: e.g. "Blend of wines from different countries of the European Community" for such wines offered for sale in the UK. Only very general rules apply to table wine production, the most important being that the finished wine must contain a minimum of 8.5% alcohol by volume, and a maximum of 15% vol. (there is a derogation to 17% vol. for Greek table wine).

Table wine can bear neither a vintage nor a grape variety.

TABLE WINE LABEL

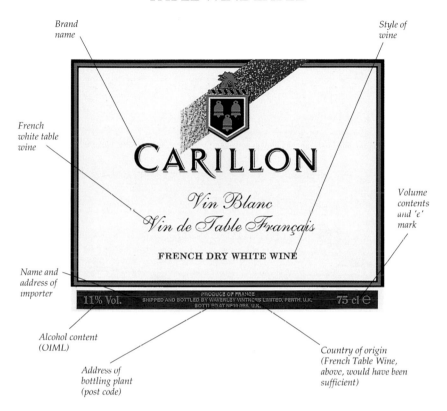

Brand name

Style of wine

French white table wine

Volume contents and 'e' mark

Name and address of importer

Alcohol content (OIML)

Address of bottling plant (post code)

Country of origin (French Table Wine, above, would have been sufficient)

4. Wine with Geographical Description

This is a wine from outside the European Community, known officially as a "third country wine", which names the specific producing region in that country: e.g. Margaret River Chardonnay from Australia or Suhindol Cabernet Sauvignon from Bulgaria. The region must be on a list approved by the European Community authorities and must not be likely to be confused with a Quality Wine name. The region might be small or quite large, such as South-East Australia, which comprises three states. A vintage may be mentioned on the label and normally up to two grape varieties if a derogation is in place (see Varietal labelling, page 69). Many countries outside the European Community have their own legally defined statements of quality, for example, Controliran in Bulgaria, and these may appear on bottles sold in the EC. Such statements do not, however, have any legal significance in the Community.

THIRD COUNTRY WINE LABEL

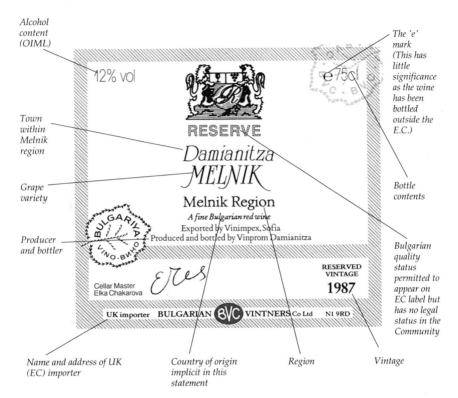

Alcohol content (OIML)

The 'e' mark (This has little significance as the wine has been bottled outside the E.C.)

Town within Melnik region

Grape variety

Bottle contents

Producer and bottler

Bulgarian quality status permitted to appear on EC label but has no legal status in the Community

Name and address of UK (EC) importer

Country of origin implicit in this statement

Region

Vintage

RESERVE
Damianitza
MELNIK
Melnik Region
A fine Bulgarian red wine
Exported by Vinimpex, Sofia
Produced and bottled by Vinprom Damianitza

Cellar Master
Elka Chakarova

RESERVED VINTAGE
1987

UK importer BULGARIAN VINTNERS Co Ltd N1 9RD

12% vol

e 75cl

5. Wine

This is a non-EC wine which does not fall into category 4. Grape varieties and vintages may not be mentioned. The blending of wines from two non-EC countries is forbidden, as is the blending of an EC wine with a non-EC wine.

For each category the Regulations specify what must be on the label and what may be on the label. Anything not specified on either list is forbidden. For example, the style of the wine may be described (e.g. sweet); on the other hand health-warnings, compulsory in the United States, are forbidden in the European Community. A full list of mandatory and optional information appears in the table at the end of this chapter.

Sparkling Wines

There are four different categories of sparkling wine laid down, which, with the exception of the first, have no still wine equivalents. As with light still wines, only those items specifically permitted may appear on the label; more information being mandatory in the higher categories.

1. Quality Sparkling Wine Produced in a Specified Region
This can only be produced from within the European Community at AC or comparative level: e.g. Crémant de Bourgogne, Moscato d'Asti, Cava, and must be made sparkling by a means of fermentation, either in bottle or tank in accordance with the local regulations.

2. Quality Sparkling Wine
This too must be produced by fermentation, either in bottle or tank. A minimum of nine months must elapse from the time that fermentation begins until the wine is put on the market for bottle-fermented wines, reduced to six months if closed tanks are used. During this time bottle fermented wines must spend a minimum of sixty days on the lees, increased to eighty days for tank fermentation, unless made in a vat with rousing paddles in which case the minimum period is only thirty days.

Whilst this category is mainly for EC wines it has been extended to a number of wines made in other countries, particularly Austria.

For these first two categories, the word "aromatic" may appear on the label if the wine is made from such a grape variety as the Moscato or Gewürztraminer.

3. Sparkling Wine
This can come from within or outside the European Community. The one stipulation is that the sparkle must come from fermentation. No geographical source smaller than the country of origin can be mentioned.

4. Aerated Sparkling Wine
This is applied to carbonated wines and the method of production must be clearly stated on the label in a phrase such as: "Obtained by the addition of Carbon Dioxide". No geographical description more precise than the country of origin may appear on the label.

General EC Regulations

Varietal labelling
Any wine produced in the EC which mentions a grape variety on the label must contain at least 85% of that variety. For most non-EC countries a wine must contain 100% of the named variety, although there are derogations for certain countries, including Australia, New Zealand and Hungary, permitting 85% and one for the United States permitting 75%. A limited number of countries outside the EC, including Bulgaria and Chile may name two varieties on the label. Unusually Australia is permitted to list up to five varieties, provided each is at least 5 percent of the blend. For EU wines any number of grapes may be listed as part of "descriptive text", but a maximum of two may appear as stand alone information.

Lot marking

Lastly, under EC regulations, in case of complaint, a consumer must be able to look at a label and recognise a distinctive reference by which the producer can check back to the bottling batch and, if necessary, recall the total parcel. Generally speaking, this will be a coded series of figures or letters. Such systems as Codedge, by which the side of the label are nicked, are not acceptable. A batch number is not needed if the total production of that particular wine is bottled at one time. This is often the case with, for example, domain bottled Burgundies, or Muscadet sur lie. Nor is it required for wines bottled before 1st July 1992.

SUMMARY OF EC REGULATIONS
Information on Labels of Still Wine

	Types of Wine				
	EC Wine			Third Country Wine	
	1	2	3	4	5
Indications appearing on any label attached to the bottle	Quality Wine PSR	Table Wine with Geographical Description (e.g. Vin de Pays)	Table Wine	Wine with Geographical Description	Wine
1 The words 'table wine'		O† M	M		
2 The words 'Quality Wine PSR' or equivalent expression (e.g. Appellation Contrôlée)	M				
3 Superior Quality Description				O	
4 The word 'wine'				O	M
5 The specified region of origin in the EC (or geographical unit in third countries)	M			M	

M = Mandatory   O = Optional   (Blank = Not permitted)   * Mandatory in Germany
O† = Optional for Vin de Pays, Landwein and similar categories where local laws allow.
Mandatory for all other Tables Wines with geographical description.

Indications appearing on any label attached to the bottle	Types of Wine				
	EC Wine			Third Country Wine	
	1	2	3	4	5
6 Country of origin (but see 7 and 8 below) when circulated outside producer state	M	M	M	M	M
7 In the case of a blend from more than one Member State, the words 'Wine from different countries of the European Community'			M		
8 In the case of EC wines not turned into wine in the Member State in which the grapes were grown, an indication of the countries in which the grapes were grown and the wine made.			M		
9 The name and address of the bottler/consignor (EC and bulk third country wines)/ importer (third country wines) as appropriate. May be coded.	M	M	M	M	M
10 The nominal volume of the contents	M	M	M	M	M
11 Lot mark (batch number)	M	M	M	M	M
12 The "e" mark	O	O	O	O	O
13 Indication as to whether the wine is red, rosé or white	O	O	O	O	O
14 The actual and/or total alcoholic strength	M	M	M	M	M

M = Mandatory   O = Optional   (Blank = Not permitted)   * Mandatory in Germany

Indications appearing on any label attached to the bottle	Types of Wine				
	EC Wine			Third Country Wine	
	1	2	3	4	5
15 A recommendation to the consumer as to the use of the wine (e.g. 'serve chilled')	O	O	O	O	O
16 Sweet/dry description	O	O	O	O	O
17 Indication of one or two vine varieties	O	O		O‡	
18 Indication of vintage year	O	O		O	
19 Vineyard name	O	O		O	
20 Indication of a geographical unit other than a specified region, or a wine-producing region in third countries	O	O		O	
21 Traditional special details	O	O		O	
22 Quality control number	O*			O	
23 Serial number of container	O				
24 Indication of method of production/type of product/special colour characteristics	O	O	O		
25 Indication of a recognised award to the wine	O	O		O	
26 Indication of bottling on the premises of production (e.g. château-bottled)	O	O		O	
27 Use of a brand name	O	O	O	O	O
28 Distributor's name and address	O	O	O	O	O

M = Mandatory   O = Optional   (Blank = Not permitted)   * Mandatory in Germany
‡ = 5 for Australia

Indications appearing on any label attached to the bottle	Types of Wine				
	EC Wine			Third Country Wine	
	1	2	3	4	5
29 A citation awarded to the distributor/ wholesaler/retailer (e.g. 'By Appointment to . . .')	O	O	O	O	O
30 History/ageing	O	O		O	O

M = Mandatory   O = Optional   (Blank = Not permitted)   * Mandatory in Germany

CHAPTER 5

FRANCE

France, today, produces something approaching 60 million hectolitres of wine each year. Though it is some years since she was the country that both produced and also consumed the most wine, France is still regarded by many around the world as the mother country for fine wine. Champagne, for example, is perhaps the only wine that is demanded in every country in the world. If imitation is the sincerest form of flattery, the numbers of "sauternes", "burgundies", "chablis" and "champagnes" that have been, and still are, produced around the world, show that consumers everywhere still look up to the wines of France.

The commercial ties between France and the United Kingdom are rooted in history and have waxed and waned over the centuries. After a long hiatus when the two countries were often at war, during which Britain looked largely to Portugal for its wine, the Anglo-French trade treaty of 1860 restored the older links. Imports of French wine grew quickly and remain strong to this day, as more wine is imported into the UK annually from France than from any other country. During the eight years up until 1995, French wines made up, on average, and without significant variation, 40% of the UK's total wine imports. Although Britain has always been an important market for the fine wines of France, the majority of French wine imported falls squarely into the inexpensive category.

HISTORY AND DEVELOPMENT OF WINE LAWS

In 1816, a contemporary commentator, André Jullien, put the total production of French wine at just over 30 million hectolitres a year; now it is approximately double that, but, in the meantime a number of dramatic changes have taken place. These developments affect both the shape and practice of the wine trade in France, and the way that the trade is controlled.

At that time, there were significant vineyards in the region of Paris, supplying the important local market. Improved transport, particularly the railways, then led to the uprooting of what were marginal vineyard areas as far as the climate was concerned. This occurred because the railways opened up the major urban markets throughout the country to the untapped potential of the Midi, where much land hitherto used for other purposes was put under vine in order to exploit these better links.

More striking, perhaps, has been the long term effects of disease and pestilence. In, 1851, just before trade with Britain resumed once more, Bordeaux was blighted by a form of rot. Powdery mildew, or oidium, wrought much damage before the cure, dusting the vines with sulphur, came widely into use in 1857.

Eighteen sixty-three saw the first reported case of phylloxera – at Arles, in Provence. Subsequently discovered to have entered the country in the south in 1860, the plague spread far and wide, and not only within France. In 1867, phylloxera was first seen in Bordeaux. One by one the different regions of France were contaminated, with first sightings in the Loire in 1876, the Bas-Médoc in 1877, Burgundy a year later and finally Champagne in 1900. Spain, Portugal, Italy and eventually Germany were hit, and by 1920 virtually every vine-growing country in the world had been affected. Small wonder the particular strain was subsequently called *Phylloxera vastatrix*, the devastator.

This name was given by a French professor of pharmacy at Montpellier University, Jules-Emile Planchon, who played a prominent part in identifying the cause of the disease, its source and, finally, the remedy. All of this took many years: Planchon was not approached until 1866, and it was two years before he discovered the aphid and *vastatrix* was christened. He went on to discover that phylloxera originated from the eastern seaboard of the United States. This discovery eventually led to the remedy, whereby scions of the European *V.vinifera* species were grafted on to rootstocks of American vine species which were resistant to phylloxera. This practice is still seen as the best way to control the voracious insect.

The introduction of grafting was not helped by the arrival, around 1880, of a new mildew, more vicious than oidium. Ironically, it was carried across the Atlantic on the new American rootstocks, and became known as "downy" mildew to distinguish it from the earlier "powdery" strain. For four years it wreaked further havoc across the embattled French vineyard areas before Bordeaux mixture was found to be the cure.

The overall physical effect of these successive traumas was immense. Bemused old hands had to learn many new skills. What had been a relatively simple task rapidly became increasingly complex and expensive. Many coped and survived, many did not. Over the latter half of the 19th century more than 30% of vines were lost. New plantings were made in the Languedoc, not only to exploit the flexibility of the railways, but also to plant vines in sand, for it had been noted that the phylloxera aphid could not move and hence sustain itself in this type of soil. These increases, however, did not compensate for the losses in the short term, although they were eventually to become a prime cause for the subsequent problems of vast over-production.

In the 1880s and beyond, the diminishing French supply could not meet the demand which was rapidly increasing both at home and abroad. Prices inevitably rose, attracting those who were happy to operate on the darker side of the wine trade. These unscrupulous winemakers and traders took advantage of the situation and passed off inferior wines exploiting the names of France's famous regions. Wine produced, for instance, from vines grown in the Midi on land that shortly before had been used for cereal production, was sold labelled "Beaune". Wine was also made from raisins and beet sugar and sold alongside inferior vinous products, made originally for vinegar or distillation, which had been "softened" by watering down and other devices. Additionally, bulk wine was imported from Spain and Italy and passed off as something that it was not. By 1905 the trade in fraudulent wines was so great that the French Government intervened.

In that year, the *Service de la Repression des Fraudes et du Contrôle de la Qualité* was established. Its first aim was to introduce legislation to prevent the misrepresentation of a product's name. It also laid the framework for the delimitation of vineyard areas and appellations. Progress was slow, but by 1923 Baron du Roy and others in Châteauneuf-du-Pape had created a set of rules for that vineyard area. Interestingly, these rules, which were subsequently adopted as the basis for the Appellation Contrôlée system, were originally intended to protect the producer rather than provide a guarantee of authenticity for the consumer.

At about the same time, across France at Château Mouton-Rothschild in the Médoc, in another move towards improving quality which was to have far reaching effect, Philippe de Rothschild introduced château bottling for his whole crop. It does not sound much today, but in 1924 it was revolutionary and seen by the trade as "an act of mistrust vis-à-vis the Bordeaux merchants" – who until that point were responsible for most of the bottling in the region. Two years later, he persuaded the owners of the *premiers crus* to do the same and also to revive their dormant informal association in order to fight frauds and provide a forum in which to discuss prices. This inspired a number of similar initiatives throughout the region.

These moves took place, progressively, against a background of severe over-production as the vineyards recovered. Most of this was at the low end of the quality spectrum and much emanated from Languedoc. The initiatives were complemented by a series of Government decrees that forbade new planting and some varieties, mainly American-French hybrids, were banned. In the drafting of these decrees, a member of the Chamber of Deputies, Joseph Capus, who represented the Gironde, came to play an increasingly significant role. It was he, in 1927, who was largely responsible for working into the legislation concerned with defining delimitation of production, the concept of local grape variety to stand alongside the accepted concept of territorial boundaries. Later, he was to be the architect of the 1935 legislation which collated much of what had gone before into a comprehensive whole and which established the *Comité National des Appellations d'Origine.*

Whilst one reason for over-production lay in the amount of production *per se*, another lay at the other end of the cycle, consumer offtake. After decades of increasing consumption rates both internal and external, demand in France began to fall whilst, externally, French wines had to compete with the wines from other countries. This situation persisted after World War II. By the early 1990s, per capita consumption in France compared with that of the mid 1950s had all but halved, almost all the reduction having taken place at the level of table wine. It seems that the days when a bottle of "vin rouge" was an essential part of most Frenchmen's lunch or dinner have long gone: indeed, over half the population now claim to drink no wine at all.

Initially, the European Community's Common Agricultural Policy, exacerbated the problems of over-production. Only very recently has the EC been actively offering subsidies to encourage the uprooting of high yielding vineyards.

As demand for everyday wine diminished, a wider demand for quality wine has occurred. There have thus been parallel movements: a reduction in the area under vines and an increase in the production of better wine. The result of this is that by the early 1990s in France, over half of the vineyard acreage and approximately 40% of the wine produced is at the QWPSR level.

THE FRENCH WINE LAWS

The production of wine in France today is tightly controlled by two organisations, which might be likened to the carrot and the stick. The carrot is the *Institut National des Appellations d'Origine* (INAO). This body succeeded the *Comité National des Appellations d'Origine* after World War II and controls the hierachy of French quality wines. The stick is the *Service de Repression des Fraudes*, which is responsible for seeing that the very complicated laws on wine production are carried out. From the moment that the grapes are picked, they must be covered by some form of documentation until, in France, the moment that they are purchased by the final consumer. (On the French domestic market, every bottle carries a capsule congé, or capsule with the government seal on it showing that the relevant tax has been paid. It also shows the wine's quality status). In addition to the organisations decribed above the *Office National Interprofessionnel des Vins de Table* (ONIVINS) is the controlling body for all French table wines.

In 1963 the wine laws of France, though in essence the same as laid down in 1935, were absorbed into the European Commmunity's wine regime and, in fact, provided much of the framework of that regime. France has two grades of QWPSR: Appellation Contrôlée and Vin Délimité de Qualité Supérieure, and two of Table Wine: Vin de Pays and Vin de Table.

Quality Wine

Appellation d'Origine Contrôlée (AC or AOC)
This is the highest level that a French wine can attain. Though the requirements may vary widely from one region to another, they are the most tightly defined and the following points will always feature:

Areas of production – the boundaries of which are based on the composition of the soil.

Grape varieties permitted – the principle being that, in the words of an earlier decree, these should be "hallowed by local, loyal and established custom".

Viticultural practices – planting distances, pruning methods and general handling of the vine.

The maximum permitted yield per hectare.

Vinification methods, including ageing.

The minimum alcoholic degree in the wine that must be achieved without must-enrichment.

Within each region there is a laid down hierarchy of appellations which, in general, are geographically based. The more specific the geographic description, the higher the appellation, and the stricter the regulations. In some areas an individual vineyard may be eligible for several ACs of different quality levels.

Some regional and district appellations have the right to the additional qualification supérieur, e.g. Bordeaux Supérieur, Mâcon Supérieur. These wines simply have an extra half or full degree of alcohol compared with the equivalent basic appellation.

Vins Délimités de Qualité Supérieure (VDQS)
This classification was established in 1949 as a stepping-stone to Appellation Contrôlée, and many wines originally classified as VDQS (e.g. Minervois, Corbières) have subsequently moved to the higher level.

On the other hand there appear to be some regions (e.g. Bugey) which seem quite happy to remain as VDQS.

The laws cover the same ground as for AC wines but are often less stringent on yields and grape varieties. In one aspect, however, the VDQS laws were initially stricter. The right to the VDQS label was only granted after an official tasting. Now this requirement has been extended to AC wines as well. Overall, though, this is a tiny category, representing scarcely more than 1% of France's production.

Table Wine

Vin de Pays
This classification was established by decree in September 1979 partly as a result of an initiative on the part of the wine trade, which wanted to give added value to certain vins de table. At the same time, a broader objective was to upgrade the quality and sharply reduce the quantity of bulk wine being produced in areas such as the Midi. At present, there are 141 different vins de pays, spread throughout all viticultural France, from the Meuse, against the Belgian frontier, to the Pyrénées-Orientales, against that of Spain, and they represent approximately 20% of the total production.

A wine must meet four qualifications to be eligible for this category:

1: *Area of production* – This can be regional, for example Vin de Pays d'Oc, which covers four départements. It can be that of a département, such as Vin de Pays de l'Aude, or it can be zonal within the same département, such as Vin de Pays des Coteaux de Peyriac.

2: *Grape varieties* – For each Vin de Pays there is a recommended list of grape-varieties. Generally, this will be much broader than that for a local AC or VDQS wine, enabling the grower to introduce classic varieties from other regions. This latter has led to much interesting experimentation.

3: *Yields* – The maximum permitted yield is 90 hl/ha, though in some areas this has been reduced to 80 hl/ha.

4: *Analytical standards* – Amongst other things, this includes the minimum natural alcoholic strength of 9% vol. in the north and 10% vol. in the south, and maximum sulphur and volatile acidity levels.

Vins de Table
Thirty per cent of the wine produced in France falls into this category. Vins de table can be produced anywhere in the country with no restriction as to grape variety, though the wine may not be chaptalised. No maximum yield is stipulated, but a proportion of production over

100hl/ha must be sent for distillation and the greater the over-production, the lower the price paid per hectolitre for distilling wine. This measure was introduced to act as a stimulus upon producers to reduce yields and plant finer grape varieties in order to improve quality. There are some signs that producers are responding.

The Abolition of the "Cascade" System

An important feature of the French Appellation system is that within a region one vineyard might have the right to two or more appellations in descending order of merit – and ascending potential yield. Prior to 1974 it was possible for a grower to over-produce, that is, exceed the permitted yield and yet still sell some of his wine under the highest appellation and the remainder under lesser ACs. A winemaker in St Estephe, for instance, who produced 50 hl/ha could sell 40 hl of that as AC St Estephe (maximum yield 40 hl/ha), a further 3 hl AC Haut-Médoc (maximum yield 43 hl/ha) and the remaining 7 hl as AC Bordeaux (maximum yield 50 hl/ha). This system was referred to as classification "*en cascade*" and it became subject to a great deal of abuse.

Under the old system, there was every encouragement for the grower to make as much wine as possible, because he had the opportunity of selling unlimited quantities, though perhaps much of it under names of steadily decreasing value. Now, the objective is to force each grower only to make as much wine as will reflect the potential quality of the appellation. As was pointed out in the chapter on viticulture, smaller yields tend to lead to higher quality.

As from 1974 classification *en cascade* was prohibited. Under the new arrangement put in its place, each appellation carried forward, unchanged, its previous basic permitted yield, the *rendement de base*. This is now the maximum to which the grower has automatic right, though it may be increased, or decreased in an individual vintage (*rendement annuel*), to take account of special conditions for that year. In addition to the *rendement de base* plus any annual adjustment, an allowance of 20%, known as *plafond limite de classement*, may be sought by the winemaker. In this case, the grower is required to submit samples of the wine for analysis and tasting. If, following these tests, the samples are rejected and the appellation is refused, the grower's entire production of this wine must be sent for distillation or vinegar production.

The grower does have the opportunity of declaring his wine as a lower appellation, if he fears that it is not worthy of the higher, or if he has exceeded the production figures. However, he must decide at the moment of the vintage under what appellation he is making his wine. Thus, if he fails subsequently, at the testing level, he cannot then aim for a lower appellation.

Burgundy provides many instances where this could occur. In a normal year, a grower with one hectare of, say, Clos de la Roche, a Grand Cru in the village of Morey St Denis, could produce one of the following:

35 hl Clos de la Roche (+ 20% if tested successfully)

or

40 hl Morey Saint Denis Premier Cru (+ 20% if tested successfully)

or

55 hl Bourgogne (+ 20% if tested successfully)

(In each case, the base could change according to the *rendement annuel* for that year.) He could not produce more than 66 hl of wine (unless it were unchaptalised and then, theoretically, he could produce a vin de table rouge).

FRENCH LABELLING TERMS

The following definitions may be useful in interpreting French wine labels:

Blanc	white
Brut	dry (usually sparkling wine)
Cave	cellar (often underground) or winemaking establishment
Cave Co-operative	winemaker's co-operative
Cépage	grape variety
Chai	warehouse for storing wine, usually in barrels, above ground level
Château(x)	estate(s), may or may not have a manor house
Clos	walled vineyard (in some cases the walls have been demolished over time, but the vineyard retains the name)
Côte	hillside
Coteaux	hillsides
Cru	"growth" (indicates a specific, usually high quality vineyard, district or village)
Cru Classé	classified vineyard (in Bordeaux especially)
Cuve	vat or tank

Cuvée	blend (this term has a special meaning in Champagne, see Chapter 16)
Demi Sec	medium dry
Département	French political region roughly equivalent to a British county. Usually named after physical features such as rivers or mountains.
Domaine	estate
Doux	sweet
Eau-de-vie	spirit
Grand vin de...	marketing term meaning "great wine of..." but having no legal significance
Manipulant	grape grower who also makes wine from those grapes, especially in Champagne
Marc	pomace, the residue of skins, stalks and pips from a press. Distilled to make eau-de-vie-de-marc
Mis en bouteille	bottled
Mis en bouteille au château	château bottled
Négociant	merchant who buys wine and matures it prior to sale
Propriétaire	vineyard or estate owner
Raisin	grape
Récoltant	harvester of grapes
Récolte	vintage/harvest
Rouge	red
Sec	dry
Supérieur	indicates an extra 0.5% or 1% vol. alcohol
Vendange	vintage/harvest
Vignoble	vineyard
Vin	wine

THE WINE REGIONS OF FRANCE

Few countries have such a long standing and developed wine culture as that of France. Not many have such a diverse range of wine growing regions or so rich a population of native grape varieties recognised to be amongst the best in the world. The next five chapters will look at these regions in some depth and will describe their climates, soils and grape varieties as well as the other factors which combine to shape their differing styles of wine.

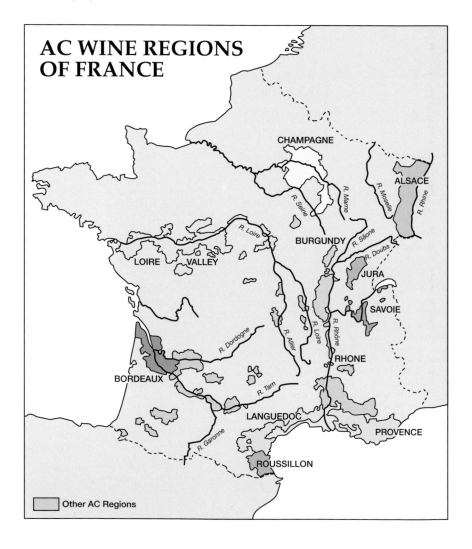

CHAPTER 6

BORDEAUX AND SOUTH WESTERN FRANCE

BORDEAUX

The Bordeaux wine region is confined to the Gironde département in the south-west of France. The Gironde itself is the confluence of the Garonne and Dordogne rivers; the city of Bordeaux lies in the centre of this region astride the Garonne.

These rivers divide the region into three broad areas. West and south of the Gironde/Garonne lie the districts of Médoc, Graves and Sauternes. Most of the area between the Garonne and Dordogne is covered by the Entre-Deux-Mers district, literally "between two seas." Finally, the principal districts north and east of the Gironde and Dordogne are Saint-Emilion and Pomerol.

In Roman times Bordeaux (Burdigala) was an important university town with a broad cosmopolitan image. Whilst it was a region of polyculture, there were many vineyards and the wine had a high reputation. One vestige of Roman times is the Saint-Emilion Château Ausone, named after the poet Ausonius.

From Roman times until Henry II's marriage to Eleanor of Aquitaine in 1152 there is a black hole as far as the wines of Bordeaux are concerned; little or no information about them survives. Even under the English, the city and its neighbour Libourne on the river Dordogne were more important as transit ports for the shipment of wines from the "High Country" up river than they were for the wines from the Bordeaux vineyards themselves. Nevertheless, the exports of these latter must still have been considerable.

It was not until the first years of the 18th century that Bordeaux wines as

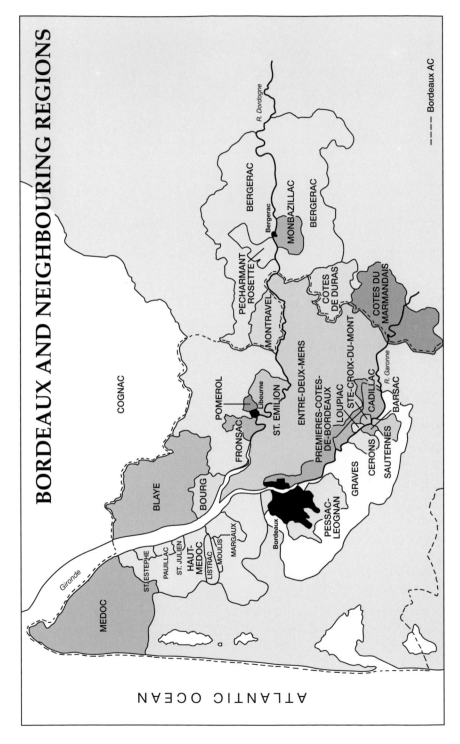

BORDEAUX AND NEIGHBOURING REGIONS

ATLANTIC OCEAN

MEDOC
ST.ESTEPHE
PAUILLAC
ST. JULIEN
HAUT-MEDOC
LISTRAC
MOULIS
MARGAUX
Gironde
BLAYE
BOURG
COGNAC
FRONSAC
POMEROL
Libourne
ST. ÉMILION
Bordeaux
PESSAC-LEOGNAN
PREMIERES-COTES-DE-BORDEAUX
ENTRE-DEUX-MERS
LOUPIAC
STE-CROIX-DU-MONT
CADILLAC
CERONS
GRAVES
SAUTERNES
BARSAC
R. Garonne
COTES DE DURAS
COTES DU MARMANDAIS
MONTRAVEL
PECHARMANT
ROSETTE
Bergerac
BERGERAC
MONBAZILLAC
BERGERAC
R. Dordogne

– – – – Bordeaux AC

we know them now began to be shipped in quantity to the English market, often as contraband from Ireland or Scotland. They were known as New French Clarets. Already, certain châteaux were becoming known: Pepys had Haut-Brion in his cellar, and as early as 1678 the philosopher John Locke visited the château and related the quality of its wines to its soils. From this time on there began to evolve a clear hierarchy among the vineyards, particularly those in the recently drained district of the Médoc.

BORDEAUX TODAY

In terms of Appellation Contrôlée wine, Bordeaux is the largest wine-producing area of France accounting for almost a quarter of the total output. In all it produces just under 5 million hectolitres of red wine and 1 million hectolitres of white each year. The single most important Appellation, at almost 2 million hl, is AC Bordeaux rouge.

Bordeaux wines are of continuing importance to the United Kingdom market and especially so at the upper end. The influence of Bordeaux is measured not only in the UK market place but also in vineyards around the world, as other important wine-producing countries have used Bordeaux as a model for their winemaking techniques. This applies particularly to the New World countries and it is of interest to note that, in turn, these are beginning to influence the Bordelais *vignerons.*

THE CHÂTEAU CONCEPT

Most vineyards in Bordeaux are not known by names attached to specific plots of land as is, for example, any premier cru in Burgundy. Rather, they are known by the names of châteaux. A Bordeaux wine château is an estate under single ownership, which may or may not have a castle or country house attached to it. Additionally, over the years, the size of the property may vary by purchase or sale of vineyard plots. For example, the very highly rated estate of Château Pétrus in Pomerol has increased in size by approximately 50% since 1969. Thus a château name is rather more of a brand than a designation of a specific vineyard.

It has been estimated that there are more than three thousand individual château names in Bordeaux and, until recently, few of these appeared on labels. Those that did were the prestigious and long-established names. The rest were blended off by the Bordeaux merchants for sale under their own labels. Today, with the demand for more individuality and the increase in the number of mobile bottling-lines, the number of so-called *"petits châteaux"* on the market has increased considerably.

THE AC HIERARCHY AND CLASSIFICATION OF ESTATES

The AC hierarchy in Bordeaux consists of three levels: generic, district and commune:

1. *Generic* – These are names which may be applied to AC wines produced anywhere within the Gironde. Examples are: Bordeaux and Bordeaux Supérieur, together with the sparkling Bordeaux Mousseux and Crémant de Bordeaux (see Chapter 16). Within this group, there are certain sub-appellations such as Bordeaux Haut-Benauge. There is also a special optional appellation for rosé wine: Bordeaux Clairet. The English generic term "claret" is thought to be derived from "*clairet*".

2. *District* – These may be the highest appellation attainable in a particular locality, such as Entre-Deux-Mers, or they might embrace a number of superior commune appellations, such as Haut-Médoc.

3. *Commune* – Excepting the particular case of Saint-Emilion Grand Cru AC, these are the highest appellations within the AC system. Château names themselves do not form part of any AC. For example, Château Latour is AC Pauillac, Château Trotanoy is AC Pomerol.

Because of the large number of châteaux, classification systems of qualitative grading grew up over the years, and in some cases long before the advent of Appellation Contrôlée. Unfortunately for the student of the subject, however, these classifications vary from district to district within Bordeaux.

Médoc and Sauternes

In 1855, on the occasion of the Paris Universal Exhibition, the Bordeaux Chamber of Commerce was approached to produce an official list of their best wines. They passed on the job to the brokers and a list was drawn up which classified the red wines of the Médoc and the white wines of Sauternes. The classification was based upon the prices that the various wines had been fetching on the market.

Over the years there have been numerous changes in the number and size of the various estates as châteaux have merged or split and also in the quality of the wines that they produce. Nevertheless the 1855 classification still stands virtually intact.

There are 61 "*crus classés*" divided into five ranks. There has only ever been one change; in 1973 Château Mouton-Rothschild was promoted from being a second growth to a first.

The red first growths (*premiers crus*) are:

Ch. Haut-Brion (AC Pessac-Léognan) – the one wine from outside the

Médoc to be included in the original list
Ch. Lafite (AC Pauillac)
Ch. Latour (AC Pauillac)
Ch. Margaux (AC Margaux)
Ch. Mouton-Rothschild (AC Pauillac)

Below this there are:

14 châteaux classified as 2nd growths (*deuxièmes crus*)
14 châteaux classified as 3rd growths (*troisièmes crus*)
10 châteaux classified as 4th growths (*quatrièmes crus*)
18 châteaux classified as 5th growths (*cinquièmes crus*)

In Bordeaux the concept of a château is perhaps more important than anywhere else. This is Château Giscours, in Margaux, classified as troisième cru classé in 1855.

The 1855 classification only accounted for a very small number of the estates of the Médoc. In 1932 a further classification of *Cru Bourgeois* was introduced, updated in 1978. Now accounting for some 203 châteaux, the classification is divided into three levels:

Grand Cru Bourgeois Exceptionnel
Grand Cru Bourgeois
Cru Bourgeois

Beneath this there is the classification *Cru Artisan*.

In these lower classifications there is more flexibility, with the possibility of promotion within the system and, indeed, of joining it.

Also classified in 1855 were the sweet white wines of Sauternes. Here Château d'Yquem was classed by itself as *premier grand cru classé* with, beneath it, nine first and eleven second growths.

Graves (including Pessac-Léognan)
The wines of the Graves were classified in 1959, with parallel but separate lists for reds and whites. There is no ranking; all listed wines may simply call themselves *Cru Classé*. Château Haut-Brion is included although it retains its 1855 classification as of right.

Saint-Emilion
The classifications for the appellation Saint-Emilion work on a rather different basis and, uniquely in Bordeaux, within the AC system. There is a separate AC called Saint-Emilion Grand Cru, which has two sub-divisions. Every ten years subsequent to the original classification in 1955, the individual estates are reclassified. This has involved both promotions and demotions.

At present there are thirteen châteaux classified as *Premier Grand Cru Classé* (with Ausone and Cheval Blanc considered to be above the rest) and a host as *Grand Cru Classé*.

CLIMATE, SOILS AND GRAPES

Climate
Bordeaux lies at 45° latitude and is therefore quite northerly in the winemaking context. Whilst, as in other vineyard regions, there are microclimates that may benefit individual sites, the overall climate is maritime. That is to say it is temperate, with frost damage a comparative rarity (a notable exception was in April 1991). Humidity is high, not only because of the proximity of the sea, but also due to the influence of the rivers Dordogne and Garonne; the latter, particularly, affecting Sauternes and Barsac. The high humidity facilitates noble rot, *pourriture noble* in French, but can also lead to undesirable grey rot being a problem, particularly for red wines. The strong prevailing winds from the Atlantic can present difficulties, though these are alleviated to some extent by the high coastal sand dunes and pine forests acting as wind-breaks.

The weather has a major effect on the quality of the grapes produced by individual vineyards in this temperate zone and can vary sharply from year to year. A sound knowledge of the difference between vintages is therefore very important.

Soils

On the borders of the rivers there is a band of rich alluvial soil. Plantings for AC wines are only allowed on this soil for the lowest appellations, if at all. The finest vineyards are found on gravel, where quartz pebbles and flint lie over a sub-soil of marl. This occurs particularly in the Médoc to the north of Bordeaux, and in the northern Graves. In parts of St-Emilion there is gravel on a limestone base. Hillside vineyards in Bordeaux are comparatively rare; where they do occur they are generally on limestone and clay.

Grape Varieties

All the red wines of Bordeaux, and almost all the whites, are the result of a blend of grape varieties. This is no accident of history. The varying microclimates that are found and the wide variations in weather pattern that can occur from year to year make vinegrowing even more unpredictable in Bordeaux than in many other wine regions. Different grape varieties are affected differently by weather phenomena: some are thicker skinned and thus more resistant to rot, others ripen later or flower earlier, some can withstand frosts or adapt to wet soil better than others, and so on. By judiciously mixing the proportions of the varieties planted the grower can hedge his bets to minimise the effects of bad weather and, hopefully, be able to salvage something out of even the worst year. This practice has been honed to a fine art in Bordeaux.

There are 14 grape varieties permitted in the making of Bordeaux wine. In practice production is almost entirely from five black varieties and three white. These are:

Black:
Cabernet Sauvignon
Merlot
Cabernet Franc
Malbec
Petit Verdot

White:
Sémillon
Sauvignon Blanc
Muscadelle

Cabernet Sauvignon (Petit Cabernet) is widely regarded as the classic black variety of Bordeaux. It accounts for three quarters of the blend in the finest wines of the Médoc where, mainly, it is found. Across the region as a whole it represents 29% of the surface area under black varieties. It gives only moderate yields and produces quality, tannic wines with a characteristic blackcurrant aroma.

Cabernet Franc (Bouchet) is mainly grown in St-Emilion and, to a lesser extent, in the Médoc and Graves. It gives higher yields than Cabernet Sauvignon but the wine has rather less body and finesse, is somewhat greener and stalkier and matures more rapidly.

Both Cabernets prefer to be planted on gravel soils.

Merlot (Sémillon Noir) produces a medium yield of full-bodied, moderately tannic wine which also matures earlier than Cabernet Sauvignon. Blended with that grape its body helps create a better balance. Merlot is particularly important in St-Emilion and Pomerol where it prefers the limestone soils.

Malbec (Cot) is mainly used for early drinking red wines such as those of Bourg and Blaye. It suffers particularly from *coulure*.

Petit Verdot gives a very deep-coloured tannic wine which ages slowly. Never more than a very minor part of any blend it can be likened to the vigneron's "seasoning," a pinch of which may be added to produce the optimum flavour.

Sémillon is the most widely planted white variety in Bordeaux and, given its thin skin and propensity towards noble rot, is used especially for sweet wines. It gives wines with a golden colour and plenty of body.

Sauvignon Blanc is a grape variety with a lowish yield. It produces wines with a distinctive bouquet and a characteristic gooseberry fruit. In Bordeaux it is increasingly used for single varietal dry white wines, the one exception to the rule that all Bordeaux wines are blends. When blended, its high acidity acts as a counterbalance to the potential flabbiness of Sémillon; this is especially the case in sweet wines.

Muscadelle has a distinctive grapey Muscat flavour and is therefore used as a minor constituent in sweet wines.

VITICULTURE

The vineyards in Bordeaux are generally densely planted with vines trained upon wires on the single Guyot system. The vines are also trained low to benefit from reflected heat off the ground. The best châteaux try to maintain a high average age among the vines planted on their property by carefully planning their replanting cycle.

Until recently it might have been said that machine harvesting was only used for cheaper wines. This is no longer the case as machine harvesting is now widely practised, even amongst some of the classed growths of the Haut-Médoc. Machines give the grower lower man-power costs and greater flexibility. If bad weather approaches, for instance, grapes can be picked speedily thus minimising damage to a valuable crop.

Hand-picking is, of course, necessary for fine sweet wines made from botrytized grapes. In the top red wine châteaux, too, picking is still by hand.

VINIFICATION

Red wine vinification in Bordeaux can be said to be classical in so far as it is that on which many other regions model themselves. However, there is a broad variation of prices and qualities within the hierarchy of Bordeaux wines. This reflects the different ways in which the winemakers approach their task. The finest clarets are amongst the most expensive wines in the world. The top producers, therefore, can afford to spend more than the owners of more humble properties on the making of their wines; they are also better placed to accept lower yields in order to produce better fruit.

Let us look at where the differences might occur. Assuming that abnormal weather has not largely dictated the course of events, the first choice concerns the proportions of the various grape varieties that will go into the blend. If one is making a wine that is designed for early maturation and sale the tendency will be to use more Cabernet Franc; if the aim is to make a longer lasting, later maturing wine then it will be the lower-yielding Cabernet Sauvignon that dominates. Merlot, depending on how it is handled, can either be forward, fruity and supple or more firmly tannic and capable of extended ageing.

The next step is to select, or not select, the grapes to be used. Selection in the top châteaux will be in the vineyard, with the pickers working to the instructions of the winemaker. Alternatively, at the moment that the grapes arrive at the winery *(cuverie)* they might be inspected by hand and any poor ones rejected. These are both very labour intensive operations.

Also within the *cuverie*, for wines that are made for keeping, a percentage of stalks may be put in the fermentation vats to increase the tannin. Nowadays this is done less and less, and the majority of winemakers destalk their entire crop.

Traditionally, the fermentation vats in Bordeaux have been of oak but, whilst there are still some properties that maintain this tradition, stainless steel is now more common for the finer wines, as is lined concrete for the rest.

The individual grape varieties are vinified separately. In the early part of the following year, they will then be blended in the necessary proportions to achieve the final style and quality of wine required by the winemaker. Many châteaux now have a second label for the wines rejected at this *assemblage* or from, perhaps, young vines. Some wine may even be sold off in bulk under the district or lower appellation.

Top quality red Bordeaux is aged in small oak *barriques*, or *pièces*, of 225 litres. Traditionally, though, production figures have been quoted in *tonneaux* (1 tonneau = 4 pièces = 900 litres.) In the finest châteaux the new wine will all be put into new casks; these cost over £400 each and represent a considerable cash investment. Lesser properties will buy a smaller proportion of new casks each year; some will age only in second-hand casks. For some of the more peripheral wines and for Bordeaux rouge, there will be no oak-ageing at all. For those that do age in oak, the period will vary, but 24 months is usual in the case of the best wines.

Cru Classé claret commencing its maturation in new oak in the first year chais of Château Mouton-Rothschild, premier cru classé.

Turning to white wines, the vinification of dry wines has improved enormously with the advent of stainless steel vats and the ability to control temperatures. The top white Graves properties have always aged their wines in oak and, often, new oak. Producers of other dry white Bordeaux wines are using this technique more and more. In so doing they are seen by some to be emulating the winemakers of the New World countries.

As far as the sweet white wines are concerned, occasionally the problem is getting a liquid so rich in sugar to ferment at all. Fermentations are usually slow, therefore lengthy, and for most châteaux in the major ACs like Sauternes and Barsac a period of maturation in wood is important.

THE PRINCIPAL AREAS OF BORDEAUX

West and South of the Gironde and Garonne

Key District ACs:	Key Commune ACs:
Médoc	Saint Estèphe
Haut-Médoc	Pauillac
Graves	Saint Julien
Sauternes	Margaux
	Listrac
	Moulis
	Pessac-Léognan
	Barsac

The Médoc

This is divided into two portions, the Médoc and the Haut-Médoc. Wines with the appellation Médoc come from north of the village of St Estèphe. The soil is predominantly clay but with significant outcrops of gravel, and the Cabernet Sauvignon is the principal grape variety. There are no 1855 classified estates in this district.

The Haut-Médoc is the centre of quality red wine production in Bordeaux. With one exception, all the red wines classified in 1855 come from here. Yields for AC Haut-Médoc are slightly lower than for AC Médoc, set at 43 hectolitres per hectare as opposed to 45. Within the district there are a number of commune appellations where one finds most of the classified growths. Those with the highest reputation are, from north to south, Saint Estèphe, Pauillac, Saint Julien and Margaux. Close behind come Moulis and Listrac. Most of these commune ACs are limited to 40 hl/ha.

Médoc and Haut-Médoc wines are blends in which Cabernet Sauvignon predominates. They are made to age for a long time before they are ready to drink.

Graves

This is a district for both red and white wines with the reds generally produced to the north and the whites to the south, though there are some châteaux that have high reputations for producing both. *Graves* is the French word for gravel and this is the dominant constituent of the soil. The whites are generally dry though some sweeter wines, often with the appellation Graves Supérieures, are made. In the reds, once again, it is Cabernet Sauvignon that dominates the blends.

In 1987 the appellation Pessac-Léognan was created. This appellation covers the northern part of the area and includes many of the finest properties. The white wines here must be dry.

Sauternes

Here some of the finest sweet white wines in the world are made from a combination of Sémillon, Sauvignon and Muscadelle grapes. Misty autumns, intensified by the influence of the river Garonne, give ideal conditions for the production of wines affected by *pourriture noble*. The vintage may be spread over several weeks with the pickers passing through the vines to collect, each time, only those bunches of grapes that have been shrivelled by noble rot. Yields are necessarily low and production costs high. By law, the must has to contain a minimum of 221 g/l natural sugar and attain 12.5% alcohol. Any wines made from must with less than this amount can only have the appellation Bordeaux. There are a number of châteaux that produce quality dry wine each year in order to utilise their grape production fully.

The botrytis-affected Sémillon grapes used for Sauternes cannot be harvested by machine, and must be selectively picked by hand.

The area of production covers five communes: Sauternes, Bommes, Fargues, Preignac and Barsac. Barsac has, additionally, its own appellation. Its wines tend to be slightly less sweet than those of Sauternes.

Adjacent to Sauternes, Cérons is a further appellation for sweet wine that overlaps with the southern part of the Graves.

Between the Garonne and Dordogne

Key District ACs:	*Key Commune ACs:*
Entre-Deux-Mers	Cadillac
Premières Côtes de Bordeaux	Loupiac
	Sainte-Croix-du-Mont

The largest appellation here is Entre-Deux-Mers. This is a dry white wine which, in the past, was often made just from the Sémillon grape. Today, however, the wine is usually a blend of this and Sauvignon Blanc. Further, a growing number of producers are opting to make a pure Sauvignon Entre-Deux-Mers to capitalise on the popularity of this variety.

St Macaire, Cadillac, Loupiac and Sainte-Croix-du-Mont are sweet wines in the Sauternes style but not as rich or intense. Premières Côtes de Bordeaux can either be a red or a medium sweet white wine. Lesser appellations for both red and white wines are Graves de Vayres and Sainte-Foy-Bordeaux and, for just white wines, Bordeaux Haut-Benauge. This area is also widely used for the production of basic AC Bordeaux wines.

North and East of the Gironde and Dordogne

This is an area of mainly red wines with Merlot and Cabernet Franc playing a more important role than Cabernet Sauvignon.

Key District ACs:	*Key Commune ACs:*
Saint-Emilion	Pomerol
Saint-Emilion Grand Cru	Fronsac
Côtes de Bourg	
Premières Côtes de Blaye	

Saint-Emilion
The most important district is that of Saint-Emilion. This wine is produced from nine communes and three distinct types of soil. First of all there are the vineyards on a plateau to the north and west of the town, with sandy, gravelly soil; here the best known châteaux are Cheval Blanc and Figeac. Secondly, come the estates on the escarpment or Côtes to the south and east, with Ausone having the highest reputation; these are mainly on chalky soil. Finally, come the sandy soils of the plain in the south of the appellation, where much lighter wines are made. The lesser villages of Lussac, Montagne, Parsac, Saint-Georges and Puisseguin can add their name before that of St-Emilion and so gain some reflected glory, although they are separate ACs.

Pomerol
The reputation of nearby Pomerol is as high as that of St-Emilion. The

wines are rather richer and have been described as the Burgundies of Bordeaux. Production is lower as the properties are very small; that with the highest reputation is Château Pétrus, which regularly produces the most expensive wine in Bordeaux. Unlike the Médoc, however, there is no classification for individual châteaux. There is a satellite appellation of Lalande de Pomerol.

All the ACs of the St-Emilion and Pomerol are for red wines only.

Fronsac, Bourg and Blaye
For those looking for excellent value in the red wines of Bordeaux, Fronsac and Côtes Canon-Fronsac is an area to search. Here the hillside vineyards give the possibility of producing very good wines at reasonable prices. Unusually, perhaps, for wines made mostly from Merlot, they are quite tannic. Nearby Bourg and Blaye offer softer early drinking red and some white *petit château* wines. The best ACs are Côtes de Bourg and Premières Côtes de Blaye. Lesser reds and whites can be found in the Côtes de Castillon and Côtes de Francs; in the latter some sweet wine is made.

THE BORDEAUX TRADE

Over the past few years there has been a distinct change in the nature of the wine trade in Bordeaux. When the city was a great port the merchants, or *négociants*, had their cellars along the quays that fronted the river, particularly the Quai des Chartrons. Here they would bottle a broad range of wines mainly under generic or village names.

Nowadays, the role of the merchant has declined dramatically as the centre of gravity has moved outwards from the city of Bordeaux towards the châteaux. The majority of wines are now bottled at the château, often on mobile bottling lines. Many of the major merchants have moved their operations out of the city centre. They will stock little wine in bulk but hold vast quantities in bottle and will probably have a monopoly on a number of *petits châteaux*. In earlier times the latter would, probably, have been sold by the growers in bulk for blending.

Other, smaller, merchants are now little more than brokers, not holding much stock themselves but having access to wine still held at the various châteaux. The brokers, or merchants acting as brokers, are responsible for the actual selling on of the wine and act as the buffer between the châteaux and the wider trade.

En Primeur Sales
As can be seen, the capital demands made upon the more prestigious properties in Bordeaux are considerable. Cash flow management can be a problem too, because of the money tied up in stock. In order to

minimise this producers will release quantities of their crop for sale during the spring following the vintage. The price will include the storage and bottling costs. These are known as *en primeur* sales. Usually there will be at least two opportunities to buy wine this way called the first and second *Tranches*; prices gradually increase with each *Tranche*. Wine bought *en primeur* will continue its maturation at the château for up to two years before bottling and release. Buyers will then have to arrange shipment and, in the case of the United Kingdom, pay duty and VAT at the prevailing rate. This system depends for its success on the availability of surplus money within the trade and therefore works best in periods of boom.

SOUTH-WESTERN FRANCE

As already noted, in earlier times Bordeaux was little more than an entrepôt for the wines of the "High Country" which were produced further up the Garonne and Dordogne rivers and their tributaries. Many of these wines have never regained the reputation that they enjoyed in the Middle Ages. Now, more emphasis is being placed on their individuality and the quality needed to justify a distinctive standing.

These wines can be split into two groups: products that come from vineyards which are a logical extension of those of Bordeaux and which are in the main made from the same grape varieties. For convenience we shall call these the "Bordeaux look-alikes". Then there is a range of wines often made from local varieties of long standing which have individual characteristics clearly distinct from those of the wines of Bordeaux. These we shall call "south-west wines".

Bordeaux Look-Alikes
Key ACs:
Bergerac
Pécharmant
Monbazillac
Côtes de Duras
Côtes du Marmandais
Buzet

To the east of Entre-Deux-Mers, in the valley of the Dordogne, is the important vineyard area of Bergerac. Here the same grape varieties are used as in Bordeaux for both red and white wines. There are, however, superior appellations from specific sub-districts for the best wines: Pécharmant for reds, Montravel and Côtes de Saussignac for dry whites, Rosette for medium and sweet and Monbazillac for sweet white wines.

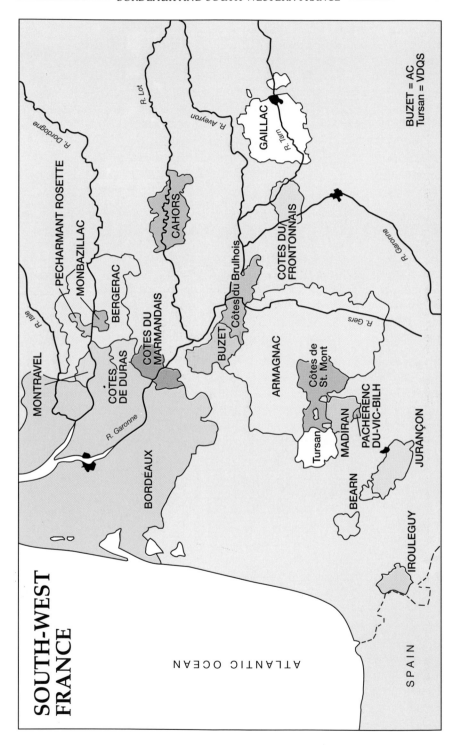

SOUTH-WEST FRANCE

BUZET = AC
Tursan = VDQS

GAILLAC

R. Lot

R. Aveyron

R. Tarn

PECHARMANT ROSETTE

MONBAZILLAC

CAHORS

BERGERAC

CÔTES DU FRONTONNAIS

R. Dordogne

CÔTES DU MARMANDAIS

Côtes du Brulhois

BUZET

MONTRAVEL

CÔTES DE DURAS

R. Isle

R. Garonne

R. Gers

R. Garonne

ARMAGNAC

Côtes de St. Mont

PACHERENC DU-VIC-BILH

MADIRAN

Tursan

JURANÇON

BEARN

BORDEAUX

IROULEGUY

ATLANTIC OCEAN

SPAIN

Produced from nobly rotted grapes, the latter are not as expensive as Sauternes and represent good value.

To the south but again adjoining Entre-Deux-Mers, are the AC areas of Côtes de Duras and Côtes du Marmandais, the latter a recent promotion. The Côtes de Duras, both red and white, wines closely resemble those of Bordeaux. The area is gaining a reputation for its pure Sauvignon Blanc dry whites, though local white grapes as Mauzac and Ondenc are also found. Local varieties like the aromatic Abouriou find their way into the blend of red Côtes du Marmandais, alongside the familiar Bordeaux names. The wine itself is soft and fruity. Some white and a little rosé is also made here.

In the valley of the Garonne the vineyards of Buzet overlap those producing wine for distillation into Armagnac. Whilst white and rosé are produced, the best wine is the red made from the classic Bordeaux grapes. Production is dominated by the local co-operative cellar.

South-West Wines
Key ACs:
Cahors
Côtes du Frontonnais
Gaillac
Madiran
Jurançon

Key VDQS:
Côtes de Saint-Mont

From the upper Lot valley come what were once described as the "black" wines of Cahors. A variety of styles and qualities of wine is to be found depending on whether the vineyard is on the fertile valley bottom, the slopes themselves or the plateau above. The dominant grape variety is Malbec known locally as Auxerrois. Blends must contain at least 70% Malbec; other varieties used are Merlot and Tannat. The wines are aged in oak and, at their best, are very deeply coloured, full-bodied and slow to mature.

Just north of the city of Toulouse are the Côtes du Frontonnais giving fruity red wines with a characteristic blackberry-like aroma, mainly from the Negrette grape. To the east lies the major district of Gaillac, one of the oldest vineyard areas of France. The majority of the production is dry white wine from the l'En de l'El and Mauzac grapes grown on chalky soils; Mauzac, sometimes known as Blanquette, is used extensively in the blends for sweet white wine. Gaillac also produces sparkling wines and reds. The main black grapes found are Gamay, Syrah, Negrette, Merlot and the two Cabernets.

The other appellations of the south-west are attached more to the Pyrenees than to the rivers of Bordeaux. Here local varieties such as the Gros and Petit Manseng (white) and Tannat and Fer (black) come to the fore. Two AC wines, the rather rustic honeyed dry or semi-dry white Pacherenc du Vic Bihl and the red Madiran, come from the south of the Armagnac region. The Tannat grape is the main constituent of Madiran. Up to 60% may be used, which provides a very tannic deeply coloured base with good potential for ageing. Cabernets Sauvignon and Franc and Fer add their seasoning to the blend.

Béarn is a fragmented district giving red, rosé and dry white wines, often made in co-operative cellars. The principal grape varieties are Tannat for reds and Gros and Petit Manseng for whites. From the same white grapes, but more noble is the neighbouring Jurançon which is said to have inspired Henri IV from the time his lips were moistened with it at his birth. At its best, this is a spicy sweet wine made from late-harvested or nobly rotted grapes. Nowadays, much more dry wine is made which must be labelled Jurançon sec. This, too, has a distinctive spicy flavour.

The last AC wine of the south-west is the phoenix-like wine from the Basque country Irouléguy. For many years until 1990 the white wine had totally disappeared and all the red and rosé wine was produced by one co-operative cellar. Recently, there has been much replanting on the steep hillsides overlooking the picturesque town of St Jean Pied de Port and the wines have taken on a new lease of life. Here Tannat is the dominant variety for the reds and is mixed with Bordeaux varieties. The main varieties for white wine are Gros and Petit Manseng. What was no more than a regional novelty now can look for broader exposure.

Finally, three local VDQS wines are worthy of mention.

Côtes du Brulhois is the latest to have been promoted to VDQS (1984). These are red and rosé wines made from a mixture of Bordeaux and indigenous grape varieties.

Tursan, which lies on the fringes of Armagnac, produces reds and rosés from a similar mixture of grapes as in the Côtes du Brulhois. The speciality, however, is the white wine made from the local grape, the Baroque.

North-east of Madiran and overlapping the Armagnac vineyards are the Côtes de St Mont whose red wines are similar to those of Madiran. The whites and rosés are less rustic in character.

CHAPTER 7

BURGUNDY

The vineyards of Burgundy lie south-east of Paris and form an arc 300 kilometres long from Auxerre to Lyon which roughly follows the route of the A6 motorway. The bulk of the region lies on a north–south line stretching for 185 kilometres between Dijon and Lyon. The regional boundary of AC Burgundy spreads over four départements, and within this are five separate vine-growing districts. The northernmost is Chablis in the Yonne département, separated by some 130–150 kilometres from the next, the Côte d'Or; which shares its name with that of its département, and is subdivided into the Côte de Nuits and the Côte de Beaune. Continuing south, both the Côte Chalonnaise and the Mâconnais are in Saône-et-Loire; the southernmost, Beaujolais, is in the département of the Rhône.

The earliest actual traces of winemaking in Burgundy date back to Roman times. The spread of Christianity in Burgundy in the third century AD then saved the vineyards when the Romans withdrew. In time, the Benedictine and Cistercian monastic orders came to be the most important factor in the production of the wines of Burgundy and the spreading of their reputation around the civilized world.

The French Revolution at the end of the 18th century, upturned the social order in France to lasting effect. As far as the vineyards of Burgundy are concerned, the major result has been the extreme fragmentation of ownership. There are two reasons for this. First, all the large vineyard estates that had belonged to the church and nobility were confiscated and auctioned off in a number of lots. This meant that what had been one large estate was transformed into several smaller ones.

More drastic, however, were the effects of the Napoleonic Law of Succession. Under this, the majority of one's possessions had to be split equally amongst one's children. Through the generations this has a mathematical progression, with vineyard and other holdings becoming smaller and smaller. This has affected the structure of the trade in Burgundy, as has the sophisticated nature of the Appellation Contrôlée system here.

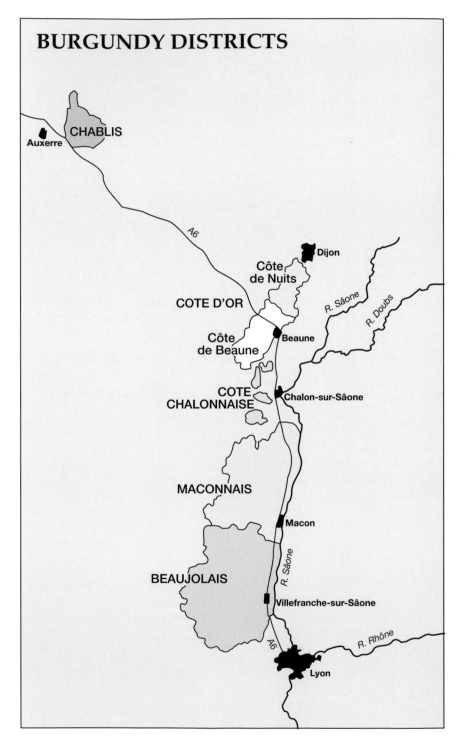

BURGUNDY DISTRICTS

CHABLIS

Auxerre

A6

Dijon

Côte
de Nuits

COTE D'OR

Côte
de Beaune

Beaune

R. Sâone

R. Doubs

COTE
CHALONNAISE

Chalon-sur-Sâone

MACONNAIS

Macon

R. Sâone

BEAUJOLAIS

Villefranche-sur-Sâone

A6

R. Rhône

Lyon

AC STRUCTURE

There are some fundamental differences between the AC structures of Bordeaux and Burgundy. In Bordeaux, a château name is largely a trademark. The owner can increase the size of his or her property by purchasing vineyard plots as they become available, and still sell the wine under the name of his château. In Burgundy, on the other hand, a vineyard name is attached to a specific plot of land, which is registered in each town hall. Its size cannot be increased. Each vineyard will also have its position in the AC hierarchy.

As an illustration, whilst Bordeaux has 91 different ACs, Burgundy has 669, and this in spite of the fact that Burgundy has only 46,000 ha under vine for AC production compared with Bordeaux's 95,000. Burgundy's total production is also correspondingly lower; its average 2.5 million hl per annum is only 45% of that of Bordeaux. Furthermore, of Burgundy's total, over half is the product of just one district: the Beaujolais.

Also, in Bordeaux a château will have one owner, all vines will be tended by the same workers, all wine will be made in the same winery by the same team of winemakers giving a high assurance of consistency in quality and style. Whereas in Burgundy, a vineyard may be split among a number of owners, each producing his individual wine. Thus, whilst it is important to know the respective merits of the individual vineyards, as in Bordeaux, it is also important to know the merits, or otherwise, of the individual growers. Putting all these factors together, it is easy to appreciate that whilst demand for fine Burgundy, as for the top Bordeaux wines, is high, that demand is less likely to be satisfied because supply is more limited.

Regional and District ACs

How are the ACs in Burgundy split up? At the base of the pyramid, there are 22 regional and district appellations, which together represent 65% of the total production.

Appellations at regional level always have the word Bourgogne in their title (e.g. Bourgogne Aligoté). Most will come from vineyards not entitled to any superior AC, though some may be declassified wines from superior appellations. The majority may be produced anywhere in Burgundy, but there are a small number of more localised appellations deemed to be of equivalent status (e.g. Bourgogne Hautes Côtes de Nuits).

District appellations are a step up in the hierarchy and do not include the word Bourgogne (e.g. Mâcon).

Commune ACs

The next level on the pyramid is that of communal appellations (e.g. Volnay, Gevrey-Chambertin). In all, there are 53 of these spread throughout the whole of Burgundy and they account for 23% of the total production. The main communes and their wines are listed towards the end of the chapter. If a wine comes from a single vineyard it may be named on the label, but does not form part of the AC.

Vineyard ACs

Appellations then exist for the best individual vineyard sites, known as *climats* in Burgundy. There are two grades: *Premier Cru* and the superior *Grand Cru*.

The labelling of these two grades is different. For *Premiers Crus*, the commune and the vineyard name will both be stated, and in the same size type:

BEAUNE GRÈVES
Appellation Beaune Premier Cru Contrôlée.

In all, there are 561 vineyards with the *premier cru* status, spread between Chablis, the Côte d'Or and the Côte Chalonnaise. They account for 11% of Burgundy's production.

At the peak of the pyramid come the *Grand Cru* vineyards, which account for no more than 1% of the production. There are 32 of these on the Côte d'Or and they can be recognised by the fact that the vineyard

The hill at Corton with woods on the summit, Grand Cru vineyards on the slopes and Commune appellation vineyards in the foreground.

name stands alone on the label, and is not attached to that of the commune:

MONTRACHET
Appellation Montrachet Contrôlée

It is important not to confuse the vineyard name and the commune name: for example, Chambertin and Gevrey-Chambertin. During the depression, the mayors of certain villages on the Côte d'Or thought it would help to sell their wines if they added the name of the best vineyard within their parish to the name of the village, thus, plain Gevrey became Gevrey-Chambertin, Puligny, Puligny-Montrachet, Vosne, Vosne-Romanée etc.

In Chablis, the *grand cru* status is a little different. There is one *grand cru*, but it is spread over seven contiguous plots of land or *climats*. Thus you have on the label:

CHABLIS LES CLOS
Appellation Chablis Grand Cru Contrôlée.

THE TRADE IN BURGUNDY

The large number of very small vineyard holdings in Burgundy has led to the individual nature of the trade in the wines.

Often the grower, or *viticulteur*, will make the wine himself as well as growing the grapes. In certain regions, particularly Beaujolais and Mâconnais, and to a lesser extent Chablis and the Côte Chalonnaise, he might take his grapes to a co-operative cellar. In a small, but growing number of cases, he might sell his grapes to a merchant, who will vinify the wine.

If the grower has made the wine there are two main options open to him. He can bottle the wine and sell it under his own label. Such wines are known as domaine-bottled (*mis du domaine* or *mis au domaine*) and account, at present, for about a third of the total production. Alternatively, he can sell his wine in cask to a *négociant*.

The role of the *négociant* in Burgundy is important. He has to produce wines in sufficient quantities to meet the commercial demands of the markets around the world. Say, for example, he has need each year of ten thousand cases of Beaune. There will be very few individual growers who will produce so much wine, so he buys lesser quantities from a number of growers and then blends the wine together so that he has a sufficient quantity of a single quality Beaune in the vintage.

Whilst there has been an increase in the sale of domaine-bottled wine over the past few years, the role of the *négociant* is still an important one. Generally speaking, he has at his disposal better facilities for the treatment of a wine and an infrastructure that enables him to maintain a network of customers around the world. Many of the major merchant companies are also important vineyard owners. Whilst there is a traditional reserve between the grower and the merchant, they both need each other.

The upshot of all of this is that there can be a marked inconsistency in style and quality in any vintage. Different *négociants*, for instance, have differing blending and maturation techniques which produce different styles of wine.

Some growers take great pride in their viticulture and, where appropriate, vinification. Others do the minimum necessary to be awarded AC knowing that even if they produce poor wine the demand for Burgundy is such that they will be paid a high price. A sound knowledge of the name and reputation of the grower or *négociant*, therefore, is at least as important as the AC when buying Burgundy.

The Hospices de Beaune
Beaune is the centre of the Burgundy wine trade and many of the major merchants are based here. It is also the site of the *Hospices de Beaune*, consisting of two charitable institutions in the centre of the town. The better known of these, the *Hôtel-Dieu* was founded in 1443, by Nicholas Rolin, chancellor of the Duchy of Burgundy. The charity's main asset is land, bequeathed to it over the years, much of which is vineyards. Wine from these vineyards is auctioned soon after the vintage, on the third Sunday in November. Prices paid are considered to be some guide to general price movements in the wines of Burgundy.

This auction is the second of what are known as the *Trois Glorieuses*. The first is the banquet of the *Chevaliers du Tastevin*, the most senior of the Burgundian wine fraternities, on the Saturday night, and the third, another banquet, the *Paulée* at Meursault on the Monday lunchtime.

CLIMATE, GRAPES AND SOIL

Climate
Burgundy experiences a northern continental climate. The winters are cold, colder than in Bordeaux which benefits from the maritime influence; the summers are hot, hotter than in Bordeaux for the same reasons and the autumns are cool. Humidity is less than in Bordeaux, the rivers in Burgundy being either too small or too distant from the vineyards to have much impact upon the microclimates.

The cool autumns and relatively low humidity mean that noble rot is rarely, if ever, found; the white wines of Burgundy are always dry. Among the natural hazards the grower faces are spring frosts, which can be as late as May in Chablis; summer rain which can cause grey rot and lastly localised but destructive summer hailstorms.

Grape Varieties

The vast majority of wines in Burgundy are produced from one or other of four grape varieties. There are two black, Pinot Noir and Gamay and two white, Chardonnay and Aligoté.

The Pinot Noir is the classic black grape variety of Burgundy. Early to ripen, it is better suited to the climate than Cabernet Sauvignon. It has very tight bunches of small grapes, which give a very sweet juice. Pinot Noir, typically, is fruity when young, but develops a vegetal fruit character with age; in colour it shows a medium intensity and tends to brown quickly. It is grown throughout the region, with the exception of Beaujolais. Particularly with this grape, it is essential that the correct clone is chosen, because there are a number of clones available which were developed in the past to give high yields, and which give poor quality fruit by today's standards.

Historically, Gamay was grown throughout Burgundy, because it was easy to grow and gave a large yield. It now thrives in the Beaujolais where it gives of its best – young, fruity wines which tend to be low in tannin.

Chardonnay, known as Beaunois in the Chablis region, provides all the great white wines of Burgundy. The bunches are similar in size to those of Pinot Noir, but rather longer and less compact. With its rich, ripe, creamy-buttery fruit, Chardonnay is a variety that has been widely planted around the world, though often outside of Burgundy, sadly, these qualities are overpowered by too zealous oaking.

Aligoté is mainly grown for Bourgogne Aligoté. In the past it tended to produce thin acid wines. Now, quality is improving and some good wine is being produced though this is unlikely ever to threaten the style and quality of Chardonnay. At best, it represents a reasonably inexpensive wine which gives value for money. It is also widely used for the production of sparkling wines, where its innate acidity is a virtue.

One final oddity is Sauvignon Blanc, whose sole Burgundian outlet is as the VDQS Sauvignon de Saint Bris in the Yonne.

Soil

Burgundy, and the Côte d'Or in particular, provides a very good example of the way grape varieties are planted according to the composition of the soil. Where limestone soils predominate, Chardonnay can be found;

where there is more marl and clay, Pinot Noir is planted. Further south in the Beaujolais, there is a natural affinity between Gamay and granitic soils.

VITICULTURE

Vines in Burgundy are among the most densely planted in the world: 12,000 plants per hectare is not unusual. Most are trained low along wires according to the Guyot system; the exceptions are some higher trained vines in the Hautes Côtes de Nuits and the Hautes Côtes de Beaune, and the gobelet trained Gamay in Beaujolais.

Summer pruning of low trained Pinot Noir growing in marl soil in Charmes Chambertin.

VINIFICATION

Climate is an important factor never far from the mind of the Burgundian winemaker. Because of the relatively cool autumn and then cold winter, fermentation will cease if the musts are not warmed. Superficially, this would appear to threaten only the red musts. However, although white wines benefit from a long cool fermentation, the temperatures in some cellars, particularly in Chablis, can drop sufficiently in winter to stop fermentation; the cellars are therefore heated if this eventuality seems likely.

Vinification techniques for red wines vary as one moves south. Traditional, open vat fermentation with pumping of juice over the cap is the norm for the Côte d'Or and Côte Chalonnaise; the use of carbonic maceration is slight in Mâconnais but widespread in Beaujolais, providing a link to vineyard regions further south.

For top quality wines, both red and white wines are matured in oak casks, for sixteen to eighteen months in the case of reds and six to nine months for whites. Most of the casks used in Burgundy are of old wood. Pinot Noir is a delicately flavoured grape by red standards, and is easily overpowered by new oak; it is only used for the very richest wines. Chardonnay's affinity with new oak is well known, but as with the reds, in Burgundy only the best wines are aged exclusively in new wood.

Burgundy is, nevertheless, an important centre for cooperage: it is conveniently placed for the oak forests of the Vosges, Nevers and Allier in particular, and exports barrels to winemakers all over the world.

REGIONAL WINES

For those wines that can come from anywhere in Burgundy, there is an ascending hierarchy:

Bourgogne Grand Ordinaire – mostly red, usually from the Gamay grape.

Bourgogne Aligoté – generally high in acidity and quite light in alcohol. The village of Bouzeron, on the Côte Chalonnaise, has the right to its own appellation, Bourgogne Aligoté-Bouzeron.

Bourgogne Passetoutgrains – loosely translated, "Burgundy – chuck all the grapes in together"; in practice, a red wine from Pinot Noir and Gamay, with the former being a minimum of a third of the blend.

Bourgogne Rouge, Bourgogne Blanc – must be made from the best grapes in the area where it is grown, effectively, this means Pinot Noir for the red and Chardonnay for the white, and with higher minimum levels of alcohol than the other regional wines.

Those appellations at regional level whose production area is restricted, for example, Bourgogne Hautes Côtes de Beaune, are covered below with the district in which they are found.

BURGUNDY DISTRICTS

The district appellation is restricted to wines from a single district within the AOC Burgundy region. Not all districts qualify for this status. Unless otherwise stated those described below do qualify.

Chablis
Key ACs:
Chablis
Chablis Premier Cru
Chablis Grand Cru

The vineyard area is centred upon the town of Chablis which lies in a hollow surrounded by hills. Here the soil has an important effect on the wine. In the best sites it is limestone overlaid with Kimmeridgian clay, which is a poor marl very high in marine fossils. Over the past few years, there has been a move to extend the area with the right to the appellation Chablis, to more outlying parts, where the soil is the similar Portlandian limestone. Some of these vineyards still carry the lesser AC Petit Chablis.

The district is prone to heavy frosts. Most of the better vineyards now have a sprinkler system installed. Whilst it is simple to operate, the high initial costs mean it is only feasible to install sprinklers in districts like Chablis where the spring frost risk is significant every year.

Vineyards are often planted following the contours of the slopes, with the best ones, those of *Grand Cru* status, all on one hillside across the river Serein from the town of Chablis. Peculiarly for Burgundy, these are exposed to the south-west. The only grape variety permitted is Chardonnay (Beaunois) and the method of pruning generally used is the double-Guyot. There is a move away from oak-ageing towards wines which have spent all their life in stainless steel.

Classic Chablis should have a greenish tinge and a distinctive acidity which, in the greatest wines, can be balanced with a rich fullness.

There are seven *Grands Crus*: Les Clos, Vaudésir, Valmur, Blanchot, Preuses, Grenouilles and Bougros and 40 *Premiers Crus* of which those most often seen include: Mont de Milieu, Montée de Tonnerre, Fourchaume, Montmains and Vaillons.

The AC Irancy covers reds and rosés from Irancy near Chablis; made from Pinot Noir. They are lighter and more acidic than other Burgundies, their style reflecting the influence of their more northern situation. Now commune level, it was promoted from AC Bourgogne Irancy in 1996.

The Côte d'Or
For Key ACs see the listing of commune and vineyard ACs below.

The vineyards of the Côte d'Or are the heartland of viticultural Burgundy, for it is here that the greatest wines are made, on east or south-east facing slopes that gain the maximum benefit from the sun and are protected from the predominant winds by the Morvan hills to the

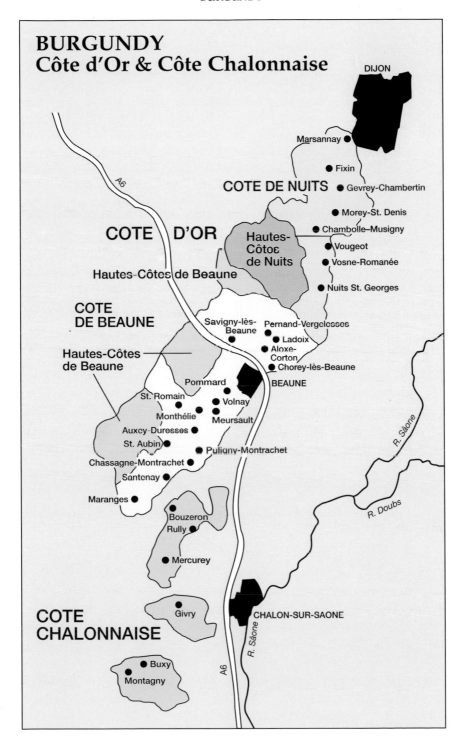

BURGUNDY
Côte d'Or & Côte Chalonnaise

DIJON

Marsannay ●

● Fixin

COTE DE NUITS ● Gevrey-Chambertin

● Morey-St. Denis

● Chambolle–Musigny

COTE   D'OR   Hautes-
Côtes
de Nuits

● Vougeot

● Vosne-Romanée

Hautes-Côtes de Beaune

● Nuits St. Georges

**COTE
DE BEAUNE**

Savigny-lès-
Beaune ●   Pernand-Vergelesses

● Ladoix

Hautes-Côtes —
de Beaune

● Aloxe-
Corton

● Chorey-lès-Beaune

Pommard ●   BEAUNE

St. Romain ●   ● Volnay

Monthélie ●   Meursault ●

Auxey-Duresses ●

St. Aubin ●

Puligny-Montrachet ●

Chassagne-Montrachet ●

Santenay ●

Maranges ●

Bouzeron ●

Rully ●

● Mercurey

R. Sâone

R. Doubs

**COTE
CHALONNAISE**

Givry ●

CHALON-SUR-SAONE

R. Sâone

● Buxy

Montagny ●

A6

west. The base of the soil is limestone mixed with marl; where the limestone predominates the finest white wines are made from the Chardonnay, where the marl, red wines from the Pinot Noir. The pruning method is the Guyot.

The Côte is split into two parts: the northern is the Côte de Nuits, stretching from just south of Dijon to the village of Corgoloin. It is here that the fullest-bodied red wines are produced from Pinot Noir. The southern part is the Côte de Beaune, from Ladoix-Serrigny in the north, to Cheilly lès Maranges in the extreme south, where the vineyards creep over into the Saône-et-Loire département. Here, a great deal of rather less full-bodied red wine is produced, but also, more importantly, what many claim are the finest dry white wines in the world.

All the red *Grand Crus* save one (Corton) are to be found in the Côte de Nuits and, likewise all the white *Grand Crus* except one (the very rare white Musigny) lie in the Côte de Beaune. This is a function of the soil. In geographical order, from north to south, here are the various village ACs of the Côte d'Or, together with some of their more important vineyards:

Côte de Nuits
There is no district AC Côte de Nuits.

Marsannay and Fixin – The communes closest to Dijon; the former known for its rosés, the latter for its reds.

Gevrey-Chambertin – The largest commune appellation of the Côte de Nuits. Red wines only including *Grands Crus* Chambertin, Chambertin Clos de Bèze.

Morey Saint Denis – Full but rather soft, red wines. *Grands Crus* include Clos de Tart, Clos Saint Denis, Clos de la Roche.

Chambolle-Musigny – Very elegant red wines. *Grands Crus* include le Musigny, Bonnes Mares.

Vougeot – This village is dominated by its one *Grand Cru*, Clos de Vougeot, which has an area of just over 50 ha and approximately 80 owners.

Vosne-Romanée – Beautiful red wines, where fruit and elegance balance, richness and body. *Grands Crus* include Richebourg, la Tâche and Romanée-Conti, reputed to be the most valuable agricultural land in the world.

Nuits-Saint-Georges – A large and popular appellation, with no *Grands Crus* but fine *Premiers Crus* in Vaucrains and les St Georges.

There are two broader appellations from the Côte de Nuits:

Côte de Nuits-Villages – These wines, virtually all red, come from vineyards which do not have the right to a commune appellation. The wines tend to be supple and may be drunk young.

Bourgogne Hautes Côtes de Nuits – Eighteen villages in the hills west of the vineyards of the Côte have the right to produce wines with this appellation. This is an area of polyculture, with cattle and soft fruit, as well as vineyards. As the vintage normally takes place a week or so later than on the Côte, there can occasionally be problems in picking fruit with optimum ripeness, but in good vintages, good wines are made which sell at reasonable prices. Some white wine is made, but red wine predominates.

Côte de Beaune
Ladoix and Pernand-Vergelesses: mainly red wines, but some good whites.

Aloxe-Corton – Fine red wines at commune level, but also two *Grands Crus* Corton (mainly red) and Corton-Charlemagne (white).

Chorey-lès-Beaune – Lying on the plain, this village produces rather firm, earthy red wines.

Savigny-lès-Beaune – An important village of which the production is 97% red. Les Lavières is a well known *Premier Cru*.

Beaune – Soft, fragrant reds and a small quantity of white. No *Grands Crus*, but many excellent *Premiers Crus* including Grèves, Cents Vignes, Marconnets, Teurons.

Pommard – Just red wines, these are amongst the most tannic in Burgundy, due to the slightly sandy nature of the soil here. Noted *Premiers Crus* are Epenots and Rugiens.

Volnay – Again just red wines, but rather softer than those of Pommard. Caillerets is among the best known of the *Premiers Crus*.

Monthélie, Auxey-Duresses and Saint-Romain – Villages lying up behind Meursault, the first two produce predominantly red wine, whilst the wines of the last are almost equally red and white. These are sound alternatives, at lower prices, to some of the more fashionable names of the Côte.

Meursault – Known for its full-bodied, nutty white wines, in particular those from *Premiers Crus* Genevrières, Charmes and Poruzot.

Saint-Aubin – Again, one of those less fashionable villages which produces very enjoyable wines.

Puligny-Montrachet – Produces white wines that have more finesse than those of Meursault. Contains the *Grand Cru* Chevalier-Montrachet in its entirety, but the boundary between Puligny and the next commune, Chassagne, runs through the *Grands Crus* le Montrachet and Bâtard-Montrachet.

Chassagne-Montrachet – Here there are two distinct soils; the chalky, which is a continuation of Puligny and gives great white wines, and marl with ironstone, which gives good red wines.

Santenay – Has an important area of vineyards, which face more south than east.

Maranges – The final commune appellation of the Côte de Beaune was created in 1989 by amalgamating three almost redundant commune appellations.

The two other appellations of the Côte de Beaune are:

Côte de Beaune-Villages – This wine, which must be red, can come from one or more commune appellations of the Côte, with the exception of Aloxe-Corton, Beaune, Pommard and Volnay.

Bourgogne-Hautes Côtes de Beaune – This is a similar appellation to that on the Hautes Côtes de Nuits. Twenty-nine villages are included in the area, and much of the wine is vinified at a co-operative cellar in Beaune.

Côte Chalonnaise
Key ACs:
Bourgogne Aligoté Bouzeron
Bourgogne Côte Chalonnaise
Rully
Mercurey
Givry
Montagny

This area, which is sometimes called the Région de Mercurey, is a continuation of the slopes of the Côte d'Or, separated from them by the valley of the river Dheune. The grape varieties are the same, as basically are the soils; the main difference is that the vineyards tend to be in pockets between meadows and woods. The wines are also similar, though they tend to mature earlier. This Côte has six Appellations exclusive to it:

Bourgogne Aligoté Bouzeron – The one village to have an individual appellation for the Aligoté grape. There are about 50 hectares planted.

Bourgogne Côte Chalonnaise – Considered to be a regional AC, this applies to wines from anywhere on the Côte, made from the noble varieties, Pinot Noir for the red and rosé wines and Chardonnay for whites.

Rully – This village makes about the same amount of both red and white wines. It is also a centre for sparkling wine production.

Mercurey – The most important of the commune appellations of the Côte. The red wines have a high reputation and sell at about the same price as some of the lesser villages of the Côte d'Or. About 4% of the wine made is white.

Givry – The smallest of the four village appellations, 90% of Givry's wines are red, full and deep in character.

Montagny – Until recently Montagny had the distinction of being the only commune appellation in Burgundy whose vineyards all had *premier cru* status. This anomaly is now being rectified! The AC is just for white wines from four villages, of which the most important is Buxy.

Mâconnais
Key ACs:
Mâcon
Mâcon-Supérieur
Mâcon-Villages
Saint Véran
Pouilly-Fuissé

Here begins the transition between the north and the south of France. The Mâconnais is a region of polyculture, with dairy farming as important as wine production. This used to be a region of red wines made from the Gamay grape. Now there is twice as much Chardonnay white wine made as red, and of this latter, a quarter is made from Pinot Noir. Many of the growers have their wines made in the co-operative cellars, of which there are a number in the region.

Mâcon (red or white) – This district appellation is now of comparatively small importance, as most producers opt for one or other of the following ACs.

Mâcon-Supérieur or Mâcon followed by a village name (red or white); Mâcon-Villages (white wine only) – These may only be applied to a wine made in one of forty-three listed villages towards the south of the region. The white wines represent some of the best value for money in Burgundy; the warmer climate gives them a softness not found further north. Certain of the villages such as Viré and Lugny have built up a considerable following for their wines. Amongst them also is the village of Chardonnay, from which the grape takes its name.

Village Appellations – Towards the south of the area there are a number of village appellations producing just Chardonnay white wines around the geologically startling crags of Solutré and Vergisson. Of these, the most

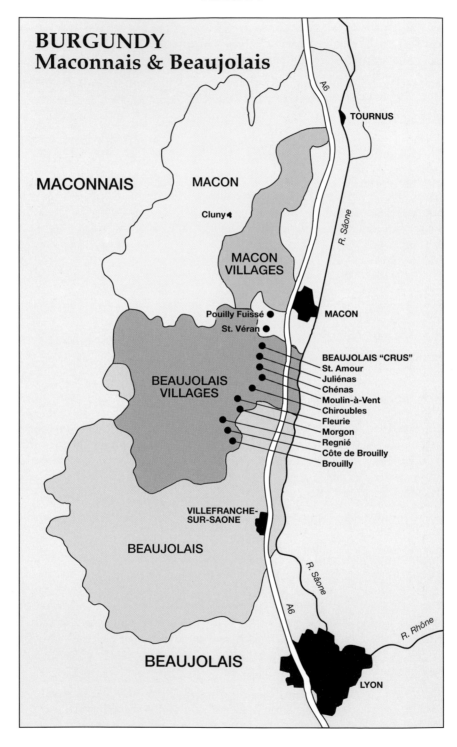

BURGUNDY
Maconnais & Beaujolais

TOURNUS

MACONNAIS

MACON

Cluny

MACON VILLAGES

Pouilly Fuissé

St. Véran

MACON

BEAUJOLAIS "CRUS"
St. Amour
Juliénas
Chénas
Moulin-à-Vent
Chiroubles
Fleurie
Morgon
Regnié
Côte de Brouilly
Brouilly

BEAUJOLAIS VILLAGES

VILLEFRANCHE-SUR-SAONE

BEAUJOLAIS

R. Sâone

A6

R. Rhône

BEAUJOLAIS

LYON

R. Sâone

A6

recently created is Saint-Véran (not to be confused with the village of Saint-Vérand, which forms part of the appellation). Then come the twin appellations of Pouilly-Loché and Pouilly-Vinzelles. The production of these wines is limited, much coming from the co-operative cellar.

The final wine of the Mâconnais is Pouilly-Fuissé, which is particularly appreciated on the American market. Here the vines are grown on a series of amphitheatre-like slopes which trap the sun, giving wines which are amongst the richest in Burgundy, achieving up to 13.5% vol.

Beaujolais
Key ACs:
Beaujolais Nouveau
Beaujolais
Beaujolais Villages
The 10 "Cru" villages listed below.

Here there is a distinct change from the rest of Burgundy. It is the Gamay grape that predominates and the vineyards are pruned in the gobelet system, with individual, free-standing vines.

The soil varies; in the north, where the better wines are made, it is predominantly granitic schist, with the vineyards planted on a series of rolling hillsides. In the east and the south, on the plain of the river Saône, where approximately half the wine is made, the soil is mainly sandy.

Carbonic maceration vats in use in Beaujolais. Whole berries, including stalks, are fermented without crushing to give a wine with good colour but little tannin.

Within Beaujolais vinification techniques vary. Cru wines are mainly vinified in the traditional way. Beaujolais Nouveau is subjected totally to carbonic maceration whilst vinification of standard Beaujolais is part traditional and part carbonic maceration. Cask-ageing is no longer practised, except for the finest wines; most wines here are made to be drunk young. About 1% of the production is white wine, made from the Chardonnay grape.

Beaujolais produces more wine than the other four districts of Burgundy put together. Co-operative cellars and a number of major merchant companies dominate production. About a quarter of the wine of Beaujolais comes from the ten cru villages at the north of the region. These, from north to south, are:

St Amour

Juliénas

Chénas: the smallest in terms of production.

Moulin-à-Vent: the longest-lived of all the Beaujolais.

Chiroubles

Fleurie

Morgon

Régnié: the most recently created

Côte de Brouilly

Brouilly: the largest production of what is generally the lightest and earliest to mature wine.

Beaujolais-Villages – Thirty-nine villages have the right to this appellation. Seven of the ten individual crus mentioned above are among them; Moulin-à-Vent and the two Brouillys are not. This appellation accounts for about a quarter of the total Beaujolais production. Occasionally the label shows the village name, e.g. Beaujolais-Charentay. The villages are all situated in the north of Beaujolais and the vineyards are on schistous soil.

Beaujolais and Beaujolais Supérieur – These come predominantly from the south and east of the region. These are the lightest of the wines of the region.

Beaujolais Nouveau – This is a wine which is specifically made for early drinking and is still the first wine of the new vintage to be released in considerable quantities. In 1990, for example, a third of the total Beaujolais crop was sold in this way. It cannot be released to the consumer until after midnight of the third Wednesday in November following the vintage, i.e. the morning of the third Thursday, and cannot be sold by growers or merchants after the following August 31st.

Beaujolais Primeur – The same wine as Beaujolais Nouveau, but may not be sold to the trade after the January 31st following the vintage. *Nouveau* and *Primeur* may only be of Beaujolais or Beaujolais-Villages quality; the ten crus cannot be sold in this way.

CHAPTER 8

ALSACE AND EASTERN FRANCE

ALSACE

As a vineyard region, Alsace stands apart from the rest of France. The reasons for this are both geographical and historical. Geographically, the province of Alsace is isolated on the west by the Vosges mountains and on the east by the River Rhine. Historically, there have been frequent disputes as to which of these two was the natural boundary of France, or of Germany, for that matter.

After the Thirty Years War Alsace came under French control and its wines were denied access to the Rhine, their historic export route northwards. At the end of the Franco-Prussian War (1871), the province became part of Germany and this had a dramatic effect on the wines produced. The traditional quality German wine producers were unhappy that Alsace, because of its more favourable climate, could produce fine wines more easily. As a result, the province was condemned to producing ordinary wines from the grossest vines.

Returned to France after the First World War, Alsace found itself unable to compete on the new domestic market, for wines of the same quality could be produced much more easily in the Midi. Consequently, a decision was taken in 1925 to ban hybrid vines and to concentrate on making fine wines from the "noble" grape varieties, with the result that in thirty years the area under vines fell by almost half.

In the early 1970s, there were further dramatic moves towards improving the quality and the image of Alsace wines. Perhaps the most important decision was taken in 1972 when it was decreed that for wines to have the appellation Alsace, they must be bottled in the region of production, the *départements* of the Haut-Rhin and the Bas-Rhin. Only one style of bottle, the Alsace *flûte*, is permitted.

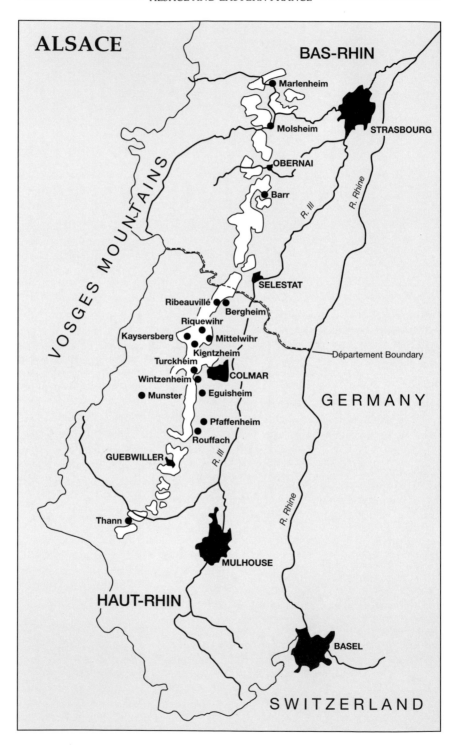

The mixture of French and German traditions lingers on. In Alsace, the yields are the highest of any AC in France (the base level is 80 hl/ha) and it is mainly German grape varieties that are grown. On the other hand, the wines are fuller and drier than those of Germany.

Soils and Climate

The Rhine flows through a vast rift valley. Some twenty-five million years ago, what was the Alsace Plain collapsed leaving on the west the Vosges Mountains, on the east the Black Forest and, ultimately, in the middle the river Rhine. As a result the eastern slopes of the Vosges, where the vineyards of Alsace lie, present a broad range of soils exposed in the collapse. These may be granitic, chalky, sandstone, loam, alluvial or even volcanic. This is one important factor in the variety of wines that Alsace produces

The Vosges mountains behind the vineyards of Alsace create a "rainshadow" and result in this being one of the driest vineyard areas in France.

Another is the climate. Although latitude and distance from the sea give a northern continental climate, Alsace enjoys almost perfect conditions for the production of wine. This is due primarily to the influence of the Vosges which shelter the vineyards from the prevailing winds which come from the west. Having crossed the Atlantic, these are high in humidity. Crossing the flat land mass of northern France the moist air forms into clouds and, as the winds rise to cross the Vosges, the first high ground encountered, most of the moisture tends to be precipitated as rain, largely on to the western slopes. Therefore, whilst the vineyards are among the most northerly of France, they are the driest after those around Perpignan on the Spanish frontier. It is the long, dry, warm autumns that enable Alsace to produce great wines.

The wine villages lie in a narrow band 140 kilometres long, at the foot of the Vosges. The better vineyards are situated on the lower slopes, which face due east and can be as steep as 65%. Exposed to the early morning sun, they gain the maximum benefit from its rays throughout the day. The lesser vineyards lie on the plain. Here, the grapes are often used for the production of Crémant d'Alsace, the local AC sparkling wine (see Chapter 16). The best wines of all come from the Haut-Rhin, around the town of Colmar, where the Vosges are at their highest and exert the strongest influence upon the climate. The average rainfall in Colmar, for instance, is only 500 mm per year – less than that in Jerez in southern Spain.

Grape Varieties
Riesling
Gewurztraminer
Pinot Blanc
Sylvaner
Tokay-Pinot Gris
Pinot Noir
Muscat
Chasselas

Alsace differs from other vineyard areas of France in that it is generally the grape variety that is the dominant feature on the label. In these instances the wine must have been made exclusively from the named grape, a rule which does not necessarily apply everywhere. Over the years, the number of varieties grown has substantially diminished. Those which produced lesser quality wine have been uprooted in favour of fewer but better quality varieties, for the growers have realised that they can best earn a living by producing wines of quality and individuality.

Riesling – With its steely clarity of flavour, the Riesling is often described as the King of Alsace wines. This is the same variety as found in Germany with the same combination of fine fruit and high acidity. The last of all varieties to ripen it is capable of sustained ripening even through spells of cooler, autumnal weather. As a result the Riesling makes exceptional late-harvest wines. Found mainly on granite or schist, it produces 23% of the crop.

Gewurztraminer – "*Gewürz*" is the German word for spice; the French spell it without the umlaut. It aptly describes this wine with its pungent aromatic spicy nose reminding many of lychees. The grape is slightly pink skinned, imparting deep colour to the wine. Gewurztraminer tends to be low in acidity and high in alcohol: 13% is not uncommon. It is a good match with strong French cheeses and frequently accompanies the local pungent "Munster" variety. Recently there has been a big increase in plantings. Mostly grown on alluvial clay, it now represents 20% of the crop.

Pinot Blanc – Plantings of this variety are expanding rapidly, particularly for making sparkling wines. It makes light, fruity wines at their best when drunk young. Wines from it are sometimes labelled Clevner or Klevner, or Pinot Auxerrois. Pinot Blanc makes up 20% of the crop.

Sylvaner – Historically the most widely planted grape in Alsace, its comparative importance has long been in decline. Grown mainly in the Bas-Rhin on loam soil, it generally gives a simple, soft wine with a hint of earthiness. It represents 18% of the crop. (Contrast the German spelling of the same variety: Silvaner.)

Tokay-Pinot Gris – In Alsace, the Pinot Gris was known before living memory as the Tokay d'Alsace – a name attributed by some to the philosopher Rousseau who on drinking it for the first time is said to have called it "the Tokay of Alsace". Others maintain that in the 16th century a local nobleman, Baron Lazare de Schwendi, introduced the variety on his return from Hungary where he had been fighting the Turks. Be that as it may, it is not related to Tokaji the wine, and the European Community objected to the use of the expression on those very grounds. The winemakers in Alsace fought to retain their "Tokay d'Alsace" on the grounds of historical usage, which eventually led to the current compromise title.

Tokay-Pinot Gris gives wine that is very rich and high in alcohol. In appearance it shows the same depth of colour as the Gewurztraminer but is less aromatic on the nose. Like the Gewurztraminer it is spicy on the palate but has higher acidity. In Alsace it often complements meat dishes. It accounts for 7% of the total crop.

Pinot Noir – Traditionally this has been used in Alsace to make a very fruity, deepish coloured rosé wine. Now more growers are making Pinot Noir in the Burgundian manner, with the juice fermenting on the skins for a week or more and a period of ageing in small oak casks. Contributing 7% of the crop, plantings are on the increase to fill the demand for red wines which is being stimulated by the often hearty Alsace cuisine.

Muscat – Difficult to grow because of its unreliable flowering, it is not widely planted and accounts for only 2% of the crop. Two branches of the numerous Muscat family are found: the higher-quality Muscat Blanc à Petits Grains and the more common Muscat Ottonel. Grown mainly on chalk they give a wine that is dry, yet full and grapey on the nose and palate. Although difficult to match with food, it is a good aperitif.

Chasselas – Generally considered to be a table grape, the only other places where this is grown for wine production in France are Savoie and Pouilly-sur-Loire. Traditionally this is a speciality of the Haut-Rhin, where it gives a light, fruity wine. No replanting of this variety is now permitted; it currently represents under 2% of the total Alsace harvest.

Finally, occasionally one comes across the expression *"Edelzwicker"* on a label. This means that the wine has been made from a mixture of grape varieties. Usually the Sylvaner, Chasselas and Pinot Blanc are used.

Viticulture and Vinification

The vines are trained high in rows which follow the contours. This gives maximum exposure to the sun and also reduces the risk of damage by late spring frosts. On the steepest slopes the vineyards are terraced. In these, planting patterns are tighter than on the plain where the rows of vines are generally further apart to give access to machinery. Pruning is generally double-Guyot.

The role of the co-operative cellars is more important in Alsace than in any other fine wine region in France. As opposed to Burgundy, for instance, where the majority of vineyard owners also make their own wine, in Alsace most wine is made either by the co-operative cellars or the merchants. The majority of the vineyard holdings are small, with more than 80% of the growers owning less than a hectare of vines and much of the work being done on a part-time basis. Even so, most growers will harvest a broad range of grape varieties. The sale of the grapes will be contracted out and advice on viticulture and, for example, the time of the harvest will come from the purchaser.

The vintage normally begins towards the middle of October. As the various grape varieties do not ripen at the same time, with the Pinot Noir and Muscat being the first to ripen, followed by the Sylvaner, and the Riesling the last, it is generally easy to programme the picking. With various qualities of late-harvest wines, this might go on until the end of November or beginning of December.

There is a saying in Alsace to the effect that the best Alsace wine is the one to which least has happened. The grapes are pressed, generally in pneumatic Willmes presses, and despite the climate, chaptalisation is widely practised. The juice ferments in large oak casks, many up to one hundred years old. On the inside of these, there is a thick tartar deposit which prevents the wood from having any influence on the wine. Stainless steel, being much more practical, is now replacing wood in many cellars.

Normally, the malo-lactic fermentation is not allowed to take place. Bottling usually takes place in the spring following the vintage so that the wines retain their maximum fruit.

Appellations Contrôlées
Alsace (with name of grape variety)
Alsace Grand Cru (with name of vineyard)
Crémant d'Alsace (see chapter 16)

Alsace was the last of the major French wine-producing regions to become part of the Appellation Contrôlée system. It did so in 1962. The basic designation in the region is Appellation Alsace Contrôlée, which may or may not be qualified by one of the grape varieties already mentioned.

Since 1975, there has also been the possibility of a qualitative statement for Alsace wine, based on the place where the grapes were grown. There are now fifty individual vineyards that have been granted the status *Grand Cru*. These are particular slopes which traditionally have produced the finest wines.

To achieve *Grand Cru* status, the wine must be made from one of four noble varieties: Riesling, Gewurztraminer, Pinot Gris and Muscat. The maximum yield is 65 hl/ha, as opposed to the more general 80 hl/ha. The minimum natural potential alcohol must be 10% for Riesling and Muscat and 12% for Pinot Gris and Gewurztraminer. The grape variety and the vintage have to be mentioned on the label.

Vendange Tardive / Sélection de Grains Nobles
Two further classifications of Alsace wine, which may be applied to either basic or Grand Cru level wines, have been controlled by law since 1983. They depend on the sugar content of the grapes when they are picked, which, in the case of *Sélection de Grains Nobles*, means that the grapes will have been attacked by noble rot. These are:

Vendange Tardive (Late Harvest) – These wines must be made from Riesling, Gewurztraminer or Pinot Gris grapes (the Muscat is also permitted, but is used very rarely) with a minimum natural must weight for the Riesling and Muscat of 95 °Oe and for the other two of 105 °Oe. Chaptalisation is forbidden. This wine can be either dry or medium-sweet.

Sélection de Grain Nobles (Selection of noble grapes) – This is similar to the *Vendange Tardive* but the must weights must be a minimum of 120 °Oe for the Gewurztraminer and Pinot Gris and 110 °Oe for Riesling. This wine is only made in exceptional vintages and is sweet.

Samples of both these styles of wines have to be submitted for tasting approval not less than fifteen months after the vintage.

Though these are the only official qualitative distinctions, merchants still create their own hierarchy with such terms as *Réserve Personnelle* or *Cuvée Spéciale*.

EASTERN FRANCE

Jura

In many ways, the vineyards of the Jura are an anachronism. They were severely hit at the time of phylloxera and many of them were not replanted. Their survival has been largely the work of one company. Included in what has survived are some very individual wines and distinctive local grape varieties.

The vineyards of the Jura lie some 100 kilometres east of Burgundy in a narrow north–south band between the towns of Arbois and Lons le Saunier. Two specialities are *Vin Jaune* and *Vin de Paille*.

Vin Jaune is produced throughout the Jura vineyards though the best known, Château Chalon, has its own AC. It is made from a local sub-variety of Traminer, known as Savagnin. This is aged in cask for a minimum of six years without being topped up. It develops a yeast growth, similar to Fino flor on its surface and increases in strength over the years. The result is an unfortified sherry-style wine with a distinctive flavour. (Flor is described in Chapter 17.)

Vin de Paille from the Jura is the last relic of a type of wine that, historically, was widely made in France, and can still be found in Italy and Austria. After the vintage, bunches of grapes are laid out on straw in the attics of the wineries. Over the winter, the water content reduces and the sugar concentrates. They are then pressed and fermented. The result is an expensive luscious dessert wine that will keep for fifty years or more.

For the other wines of the Jura, the local white Savagnin grape is joined by the black Poulsard and the Burgundian varieties Chardonnay, Pinot Noir and Gamay. The principal appellations are Côtes du Jura and Arbois.

Savoie

The vineyards of Savoie lie east of the river Rhône and to the south of Lake Geneva. Much of what is made is consumed in the local ski resorts.

The grape varieties, often evident on the label, include for red wines,

Gamay, Mondeuse and Pinot Noir and for whites, Jacquère, Altesse, Mondeuse Blanc, Chardonnay, Aligoté and Chasselas.

The appellations reflect the fierce individuality of the local villages, for fifteen of them have the right to add their name to the basic AC Vin de Savoie. The most commonly seen are: Abymes, Apremont, Chignin and Ripaille.

Other individual AC appellations are:

Crépy – A light faintly petillant wine made from Chasselas on the south bank of Lake Geneva.

Seyssel – A dry white and, more often than not, sparkling wine from the small town of the same name on the Rhône. Made from the Altesse grape planted on steep chalky slopes, it is a light and very flowery wine.

CHAPTER 9

THE LOIRE VALLEY

With a length of more than 1,000 kilometres, the Loire is the greatest of the French rivers. Rising in the Ardèche *département*, west of Valence, the river flows north until it turns to the west between the towns of Gien and Orléans before flowing, some 500 kilometres on, into the Bay of Biscay at Nantes.

It is not certain when the first vines were planted, but records show that during Roman times there were vineyards at Sancerre and at St-Pourçain-sur-Sioule, close to the Allier, a tributary of the Loire. Monks of the Benedictine order are known to have been planting vineyards not far from Nantes as early as the seventh century. By the 12th century, Dutch merchants came to the French Atlantic coast to buy sea-salt and they soon established an important trade in wine. Most of this was produced close to the mouth of the Loire as additional taxes had to be paid at the town of Ingrandes, downriver from Angers, on wine shipped from further up the river. England, too, was an important customer until she developed the vineyards of the Bordeaux region having acquired Aquitaine upon the marriage of Henry II to Eleanor of Aquitaine in 1152. The Dutch influence declined following the Franco-Dutch war of 1672 after which the winemakers of the region looked almost exclusively to the home market. It was not until after World War II that Loire wines again became well known outside France, this time on both sides of the Atlantic.

The 600 kilometre stretch of the Loire under consideration extends eastwards from Nantes through Orléans and then a short way southwards towards the Massif Central. There are vineyards along almost the total length of this lower stretch. These can loosely be grouped into four blocks or sub-regions: Nantais, Anjou-Saumur, Touraine and the Centre.

Appellation Contrôlée
Unlike other areas there is no regional generic Appellation for the Loire such as AC Bordeaux or AC Bourgogne. Just two AC wines include the

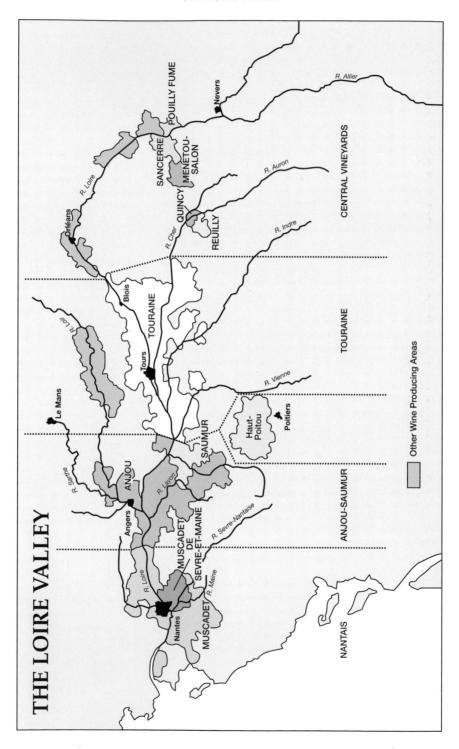

THE LOIRE VALLEY

Other Wine Producing Areas

name of the region in their title: Rosé de Loire and Crémant de Loire. However, the labels of virtually all other AC wines from the region are entitled to carry the added description "Val de Loire". As far as AC wines are concerned, approximately 60% are white wines, 30% red and 10% rosé.

There are also a number of VDQS wines and vins de pays, particularly Vin de Pays du Jardin de la France which covers the whole region. Approximate production figures are:

AC	2.5 million hectolitres	
VDQS	0.4 "	"
Vins de Pays	0.4 "	"

Climate

The vineyards of the Loire lie between 47 and 48°N; the cool climate found at these latitudes means that noticeable acidity is a feature of Loire wines. There are significant variations across the region from coast to hinterland as the Atlantic influence recedes and there can be significant variations in weather patterns from year to year. Vintages, therefore, are important, and in some cases affect the styles of wine produced.

NANTAIS

Key wines:
Muscadet AC
Muscadet de Sèvre-et-Maine AC
Muscadet de Sèvre-et-Maine AC Sur Lie
Gros Plant du Nantais VDQS

The vineyards of the Nantais are Brittany's only vineyards. They lie on both banks of the river Loire close to its mouth, with the major city of Nantes as their centre. The vineyards are split between four ACs: Muscadet, Muscadet de Sèvre-et-Maine, Muscadet des Coteaux de la Loire and Muscadet Côtes de Grandlieu. Qualitatively, the finest of the wines comes from the second of these regions which lies to the south and east of Nantes. This is also the most important Appellation in terms of quantity, not only in the Nantais but in all the Loire valley.

The vineyards are on a series of rolling slopes, with the soil a mixture of sand and clay. Many of the better vineyards in the Sèvre-et-Maine are planted on a gravelly sub-soil over granite bedrock, which makes for better drainage. Pruning is generally in the free-standing gobelet style, though to facilitate machine picking, most newly planted vines are trained on wires.

The vineyards of the Nantais are relatively flat, with gentle slopes only, and the vines are often trained as free-standing bushes.

The climate is influenced by the Atlantic Ocean and is moist and temperate, with neither aggressive summers nor winters. Severe frosts are rare.

The Muscadet Grape

All Muscadet is made from the grape of the same name, for here the wine is named not from the region where it is produced, but from the grape from which it is made. This is none other than the humble Melon de Bourgogne, reputedly brought to the region by the Benedictines. Regarded as a neutral variety, its best wines nevertheless display attractive green apple or grassy aromas. The fact that it ripens early helps in this almost marginal region for the production of wine.

All wines from the Muscadet should be dry. Indeed, not so long ago, the wines were notorious for their acidity. Sadly, perhaps, they are now generally vinified in a softer, more commercial style. Chaptalisation is widely practised, but in order to maintain the fresh nature of the wine the maximum final alcoholic strength permitted is 12%. Historically, the wines were fermented in casks, though because of cost, stainless steel is now playing a much more important role. The wine should be drunk young and is an ideal accompaniment to seafood.

Muscadet Sur Lie

A speciality which is growing in importance is Muscadet sur lie. This is wine which is bottled directly from the cask, or tank, in the spring following the vintage (*lie* is the French word for lees). It is bottled without racking, though it may be filtered. Theoretically this means that much of it is domaine bottled and, during the bottling season, mobile bottling lines go from property to property. Because the wine is handled very little it retains its delicacy and freshness, and may have lazy bubbles beading the rim of the glass. Contact with its lees gives it fuller body and a slightly yeasty character. Any Muscadet appellation may use the technique, but it is a particular feature of Sèvre-et-Maine.

Gros Plant

Gros Plant du Nantais is a local VDQS wine made from the Folle Blanche grape, known locally as the Gros Plant. Historically, this was the main variety used for distillation into Cognac because of its low alcoholic content and high acidity. These qualities are reflected in this wine, which comes mainly from the vineyard areas south-west of Nantes and towards the coast.

ANJOU-SAUMUR

Key wines:

Anjou AC (Rouge, Blanc, Rosé)	Quarts-de-Chaume AC
Cabernet d'Anjou AC	Savennières AC
Coteaux du Layon AC	Saumur AC (Rouge, Blanc, Mousseux)
Bonnezeaux AC	Saumur-Champigny AC

This is the heartland of the Loire. The vineyards to the west adjoin those of the Muscadet; to the east they extend some 10 kilometres beyond Saumur. The climate, somewhat humid without extreme variations between summer and winter, reflects the continuing maritime influence. The dampness in the west recedes noticeably as one moves further inland. The soil changes also from a schist sub-soil in the west to limestone chalk and tufa (chalk boiled by volcanic action and full of holes resembling pumice) in the east.

Of the sub-regions of the Loire valley, this is the most productive, with red, white and rosé wines being produced in almost equal proportions. All the best wines, with one exception, come from vineyards to the south of the river.

Grape Varieties

A number of different grape varieties are planted here and in the Touraine, and are described below. Chenin Blanc and Cabernet Franc, in

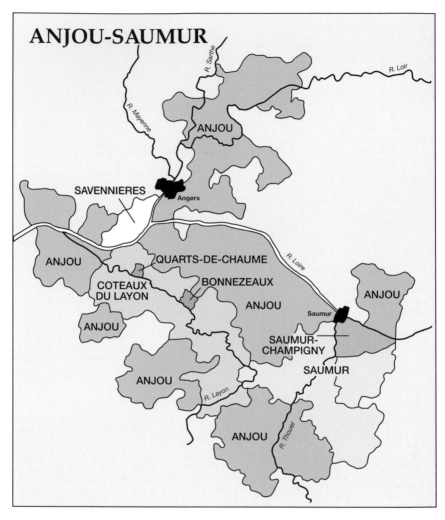

particular, are important varieties for which the Loire is the classic source.

Pineau de la Loire is the local name for Chenin Blanc, which is the grape that is responsible for the greatest white wines of Anjou-Saumur, be they dry or sweet, sparkling or still. The variety in styles of wine produced here from this versatile classic is directly related to the ripeness of the grape when picked. Barely ripe fruit is used for sparkling wines whilst the dry, medium and sweet styles of still wine reflect the use of increasingly ripe berries, including those affected by noble rot. Chenin Blanc grows best on limestone soils and, because of its high natural acidity, ages well.

Cabernet Franc (Breton) is the main red wine grape of the Loire. It is similar to Cabernet Sauvignon, with which it is often blended, but is more suited to the cooler Loire climate and appears greener and more stalky on the nose and palate. It is also used for rosé wines.

Gamay, the classic Beaujolais grape, here gives fresh, fruity wines, best drunk young.

Malbec (Cot) is of declining importance because of its sensitivity to frost and coulure. It produces deeply coloured, tannic wines.

Grolleau (Groslot), is only found in Anjou where it is the workhorse black grape producing high yields of undistinguished wine. It often forms the base of Rosé d'Anjou, or of sparkling wine.

Anjou
The broad appellation Anjou covers red, white and rosé wines. The best known are Gamay d'Anjou, Anjou Rouge, made from Cabernet Franc, Anjou Blanc, made from Chenin Blanc in both dry and medium-dry styles, and three rosés. The first of these, Rosé d'Anjou, is a blend of Grolleau, Cabernet Franc and/or Gamay and generally slightly sweet; it is declining in importance. The second is Rosé de Loire which must have at least 30% Cabernet grapes in the blend and is dry. Finally, the superior Cabernet d'Anjou, always medium, is a blend of Cabernets Franc and Sauvignon.

Vineyards in Anjou-Saumur overlooking the River Loire.

The best wines of Anjou-Saumur are white and made from Chenin Blanc. Most of these have some residual sweetness, as botrytis develops well in the sheltered valleys. This is particularly true of the deep valley of the Layon, which flows into the Loire from the south, west of Angers; from here come the sweet wines of Coteaux du Layon. In style these are never as luscious as Sauternes because of the Chenin's acidity but are more alcoholic than German sweet wines. The two most favoured sites, each shared by a handful of growers, Quarts-de-Chaume and Bonnezeaux, have their own Appellations and rank amongst the great sweet white wines of the world.

On the north bank of the Loire, again to the west of Angers, lies Savennières, with its two *grands crus* Coulée de Serrant and La Roche-aux-Moines, complex dry wines, which show the versatility of the Chenin Blanc grape. Quality reflects the low yields and the volcanic subsoil.

Saumur

At the eastern frontier of Anjou, and growing the same grape varieties, lie the vineyards of Saumur. Here the white wines range from dry to, in the best vintages, sweet. The best of the local red wines, made from the Cabernet Franc, is the fruity Saumur-Champigny. Plain Anjou rouge and Saumur rouge can represent good value for money. Many of the cellars are cut into the steep banks of tufa on both sides of the river.

Saumur is also an important centre for sparkling wine production (see Chapter 16).

TOURAINE

Key wines:

Touraine AC (Rouge, Blanc)	St-Nicolas-de-Bourgueil AC
Sauvignon de Touraine AC	Vouvray AC
Chinon AC	Montlouis AC
Bourgueil AC	Cheverny AC

Tours, the capital of Touraine, has an important place in wine history, for it was here that St Martin of Tours established his abbey, which, with its daughter houses, was responsible for planting many of the vineyards of Anjou. Indeed, locally, drunkenness is still known as the "illness of St Martin."

The temperate influence of the Atlantic, important in the western Loire, is not a factor in the climate here as Tours is some 200 kilometres from the coast.

The vineyards of Touraine fall into two main groups; to the west adjoining Saumur is the red wine area of Chinon/Bourgueil, to the east the white wine area of Vouvray. The Appellation Touraine covers the whole sub-region with the red wines being made largely from the Cabernet Franc or Gamay grapes and the dry, white wines from Sauvignon Blanc and Chenin. These often appear under a varietal label, e.g. Sauvignon de Touraine, Gamay de Touraine.

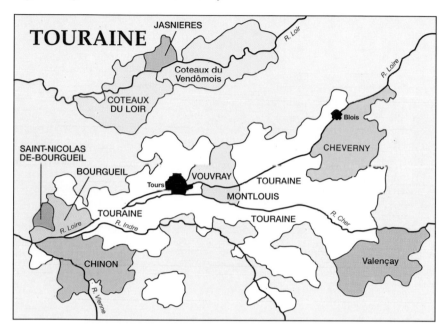

Red Wines

The most important red wine of the Loire is that of Chinon, which is produced around the town of the same name. Production is almost totally red (there is a little rosé) from the Cabernet Franc grape, known locally as the Breton. The wine comes in three distinct styles, depending on where the grapes are grown. The lightest wines come from the vineyards on the sandy soils of the valley of the Vienne. This river joins the Loire from the south some 15 kilometres west of Chinon. On the plateau to its north the soil is more clay and gravel and the wine firmer. The finest wines, however, come from the slopes where limestone predominates. These are wines for keeping.

North of Chinon, on the other bank of the Loire lie the vineyards of Bourgueil and St-Nicolas-de-Bourgueil. These are protected from north winds by a wooded plateau and have their own favourable microclimate.

The Cabernet Franc grape gives all three appellations a certain rusticity and many of them need some bottle age before they can be appreciated. It is probably Chinon that is the most forward, with the Bourgueils capable of greater development in bottle, although none could be described as needing long term cellaring.

Tufa cliff face in Vouvray, behind which the cellar is cut. The vineyard is planted above.

Vouvray

For centuries much of the production of the wines of Vouvray was shipped to Holland, where the sweet white wines of the Loire have long been appreciated. Vouvray can appear in a range of styles from *sec* (dry) to *moelleux* (sweet) though the latter are only produced in the finest vintages, when botrytis affects the Chenin Blanc grapes. Here the harvest is amongst the latest in France. Tufa is a particular feature in Vouvray, and many of the cellars are cut into the chalky cliffs that border the river.

On the other, south, bank of the river, Montlouis produces wines that are similar to those of Vouvray, though never attaining the peaks of which the best examples of the latter are capable.

Outside Touraine to the north of Tours, running parallel to the Loire is the river Loir. Here there are two ACs: the first is the austere dry white Jasnières, from Chenin Blanc; the other is the red and rosé Coteaux du Loir, which have a rather rustic bitter taste.

Upstream on the Loire south of the town of Blois are the regions of Cheverny (whites mainly from the Romorantin grape, though some Sauvignon Blanc is grown) and Valençay VDQS, which is mainly red from Gamay.

THE CENTRE

Key wines:
Sancerre AC
Pouilly Fumé AC
Menetou Salon AC
Quincy AC
Reuilly AC

At the eastern end of the viticultural Loire, well upstream from Touraine and beyond Orléans, is the area widely known as the Central Vineyards. In terms of production it is the smallest of the four sub-regions. The finest quality wines of this area are found around the twin towns of Sancerre and Pouilly-sur-Loire almost facing each other across the Loire. Here the climate is continental with warmer summers and colder winters and with a greater risk of ill-timed hail and spring frosts than in those areas closer to the Atlantic.

Sancerre
For many wine lovers, Sancerre makes the finest white wines of the Loire. The vineyards are spread over fifteen villages on very chalky stony soil, much of it rich in marine fossils, which drains well. They mainly lie on the slopes of a series of hills which face south-east and south-west. The vineyard holdings are small and generally split into a number of minute parcels of vines. Because of the nature of the soil, chlorosis is a regular problem.

Most Sancerre is dry white, made from Sauvignon Blanc and fermented slowly in 600 litre wooden casks. It often has a distinctive herbaceous taste, known to those who do not like the style as "cat's pee" (euphemistically known as elderflower or gooseberries). It also has a high acidity and, generally, does not age well. Certain individual vineyard names such as Les Monts Damnés in probably the best rated village, Chavignol, have created a reputation for themselves.

About 20% of Sancerre is red or rosé wine made from Pinot Noir. This variety is not found elsewhere in the Loire valley; perhaps the proximity of Burgundy and Champagne accounts for its presence here. Be that as it may, the reds of Sancerre made from Pinot Noir are of a distinctly lighter style than those of Burgundy.

Pouilly Fumé
On the other bank of the river Loire two AC wines are produced on soils much the same as in Sancerre but with the notable addition of flint. These are Pouilly Fumé (or Blanc Fumé de Pouilly) and Pouilly-sur-Loire. The area of production for both these wines is the same, though the first is made from the Sauvignon Blanc grape and the second from Chasselas, a

relic of the days when they were supplied as table-grapes to the gentry of Paris before the new railways brought riper mediterranean fruit within reach. Both wines are dry; the former is very similar to Sancerre, though styles may vary according to the practices of the grower. It can benefit from limited ageing. Pouilly-sur-Loire bears some resemblance to wines made from the same grape in Alsace and Switzerland: gentle, easy drinking, best when young.

To the west and south of Sancerre, on tributaries of the Cher, are the three small areas of Menetou Salon, Quincy and Reuilly. The first, which sits on kimmeridgian clay as found in Chablis, is growing in importance, whilst the other two are slowly declining. All three produce white wines from Sauvignon, those of Quincy having a more rustic style. Reds and rosés are made from Pinot Noir and Pinot Gris.

HAUT-POITOU

Whilst the VDQS Vins du Haut-Poitou certainly do not come from the Loire valley itself but from further south near Poitiers, for want of any other region adopting them they are often grouped with the Loire. Here a range of varietal wines is produced, mainly by one co-operative cellar. The most successful are Gamay, Sauvignon Blanc and Chardonnay.

CHAPTER 10

THE RHONE VALLEY AND SOUTHERN FRANCE

THE RHONE VALLEY

The Rhône is one of the most interesting wine rivers in the world. Rising in the Alps, south of the Swiss city of Luzern, it flows west through the vineyards of the Valais, and then north-west into Lake Geneva. From there it flows south through the vineyards of Savoie (notably Seyssel), and then west to join the Saône at Lyons. There it turns due south for some 400 kilometres to flow into the Mediterranean Sea west of Marseille. It is on this last stretch, between the old Roman city of Vienne in the north and the city of Avignon in the south, that what are known as Rhône wines are produced. Of these, 98% are either red or rosé.

Though the Rhône is considered as one vineyard region, effectively it is split into two distinct parts, with different climates and, for the most part, different grape varieties. The northern Rhône vineyards lie between Vienne and Valence, a distance of about 70 kilometres. There is then a gap of 60 kilometres, before the vineyards begin again at the village of Donzère, just south of Montélimar.

The AC structure is in three steps. In ascending order of quality these are as follows: first, the generic level Appellation Côtes du Rhône Contrôlée may be found throughout the region but in practice comes predominantly from the south. Secondly, Côtes du Rhône-Villages is an appellation reserved for certain villages in the south only. Finally, at the commune level, there are thirteen "*Crus,*" that is villages with individual AC status. Eight of these lie in the north and five in the south.

The Northern Rhône

Key wines:
Côte-Rôtie AC
Condrieu AC
St Joseph AC
Hermitage AC
Crozes-Hermitage AC
Cornas AC

As far as reputations are concerned, most of the truly great Rhône wines come from the north. It is, however, a much smaller area than the south, and in fact only produces 5% of the region's total.

Here the valley is quite narrow, with steep sides. The soil is basically granitic. For the most part, the vineyards are planted on the western bank, much closer to the river than in the south, on steep narrow terraces. Occasionally, soil has to be carried back up the slopes having been washed down by heavy rain. There are frequent lateral valleys, which means that the vines gain maximum exposure to the sun, and shelter from one of the significant features of the climate here, the Mistral. This is a regular, strong wind, which whistles down from the north, and has a particularly strong chill factor. Because of the Mistral, vines are often staked so that even bush trained vines will each have a post. Taking the wind into account, the climate is similar to that of the Beaujolais: southern continental, where the heat of summer is not excessive. Indeed, peaches and cherries are also widely grown here.

In all the red wines of the northern Rhône, Syrah is the principal grape. It gives full-coloured, tannic wines that age well, with a distinct flavour of soft, black fruit, like bilberries and blackberries.

The most interesting of the white grapes is Viognier, notorious for its small yield of wine with musky, apricot hints. As a variety, this had become all but extinct, with the exception of small plantings here in the Rhône valley. However, it has now become something of a cult grape and is being planted in Languedoc and California.

The Roussanne is also a quality grape, though again its plantings have declined. It gives quality to a blend. The final white grape of the northern Rhône is the much higher yielding Marsanne, which adds body and alcohol. Sadly, unless it is picked early, the resulting wines have a tendency to oxidise.

Red winemaking in this part of the valley remains traditional: open vat fermentation with pumping over after which most of the red wines will be aged in old wood for up to two years before bottling.

Of the eight crus in the region, five are red and three white. Rather than

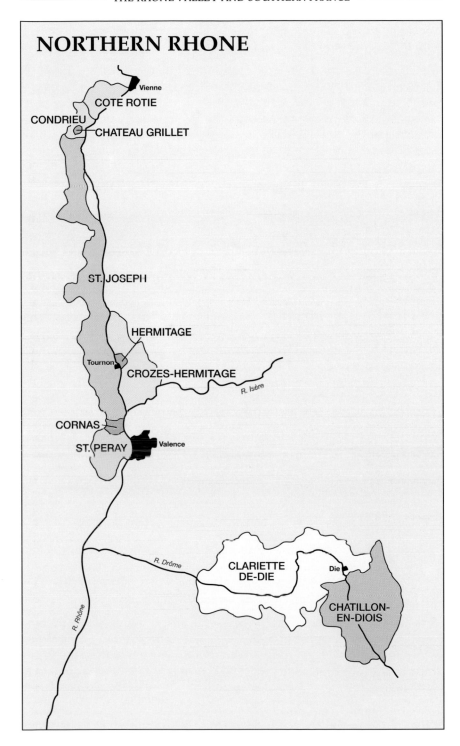

NORTHERN RHONE

Vienne

COTE ROTIE

CONDRIEU

CHATEAU GRILLET

ST. JOSEPH

HERMITAGE

Tournon

CROZES-HERMITAGE

R. Isère

CORNAS

ST. PERAY

Valence

R. Drôme

CLARIETTE DE-DIE

Die

CHATILLON-EN-DIOIS

R. Rhône

by colour, it is easier to consider these in geographical order as one moves with the river southwards down the valley.

The most northerly vineyards producing Rhône wines are those of AC Côte-Rôtie, literally "roasted slope", around the town of Ampuis where they are sheltered from the Mistral and enjoy a sunny aspect. These are just red wines made from the Syrah grape, into which up to 20% Viognier may be blended. Perhaps because of this, the wines of Côte-Rôtie are considered to be the most elegant Rhône wines. The finest vineyard areas are known as the Côte Brune and the Côte Blonde. Vines here may still be seen trained along sticks into a strong tepee shape *(taille en archet)*.

Tying vines in to stakes with raffia in steep Côte-Rôtie vineyards to form the traditional taille en archet or "wig-wam" shape.

Condrieu is a dry white wine made solely from the Viognier grape. It has an individual rich, opulent fruitiness, at its best when drunk young. Within the Appellation, there is the tiny enclave of Château-Grillet, also making white wines from Viognier, and ageing them in oak.

Saint-Joseph, Hermitage and Crozes-Hermitage are more important Appellations, the first being on the west side of the Rhône and the other two on the east. All three make predominantly red wines from the Syrah grape and a much smaller proportion of white from Roussanne and Marsanne.

In Victorian times, Hermitage was perceived to be two of the great wines of the world, for both the red and the white were highly appreciated. The vineyards of Hermitage lie on a steep, south-facing hillside, behind the town of Tain-l'Hermitage, where the river bends sharply eastward briefly before resuming its southward flow, inviting comparison, albeit on a reduced scale, with the Rheingau in Germany. There are a number of individual sites, known locally as "*mas*", of which, historically, each had its own reputation. Now, few such names are seen on the labels, though Chante-Alouette and la Maison Blanche can still be found.

Red Hermitage is one of the most full-bodied of French red wines and can age for a very long time, with the best vintages keeping for fifty years or so. Though up to 15% of white grapes are permitted alongside Syrah in the blend, this in effect rarely occurs.

About a fifth of the production of Hermitage is white wine, with Roussanne being the predominant grape. Here again, the wines can last well, though they scarcely seem to merit the status that they enjoyed a century or so ago, as one of the five great white wines of the world.

The broader Appellation of Crozes-Hermitage surrounds Hermitage on hilly terrain. Though excellent wines are often produced, these are in a lighter, more forward style which never threatens the reputation of their illustrious neighbour.

The final two Appellations of the northern Rhône are Cornas and St-Péray. The former is perhaps the most under-appreciated wine of the Rhône. Due to its southern and particularly well-sheltered situation, it is a full-bodied red, which, at its best, can rival the wine of Hermitage. St-Péray makes mainly bottle-fermented sparkling wine from the Marsanne grape. It lacks the leanness and finesse that one would expect from a Champagne, but substitutes for this a full nuttiness.

The Southern Rhône
Key wines:
Côtes du Rhône AC
Côtes du Rhône-Villages AC
Châteauneuf-du-Pape AC
Gigondas AC
Lirac AC
Tavel AC
Vacqueyras AC

Here the climate changes from continental to mediterranean, with milder winters and hotter summers. The valley of the Rhône spreads out giving pockets of sandy soil amongst the rough, rocky scrubland. With there being no steep slopes to protect the vines from the Mistral, windbreaks of trees have often to be planted.

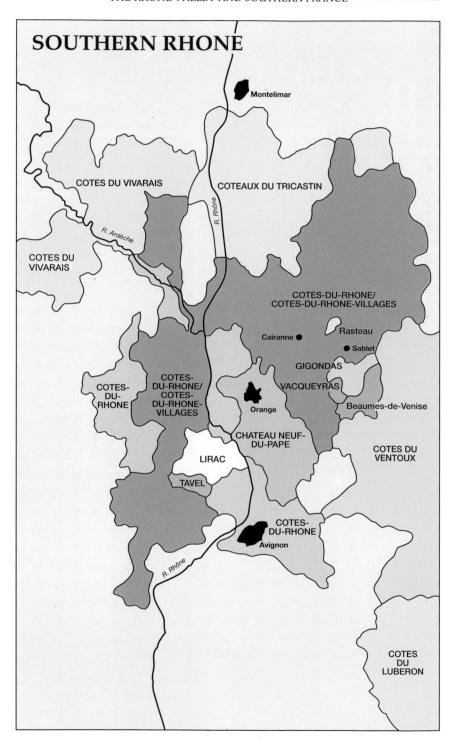

SOUTHERN RHONE

Montelimar

COTES DU VIVARAIS

COTEAUX DU TRICASTIN

R. Rhône

R. Ardèche

COTES DU
VIVARAIS

COTES-DU-RHONE/
COTES-DU-RHONE-VILLAGES

Cairanne ●

Rasteau

● Sablet

GIGONDAS

COTES-
DU-
RHONE

COTES-
DU-RHONE/
COTES-
DU-RHONE-
VILLAGES

VACQUEYRAS

Orange

Beaumes-de-Venise

CHATEAU NEUF-
DU-PAPE

COTES DU
VENTOUX

LIRAC

TAVEL

COTES-
DU-RHONE

Avignon

R. Rhône

COTES
DU
LUBERON

The wines are made from a blend of a number of different varieties. Here, the Syrah is joined by at least a dozen other varieties, of which the most important is Grenache. This is high in sugar and hence alcohol, and thin skinned with low colour and tannin. It matures quickly and is a good base wine for blending. Also significant are Cinsault and Mourvèdre: the former is low in tannin, and its fruitiness and high acidity mean that it, too, is useful in a blend, and particularly in rosés. Mourvèdre's deep-coloured, tannic wine on the other hand, provides good backbone.

For the white wines the Roussanne is joined by Clairette, Ugni Blanc and seven other varieties.

All these varieties, because they need plenty of warmth to ripen, are pruned low, in order to maximise the reflected heat. Syrah is wire trained in the single-Guyot system, whilst the others are spur pruned to form a free-standing bush.

By far the most important wine here, in terms of production, is the ubiquitous Côtes du Rhône AC. Four-fifths of the entire region's output consists of this generic level Appellation. There is some movement towards the use of carbonic maceration, particularly at this basic level, but not to the degree seen in Beaujolais or the Midi. Due to the range of different soils and grape varieties, there can be a broad variety of styles of red wine, ranging from the youthful and fruity (made by carbonic maceration) to the meaty and oak-aged (made by more traditional methods). Much of the production is carried out by co-operative cellars.

Within the southern Rhône there are a number of villages entitled to call their red (and in some cases rosé) wine Côtes du Rhône-Villages if they meet the higher criteria set out in the regulations for the AC. Compared with the Côtes du Rhône Appellation, the minimum alcohol is 12.5% vol. instead of 11%, and the maximum yield is 42 hl/ha, rather than 52 hl/ha. Where the wine is produced by blending a number of village wines together, the Appellation is simply Côtes du Rhône-Villages; but there are sixteen villages which may append their name to the AC if the wine comes exclusively from the stated village, for instance Côtes du Rhône-Villages Cairanne AC.

Two of these villages, Beaumes-de-Venise and Rasteau, have separate ACs for Vins Doux Naturels (see Chapter 18). As far as red light wines are concerned, the best known of the sixteen villages are: Beaumes-de-Venise, Cairanne, Rasteau, Sablet, Saint-Gervais, Séguret, Visan, Valréas and Vinsobres; Chusclan has a reputation for its rosés. Two former villages, Vacqueyras and Gigondas, now have individual AC status.

The third cru and, perhaps, the best-known Appellation of the southern Rhône is Châteauneuf-du-Pape. Whilst the soil in the region varies, the vineyards here are well known for their surface of rounded stones

Pudding stones in Châteauneuf-du-Pape in the flat southern Rhône during winter, showing bush trained Grenache vines, after pruning.

(pudding stones or *galets*) which store heat and aid the ripening of the grapes. Châteauneuf is also known for the multiplicity of grape varieties permitted – up to thirteen can be in the blend, though Grenache, Cinsault, Mourvèdre and Syrah still predominate. There is also a small amount of white wine made which can be much sought after. Both tend to be full-bodied and high in alcohol.

Châteauneuf-du-Pape has the distinction of having pioneered AC under the guidance of Baron le Roy de Boiseaumarie in the 1920s.

To the west of Châteauneuf, where the soil includes more limestone, are the remaining two individual ACs, Lirac and Tavel. The latter is an Appellation for rosé wines only, reputed to be the finest in France. Made largely from Grenache and Cinsault, Tavel can attain a high degree of alcohol. Lirac produces a similar rosé as well as full-bodied red and some white wines.

Around the boundary of the southern Rhône are a number of "satellite" Appellations producing wines in a similar but lighter style, from the same mix of grapes. They include Coteaux du Tricastin to the north, with Côtes du Ventoux and Côtes du Lubéron to the east and south.

Between the northern and southern Rhône, the Chatillon-en-Diois AC produces light red from Gamay and whites from Aligoté and Chardonnay.

THE SOUTH OF FRANCE

The vineyards of the Rhône lead naturally into those of the south of

France: to the east of the mouth of the Rhône lie the vineyards of Provence and, to the west, separated by the marshy Camargue delta, those of Languedoc-Roussillon. This continuation is also carried through with many of the vine varieties. To the list, though, should be added Carignan, a black grape easy to overcrop but capable of a robust fruitiness when yields are restricted.

The climate is again mediterranean. Not surprisingly, given the size of the area being considered, the soils are very varied. Rich in the river valleys, clay and gravel in the plains, sandy nearer the sea, whilst, inland, the hillier terrain shows granite and schist. A common factor linking the best areas is the incidence of limestone, a good example of which is the barren *garrigue* (moorland) where the vine struggles to survive, but produces good wine. All in all, the combination of soils and good consistent climate is excellent for wine growing as is evidenced by the relatively small variations in vintages.

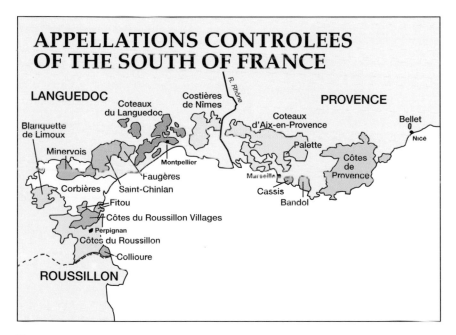

Provence
Key wines:
Côtes de Provence AC
Coteaux d'Aix-en-Provence AC
Bandol AC
Vin de Pays des Bouches du Rhône
Vin de Pays de Vaucluse

By far the most important appellation here is Côtes de Provence. This wine comes from vineyards to the east of Toulon, split into two strips, one along the coast and the other to the north of the Massif des Maures. Traditionally, much of the wine has been rosé with quite a high alcohol content and a somewhat orange colour, both derived from fully ripe grapes. Bottled in the distinctive Provence bottle, this has been aimed largely at the tourist market of the Riviera. Now, a number of producers are concentrating on quality red wines, bottled in Bordeaux bottles. Indeed, the Appellation regulations here, and almost everywhere else in Provence, allow for up to 30% Cabernet Sauvignon alongside the traditional southern varieties.

From close to Aix-en-Provence come AC Coteaux d'Aix-en-Provence and the tiny AC of Palette. Both make acceptable red, white and rosé wines. The other ACs of the region are Bandol, near Toulon (mainly Mourvèdre based meaty reds), Cassis,to the east of Marseille (the white is the best known) and the minute Bellet, just inland from Nice (all three colours, but the white is best – at a price).

Two vins de pays are worthy of mention, the mainly red Vin de Pays des Bouches du Rhône found to the north of Marseille and, further north again, in the region of Orange, the reds and whites of Vin de Pays du Vaucluse.

Languedoc-Roussillon
Key wines:
Costières de Nîmes AC
Coteaux du Languedoc AC
Fitou AC
Minervois AC
Corbières AC
Côtes du Roussillon AC
Côtes du Roussillon-Villages AC
Vin de Pays d'Oc
Vin de Pays de l'Hérault
Vin de Pays du Gard
Vin de Pays de l'Aude

Whilst these two regions are grouped together, they have a separate history, with Roussillon (for wine purposes, the *département* of Pyrénées-Orientales) having formed part of the Kingdom of Majorca. Languedoc, to the east, which takes its name from the language that was spoken there, Oc, comprises the *départements* of Gard, Hérault and Aude.

From the second half of the 19th century, until Algerian independence and the coming of the European Community, this was the heartland of French viticulture. A sea of vines produced vast quantities of low-strength wine from such grapes as Aramon, for blending with the deeply coloured, highly alcoholic wines of North Africa, which were shipped into local ports such as Sète. Between them they created the widely drunk litre vins de table.

With the North African source for blending wine having dried up, and Italy being better positioned for providing ordinary table wines within the European Community, Languedoc-Roussillon has had to find a new viticultural vocation. The situation has been exacerbated by the decline in wine consumption – particularly at the bottom end of the market.

Great swathes of vineyards have been uprooted with financial support from the European Community, and those growers who have remained have sought to produce wines that are more saleable. Their moves have been in three distinct directions.

First, there has been a more rigorous selection in the varieties that are being planted. High yielders like Aramon are being discarded in favour of such traditional quality grapes as Syrah, Cinsault and Mourvèdre, which produce less, but better, wine. The dominant grape variety, however, is still Carignan. Much of this improved wine is now classified as Vin de Pays.

Secondly, many of the long-standing VDQS areas such as Corbières and Coteaux du Languedoc have been upgraded to AC status, with the extra quality controls that such a promotion implies. In north-east Languedoc, from Narbonne round to the river Rhône, the principal appellations are

Limestone outcrops behind vineyards of Syrah trained on wires in Corbières, just prior to harvesting.

Costières de Nîmes and Coteaux du Languedoc, which contains the more local ACs of Faugères and St-Chinian.

From Narbonne south to the Roussillon, come the well-known trio of Appellations grouped around the Corbières hills: Fitou, Minervois and Corbières proper.

In the Roussillon itself, the main Appellation is Côtes du Roussillon, with higher quality wines being made in the Agly valley under the Côtes du Roussillon-Villages AC. Right in the south, Collioure produces a small quantity of full tannic wine from the Grenache grape on the steep hillsides where the Pyrenees meet the Mediterranean.

AC status, however, does tend to restrict the production to such grape varieties as have historically been used in the making of the wine. Thus, for example, a Minervois which had won the title as the best wine of the year, was subsequently disqualified because it was discovered that a small proportion of Cabernet Sauvignon had entered into the blend. There is a contrast here between Languedoc-Roussillon and Provence, where Cabernet is encouraged.

This has led to the final and perhaps most exciting development. There has grown up a whole new ethos of making quality wine outside the AC system, with no higher a classification than vin de pays. The Australians, in particular, have suddenly discovered the Midi as a place to make wine, and have provided the region with a number of winemakers keen to have two vintages a year, one in each hemisphere, and investment in the form

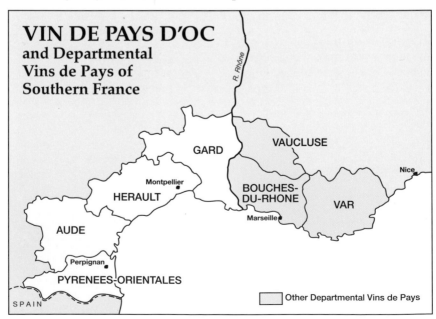

VIN DE PAYS D'OC
and Departmental
Vins de Pays of
Southern France

R. Rhône

GARD

VAUCLUSE

Nice

Montpellier

HERAULT

BOUCHES-
DU-RHONE

VAR

Marseille

AUDE

Perpignan

PYRENEES-ORIENTALES

Other Departmental Vins de Pays

SPAIN

of new plantings and wineries. In parallel with this foreign interest, some of the traditional names in bulk French wine are now developing better wines, particularly under the varietal banner.

Better grape varieties, such as Cabernet Sauvignon, Merlot, Syrah and Mourvèdre, for the reds, and Chardonnay, Sauvignon Blanc and Viognier, for the whites, allied to better winemaking, including carbonic maceration for red wines, and temperature controlled fermentation for whites, have made Languedoc-Roussillon a source of some of the most exciting wines in France. For the first time, small oak casks are appearing in cellars, to replace lined concrete vats.

This pride in the wines has led to an upsurge in individual property names appearing on the labels. This has also enabled a predominantly red wine region now to produce many excellent white wines.

The vin de pays classification thus embraces not only these new style wines, but also the more traditional ones. There is one Vin de Pays designation which covers the entire region, Vin de Pays d'Oc, as well as a master one for each *département* (examples of which are Vin de Pays de l'Hérault, Vin de Pays du Gard and Vin de Pays de l'Aude), and a number of smaller ones reflecting tighter geographical areas. It is often the varietal name on a label which identifies a new style wine.

Corse (Corsica)
Key wines:
Vin de Corse AC
Vin de Pays de L'Isle de Beauté

The dominant feature of the island of Corsica is its mountainous spine. This leaves comparatively little space for the planting of vineyards. Local grape varieties for red wines are Sciacarello and Niellucio (a close relation of the Tuscan Sangiovese). These are joined by such southern French varieties as Grenache, Syrah and Mourvèdre. White wines come mainly from Ugni Blanc and Vermentino.

In addition to the main Appellation, Vin de Corse, which may have one of five regional names appended (e.g. Vin de Corse Figari), there are two crus, Ajaccio and Patrimonio. There is also a large production of Vin de Pays de l'Ile de Beauté.

SPARKLING WINES AND VINS DOUX NATURELS
Throughout both the Rhône valley and the South of France, there are a number of sparkling and liqueur wines produced, which are given fuller coverage in the relevant chapters.

The sparkling wines include Clairette de Die from the Rhône and both Blanquette and Crémant de Limoux from the hinterland of the Languedoc (see Chapter 16).

The sweet fortified wines known as Vins Doux Naturels are quite common in this part of France, with the best known probably being Muscat de Beaumes de Venise, from the southern Rhône (see Chapter 18).

CHAPTER 11

NORTHERN EUROPE

This chapter covers Germany, Luxembourg, England and Wales, the main vineyard areas of which lie between latitudes 48 and 52° North. All four countries experience a cool northern climate, with local variations in individual vine-growing areas; with the exception of Baden in southern Germany, all are in EC Climatic Zone A. Due to their climate, they each produce delicately flavoured wines which are predominantly white and light in alcohol, with high acidity. Of the four, Germany is by far the largest producer with the longest established vineyards and wine-making infrastructure.

GERMANY

Of the ten largest wine-producing countries, Germany is the one that exports the highest proportion of its production. Britain is its most important export market, a situation which has existed for well over a century and has survived the impact of two world wars. However, whereas once quality and distinction were the bywords which influenced the British market, today quantity and accessibility are the main criteria, allied to price.

The reasons for this are complex and can be found to lie in both countries. In Germany, since World War II, much fertile land which had previously been devoted to general agriculture has been converted into easy to manage vineyards. With the growth of co-operatives, the expanding market has become more easily reached by smallholders who have seen little reason to contain the size of yield. New grape varieties, increasingly better suited to Germany's climate, which give high yields have been introduced. On the other hand the older established growers have continued to manage more difficult grape varieties often on steep slopes which preclude mechanisation and have struggled increasingly to cover the high costs implicit in the quality of their product and the manpower-intensive way in which it is made. Furthermore, and ironically in the light of Germany's large export volume, many labels have been designed solely with the home market in mind. Teutonic bureaucratic thoroughness has ensured that labels have not only been comprehensive, but also indigestible to the consumer; especially so where the producer has persisted in using the traditional Gothic script.

At the same time the British market place was, and is, changing. Through large retail chains and supermarkets wine has become more accessible to the British consumer. The light, fruity, slightly sweet style typical of many German wines has appeal to the novice wine-drinker and, by clever use of brand names and simplified labelling, the producers and suppliers have capitalised upon this trend. Today, for instance, Liebfraumilch is the best selling style of wine in the United Kingdom.

That wine should be accessible and enjoyed by more people is an excellent thing. What is sad is that these styles of wine have come to be taken by many consumers as the only style of German wine. The much wider range of wines, capable of satisfying the most discerning of palates with variety and subtlety, have tended to become hidden from almost all save the most knowledgeable winelovers. Fortunately, it appears that this state of affairs may slowly be correcting itself.

Whilst the vine has grown wild in Germany since prehistoric times, it is likely that it was not cultivated there until the arrival of the Romans. Trade continued to flourish after their defeat and expulsion. Then, as elsewhere in Europe, the dominant forces in wine production became the nobility and the Church. Just as in Burgundy, however, the arrival of Napoleon changed the whole face of German viticulture. The large holdings of the Church and nobility were split up and the introduction of the Napoleonic law of inheritance led to further fragmentation.

Since the late nineteen-fifties, though, there has been a dramatic change in the structure of German vineyards. What had become a patchwork of minuscule plots of vines has now been largely consolidated into a smaller number of more workable vineyards; this immense Government-funded scheme is known as *flurbereinigung*, meaning "reparcelling of the agricultural land of a community". The fact that there has also been increased planting on flat land in valley bottoms has made life easier, but has done nothing to improve overall wine quality.

The wines of Germany are predominantly white although the proportion of vineyards under black grapes is steadily increasing. The majority of white wines have a degree of sweetness but there is, in Germany itself, a move towards dry or medium-dry styles, *trocken* or *halbtrocken*. Now, for instance, 40% of production is of *trocken* or *halbtrocken* wines, and in terms of consumption within Germany, these wines account for some 60%, and the trend is upwards. This reflects a growing move by younger Germans, in particular, towards taking wine with food; hitherto in Germany, wines were mainly drunk socially, before and after food, rather than with it. A more modern approach to labelling and marketing is also taking place.

CLIMATE

Germany's continental climate gives warm summers, cold winters and clearly defined spring and autumn seasons. Rain falls throughout the year, the two wettest months being July and August. In spring late frosts present a potential hazard, as do storms and isolated hailstorms in summer. Autumns are normally long and warm. Within this broad framework, however, weather patterns can vary greatly from year to year. The climate also encourages the prudent grower to match carefully grape, microclimate and soil, and to plant a judicious mix of vine types.

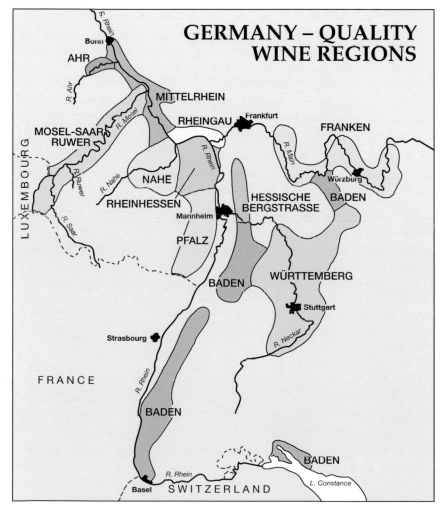

GERMANY – QUALITY WINE REGIONS

The combination of warm summers and abundant rainfall facilitates the production of high yields in German vineyards. The climate in summer and autumn also helps to shape the style of wines produced, encouraging the grapes to ripen slowly, and thus retain their acidity whilst developing characteristic delicate flavours. In river areas the long warm autumns combine with a humid microclimate, fostering the development of noble rot known in Germany as *Edelfäule*.

Due to the variance in weather patterns, the quality of wine produced can also differ sharply from year to year; some years see a high proportion of top quality wines produced, others do not. For in Germany, quality is inextricably linked to ripeness, not only in the mind of the producer, but also in the country's wine laws.

GERMAN WINE LAWS

In 1971, the German wine legislation was reorganised to harmonise with those of other EC countries. As in the other countries, geographical location and grape variety are factors governing the classification of German wines. A third factor, however, distinguishes the German scheme from any other. The sugar content of the grapes when harvested, is the primary factor governing the classification of a German wine. So, whereas in France, for example, it is the geographical location of the vineyard that principally governs the classification of the wine, in Germany it is the degree of sugar of the grapes picked, which is expressed in degrees Oechsle (°Oe).

As grapes ripen so their sugar content increases which, in turn, is reflected in a higher °Oe reading. The various grades of quality stipulate minimum must-weights expressed in °Oe. Three important consequences flow from the German approach. First, and most significant, each vintage must be assessed for granting of quality status. Second, because of this annual assessment, no vineyard is guaranteed to produce QWPSR every year, almost by rote, which happens in other countries. Third, and conversely, any vineyard in Germany is potentially eligible to be awarded QWPSR for its wines if the grapes are ripe enough.

Table and Quality Wine Grades

As with other European Community countries, the production of wines is split into two different classifications, Table Wines and Quality Wines. In Germany's case, each of these is further split into two.

Before considering the German wine classifications, however, it is perhaps convenient at this stage to look briefly at Euro-Tafelwein. This is a blend of wines from various countries in the European Community, often largely Italian. Whilst the labels frequently look Germanic, and the wine is frequently made in the medium-dry German style, there must be a statement in the language of the country for which the wine is destined, stating clearly the nature of the product (see Chapter 1).

The two German categories of Table Wine are:

1. *Deutscher Tafelwein* – The lowest classification, this can be blended only from wines originating in Germany. A geographical description may be shown but, if so, it may only be one of the four designated Table Wine Regions, *Tafelweingebiete*, or their sub-regions, and all the wine must come from the area stated. The four *Tafelweingebiete* are Rhein-Mosel, Oberrhein, Neckar and Bayern. The minimum must weight permitted is 44 °Oe for everywhere other than Oberrhein, the one region in climatic Zone B, which therefore has the higher minimum requirement of 50 °Oe.

2. *Landwein* – The second classification of German Table Wine, this was created in 1982 and is the equivalent of the French Vin de Pays. *Landwein* must come solely from one of seventeen designated areas called *Landweingebiete* and the name of the *Landweingebiet* in which the wine has been produced must be shown on the label. The must weight has to be a minimum of 47 °Oe, except in the areas in Zone B, where it must be at least 53 °Oe. Also, importantly, the wines have to be either dry, *trocken*, or off-dry, *halbtrocken*.

These two lowest classifications for German wine rarely, if ever, account for even 10% of total production. Most wine produced falls into the QWPSR category. Quality wine, too, is split into two classifications:

1. *Qualitätswein bestimmter Anbaugebiete* (QbA) – Literally means "quality wine from a particular area under cultivation" or, put more simply, "wine from designated Quality Regions". This wine has to be produced from specific grape varieties from a single *Anbaugebiet* since no blending between regions is permitted. Depending upon the geographic area and the grape variety, the minimum must-weight should be between 50 and 72 °Oe. There are thirteen *Anbaugebiete* which are considered at the end of this section of the chapter.

The name of the *Anbaugebiet* must always be shown on all QbA labels and this gives a very useful initial pointer to the style of wine. The northern regions produce more delicate wines with a higher acidity, for instance, whereas the wines from southern *Anbaugebiete* incline towards the fuller bodied, more alcoholic style.

2. *Qualitätswein mit Prädikat* (QmP) – The finest quality German wines are classified as QmP, that is "wine with special attributes of quality", or "superior quality wine". As with QbA wines, these wines must be made from specified grapes from a single *Anbaugebiet*, the name of which must

READING A GERMAN WINE LABEL

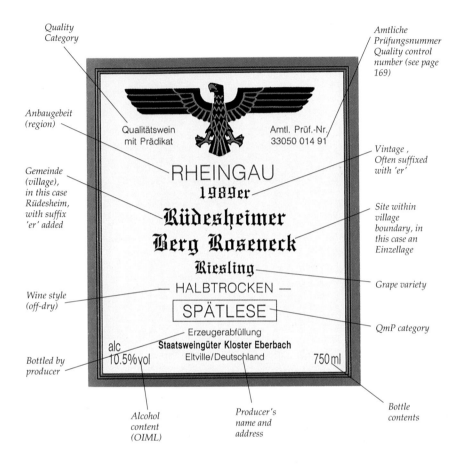

Quality Category

Amtliche Prüfungsnummer Quality control number (see page 169)

Anbaugebeit (region)

Gemeinde (village), in this case Rüdesheim, with suffix 'er' added

Vintage , Often suffixed with 'er'

Site within village boundary, in this case an Einzellage

Wine style (off-dry)

Grape variety

QmP category

Bottled by producer

Alcohol content (OIML)

Producer's name and address

Bottle contents

Qualitätswein mit Prädikat

Amtl. Prüf.-Nr. 33050 014 91

RHEINGAU

1989er

Rüdesheimer Berg Roseneck

Riesling

— HALBTROCKEN —

SPÄTLESE

Erzeugerabfüllung
Staatsweingüter Kloster Eberbach
Eltville/Deutschland

alc 10.5%vol

750 ml

be shown on the label. In addition, the grapes must all come from a single *Bereich*, or district. The grapes will have higher natural must-weights because, for wines of this quality, chaptalisation, or must-enrichment, is forbidden. Even here there is a graduated hierarchy of wines denoted by different Prädikat grades. These are dependent on the minimum must-weight, which is set for each grape variety in each region. In ascending order, together with their range of minimum must weights, the different Prädikat grades are:

Kabinett (67–85 °Oe) – The lowest of all QmP classifications is *Kabinett*. *Kabinett* signifies that the grapes were picked at normal harvest but were riper than grapes for QbA, possibly due to a more favourable site, and that the must was not enriched. The wine cannot be sold before the beginning of the January following the vintage. *Kabinett* wines are among the most delicate of German wines since, after enrichment, QbA must will have a higher Oe level than *Kabinett* must.

Spätlese (76–95 °Oe) – The German word for "harvest" is *lese*, whilst *spät* means "late" and a *Spätlese* wine is, therefore, one made from late-harvested grapes. The resulting extra ripeness will produce not simply more sugar, but more importantly, extra flavour. By regulation, the wine cannot be sold until the March following the vintage.

Auslese (83–105 °Oe) – Literally this means "harvested from" or "selected", and indicates that an *Auslese* wine is made from specially selected extra-ripe bunches of grapes. Some of the grapes used may well have been affected by *Edelfäule*, noble rot.

Beerenauslese (110–128 °Oe) – *Beeren* means "berries" and *Beerenauslese*, therefore, indicates that the wine has been made from grapes which were individually selected. Most commonly, these will have been affected by *Edelfäule*. To give an idea of the sugar content, if fermented out fully the must would achieve at least 18.1% vol.

Trockenbeerenauslese (TBA) (150–154 °Oe) – *Trocken* means "dry" but is used here not to describe the finished wine but the physical condition of the grape when it was picked. This classification is the peak of the quality wine system in Germany and *Trockenbeerenauslese* wines are only produced in the greatest vintages, with a very long ripening season. The expression implies the selection of individual grapes which have been so affected by *Edelfäule* as to be shrivelled and raisin-like in appearance with little remaining juice. There will be a high concentration of acid and the wine will have a potential alcohol content of at least 21.5% vol. As sold, however, these wines often have an actual alcohol content of less than 8%

Severely botrytised Riesling grapes, destined for Beerenauslese or Trockenbeerenauslese wine.

vol., leaving very high levels of sweetness. With this amount of residual sugar, the wine is also very high in glycerine. It is generally sold in half-bottles because of its price and rarity.

It will be seen from the above that the ranges of minimum must-weight required in the different regions and for different grape varieties overlap each other as far as the categories of *Kabinett*, *Spätlese* and *Auslese* are concerned. Thus, for example, a Mosel-Saar-Ruwer Riesling of 85 °Oe would be entitled to *Auslese* level but wine from the same grape in Baden would be entitled only to *Kabinett* level.

Eiswein – literally "ice wine" – is made from grapes, with a sugar content of at least *Beerenauslese* level but, most significantly, which are unaffected by *Edelfäule*, and which have been picked deep into the winter during heavy frost. Timing is critical to the making of *Eiswein*. At a temperature of –8 °C or lower the water in the grapes will freeze. They should then be picked and quickly pressed whilst still frozen; often these operations will all take place in the early hours. The wine made from the resulting liquid has an intriguing balance of highly concentrated sweetness and acidity.

Geographical Descriptions
Each *Anbaugebiet* is sub-divided further and progressively to form the geographical hierarchy shown below:

German Term	Meaning	Example from a Label
Anbaugebiet	Designated Quality Region	Liebfraumilch Pfalz
Bereich	A district within an *Anbaugebiet*	Bereich Bernkastel
Gemeind	Commune	Bernkastel
Grosslage	A group of adjoining vineyards	Piesporter Michelsberg
Einzellage	An individual vineyard	Piesporter Goldtröpfchen

Thus, each of the thirteen *Anbaugebiete* may contain one or more *Bereiche* which, in turn, are themselves split into a number of *Grosslagen*. Finally. each *Grosslage* is made up of individual sites or *Einzellagen*.

In addition to the name of the *Anbaugebiet*, the name of the *Bereich, Grosslage* or *Einzellage* may be shown on the label provided that in each case 85% of the blend comes from grapes grown in that particular area. Another word occasionally found on labels is the name of the *Gemeind*, or commune, either in conjunction with *Grosslage* or *Einzellage* names when these are shown, or by itself.

A number of the most popular German wines' names are *Grosslagen*. When a *Grosslage* or *Einzellage* name is shown, it must always be preceded by the name of a *Gemeinde* lying within its boundaries. In the example above, for instance, Michelsberg indicates the *Grosslage* whilst Piesport is the *Gemeinde* (the suffix "er" in German indicates the possessive case). The label does not mean that the wine was made in Piesport, simply that the *Grosslage* "belongs to Piesport". Similarly, the example of Bereich Bernkastel shown in the table above does not indicate a wine made from grapes grown in the *Gemeinde* Bernkastel but merely that the *Bereich* in question has taken for its name that of its most famous community.

From the examples shown above it may also be noted that the difference between a *Grosslage* and an *Einzellage* may not be apparent from the label. It should also be remembered that, as with Burgundian vineyards, the majority of *Einzellagen* are likely to have a number of different owners.

GRAPE VARIETIES

Germany is distinctive in that its often marginal climate and difficult growing conditions have led it to develop new crossings particularly suited to its needs. The research station at Geisenheim in the Rheingau has had a major role to play in this programme.

White Grapes
Overall, white grapes amount to some 84% of total plantings, the major grape varieties planted are:

Riesling – The noble grape of Germany, and acknowledged as one of the greatest varieties in the world, Riesling accounts for 21% of the total. Most widely planted in the prestigious sites in the Rheingau and Mosel-Saar-Ruwer, it ripens late, normally between October and early November, and needs careful siting in order to mature properly, but it is ideal for late-harvest wines. No other native variety can approach its great potential to age and its pre-eminence among German vines is testified by the fact that virtually all of the many crossings that have been developed in the country contain the Riesling strain in one form or another. It gives very clean, floral, crisp wines with a fresh acidity. As it ages it can develop a distinctive aroma reminiscent of petrol or diesel fuel.

Müller-Thurgau – Developed in the early 1880s, this is now the most widely planted variety in German vineyards amounting to 24% of total plantings. Depending upon the authority followed, the Müller-Thurgau is thought to be a cross between either Riesling and Silvaner or between two clones of the Riesling. The advantage of the grape is that it ripens early, in September, and, provided the summer has not been abnormally wet, it is very reliable even if the autumn weather is bad. Against that must be set, however, its susceptibility to rot and to damage from frost. High in yield, up to 120 hl/ha without undue loss of quality, it provides the backbone of Liebfraumilch blends. It gives a wine of medium acidity which admirers describe as flowery with a hint of Muscat and which its detractors describe as mousy.

Silvaner – A fading classic, having lost ground to Müller-Thurgau, Kerner and other new crossings, it now accounts for only 8% of plantings and is found mainly in those areas where it has always been the most important, if not sole, variety. Silvaner ripens in early October but, except in outstanding sites, the wine tends to low acidity and neutral fruit.

Kerner – This is the improbable result of crossing the black Trollinger with Riesling; nevertheless, it is a happy result, for the grapes ripen early, are resistant to frost, give generous yields and, best of all, give a wine with a lot of character. Developed in Württemberg, and only introduced in 1969, it is now widely cultivated and accounts for 7% of total plantings. Not often seen as a varietal, it is used in Liebfraumilch blends.

Scheurebe – A cross between Silvaner and Riesling, developed in 1916, this variety is late to ripen and needs good sites. Because of its high sugar content, it is particularly suited to the production of late-harvest wines. In the better vineyards, Scheurebe is capable of giving top quality wines, but if harvested when not fully ripe, it tends to give a bitter taste to the wine. Plantings amount to 4% of the whole.

Ruländer (Pinot Gris) – This is at its best in the warmer vineyard zones, where its higher must-weights and ability to ripen early make it popular. It accounts for 3% of plantings and gives smooth, rounded wines.

Black Grapes

Spätburgunder (Pinot Noir) – A late-ripening variety in Germany that gives full fruity wines which are at their best, perhaps, in the Pfalz and Baden. It provides 6% of plantings.

Portugieser – With 3% of plantings, this early ripening vine gives exceptionally high yields of light, flavoursome wine.

Trollinger – Grown almost exclusively in Württemberg, with 2% of planting overall, the Trollinger produces a dry wine, rather light in colour. One disadvantage is that it is very late to ripen.

Dornfelder – This is a recent arrival on the scene, having been created in 1956, and currently accounts for only 1% of planting. The Dornfelder grape has a red-coloured flesh and as a result produces wines which are deep in colour for German red wines. It is perceived to have great potential.

VITICULTURE

In terms of total wine production, Germany is number seven in world ratings. However, in terms of total area under vines it comes no higher than fifteenth. When these two figures are put side by side it means that Germany has by far the highest yields per hectare of any major European wine-producing country. In the 1986 vintage this was as high as

108 hl/ha. If one considers that many German vineyards, especially the best sites, are planted on steep hillsides, where the yields are by necessity limited, one can only conclude that the yields from some of the vineyards on the plains must be gargantuan.

Until very recently, German growers have resisted the concept that lower maximum yields should form an essential part of their wine law in an effort to improve quality. Indeed, apart from the contribution of nature by way of high rainfall and fertile soils, there are other good reasons why crop levels should be higher than in other countries. German vines tend to be among the most healthy in Europe, vineyards are replanted more frequently and almost invariably with top quality virus free vines and rootstocks. Germans claim, and with some justification, that in France, for instance, there are many old vines infected with virus and that as a result some French vineyards contain many plants that produce virtually no grapes; therefore, the argument goes, French plants produce more grapes than their German counterparts even though the vineyard's total yield is lower. Be this as it may, there is a move within Germany, as in other member states of the European Community, to reduce yields.

Different cultivation techniques are employed, depending largely on the topography of the vineyards. The longest established sites tend to be found close to rivers and often on steeply graded slopes, in order to take maximum advantage of the most favourable aspects and best soils for the grape variety in question. These sites are frequently devoted to the production of the richer categories of QmP wines from grapes which are picked late. On these steep and sometimes terraced slopes, where material often can only be brought up by cableway, the vines are individually planted, perhaps 1.3 metres apart, and attached to a single stake.

Much of the work is therefore performed manually; it requires skill, and is of course costly. As a result, a major problem vinegrowers on steep slopes face is that the price differential between their wines and those from other vineyards does not adequately reflect production costs. For this reason it is

Post training on steeply sloped, slate soil vineyards in Mosel-Saar-Ruwer. Bernkastler Doctor vineyard.

possible to see in places, the lower Mosel, for instance, many abandoned vineyards.

Other vineyards, including most if not all newly planted ones, tend to be located on the plains and in flatter river valleys. Here mechanisation can more easily be employed and the vines are trained along wires and may be planted 3 metres apart to facilitate the movement of equipment. The emphasis is upon maximising yields and producing wines which are accessible and easy to drink.

In the final days before the harvest, the vineyards are closed even to the owners, with the vines having to be protected from bird damage, either by netting or alarms. No grapes may be picked before the official starting date for the vintage, which is announced generally by the local trade association. It is up to the growers to decide when they want to pick after that date. Depending on the weather prospects, they may choose to leave them on the vines to ripen further and so qualify, hopefully, for QmP status. Picking is done by hand and machine depending upon the situation of the vineyard and the type of wine to be made.

VINIFICATION

Because of the low degree of natural sugar occurring in German wines, must-enrichment, *Anreicherung,* is widely used for qualities up to and including QbA – it is forbidden for QmP wines. In the more northern regions the alcohol content can be increased by up to as much as 4.5% vol.

The wines also tend to have high natural acidity and this can be countered in two different ways. The first method is by de-acidifying the wine by the addition of calcium carbonate or some proprietary product. Both de-acidification and *Anreicherung* can only be carried out with an official permit. The second way is by the addition of unfermented grape juice known as *Süssreserve* to sweeten the wine. This is permitted even with QmP wines and commonly occurs up to *Auslese* quality. The grape juice used has to be of at least the same quality as the wine to which it is being added and, ideally, should be of the same grape variety and from the same site.

In the winery, grapes are weighed and assessed for sugar content before pressing; in a co-operative, payment is related not only to weight but also to the type of grape and its ripeness. After pressing, the must may be enriched if this is thought necessary. A small percentage of the must may be drawn off to be kept unfermented for later use as *Süssreserve* and the remainder is then fermented to dryness. Wine stored in this dry state is more stable, both chemically and biologically, than a light alcohol wine that contains sugar. The unfermented must is filtered and also stored, in sterile conditions at low temperatures or under pressure to prevent fermentation. The volume involved is small so it is easy to keep this must stable. Immediately before bottling, a proportion of the *Süssreserve* is blended into the dry wine to sweeten it, this and the subsequent bottling operation being performed in totally sterile conditions.

Anreicherung and the use of *Süssreserve* should not be confused. The must is enriched in order to increase the alcoholic strength of the wine, whilst *Süssreserve* is used to balance natural acidity by sweetening the wine.

LABELLING DETAILS

The geographical and varietal descriptions above will, indeed must, be seen on a German wine label. Other details and terms which will be seen include:

AP No – Both QbA and QmP wines have to be submitted for testing which involves both tasting and chemical analysis. The label will bear the reference number for that test, known as the AP number or *Amtliche Prüfungsnummer*. The last two digits indicate the year of application which is usually the year of bottling.

Producer's name – Only a quarter of all the growers in German vineyards actually make wine themselves, many of them sending the grapes to a co-operative cellar, *Winzergenossenschaft*. If the wine has been made and bottled by the grower, or the co-operative cellar, the label might state that it is *Erzeugerabfüllung*. Alternatively, if it is not bottled by the producer, the shipper or bottler might identify himself with the term *Abfüller*.

Vintage and grape variety – The 85% rule applies in these cases. In order for a vintage to be shown a minimum of 85% of the wine must have been made from grapes harvested during that year. Similarly, if a single grape variety is shown that variety must comprise at least 85% of the grapes used. If only two grape varieties are blended, they may be shown on the label; in which case the major constituent must be listed first. When more than two varieties are blended, no variety may be displayed.

Dry wines – As has been seen, demand for dry wines from the German public is increasing, and some are finding their way into the British market. These are distinguished with the terms *trocken*, dry, with not more that nine grams of residual sugar per litre, and *halbtrocken*, off-dry, with a maximum 18 grams per litre. They are produced at all quality grades.

Awards – The German Wine Seal, *Deutsches Weinsiegel*, is awarded to wines that have succeeded in further taste tests over and above that for the AP number. The seals come in three colours, yellow for dry wines, green for medium-dry and red for sweeter ones. There are also both regional and national competitions, with gold, silver and bronze neck-labels. The outstanding award of all is the national *Grosser Preis*.

The remaining important detail to be found on the label is the wine's point of origin.

THE QUALITY WINE REGIONS (*ANBAUGEBIETE*)

With the absorption of the vineyards of what was the German Democratic Republic (East Germany), there are now thirteen *Anbaugebiete* in the unified Germany. These vary considerably in the size and style of the wines that they produce, and not all are commercially significant in the United Kingdom.

Because the quality grade of German wines from a specific location may change from year to year, the key wine listings that follow omit quality levels. All the wines mentioned will, however, be of either QbA or QmP status. Important *Bereiche* are listed first. Key *Grosslage* names are followed by the name of the community with which they are most often associated in brackets. Finally, the most important communities (*Gemeinden*) are listed.

Ahr (approximate area under vine 400 ha)
Although it is one of the most northerly vineyards in Europe, the Ahr produces predominantly light, fruity red wines from the Spätburgunder (Pinot Noir) and Portugieser grapes on volcanic slate, tufa and loess.

Mittelrhein (800 ha)
The vineyards lie on the steep, slaty slopes of both banks of the Rhine between Bonn and Lorch, some 100 kilometres to the south. Almost 75% of the production of fresh, crisp wines is from the Riesling.

Mosel-Saar-Ruwer (12,900 ha)
Key wines:
Bereich Bernkastel
Key Grosslage:
Michelsberg (Piesport)
Key Gemeinden:
Piesport
Bernkastel
Graach
Zeltingen

This region comprises the valley of the river Mosel from where it joins the Rhine at Koblenz, to the Luxembourg frontier, and those of its two small tributaries, the Saar and the Ruwer. The best wines come from the mineral-rich, slaty slopes and are made from Riesling, which accounts for some 55% of total plantings. In the valley floor of sand and gravel, wines

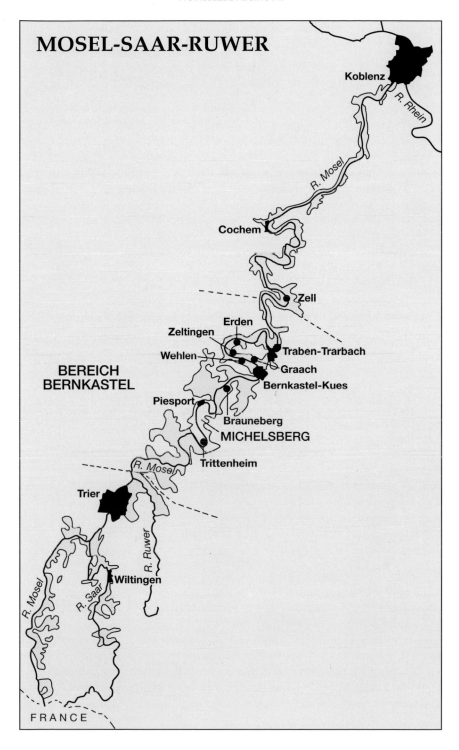

MOSEL-SAAR-RUWER

Koblenz

R. Rhein

R. Mosel

Cochem

Zell

Erden

Zeltingen

Wehlen

Traben-Trarbach

Graach

**BEREICH
BERNKASTEL**

Bernkastel-Kues

Piesport

Brauneberg

MICHELSBERG

Trittenheim

R. Mosel

Trier

R. Ruwer

R. Mosel

R. Saar

Wiltingen

FRANCE

of lesser quality are made from Müller-Thurgau and, traditionally in the upper Mosel, from Elbling.

The wines are bottled in green bottles, as opposed to the more general brown and are often quite delicate with a hint of gas in them (*spritzig*).

The finest Rieslings come from the south facing slopes of Wiltingen and the Scharzhofberg on the Saar and the villages of Trittenheim, Piesport, Brauneberg, Bernkastel, Graach, Wehlen, Zeltingen, Erden and Traben-Trarbach. The Saar-Ruwer wines show a steely acidity and tend to be more robust than those of the Mosel. The best of the latter, from the middle and upper stretches of the river, are lively, fragrant and elegant wines with a subtle fruitiness and, sometimes, an earthy flinty taste.

Nahe (4,600 ha)
Key wines:
Bereich Schloss Böckelheim

Key Grosslage:	*Key Gemeinden*:
Kronenberg (Bad Kreuznach)	Bad Kreuznach
	Schloss Böckelheim

The valley of the Nahe, to the west of the Rhine and south of the Mosel, protected by the Hunsrück Mountains to the north, comprises a variety of soils. In the north it is predominantly sandy loam. Here Müller-Thurgau and the Silvaner give agreeable, uncomplicated wines. On the slopes of the valley around the towns of Schloss Böckelheim and Bad Kreuznach, on porphyry, quartz and coloured sandstone soils, Riesling produces wine of delicacy and distinction.

Rheingau (2,900 ha)
Key wines:
Bereich Johannisberg
Key Gemeinden:

Rüdesheim	Oestrich
Geisenheim	Erbach
Johannisberg	Eltville
Winkel	Hochheim

This is the finest region for the production of Hocks. Indeed the word, now meaning any Rhine wine, comes from the local village of Hochheim and was coined by Queen Victoria who liked the wine but had difficulty in pronouncing its full name. The Rhine flows west at this point so that the Rheingau vineyards on its north bank face south and are protected from the cold northerly winds by the Taunus mountains, so giving ideal conditions for ripening of the grapes.

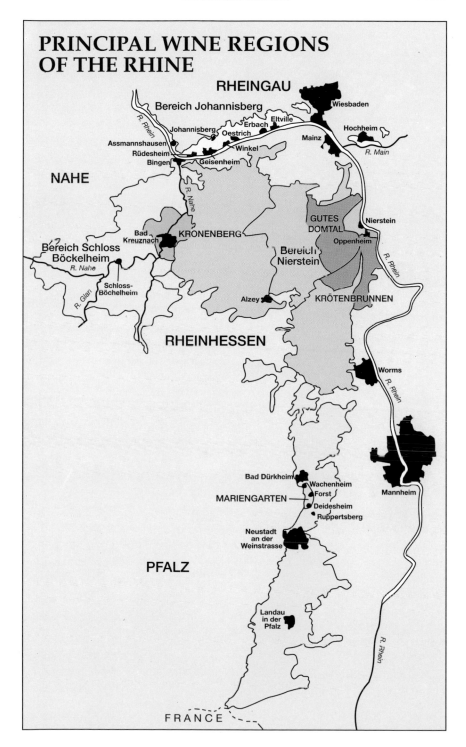

PRINCIPAL WINE REGIONS OF THE RHINE

RHEINGAU

Bereich Johannisberg

Wiesbaden

Eltville

Erbach

Johannisberg

Oestrich

Hochheim

Assmannshausen

Mainz

Winkel

Rüdesheim

Bingen

Geisenheim

R. Rhein

R. Main

NAHE

R. Nahe

GUTES DOMTAL

Nierstein

Bad Kreuznach

KRONENBERG

Oppenheim

Bereich Schloss Böckelheim

Bereich Nierstein

R. Nahe

R. Rhein

Schloss-Böckelheim

R. Glan

Alzey

KRÖTENBRUNNEN

RHEINHESSEN

Worms

R. Rhein

Bad Dürkheim

Wachenheim

MARIENGARTEN

Forst

Deidesheim

Mannheim

Ruppertsberg

Neustadt an der Weinstrasse

PFALZ

Landau in der Pfalz

R. Rhein

FRANCE

Schloss Johannisberg vineyard in the Rheingau: the best vineyards are on the steepest slopes, with flatter land down towards the river.

The soil is a combination of weathered slate, loess and loam on the slopes and gravel and sandy loam in the valley. Slate is an excellent soil for growing grapes and Riesling has a special affinity seeming to thrive on its high mineral content. Furthermore, slate is a dark soil which absorbs the heat of the sun by day and then radiates the warmth to the vines by night so helping the ripening process. This is particularly important for the varieties which ripen later and, as a result, Riesling predominates, accounting for over 80% of plantings.

The vineyards of the celebrated villages of Rüdesheim, Geisenheim, Johannisberg, Winkel, Oestrich, Erbach and Eltville embrace many of Germany's best-known estates and, in this area, many of the most distinguished German wines are produced. The hillside sites tend to produce racy wines with an elegant and balanced fruity acidity whilst the wines produced in the valley tend to be fuller bodied and richer with good acidity. In 1984, a number of the more prominent winemakers formed the Charta Group to promote the drinking of wine with food. Making wines from only the Riesling grape, they have led the move within Germany towards drier wines.

Beyond Rüdesheim, where the Rhine bends northwards once more, is the town of Assmannshausen which is more famous for its red wines than white. Once said to be the finest in Germany, these are now being challenged, if not eclipsed, by those being made in the Pfalz and Baden.

Rheinhessen (24,900 ha)
Key wines:
Liebfraumilch Rheinhessen
Bereich Nierstein

Key Grosslage:	*Key Gemeinden:*
Gutes Domtal (Nierstein)	Oppenheim
Krötenbrunnen (Oppenheim)	Nierstein

The largest vine-growing region in Germany both in terms of vineyard and total area, it is from here that many of the labels most commonly seen in Britain come; it was here, in a small vineyard now lying in the city of Worms, that Liebfraumilch was first produced.

The region lies across the Rhine from Rheingau and extends southwards from the river through undulating mixed farming land. The Rhine borders the area on the east as well as the north. To the west and south the Rheinhessen is bordered by the wine regions of the Nahe and Pfalz respectively. Like Rheingau, Rheinhessen is protected to the north by the Taunus mountains: to the east, across the Rhine, the Odenwald gives further protection. The often sandy soil gives soft wines that are easy to drink. No grape variety predominates, though Müller-Thurgau is the most common, with something under a quarter of the total production, followed by Silvaner. Throughout the region, co-operative cellars are important. Names commonly found include Bingen, which lies opposite Rüdesheim, and Nierstein and Oppenheim south of Mainz, whose finest vineyards are on the Rhine Terrace, sloping down to the river.

Up until the early 1950s vineyards were, in the main, only found alongside the Rhine and the reputation of Rheinhessen was built on the often excellent wines produced there. Since then, as more land has been converted to vine-growing from other agricultural use, cheaper wines of much lower quality have slowly eroded the region's reputation. Nowhere has this been more obvious than in the Bereich Nierstein. Here along the west bank of the Rhine, in a narrow stretch from just north of

Whilst the very best German vineyards are planted on steep slopes there are many on flatter land, especially in Rheinhessen, where mechanical harvesting is possible.

Nackenheim to just south of Oppenheim, most of the region's 7% of Riesling is found planted on sloping beds of red sandy soil. From these grapes much of the best Rheinhessen, and indeed some of Germany's finest wines, are made. The area has, however, been overshadowed by the popularity of the wines from the vast *Grosslage* Gutes Domtal which is made up of some fifteen villages, none of which produces any wine of distinction.

Pfalz (22,600 ha)

Key wines:
Liebfraumilch Pfalz
Key Grosslage: Mariengarten (Forst)
Key Gemeinden: Forst   Deidesheim

Traditionally known as the Palatinate or Rheinpfalz, this region stretches northward from the French border and is protected by the Haardt mountains, a continuation of the Vosges of Alsace. Quantitively speaking, this is the most important area for the production of wine in Germany. The best wines come from a few villages on the *Deutsche Weinstrasse* (the German wine route): Wachenheim, Forst, Deidesheim and Ruppertsberg. Some 80 kilometres south of the Rheingau, the favourable climate which gives mild winters and hot summers enables the production of Germany's finest red wines, and means that white wines tend to have a fuller roundness than those of the more northerly vineyards of Germany. The soil is mainly weathered sandstone and limestone. The most important grape varieties are the Müller-Thurgau, Riesling and Kerner.

Hessische Bergstrasse (400 ha)

Until unification this was the smallest of all the German wine regions as far as production was concerned. Riesling dominates in the vineyards, which lie in on a narrow band of loess, to the east of the Rhine between the cities of Darmstadt and Heidelberg.

Franconia (Franken) (5,200 ha)

These vineyards are east of Frankfurt in the valley of the river Main. The wines, made largely from Müller-Thurgau and Silvaner, generally have a firm steely taste to them and long before the current trend in Germany towards dry wines, Franken was renowned for its *Fränkisch Trocken* bottled into the traditionally flat flagon-shaped *bocksbeutel*.

Württemberg (9,800 ha)

The majority of the vineyards of this region lie to the north of the city of Stuttgart in the valley of the river Neckar. The production is almost equally split between light, grapey red wines, mainly made from Trollinger and Müllerrebe (Pinot Meunier), and spicy whites, from Riesling and Müller-Thurgau. These are grown on a variety of soils including limestone, loess and clay.

Baden (15,300 ha)

The wines of Baden, the most southerly of Germany's vineyard regions, have not been well known in the United Kingdom but are now being seen more frequently. Whilst the majority of the vineyards stretch along the east bank of the Rhine, from Heidelberg to Basle, there are odd pockets to the north of Lake Constance and even far to the north between the vineyards of Württemberg and Franken. In such a diverse area it is hard to generalise. Ninety per cent of the wine is vinified in co-operatives – most of which belong to the central co-operative cellar, the Badischer Winzerkellerei, which is the largest co-operative winery in western Europe.

The outstanding wines, both red and white, come from the Kaiserstuhl-Tuniberg region, between Freiburg and the Rhine, where the volcanic soil appears to impart extra body. The major varieties planted are Müller-Thurgau, Spätburgunder (Pinot Noir) and Ruländer (Pinot Gris). An interesting speciality of the south of the region is *Weissherbst*, a pale rosé.

Finally, with the recreation of a unified Germany, two new quality wine regions have now been integrated into the legislation:

Saale-Unstrut

This is now the most northerly of the German wine regions, with the vineyards lying south-east of Leipzig in the valleys of the two rivers that give the region its name. Müller-Thurgau is the main grape variety grown with about 46% of the total, followed by Silvaner and Weissburgunder (Pinot Blanc). Sturdy, mainly dry, fresh wines are produced on limestone and red sandstone soils.

Sachsen

Sachsen stretches for about 50 kilometres along the steep banks of the Elbe, around the city of Dresden. Müller-Thurgau, with about 40%, predominates, followed by Weissburgunder and Traminer. Soils vary and include loam, loess, sandstone and granite. The wines are robust and mainly dry.

Both these regions are very small. As with so much else in the eastern parts of Germany, the wine industry is very backward when compared with its counterpart in the west. At present, the wines are best when drunk young; it is likely to be some years before many of them are seen in the United Kingdom.

LIEBFRAUMILCH AND REGIONAL WINES

Liebfraumilch was originally produced from the Liebfrauenstift vineyard in Worms, which belonged to the Liebfrauenkirche. Now it has become a generic term for a medium-sweet white wine (minimum 18 g/l residual sugar) produced in one of the four regions of Rheinhessen, Pfalz, Rheingau or Nahe only. Of these four, the first two are the most important sources. The region, but no other geographical mention, will be on the label. No mention of the grape variety can be made and the wine will be of QbA quality.

Certain other regions have also tried to create regional names that can be used in a similar way – each having specific production requirements. These include Moseltaler from the Mosel-Saar-Ruwer, Nahesteiner from the Nahe and Rheinhess from Rheinhessen.

LUXEMBOURG

In all there are about 1,350 ha of vines along the west bank of the Moselle as it forms the frontier between Luxembourg and Germany, with an average annual production of 140,000 hl. The dominant grape varieties are Rivaner (Müller-Thurgau, 47%), Elbling (25%), Auxerrois (10%) and Riesling (8%). The wines are generally light and dry, and much is turned into the local, bottle-fermented sparkling wine Crémant de Luxembourg (see chapter 16). Most of the wine is consumed within Luxembourg itself, but Belgium is a very important export market. Little finds its way to the UK.

The classification system for wines in Luxembourg was established as long ago as 1935 and is based on analysis and tasting, which is scored as points out of 20. On average, approximately half of the production is Table Wine and the rest Quality Wine.

The classifications for quality wine and their associated minimum tasting scores are:

Marque Nationale – Requires a minimum of 12/20 in the tasting. No wine made from the Elbling can have a higher classification than this.

Vin Classé – Minimum required is 14/20. No wine made from Rivaner can be classified higher than this.

Premier Cru – Minimum requirement of 16/20.

Grand Premier Cru – Must score a minimum of 18/20.

The style of wine produced is light and fruity, similar to the dry wine of the upper Mosel-Saar-Ruwer in Germany or dry English and Welsh wines.

ENGLAND AND WALES

The main vine-growing areas in England and Wales lie above 51° North which would seem to make the chances of successful wine production very slim. Fortunately for the vineyard owner, the Gulf Stream tempers the climate which, nevertheless, still presents a considerable challenge. Spring can bring late and sharp frosts, and the normally cool to warm summers barely provide the vines with sufficient energy to ripen properly. The mercurial nature of the British weather permits nothing to be taken for granted, even from day to day, and, as if all this were not a sufficient challenge, the high rainfall encourages fungal diseases. Notwithstanding this, vines have been grown in Britain on and off for centuries.

Wine was probably first produced under the Romans and, later, vineyards were widely spread throughout the southern half of the country, often attached to church premises. The Dissolution of the Monasteries in 1536 started a steady decline; by the early years of this century production was on a minute scale, and it finally petered out some time after the First World War. It was not until 1951 that wine was again made commercially in Britain, with the planting of a vineyard at Hambledon, in Hampshire, by Major-General Sir Guy Salisbury-Jones.

Since then, there has been a steady expansion of the area under vines for the commercial production of wine. There are now over 1,000 ha spread throughout the southern counties of England and Wales, with small plantings as far north as Yorkshire.

With the mild, damp climate of Britain there has had to be an adaptation of traditional European techniques. Over the years there has been a move away from the Burgundian varietals and French pruning methods with which production was re-started at Hambledon, to more Germanic practices. The two main methods of pruning used now are the Pendlebogen, an adaptation of the double Guyot system but with vines growing up to 2 m high and the rows about 2 m apart, and the Geneva Double Curtain, where the rows and the vines are further apart. Whilst the latter has the advantage of lower initial capital costs, it takes longer for maximum yields to be reached. There is also increasing use being made of polythene tunnels for the growing of vines. This is particularly useful for the production of grapes for *Süssreserve* and red wine.

Grape Varieties

Whilst five white grape varieties are recommended for making Quality Wine in the UK, there are also around twenty authorised varieties. The five which are recommended are:

1. *Müller-Thurgau* – Potentially good for English vineyards, as it ripens early, but it needs good weather during flowering. The most widely planted variety, though less popular than it has been, possibly because of its susceptibility to fungal disease.

2. *Huxelrebe* – The big attraction of this grape is its high sugar content and big yields. The wine has a distinctive taste.

3. *Madeleine-Angevine* – A variety that supports the British climate and gives a good yield. It is perhaps best used for blending as it is low in acidity.

4. *Reichensteiner* – A vine which crops well even in poor summers. Good sugar content.

5. *Schönburger* – Developed at Geisenheim, it adapts well to the British climate and gives spicy wines.

Wine Laws

Since Britain joined the European Community in 1973, it has been subject to its laws for the making of wine, and all English and Welsh wine was classified strictly as Table Wine until the vintage of 1991. However, there was a great deal of flexibility permitted because, due to the small area under vines, we benefited from so-called "experimental" status. The only form of quality distinction that had any official blessing was the English Vineyards Association (EVA) Seal of Quality, awarded on the assessment of chemical analysis and tasting by a panel of experts.

With annual production now arriving at the crucial figure of 25,000 hl at which the experimental status must be forfeited, the UK must enter into full EC legislation. With the 1991 harvest, therefore, a pilot Quality Wine Scheme came into effect and the first Quality Wine became available in the autumn of 1992.

The initial arrangement allowed for just two demarcated regions: Southern Counties (which went as far north as Cheshire), and Northern Counties. This was modified with effect from the 1993 vintage with the change to two different designations: English Vineyards Wine and Welsh Vineyards Wine. It is likely that there will be further alterations to the system in the future.

The regulatory authority of the Quality Wine Scheme is the Wine Standards Board of the Vintners Company. All wines have to be submitted to a tasting panel before achieving quality wine status. Must-enrichment and the addition of *Süssreserve* are permitted.

The main implication of the new laws is that much of the wine that is being produced cannot be submitted for selection as "Quality Wine." This is because the EC does not permit QWPSR to be made from inter-specific crosses (hybrids). These include Seyval Blanc, widely planted in Britain because of its high yields and resistance to disease. Mainly for this reason, the UKVA (successor to the English Vineyards Association) system of certification will run in parallel with the trial scheme, and may continue afterwards unless the Community rules proscribing the use of hybrids in quality wines are relaxed to allow Seyval Blanc to be made into a QWSPR.

British Wine
It should be noted that there is a great deal of difference between English wine and British wine. The former is wine made from freshly picked grapes grown in England. The latter is made in Britain from imported grape concentrate, usually from Cyprus or southern Europe, and therefore does not fall within the EC's definition of wine. Accordingly, it may not be described as wine but the term British Wine may be used; thus "red British Wine" is correct but "British red Wine" is not. Until quite recently most British wines were fortified and competing with Ports and Sherries, now there are several light British wines. Often, only close study of the label can show the difference.

CHAPTER 12

ITALY

Italy is often both the largest producer and the largest exporter of wine in the world; its annual production of around 60 million hl is similar to that of France. Italy is also important on the United Kingdom market, ranking third behind France and Germany; although declining, Italy's Lambrusco is still Britain's fourth biggest selling type of wine.

The history of Italian wine is just as impressive, with vineyards first having been planted by Greek settlers, probably as early as 800 BC. The Etruscans grew vines and made wine both for their own consumption and to be traded. The Romans, too, recognised the commercial possibilities of wine production. Cato the Censor, in his work "On Agriculture", laid down detailed instructions as to how to run a vineyard profitably, by producing as much wine as possible. The Romans are also known to have made technical strides in wine-preservation and covered wine in amphorae with a layer of olive oil to inhibit what today we would recognise as oxidation. So high was the reputation of Italy in classical times that it came to be dubbed by the Greeks "Oenotria" or wine land.

However, it is really only over the last thirty years or so that Italy has perceived its true vocation to be in the production of quality wine. Italy's quality regime, *Denominazione di Origine Controllata* (DOC) was introduced as recently as 1963, with the first wine, Vernaccia di San Gimignano, granted its DOC in 1966. Since then advances along the quality path have been significant.

There are, though, contradictory forces at work in Italy. On the one hand, much of the country's grape crop is grown by smallholders who are part of the rural tradition and resistant to any change. There is sometimes little incentive to produce higher quality wine when the local market is so undemanding: wine is simply a natural part of the daily meal in Italy, as in many mediterranean countries, and is not considered as special or worth much attention.

The other side of the coin is the native creativity and individuality of the Italian character. In the field of wine, this has led to the creation of numerous idiosyncratic wines of high quality which are widely discussed, even if they are only available in very small quantities.

ITALIAN WINE LAWS

The variety of Italian wines is enormous. Even within the DOC system, more than 900 different types of wine are being produced from over 240 different geographical locations. For the student, it is this very diversity that causes complications. Whilst the 1992 wine legislation, the "Goria Law", is changing much, a number of Italy's finest wines still fall outside the quality classification and have to be labelled simply as *vino da tavola*, usually because they are made outside the traditions of the region in which they are produced. Italian wine legislators, particularly in the past, have not been generous towards innovators.

The Italian wine laws recognise four different quality levels. These are, in descending order:

1. Denominazione di Origine Controllata e Garantita (DOCG) – DOCG wines must meet all the requirements of DOC and, additionally, be bottled in the region of production and be subject to a Ministry of Agriculture tasting and seal of approval. There are now well over a dozen wines that have achieved this status, and the number is growing steadily. Among the most important are:

Asti and Moscato d'Asti

Barbaresco

Barolo

Brunello di Montalcino

Carmignano (for its red wines only)

Chianti Classico

Chianti (including the other six sub-regions)

Taurasi

Vernaccia di San Gimignano

Vino Nobile di Montepulciano

2. Denominazione di Origine Controllata (DOC) – This was the first designation to be introduced, and it is similar to *Appellation Contrôlée* in France, specifying geographical zone, grape varieties, yields and the like. There are more than 230 individual geographical entities now entitled to their own DOC. The wines may then be further differentiated in a number of ways: whether they are still or sparkling, sweet or dry, young or old; by a geographical sub-region; or by the grape variety from which they are made.

Until now, these two highest classifications have accounted for no more than 15% of Italian wine production.

3. *Indicazione Geografica Tipica (IGT)* – A new qualification in the 1992 laws, IGT is designed to absorb those *vini da tavola* that are allowed to specify their region or district of origin, for example *Vino da Tavola di Sicilia*. As with the French *Vin de Pays*, of which it is the equivalent, it includes many wines that are made from grape varieties and vinification techniques not traditional to the area of production, and which are therefore not entitled to a higher designation.

4. *Vino da Tavola* – As a market segment, this is in decline, partly as a result of the European Community policies to reduce the wine lake and partly due to the absorption of the better end of the production into higher classifications.

LABELLING

There are factors other than geographical location that play their role in the DOC system. To recognise what these are, it is useful to have a small Italian vocabulary. Amongst the words that might be seen on a label are:

Abboccato	Medium-sweet and full-bodied
Amabile	Medium-sweet
Annata	Vintage
Azienda (or Casa) agricola	An estate that uses only its own grapes in the production of its wines
Azienda (or Casa) vinicola	A producer who buys in and vinifies, usually a large scale operation
Azienda (or Casa) vitivinicola	An estate that grows vines, buys in grapes and makes wine
Bianco	White
Botte	Cask
Bottiglia	Bottle
Cantina Sociale	Co-operative cellar
Cascina	Farmhouse (has come to mean estate)
Cerasuolo	Cherry-red
Chiaretto	Deep rosé
Classico	The original centre of a DOC region, making the most typical wines

Consorzio	Producers' trade association, whose members' wines are identified by a neck-label
Dolce	Sweet
Fattoria	Estate
Fermentazione naturale	Natural sparkle in a wine
Frizzante	Slightly sparkling
Imbottigliato all'origine	Estate bottled
Invecchiato	Aged
Liquoroso	Strong, often fortified, wine
Maso, Masseria	Estate
Metodo charmat	Tank-method sparkling wine
Metodo classico, Metodo tradizionale	Traditional method, bottle-fermented sparkling wine
Passito, Passita	A generally strong, sweet wine made from part-dried grapes
Podere	A small estate
Produttore	Producer
Recioto	Similar to *passito*, made with part-dried grapes
Riserva	Reserve, for DOC wines, one that has been aged in cask and/or bottle for a particular length of time
Rosato	Rosé
Rosso	Red
Secco	Dry
Semisecco	Medium-dry
Spumante	Sparkling wine made by any method
Stravecchio	Very old, particularly of marsala and spirits
Superiore	Superior. This term is being suppressed by the new laws. For DOC wines this might have meant that it came from the best vineyards within the region, had been aged longer, or had a higher alcoholic content
Tenuta	Estate

Uva	Grape
Vecchio	Old; with DOC wines there are restrictions as to how this may be used
Vendemmia	Vintage
Vigna, Vigneto	Vineyard
Vigniaiolo, Viticoltore	Grower
Vino novello	New wine, bottled less than a year old
Vitigno	Grape variety
Vivace	Slightly sparkling

CLIMATE AND WEATHER

Given the country's location, size and shape it is not surprising that the climates of Italy's wine regions vary as they do. Between the Brenner pass in the north, and the southern part of Sicily, there is a full 10 degrees difference in latitude (47–37°). The climatic variations, which would otherwise be even greater, are moderated by the effects of the Mediterranean and Adriatic on the one hand and by mountains on the other.

In the north the Alps and the Dolomites give protection from the bitter north winds in the winter and stimulate cool down draughts in the summer; here also, lakes Como, Garda and Maggiore create beneficial microclimates. The Appennines form the backbone of Italy from just south of the River Po to its toe. Their slopes provide sufficient altitude for cooler growing conditions to be found.

In summary, the climate in Italy ranges from continental in the north, with cold winters and long, hot summers, to mediterranean in the south, where winters are warmer and summers very hot and dry.

Although weather patterns do vary from region to region, overall the weather is generally consistent. Differences in quality between vintages are therefore less marked than, say, in France or Germany.

SOILS

Many types of soil are found across Italy's regions, from the volcanic slopes of Etna and Vesuvius to the glacial moraines of the north. The link between soil type and grape variety planted is less well explored than in France. Nevertheless, on hillier ground, in particular, the soils tend to be poor, with good drainage, making them ideal for viticulture.

GRAPE VARIETIES

One of the principal reasons for the diversity of Italian wines, and one of the keys to understanding the subject, is the number of grape varieties planted. In excess of 1,000 varieties of *Vitis vinifera* are said to exist in the country. More importantly, many are native to Italy and not planted anywhere else in the world. Not all, it must be said, are top quality, but black grape varieties such as Nebbiolo and Sangiovese are capable of producing world class wines. Grape varieties are given full coverage in the sections on individual regions.

VITICULTURE

The diversity of climate, soil and vine inevitably means that there are many different methods of growing vines in Italy.

Fortunately, and perhaps, simplistically, these can be grouped into two broad headings. Both have their roots in history, reflecting to this day the influence of the Etruscans and Greeks.

In central and north-east Italy vines, historically, were trained high. The Etruscans used natural supports: olive, fig, walnut and poplar trees for instance. Density of planting was low and, with little pruning performed, vines were high yielding. When grapes were regarded as merely another product, this inefficient method of mixed cultivation was accepted. Now, with the move towards quality, it has virtually disappeared. The Etruscan influence, however, does survive in the use of high trellising systems in north-east Italy, in particular.

High cordon trained vines in Trentino during the winter; with the Alps in the background.

The Greeks planted specialist vineyards where the vines were trained low and planted densely to give small yields of high quality fruit. The regions in the north-west and in the south of Italy have favoured this approach historically, and continue it today by training their vines on wires using the cordon (*spalliera*) or cane (Guyot) methods, or by using the bush method (*alberello*).

The two schools are now drawing closer. In the north there is a move away from the Etruscan towards the Greek tradition. Conversely in the south it has been found beneficial, given the hotter climate, to train the vines high. Elsewhere, methods combining both are being tried. Yields still tend to be high but the emphasis is on reducing them.

VINIFICATION

The juxtaposition of modern technique and traditional practice is, if anything, more obvious in the winery than in the vineyard. Especially for reds, traditional methods of open vat fermentation, long maceration and the use of old wood are still very evident. Nevertheless, with the advent of "foreign" grape varieties and the move to quality, experimentation is in many places well advanced, and indeed now firmly translated into practice. Temperature controlled stainless steel vats, control of malo-lactic fermentation and ageing in new oak *barriques* are becoming the tools of Tuscan, Pied-

Many Italian wine producers, especially those in Tuscany, find the DOC and DOCG regulations too restrictive, and are "breaking the rules" to produce high quality vini da tavola, often aged in 225 l barriques alongside the DOCG wines maturing in botti.

montese and other winemakers. The use of these newer methods is particularly widespread in the making of Italian white wines.

REGIONS AND WINES

Politically, Italy is divided into twenty regions each with a certain amount of autonomy. Every one of these regions produces wine, with at least some of DOC quality. All are covered below, though not all are significant enough to warrant a key wines list.

Valle d'Aosta

This is the smallest of Italy's regions, in size, in vineyard area and in wine production. Valle d'Aosta is a veritable vinous Tower of Babel, with French, Italian, German and Swiss grapes being grown to make wines that are as likely to be labelled in French as Italian. Perhaps the two best-known DOCs are the reds Donnaz and Enfer d'Arvier.

Piedmont (Piemonte)

Key wines:

Barolo DOCG	Barbera d'Asti DOC
Barbaresco DOCG	Dolcetto d'Alba DOC
Gattinara DOCG	Gavi DOC

"At the foot of the mountains" is what Piemonte means and the whole region is dominated by the Alps to the north and the west. The local capital is Turin and the vineyards lie in two distinct groups: to the east of the city in the direction of Lake Maggiore, and to the south in the Langhe and Monferrato hills, both DOC zones, where the wine towns of Asti and Alba are found. The climate is severe in winter, but there is a long ripening season in summer and autumn, though fogs are common in the latter.

Piedmont has the largest area under vines for the production of DOC and DOCG wines and also the most denominations, with over forty. Whilst a number of good white wines are made, more red wine is produced and this includes the four wines of DOCG status: Barolo, Barbaresco, Gattinara and Asti (spumante).

Barolo, made solely from the Nebbiolo grape, is considered to be one of the finest of all Italian red wines. It takes its name from the village of the same name, to the south-west of Alba. Traditionally, Barolo is aged for long periods in large oak casks (a minimum of two years, plus a further

one in bottle, to have the designation), but certain modernists are now moving towards smaller *barriques*. The wines have a great concentration of fruit and flavour with high tannin, acid and alcohol. Because of this they benefit from further ageing in bottle to reach their peak.

Nebbiolo is also the sole grape used in the production of Barolo's sister wine, Barbaresco. This is similar in style, though the wine is generally less full-bodied and the regulations demand less ageing in cask as a result.

The third of the DOCG wines from Piedmont, Gattinara, is also based on Nebbiolo, here called Spanna. However, up to 10% of the Bonarda grape may also be used. Minimum ageing is as for Barolo and the wines are similar in style, though rarely achieving the heights of which Barolos are capable.

Notable DOC reds based on Nebbiolo are Boca and Ghemme near Gattinara, and Carema where mountainside vineyards give a distinctive and refined wine.

Whilst Nebbiolo is the monarch of Piedmontese black grape varieties, there are a number of others producing good wines. Amongst these, Barbera with its good acidity levels (Barbera d'Asti, Barbera d'Alba, Barbera del Monferrato, all DOC) has a rapidly improving reputation, sometimes giving wines for ageing but more often young, fresh and fruity wines in the "Beaujolais" style for early consumption. Freisa (Freisa d'Asti DOC) produces light, often slightly sparkling wines, Grignolino, lighter wines still, and Brachetto something on the Lambrusco model, particularly around the small spa town of Acqui Terme. The wine from Dolcetto is most often soft and fruity (its name means "the little sweet one") but some growers produce a more concentrated tannic wine. The best-known DOC is Dolcetto d'Alba.

For the British consumer, the most famous white grape of Piedmont must be Moscato. This is the base for the DOCGs Moscato d'Asti and Asti. Sparkling, highly aromatic and grapey, it needs to be drunk whilst young and fresh (see Chapter 16).

The finest still white wine of the region comes from the southern hillside vineyards around the town of Gavi, made from the Cortese grape (Cortese di Gavi DOC). This has good acidity and is exceptionally dry, with a steeliness uncommon in Italian wines and a lime-like flavour.

Piedmont is also an important region for the production of vermouth, with major centres in Turin, Canelli and Asti (see Chapter 17).

Lombardy (Lombardia)

Key wines:
Valtellina DOC
Franciacorta DOC
Oltrepò Pavese DOC

Whilst Lombardy is the most populous region of Italy and has important vineyard areas, the wines have not generally received the recognition they might deserve. Less wine is made than in Tuscany or Piedmont; the dampness of the fertile soils near the Po, for instance, makes them unsuitable for viticulture.

Among the best-known wines are the reds made from the Nebbiolo grown in the Valtellina DOC zone. These hillside vineyards are virtually on the Swiss border. A perfect southern aspect ensures that the Nebbiolo can still ripen, and gives the four superiore zones of Grumello, Inferno, Sassella and Valgella an international following. A local speciality is the Sfurzat made from semi-dried grapes, giving wine of at least 14.5% vol.

Further south, the Franciacorta DOC covers still reds and whites as well as sparkling wines; these latter, made largely from the Pinot Bianco grape, can be either tank or bottle fermented, but have a wide market.

Oltrepò Pavese DOC is a large vineyard area south of the city of Pavia, making wines from a wide range of grape varieties and with a corresponding breadth of styles.

Trentino–Alto Adige

Key wines:

Alto Adige DOC	Santa Maddalena DOC
Trentino DOC	Teroldego Rotaliano DOC
Lago di Caldaro DOC	

This is Italy's most northerly region, and is so mountainous that only 15% of the land, that part which forms the valley of the Adige, can be cultivated. Historically, the south of the region (Trentino) around the city of Trento has always been Italian, whilst the north, the Alto Adige round the city of Bolzano (Bozen), was part of the Austro-Hungarian Empire. In this latter part of the region, sometimes referred to as the South Tyrol, German is still spoken and used for many of the wine names. Indeed, the term *Qualitätswein bestimmter Anbaugebiete* may be used as well as DOC for certain wines.

Whilst in terms of quantity this region is not the most important, it has both the highest proportion of DOC wine production in Italy and of exports; most of the latter goes to Austria where there is a shortage of red wine production. Much of the wine is sold under varietal names; the two major DOCs are Trentino in the south and Alto Adige (Südtiroler) in the north.

The finest reds are perceived to come from DOC Santa Maddalena (Sankt Magdalener) and the most popular from DOC Lago di Caldaro (Kalterersee). Both use the Schiava grape (Vernatsch). Other grapes found in the region include the local Teroldego and Lagrein as well as more international favourites such as Cabernet Sauvignon, Merlot and Pinot Nero (Pinot Noir). Teroldego Rotaliano DOC is a wine with lots of colour and soft fruit.

Climatically and commercially, the future would seem to be more in the field of flavoursome white wines. This has led to the planting of quality varietals including Traminer Aromatico (Gewürztraminer), Moscato, Chardonnay, Pinot Bianco (Pinot Blanc), Pinot Grigio (Pinot Gris, a particular success), Sauvignon Blanc and Riesling.

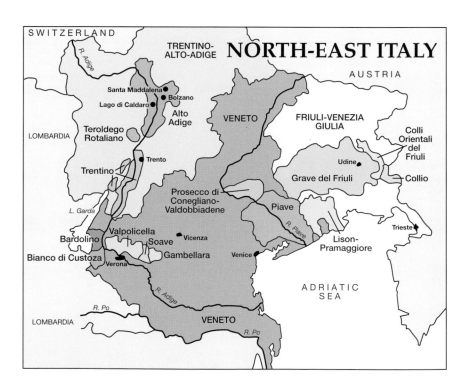

Friuli–Venezia Giulia
Key wines:
Collio DOC
Grave del Friuli DOC
Colli Orientali del Friuli DOC

The hillsides of this region, on the borders of the Balkans, benefit from contrasting airflows from the Alps and the Adriatic. Whilst more red wine is made, it is the whites which have the higher reputation, with varietal names being prominent on the labels. The climate enables wines to be made that are crisp and fruity, showing the individual styles of the grape varieties. It is rare for the wines to be aged in cask.

There are seven DOCs but the most important, in terms of quantity, is Grave del Friuli, though the best wines come from the Collio Goriziano (or simply Collio) and the Colli Orientali del Friuli.

In all, up to twenty grape varieties are accepted; a mixture of local specialities and celebrated imports. The former include the widely planted Tocai Friulano, which appears to have little to do with either Tokaji in Hungary, or Tokay-Pinot Gris. This gives a full-bodied, rather neutral tasting wine. Picolit makes prestigious and pricey dessert wines, Ribolla, full-flavoured, and Verduzzo, attractively fragrant and flowery, generally dry wines. Also among the more widely planted grapes are Pinot Grigio and Pinot Bianco, Riesling, Traminer Aromatico and Chardonnay.

Of the local black grapes Refosco has the highest reputation. It gives wines that age well. Cabernet Franc, Cabernet Sauvignon and Merlot are the most widely planted imports.

Veneto
Key wines:
Soave DOC
Valpolicella DOC
Valpolicella Amarone DOC
Bardolino DOC

Whilst the province of Veneto stretches from the Alpine resort of Cortina d'Ampezzo in the north to where the river Po enters the Adriatic in the south, the DOC vineyard area stretches across the centre from the mouth of the Piave east of Venice, to Lake Garda in the west. The climate is tempered by the mountains to the north and the sea to the east. Veneto produces more DOC wine than any other region. As far as the British market is concerned, the three most important wines all come from the west, around the city of Verona. These are: Soave, Bardolino and Valpolicella.

Quantitatively, Soave is the second most important DOC of Italy after Chianti. Its importance, particularly outside Italy, may sadly be due to the fact that it is a wine that is likely to offend nobody. Soave is made mostly from Garganega, a grape with a delicate fruit, with hints of almond, and some acidity. This is normally blended with up to 30% Trebbiano, an undistinguished neutral grape found as the base in many Italian white blends. When inexpensive, Soave is all too often a bland and uninteresting wine. It is capable of doing better, however, particularly in the classico region around the town of Soave itself. The DOCs Gambellara and Bianco di Custoza produce similar wines to Soave.

Valpolicella DOC is the second most important red wine in Italy – at least as far as quantity is concerned. The vineyards lie east–west in a band to the north of Verona. The black Corvina, with a sour cherry or herb flavour, is normally blended with Rondinella and Molinara to produce a range of styles of wines.

Basic Valpolicella is a light, fruity wine best drunk young. DOC Amarone della Valpolicella is rather more distinguished. It is produced from semi-dried grapes which, fully fermented, give a wine that is intense and long on the palate, rich, yet dry with a hint of bitterness and with 14 – 15% alcohol by volume.

Recioto della Valpolicella DOC is also made from semi-dried grapes, but a stopped fermentation results in a distinct sweetness which comes as a shock to traditional red wine drinkers.

Bardolino DOC, from the shores of Lake Garda, which has its own cooler climate, is typically a light, uncomplicated wine made from the same grapes as Valpolicella. It is increasingly found as a *vino novello* or as a *chiaretto*.

Elsewhere in the Veneto, a wide range of varietal wines are made under the Piave DOC, dominated by Merlot and Cabernet Franc. DOC Prosecco di Conegliano-Valdobbiadene is a dry to medium-sweet white wine, usually sparkling.

Emilia-Romagna
Key wines:

Albana di Romagna DOCG	Sangiovese di Romagna DOC
Lambrusco di Sorbara DOC	Trebbiano di Romagna DOC
Lambrusco Grasparossa di Castelvetro DOC	Lambrusco Vino da Tavola

This province lies to the south of the river Po, where the land is relatively fertile and capable of high yields. The region's best-known grape variety is, of course, Lambrusco, which as a *vino da tavola* has been one of the most commercially successful Italian wines on export markets.

Lambrusco Vino da Tavola has a screw top, and the fermentation will have been stopped artificially to leave residual sugar, between 7 and 9% alcohol and a gentle sparkle. White Lambrusco will also have been vinified from the same black grapes, with the skins eliminated.

There are four DOCs for Lambrusco, and they are excellent examples of a wine style developing to match local cuisine. The area is rich gastronomically, and Bolognese sauces, parma ham, parmesan cheese and balsamic vinegar need a wine to cut through their richness and refresh the palate. The drier DOC versions of the light sparkling Lambrusco with their soft fruit, good acidity and low tannin perform this role admirably.

The four Lambrusco DOCs come from around the cities of Modena and Reggio Emilia. The best known are Lambrusco di Sorbara and Lambrusco Grasparossa di Castelvetro. The vines are trained high on trellises to maintain acidity and the wine, at its best, is purple, dry, lightly sparkling, low in alcohol, fruity and refreshing. Amongst other things, the wine must have a bottle with a mushroom stopper to qualify for DOC status.

To the south-west, from the hills around the motor-racing town of Imola comes Italy's first white DOCG, Albana di Romagna. Made from the Albana grape, the wine can be either *secco*, with hints of marzipan on the palate, or *amabile*.

Perhaps the most popular still wine within the region is Sangiovese di Romagna. This is made from a high yielding clone of Sangiovese which is widely planted outside Tuscany. The result is a more dilute, rather straightforward fruity red wine. In the same part of the region, Trebbiano di Romagna gives a light, refreshing, still or sparkling white wine.

Liguria
This province consists of a narrow strip along the Mediterranean coast between the French frontier and the city of La Spezia. Wine production is of minimal importance in the region and much of what is produced is blithely consumed by the myriad of tourists in the local beach resorts.

The best known DOC wines are the dry white Cinqueterre, and the soft, floral red wines of Rossese de Dolceacqua.

Tuscany (Toscana)
Key wines:

Chianti Classico DOCG	Carmignano DOCG
Chianti DOCG and its districts	Vernaccia di San Gimignano DOCG
Brunello di Montalcino DOCG	Vino Nobile di Montepulciano
Vin Santo	DOCG

Home of the new wave of talented and creative young oenologists,

Tuscany, together with Piedmont, is the foundation upon which Italy's reputation for producing fine wines is being built. Within its boundaries lie six of the country's DOCG areas and it is here also that many of the best premium *vini da tavola* have been created.

The classic wine of Tuscany is Chianti. Paradoxically, it is probably Chianti's straw flask of tradition, bought more for future use as a candlestick or lamp base than for what was in the bottle, that did more than anything else to harm the image of Italian wines. Happily, from this nadir, the quality and the reputation of the wine have deservedly regained stature in the international marketplace.

Chianti is a single DOCG in its own right, yet within its boundaries there are seven distinct sub-regions. Of these, the best-known is the classico

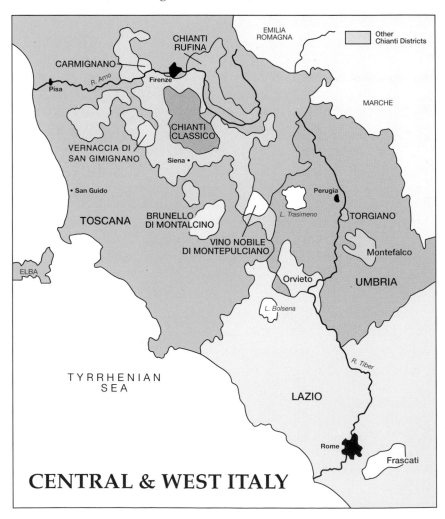

There are six DOCG wines produced in Tuscany, Chianti being the most famous. Classico wines are grown on the Tuscan hills between Florence and Siena.

zone, whose consorzio is identified by a black cockerel label. This now has its own, separate, DOCG. This lies between Firenze (Florence) and Siena, and from its beautifully rolling hillsides come many of the best-known Chiantis. The vineyards are situated on the western foothills of the Appennines. The comparatively high altitude, between 350 and 500 m, tempers the long and very warm dry summers and imparts more finesse to the wines.

The other six sub-regions, which are grouped together in the Chianti Putto Consorzio are:

Colli Aretini

Colli Fiorentini

Colli Senesi: the largest area

Colli Pisane: closest to the sea, giving, perhaps the lightest Chiantis

Montalbano

Rufina: the smallest zone producing some of the greatest wines

The principal grape variety is Sangiovese, a grape that is believed to have been known to the Etruscans in this area. Over the centuries it has spawned many clones of varying quality which can produce wine not only of the highest, but also of the most execrable standard. Typically, it produces a wine of medium-deep colour with a warm herbal, nutty or savoury character on the nose which is repeated on a dry palate. It is capable of great finesse and can age well.

Chianti Classico DOCG may be made entirely from Sangiovese. Other Chianti DOCG wines must contain between 75 and 90% Sangiovese. The clone most likely to be used is the quality Sangioveto, or Sangiovese Grosso. Any balance will include varieties like Canaiolo and the white Trebbiano, though the use of the latter has recently been severely restricted. Some of the local producers have created a jointly owned name, Galestro, to cover dry, white wines made from the resulting surplus of Trebbiano.

Traditionally many of the better wines of Chianti have been given added glycerine by the inducement of a slight secondary fermentation in cask, ideally by the addition of some must from semi-dried grapes. This technique is called *governo*. Ageing, too, has been a matter of taste; some growers have believed in using the traditional large oak casks known as *botti*, some favour small oak *barriques*.

Normally, two different styles of wine are made: basic Chianti for early drinking, and *riserva*, aged in oak and bottle for at least three years before release, which usually needs further bottle-ageing to reach its peak.

Another quality clone of Sangiovese is Brunello and this produces its greatest wine in the DOCG Brunello di Montalcino, the best of which vie with the best Barolos for the accolade of finest and most long-lived of all Italian wines. Produced only from Brunello in limited quantities around the town of Montalcino, to the south of Siena, it is an intensely robust wine which needs ageing before being consumed. The bottle should also be opened well in advance, to allow the complex bouquet to develop fully.

By law the wine has to be aged for four years, of which three must be in cask, before it can be sold. To give producers more flexibility, a more quickly saleable wine, DOC Rosso di Montalcino has recently been developed. This is also made from Brunello, but higher yields are permitted and only one year's ageing is required. Some producers use this DOC rather as a top Bordeaux château would use a second label.

Vino Nobile di Montepulciano was the first wine in Italy to be classified DOCG. It is made around the town of Montepulciano from another Sangiovese clone, called Prugnolo, in a blend similar to a Chianti *riserva*, which it resembles in style.

The final red DOCG of the region is Carmignano. In this small vineyard zone the quality of the Sangiovese is heightened by the addition of up to 10% Cabernet Sauvignon. The result combines Bordeaux finesse and elegance with Italian warmth.

Tuscany's only white DOCG wine is Vernaccia di San Gimignano, from an area west of the Chianti Classico zone. Now made for drinking young and fresh, traditionally it was a wine for ageing.

In all there are over 20 wines with DOC status produced in Tuscany, many of them with small production and largely local consumption.

A final speciality of Tuscany, though it is also produced elsewhere, is the dessert wine Vin Santo which is deliberately oxidised in a traditional manner. Grapes are left to dry on racks in lofts throughout the winter. The pressed juice is very sweet and is sealed in tiny (50 litre) casks with some lees from a previous batch. Often left under the roof, the sealed casks are not topped up during the subsequent slow fermentation and maturation which lasts for a minimum of three, but can extend to five or six, years. Vin Santo is not a DOC in its own right, but might be included in certain DOC legislation (that of Carmignano or Chianti Classico, for instance); most often it is seen as *vino da tavola*.

Many Tuscan producers make prestige wines, largely based on

Steam cleaning of new oak barriques prior to their first filling.

Sangiovese, Cabernet Sauvignon or Chardonnay, outside the DOC system. These are the so-called new wave winemakers who have questioned tradition and whose influence is now extending throughout Italy.

The movement started as long ago as 1948 in San Guido on the coast of Tuscany with the planting of Cabernet Sauvignon. The resultant wine, a pure Cabernet varietal called Sassicaia, was quite unique in the Italy of the day. This was followed most significantly in 1971 by Antinori's Tignanello, a blend of Sangiovese and a little Cabernet Sauvignon, aged in *barriques*. The introduction of Sassicaia and Tignanello may now be seen as a watershed in the Italian wine scene both nationally and internationally. Many of the changes in viticulture and vinification already described in this chapter result from these initiatives; with these wines, high in profile but with small production, Italy reached out to the discerning end of the world market.

Initially, the official status of these two wines and those they have inspired was no more than *vino da tavola*. They were sold either under individual brand names, often designed to catch the eye, or with one of a number of unofficial joint brand names known as *Predicati*. The new legislation of 1992 attempts to reconcile this anomaly whereby some of Italy's best wines lie outside its quality system. The introduction of the new category, IGT, addresses this dichotomy and Sassicaia has been promoted to DOC.

Marches (Marche)
Key wines:
Verdicchio dei Castelli di Jesi DOC
Rosso Conero DOC
Rosso Piceno DOC

The most famous wine of this region, which borders the Adriatic, is Verdicchio, traditionally sold in a green amphora-shaped bottle. This presentation may well have put off many consumers, but this dry, white wine can be very good. The use of cold fermentation and stainless steel is becoming more widespread amongst exporting producers. There are three DOCs incorporating the Verdicchio grape variety in the name; the most readily found is Verdicchio dei Castelli di Jesi which has a light fresh grassy aroma.

The two most important red wine DOCs in the region are Rosso Piceno, made from a blend of Sangiovese and Montepulciano grape varieties and Rosso Conero, made around the city of Ancona, almost totally from the Montepulciano grape. This grape is in many ways similar to the Sangiovese, but it produces wines that are deeper coloured, less fine and lower in tannin, though often fuller bodied. It should not be confused with the town of Montepulciano in Tuscany.

Umbria
Key wines:
Torgiano Rosso Riserva DOCG
Sagrantino di Montefalco DOCG
Orvieto DOC

Umbria has a topography and climate similar to Tuscany but without any maritime influence. Its main wine town is Perugia. Historically, Umbria is known for its white wines from Orvieto. These used to be predominantly sweet but the modern tendency is for them to be dry, and rather bland. The better producers, however, bring out the fruit characteristics of the blend of grape varieties from which Orvieto is made; these include the Trebbiano, Malvasia and Grechetto.

The finest red wine from Umbria is undoubtedly from Torgiano, a DOC dominated by just one producer. The *riserva* has now been awarded DOCG status; it is made from the traditional Chianti blend of Sangiovese and Canaiolo.

From the heartland of the region, around the town of Montefalco, a local red varietal, the Sagrantino, produces exceptional sweet and dry red wines. These, too, now have DOCG status.

Latium (Lazio)
Key wine:
Frascati DOC

White wines dominate in Latium and of these it is Frascati DOC that is widest known having built its reputation originally on draught in the *trattorie* of Rome. Now its fresh, clean taste and pale colour appeal to many wanting to play safe. The basic grapes in the blend are Malvasia, which develops quickly and shows pleasing light aromas, and the ubiquitous Trebbiano. The better wines with most character tend to be those in which Malvasia predominates.

Abruzzo (Abruzzi)
Key wines:
Montepulciano d'Abruzzo DOC
Trebbiano d'Abruzzo DOC

On the leg of Italy, Abruzzo is behind the knee, a region of mountains sliding down through hills to the sea. Whilst the wine-growers of most of Italy have realised that fragmentation in the DOC system generally means higher prices, here they have gone for simplicity and there are only two: Montepulciano d'Abruzzo for the red wines and Trebbiano d'Abruzzo for the white. The Montepulciano is a typical product of that grape, rich and full with low acidity and relatively low tannin.

Molise

The small province of Molise has been long neglected in the family of Italian wines, and for some time it was the only region not to have any DOC wines. Now there are two, both giving red, white and rosé wines. Biferno is produced towards the coast, with the reds from Montepulciano being thought to have more potential. The other DOC, Pentro di Isernia, is produced up in the hills.

Campania

Key wines:
Taurasi DOCG
Greco di Tufo DOC
Fiano di Avellino DOC

It was in Campania, with the Bay of Naples at its centre, that the finest classical wines were made, with the name of one of the local grapes, the Greco, bearing witness to their origins. The volcanic soils are ideal for the production of fine wines; at the beginning of the last century, Lacryma Christi was considered to be one of the great sweet wines of Italy. Sadly, since then, standards have declined and it is only in the past few years that a small number of growers have sought to make better wines.

The three wines with the finest reputations come from around the town of Avellino: Taurasi, a red wine made from the high quality Aglianico grape, has now been promoted to DOCG status. It must be aged for three years, with at least one year in cask, before sale. This is a full-bodied red with great ageing potential. Greco di Tufo and Fiano di Avellino are both top quality DOC dry white wines, named after the grape varieties from which they are made. The classical Greco is a quality grape which ripens late and produces a deep-coloured wine which matures in the bottle. Fiano was known to the Romans. Grown today in the hills about Avellino, it produces a distinctive wine whose flavour has been said to reflect the hazlenuts for which Avellino is also famous and amongst which the vines are planted.

Apulia (Puglia)

Key wines:
Salice Salentino DOC
Castel del Monte DOC

Lying on the heel of Italy at 41° latitude, Puglia has a hot rather than warm climate. With Sicily it has the largest wine production of all Italy and historically it was the source for much of the blending wine that was shipped around the world. Even now, DOC production represents less than 2% of Puglia's total, though there is a distinct movement towards the production of quality wines, with the planting of many of the best-known French varieties.

The two DOCs with more than a purely local reputation are Salice Salentino, a deep red from Negroamaro and Malvasia Nero grown near Brindisi, and Castel del Monte, whose best wine is the red made from Uva di Troia.

Basilicata
Key wine:
Aglianico del Vulture DOC

This is a desolate mountainous region in the instep of Italy. Here it is the Aglianico grape which dominates and is responsible for the one DOC wine, Aglianico del Vulture, which appears under a variety of guises, a young red, a Vecchio aged for 5 years, and even a slightly sweet sparkling wine.

Calabria
The mountainous toe of Italy also produces predominantly red wine, which varies greatly in quality according to the climate; cooler up in the mountains and hotter on the coastal strips. Two good DOC red wines are made from the Gaglioppo grape, Cirò and Melissa. Of the whites, the sweet Greco di Bianco rates amongst the best.

Sicily (Sicilia)
Key wine:
Marsala DOC

The largest of Italy's provinces also has the largest area under vines. Production is concentrated at the western end of the island. Co-operative cellars, particularly, have profited considerably from European Community financial assistance. The region has its own quality award, shown by a Q on the label, which can be applied to all classifications of wine. Indeed, there is a great deal of excellent *vino da tavola* produced. Many of the better wines come from the mountainous interior of the island, where the cooler climate adds finesse.

The fortified wine, Marsala, named after the Sicilian port of the same name near where it is made, is described in Chapter 17.

The remote island of Pantelleria off the North African coast, produces a superb Moscato, and another great dessert wine is the Malvasia delle Lipari from the Aeolian Islands.

Sardinia (Sardegna)
Key wines:
Cannonau di Sardegna DOC
Vermentino di Sardegna DOC

The international flavour of Sardinia's wines reflects the island's history and situation. Many of the grape varieties grown are found nowhere else in Italy whilst links with France and Spain can be traced. Traditionally, much of the wine has been made for blending purposes and enormous yields have not been uncommon from the Campidano plains of the south of the island. Here, as in Sicily, co-operative cellars play an important role.

Two-thirds of the production is white wine and nearly all wines are named after the grape variety from which they are made. The main white grapes are Nuragus, giving a rather bland, dry wine, the more characterful Vermentino and Moscato. Of the reds, the best probably come from Cannonau (Grenache), which must be aged in wood for a year to obtain the DOC.

CHAPTER 13

SPAIN AND PORTUGAL

Whilst it is convenient to consider the wines of the Iberian peninsula in one chapter, the differences between the two countries of Spain and Portugal are immense. Their fierce independence, the one from the other, is continued in their wines. With a few exceptions there is little similarity between them. At the root of this difference is the climate although, not surprisingly, the further south one goes throughout the peninsula, the hotter is the climate in both countries.

In Portugal, it is the Atlantic Ocean that is the dominant feature. As a result there is predominantly high rainfall, with mild winters and warm but not excessively hot summers. Spain, on the other hand, has a vast mountainous interior bordered to the east and south by coastal plains which are seldom wider than 45 kilometres; interior and coast have continental and mediterranean climates respectively. Except in the north-west, rainfall is lower in Spain than in Portugal, and central Spain, where much of the wine is produced, is very arid. Here, in the interior, several hundreds of kilometres from the coast and separated from the sea by mountain ranges, the winters are cold and the summers extremely hot, with temperatures varying from –10 to +45 °C over the year. Even in summer, temperatures at night can be low because of the altitude. On the coastal plains, the Mediterranean moderates temperatures especially in winter, giving mild or, in the south, warm conditions; westerly winds are moist and bring rain.

SPAIN

The history of wine in Spain goes back to the earliest of times. It was probably the Phoenicians who first introduced the vine; they planted considerable vineyards in the south around the city of Gades (Cádiz) and are known to have navigated the river Ebro as far as Rioja. During the subsequent settlement of much of Spain by the Moors, production of wine continued, being carried on by Jews and Christians who were allowed considerable freedom by their Moslem rulers.

In modern terms, the turning point for the vineyards came with the arrival of phylloxera in France, which led to the emigration of many merchants who came to settle in northern Spain, predominantly in Rioja and Penedés. It is for this reason that so many Spanish wine companies still have French names. Also, because the settlers were largely merchants not growers, it meant that the concept of individual wine-estates has scarcely developed in Spain. It is the merchant's or brand name that is known. The French introduced their own techniques where they settled, in particular the use of small oak barrels for ageing their wines.

With Spain now in the European Community, the country is perceived as a prime source of good value, inexpensive wine. Pressure and promises from major buyers have led to dramatic improvements in standards, not just in the traditional quality regions, but also in formerly despised areas such as La Mancha and Valencia. European Community funds have been poured into the Spanish wine trade – and the results have been dramatic: refrigeration and stainless steel have worked miracles.

In contrast to this is the traditional nature of much of Spain's viticulture. Whilst it has a much larger area under vines than Italy or France, it produces considerably less wine than either. The annual production varies more significantly than that in these two countries, as occasional rainfall in the generally arid centre of the country can make a big difference to the size of the crop, but the average figure is in the region of 33 million hectolitres a year. Growers, and even the local trade associations, have often been unwilling to accept that more wine, and better wine, can be made by denser planting and the training of vines along wires. The other factor that contributes to the low yields is the age of the vines. Fifteen per cent of these are reputed to be forty-five years old or more.

WINE LAWS

Spanish growers, on the other hand, have not been slow to realise some of the merits of European Community law, particularly when it comes to the creation of specific appellations or *Denominaciónes de Origen* (DOs) as they are called. Now there are more than forty of them, some representing very small areas.

There is now also a higher classification of wines, *Denominación de Origen Calificada* (DOCa or DOC), and the first region to benefit from this was Rioja in 1991. Similarly, a lower classification, *Vino de la Tierra*, has been created, for a number of regions that have aspirations towards DO status. This classification approximates to the French *Vin de Pays* or German *Landwein*.

Below this comes the lowest classification, Table Wine or *Vino de Mesa*.

Ageing
Every bottle of DO or DOCa wine carries a seal issued by the local *Consejo Regulador*, or controlling body, guaranteeing the classification of the wine. As well as certifying the region of origin, the extent to which the wine has been aged may also be noted. There are minimum requirements for each of the four different categories, and as a general rule these apply nationally to all DOs.

Vino Joven – Literally "young wine", this is a wine which may or may not have spent some time in cask before being bottled in the year following the vintage, for immediate release.

Crianza – Red wines must be at least two years old, and have been aged in small oak casks for a minimum of six months. White and rosé wines must be at least one year old.

Reserva – These are wines generally produced in the better vintages, from selected vats of wine. The reds must have been aged in cask and bottle for a minimum of three years. The balance of ageing between wood and glass will depend on the policy of the individual shipper, though the wine must spend a minimum of 12 months in cask. White and rosé *Reservas* must be aged for two years, of which six months must be in oak.

Gran Reserva – These wines are only produced in exceptional vintages. Reds must have aged for at least two years in cask, followed by a further three years in bottle or vice versa. White and rosé wines are aged for four years, of which six months must be in oak.

Some regions, Rioja for instance, stipulate additional ageing beyond these national requirements.

REGIONS AND WINES
In the survey that follows, Spain's principal DO regions are grouped geographically by similarity of climate and, to an extent, wine style. The six unofficial groups are the Upper Ebro, Catalonia, the Duero valley and the Atlantic coast in northern Spain and Levante and Castilla-La Mancha further south.

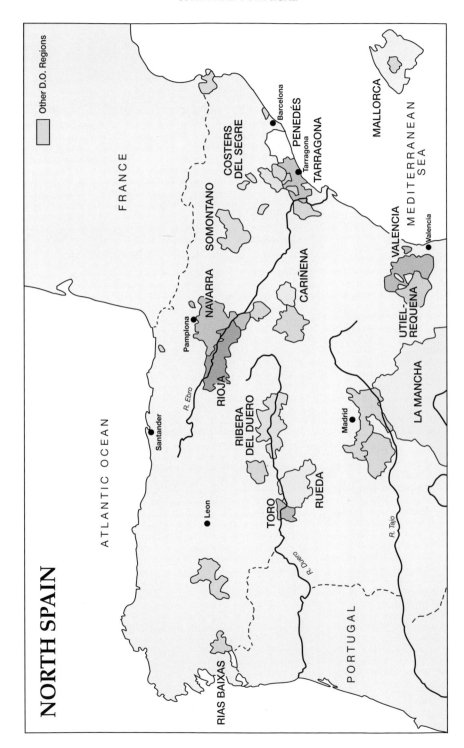

NORTH SPAIN

Other D.O. Regions

FRANCE

ATLANTIC OCEAN

Santander

R. Ebro

Pamplona

NAVARRA

RIOJA

SOMONTANO

COSTERS DEL SEGRE

Barcelona

PENEDÉS

Tarragona

TARRAGONA

CARIÑENA

VALENCIA

Valencia

MEDITERRANEAN SEA

MALLORCA

UTIEL-REQUENA

LA MANCHA

Madrid

RIBERA DEL DUERO

RUEDA

TORO

Leon

R. Duero

R. Tajo

PORTUGAL

RIAS BAIXAS

The Upper Ebro
Key regions:
Rioja DOCa
Navarra DO
Cariñena DO
Somontano DO

Rioja
There are vineyards along much of the river Ebro from the Cantabrian mountains to the Mediterranean, but the finest wines, perhaps of all Spain, come from its upper reaches, in the region of Rioja, where mountains give protection on three sides. The region takes its name from the Rio Oja, a tributary of the Rio Ebro.

The capital of the province of La Rioja is the city of Logroño which is used as a reference point for the three distinct sub-regions of the area described below.

Rioja Alavesa – This area is situated to the west of Logroño and on the northern side of the river Ebro. The climate is influenced by the Atlantic and is cool, with the highest rainfall of the three sub-regions. The soil is very chalky and the wines are perhaps the lightest of the region but with the most finesse. Tempranillo is the dominant grape variety. Alavesa wines have the best overall balance and one or two single vineyard Riojas are made in this district.

Rioja Alavesa vineyards. Tempranillo grapes planted in chalky soil with the Cantabrian mountains in the background.

Rioja Alta – This area is also to the west of Logroño but lies to the south of the Ebro. The largely clay soil varies from the more chalky to the richer red with a proportion of iron in it. The former is better for the white Viura, and the latter for Tempranillo. In the river valley there is some alluvial soil, ideal for Malvasia. Many of the major *bodegas*, or wine-producing companies, are based in la Rioja Alta, particularly in the town of Haro. The climate is rather warmer and drier than the Alavesa, but is still Atlantic influenced. Wines from this area provide the backbone of most blends, being full of body and colour.

Rioja Baja – The final sub-region is situated mainly on the south bank of the Ebro downstream of Logroño. Here the soil has a higher proportion of clay and the climate is more continental with very hot summers, drier still than Rioja Alta. The dominant grape variety is Garnacha, giving rather coarser, early maturing wines. Baja wine may be added to both Alta and Alvesa wines in light years in order to increase alcohol levels.

Classic Rioja is a blend created from the wines of these three sub-regions. Very occasionally, it is produced from a single grape variety. There are severe limitations on the varieties that may be used: all are traditional to the region. For example, Cabernet Sauvignon is only permitted for two producers who planted it many years ago; recently a move to have Cabernet more generally accepted was rejected. Rioja produces red, white and rosé light wines, and some Cava (see Chapter 16) is also made. The breakdown of light wine production is 75% red, 15% rosé and 10% white.

The permitted black varieties in Rioja are:

Tempranillo – This takes its name from the Spanish word temprano – early, and its advantage is that it is early ripening. Although not the most extensively planted variety in Spain, Tempranillo is the premier Spanish grape and can be found under a number of local synonyms. It likes chalky soils and grows well in a cool climate. Quite low in acidity, it nevertheless ages well.

Garnacha (or Garnacha Tinta) – Known as Grenache in the south of France, this is the most widely planted red grape in Spain. It gives a big yield, and makes wines of high alcohol with a tendency to mature early. It is widely used for rosé wines.

Graciano – With low yields, plantings of this grape are now very limited. Graciano gives very full-bodied wines with a powerful nose, which age well.

Mazuelo – The French Carignan, giving a wine high in acidity, tannin and colour. This balances well when blended in a small proportion with Tempranillo.

The white varieties permitted are:

Viura – The same grape as Macabeo and Maccabeu of the south of France, this produces wines with good fruit and acidity. The yields can be high.

Malvasia – This makes full-bodied heavy wines which balance out the frequent lightness of Viura.

Garnacha Blanca is also permitted.

Bush training is obligatory throughout Rioja except for experimental vineyards. Most of the vineyards are in the hands of small growers, many of whom will send their grapes to the co-operative cellar, or alternatively to one of the merchant *bodegas*.

Sample of wine being taken from a new oak cask in Rioja.

There has been a distinct move by a number of producers to reduce the tradition of long wood-ageing, in which the minimum ageing stipulations have been widely exceeded for all categories of wine, in some cases with a detrimental effect on quality. In practice now, the ageing period is still significant, and indeed may still exceed the minimum requirements, but is much more in tune with the wines. Red Crianza Riojas, for instance are required to have at least twelve months oak-ageing rather than the six months stipulated for other DOs, and most *bodegas* will actually age them in cask for eighteen months to two years and then further in bottle. For the whites, it is often a case of fermentation at low temperature, storage in stainless steel and bottling when young to preserve the maximum amount of fruit. Interestingly enough, some of the most modern *bodegas* are going back to what for them are more old-fashioned oak-aged white wines, but using new French rather than Amercian oak for just a short period.

Navarra

Twenty years or so ago, Navarra suffered from regular over-production of rosé wines, made from the Garnacha grape, which often had an alcoholic content of 15% or more and a tendency to oxidise. With demand for such wines being in rapid decline, the whole region has had to move in another direction. This is firmly towards the production of quality red wines; whites only account for approximately five per cent of the production. The quantities of rosé wine made are still important, but they are now of a lighter, fruitier style than hitherto.

The 18,000 ha of Navarra vineyards lie down the Ebro valley from Rioja, stretching from that valley to the Pyrenees. There is a variety of soils and the climate ranges from the cooler areas in the foothills of the Pyrenees to the hotter, drier parts south of the Ebro.

Whilst the vineyards of Navarra have traditionally been planted with the same grape varieties as those of Rioja, with the Garnacha predominating, there is a pragmatism with regard to the introduction of other varietals that is totally absent in Rioja. The policy is for Tempranillo to become the major red varietal, but there are now substantial plantings of Cabernet Sauvignon and Merlot. Chardonnay is also being planted to liven up the sometimes rather neutral Viura white wines.

This investment in the vineyards is being matched in the cellars, where small oak barrels are coming in to wider use and where temperature controlled fermentation tanks are being used for the rosé and white wines. Hopefully this will lead to a more balanced output of quality wines at reasonable prices.

Other regions
Cariñena lies south of the city of Zaragoza in the province of Aragon. Ninety per cent of the production is in the hands of the co-operative cellars. Whilst red, white and rosé wines are made, the best are generally the reds made from Garnacha and Tempranillo.

Somontano is north of Zaragoza in the foothills of the Pyrenees. It has a cool climate and no shortage of rainfall. Although reds are produced, Somontano is best known in the UK for high quality white wines from French varieties.

Catalonia
Key regions:
Penedés DO
Costers del Segre DO
Tarragona DO

Penedés
This is the most important of the Catalan appellations, lying to the south-west of Barcelona. Largely due to the efforts of one local company, it has been in the forefront of viticultural and winemaking advances in Spain and it was one of the first areas to make large scale use of "foreign" grape varieties. Penedés, additionally, is the principal centre of sparkling wine (Cava) production.

Within the region, there is a broad selection of grape varieties planted, both traditional and imported. The reputation of the region in the past has rested on its white wines made largely from the local Parellada, Xarel-lo and Macabeo grapes. Over recent years, there has been a positive move towards improving quality by planting Chardonnay, Riesling, Gewürztraminer and Sauvignon Blanc. Often these are used to improve the quality of blends, or sometimes as single varietal wines. Cask-ageing of wines is much less important in Penedés than in Rioja, and most of the area's production is *Vino Joven*.

Traditionally, vines have been pruned *en vaso*, a method similar to the Beaujolais gobelet system. The more recently introduced French and German varieties, however, are normally trained along wires.

Red wine production is dominated by Spain's two most planted red wine grapes, Garnacha and Monastrell. Tempranillo is also found and is occasionally seen on labels under its Catalan name, Ull de Llebre. Just as noble white varieties have been introduced, so too with the reds; Cabernet Sauvignon, Cabernet Franc, Merlot and Pinot Noir have all been planted by the better producers in the cooler vineyard areas.

Climatically, the region can be split into three zones which correspond to strips that run parallel to the coast. Between the coastal range of hills and the sea, the summers are hot and dry. Here, mainly red wines are produced. Inland, in the valleys of the Foix and Noya rivers, the climate is more temperate; much of the white wine used in Cava production is made here. Further into the hills in the Alt Penedés, where vines are grown up to 800 metres, the climate is cool, and there has been a move to plant varieties such as Pinot Noir and Riesling, where their full finesse can be developed.

Other regions
Costers del Segre lies inland close to the town of Lérida. Production is dominated by just one company which has extensive plantings of Tempranillo, Cabernet Sauvignon and Chardonnay. The climate is continental and rainfall is low, but because the vineyards are classified as "experimental", irrigation is permitted.

Tarragona was traditionally known in Britain for producing a strong, sweet, red wine sold in flagons. Today, the region's inexpensive red and white wines are more often seen.

The Duero Valley
Key regions:
Toro DO
Rueda DO
Ribera del Duero DO

Whilst the valley of the river Douro is perhaps best known for Port wines, in Spain, under the name of the Duero, it has vineyards producing some truly outstanding wines. This part of the country experiences a continental climate which can often be very harsh. Altitude gives the nights a certain coolness, but there is also an ideal long, dry ripening season for the grapes.

Toro is the first DO region upstream from the Portuguese frontier. Here the dominant grape is Tinto de Toro, another manifestation of the ubiquitous Tempranillo. The extreme summer heat gives wines of very high alcohol, 14.5% is common, which are more full-bodied and richer than Riojas but without, arguably, quite the same long term ageing potential in the very best wines. In the *Vino Joven* style for drinking young, there is likely to be a proportion of Garnacha in the blend; *Reservas* and *Gran Reservas* for ageing are very deep in colour and tannic when young.

Rueda lies to the south of Valladolid. Its reputation for dry, white wines dates from 1972, when a leading Rioja company established cellars here for the production of white wines. In taking this decision the company was attracted by the area's chalky soil and good spring and autumn rainfall. The grape of the region, the Verdejo, produces surprisingly elegant wines, whilst two "new" varieties, the Viura and the Sauvignon Blanc, may also now be grown. All this, together with modern vinification techniques, combine to produce some of Spain's finest white wines which have a distinctive earthy or nutty fruit character and very good acidity. These wines are usually drunk young though there are some cask-aged wines available.

Ribera del Duero is a comparatively young DO, still expanding to take in further producers. It spreads in a narrow band along both banks of the Duero and can justifiably claim to produce some of the greatest red wines of Spain. There are two main reasons for this: the summer nights are cool, giving grapes with more finesse, and, since the end of the last century, there have been plantings of Bordeaux varieties, such as Cabernet Sauvignon, Merlot and Malbec, alongside the local Tinto del Pais (Tempranillo) and Garnacha. The top brand of the vineyard of Vega Sicilia, "Unico", is, reputedly, the most expensive wine in Spain. The wines are slightly lighter in weight than those of Toro but are fuller than Rioja reds. They have a potential to age similar to the latter. Traditionally, the best wines have been rotated between barrels, wood and concrete vats for several years before bottling. This has given them a great deal of complexity. Some more modern bodegas, however, appear capable of arriving at the same quality level with earlier bottling.

The Atlantic Coast
Key region:
Rias Baixas DO

The exceptionally damp climate of the northern Atlantic coast of Spain is scarcely conducive to the production of fine wine. Indeed, there is a considerable cider production in the area.

Of most interest is the Rias Baixas of Galicia, made from the Albariño grape, which, as Alvarinho, also gives the best Vinhos Verdes just across the river Minho, which is the frontier with Portugal. Rias Baixas wines improve for up to two years in the bottle and, compared with Vinho Verde, have more alcohol and much more intense fruit.

Levante
Key region:
Valencia DO

Historically, Valencia has been an exporter of bulk wine of little reputation. There has, however, been considerable investment and recently, successful efforts have been made to give the wines of the region their own image. This has meant considerable replanting in the vineyards, where, until the early 1980s, hybrid vines were still in the majority. For red wines, Cencibel, a local synonym for Tempranillo, is taking over from Bobal and Garnacha, and for whites, Macabeo from Mersguera. It is in winemaking, however, that most of the improvements have come and the region is now making clean, simple wines that sell at affordable prices.

A speciality of the region is Moscatel de Valencia, which by law can either be fortified or not.

Lesser DOs in the region include, Alicante, Utiel-Requena, Jumilla, Yecla and Almansa. Their heavy red wines have traditionally been used for blending, but better producers are now creating individual reputations for their wines.

Castilla-La Mancha
Key regions:
La Mancha DO
Valdepeñas DO

Almost half of Spain's total wine production comes from this vast central plateau. Most vines are grown by smallholders and much of their produce is vinified in co-operative wineries. In the main, these wines are made to be drunk young. La Mancha is the home of the world's most widely planted grape variety, Airén; that this is so might seem incredible given that Airén is seldom seen outside Spain, indeed seldom seen

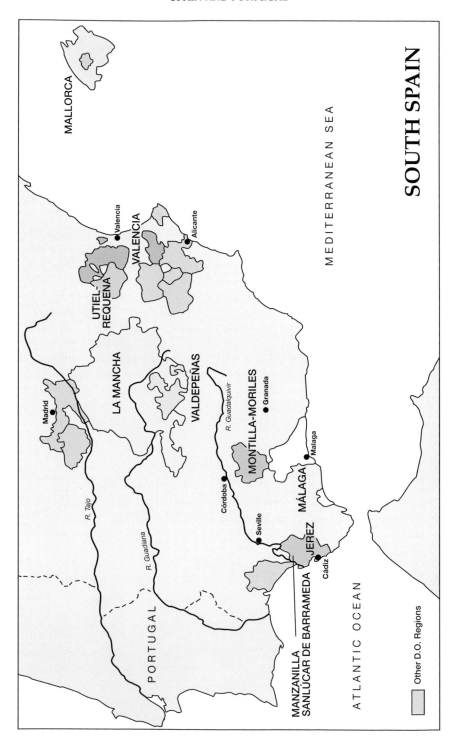

SOUTH SPAIN

MALLORCA

MEDITERRANEAN SEA

Valencia

VALENCIA

Alicante

UTIEL-REQUENA

LA MANCHA

VALDEPEÑAS

MONTILLA-MORILES

Granada

R. Guadalquivir

Madrid

R. Tajo

R. Guadiana

Málaga

Córdoba

MÁLAGA

Seville

JEREZ

Cádiz

MANZANILLA
SANLÚCAR DE BARRAMEDA

PORTUGAL

ATLANTIC OCEAN

Other D.O. Regions

outside La Mancha and Montilla. The scope of this grape is matched by its anonymity, for much of the undistinguished wine that it makes is distilled for ageing as brandy or sold as house wine in bars and restaurants in Madrid.

The climate is hot and dry; the vines are planted far apart and grow so close to the ground that the leaf canopy gives permanent shade both to the fruit and to the ground surrounding the foot of the vine. This keeps the grapes as cool as possible, and preserves whatever moisture there might be in the soil. Traditionally, and again to keep it cool, the wine was stored in enormous *tinajas* made of clay, like monumental Ali Baba baskets, buried so as to leave only the narrow neck and opening visible.

Widely spaced, low bush trained vines in La Mancha, in late spring. Note the vast expanse of flat, arid vineyards.

Now, much is changing. Under pressure from foreign buyers, the white grapes are picked earlier, by anything up to fourteen days, and as a result have lower potential alcohol and higher freshening acidity. Fermentation takes place at low temperature to preserve the fruit. The result is wines that have a broad international acceptance, at reasonable prices.

There are two DOs of importance: La Mancha itself and the much smaller Valdepeñas. This is a hilly enclave in the south of the region around the town of the same name. Its reputation rests securely on its red wines made mainly from the Cencibel (Tempranillo) grape, though some Airén is frequently included in the blend. The best wines are now aged in oak, though there are also some interesting, fruity young wines made by carbonic maceration.

SPANISH LABELLING TERMS

The following expressions are commonly found on Spanish wine labels:

Bodega	winery
Blanco	white
Brut	dry sparkling wine
Cava	DO sparkling wine made by the traditional method (see Chapter 16)
Dulce	sweet
Elaborado	produced by
Embotellado	bottled
Granvas	tank method sparkling wine
Rosado	rosé
Seco	dry
Semi-seco	medium-dry
Tinto	red
Vendimia	vintage
Viejo	old
Viña	vineyard
Vino	wine

PORTUGAL

The history of the wine trade in Britain has for long been closely tied to that of Portugal. One of the main reasons for this has been that at time of war with France, it was easy to ship wine from the ports of Portugal. A special boost was given to the importation of Portuguese wines, when for eight years from 1678, the importation of French wines was prohibited. Preferential treatment for Portuguese goods was confirmed by the Methuen Treaty of 1703. Today, Portugal is the world's ninth largest producer of wine, with an annual average crop of 9 million hectolitres a year. This places it below Germany but above South Africa in most years.

As a general comment, the choice of grape variety is a less significant factor in the style of Portuguese wines than, say, in France. Most wines are made from blends of grapes and no Portuguese grape has the combination of a distinctive fruit character and structure to allow it to stand on its own. Also, it must be said, many vine-growers are not totally sure which varieties are planted.

WINE LAWS

A small but increasing percentage of the total production has the highest classification of *Denominação de Origem Controlada* (DOC).

In 1989, a new category of Quality Wine below DOC was introduced, for regions that have the potential for promotion to DOC status. These regions are presently classified as *Indicacão de Proveniencia Regulamentada* (IPR). This is roughly equivalent to the VDQS category in France. Finally, there is *Vin de Pays* equivalent, *Vinho Regional*.

DOC and IPR wines are identified by a paper seal, the *Selo de Origem*, which is issued by the authorities of the appropriate region. Forming part of the quality control system, each seal is numbered. This takes the form of a paper disk on the bottle's neck with a "tail" that goes under the capsule and over the cork.

All other wine is classed as *Vinho de Mesa* (Table Wine).

The terms *Reserva* and *Garrafeira* are used to denote wines of superior quality. A *Reserva* wine must come from one vintage, which must be stated on the label, and must pass a tasting panel. If DOC, it must be of a higher alcoholic strength than the minimum laid down for that DOC.

The term *Garrafeira*, which can also be applied to all wines, not just those of DOC status, must in addition to the requirements for a *Reserva* wine, be aged at least two years in cask and one in bottle if it is a red wine, and six months in cask and six in bottle, if it is a white.

REGIONS AND WINES

DOC wines
Key regions:

Vinho Verde	Douro
Dão	Borba
Bairrada	

Vinho Verde
This region lies mainly between the river Douro and the Spanish border in the north, and from the coast up to 90 kilometres inland. The climate is hot in the summer, but there is an exceptionally high rainfall during the

winter which can also be a problem during the vintage. The main soil is granite.

Traditionally, and a living testament to early Roman influences, the vineyards were smallholdings with, in some areas of polyculture, vines grown up trees, as hedges or on pergolas. Indeed, until the revolution of 1974, it was forbidden to plant whole fields with vines, they could only be planted round the edges. Nowadays, vineyards are more systematically planted. Growers use either the *Cruzeta*, a high trained (2 m), spur-pruned double cordon system, or the *barra*, a single, spur pruned cordon trained to between 1 and 1.5 m, similar to some French systems. Modern vinification methods are practised. Fermentation takes place in large vats; the best wineries use stainless steel, others concrete vats lined with tiles.

Vinho Verde translates as "green wine" but this has nothing to do with its colour. Indeed, whilst we may not see it in Britain, more red wine is produced than white. Rather, "Verde" refers to its youth, or greenness.

The traditional high trellising system, in combination with the influences of climate and soil, gives grapes which even when fully ripe have low sugar and high acidity. It used to be the practice to let malolactic fermentation occur. The wine was then bottled in the winter, which meant that there would still be gas in suspension. This gave the wine its characteristic prickle.

Cruzeta training in Vinho Verde, with two vines planted against each post.

Nowadays, the wine is not normally allowed to undergo its "malo" which is prevented by the careful use of SO_2. At bottling, CO_2 is injected into it to create the light sparkle. To satisfy foreign consumers' taste, the wines are often sweetened and, as a result, scarcely resemble those drunk in Portugal. Certainly, the tannic acidity of a red Vinho Verde can come as a surprise to the unsuspecting. The sweetness is achieved by arresting fermentation of certain vats and blending this sweeter wine with dry wines immediately before bottling.

Except on the south bank of the river Minho in the extreme north, where the Alvarinho makes the most complex and expensive wines, often bottled under the name of a single *quinta* or estate, the main grapes for the white wines are Loureiro and Trajadura. For the red wines the main grape variety is Vinhão.

Douro

As only a proportion of grapes grown in the schistous vineyards of the Douro valley are permitted to be made into Port, and this proportion can change from vintage to vintage, the majority of grapes are now used for the production of light wine. This has become more rewarding since the award of DOC status in 1982 and indeed there is now a small number of vineyards dedicated to nothing else, including those producing Portugal's most expensive light wine, Barca Velha.

Generally speaking, the grapes used are the same as for making Port, particularly Tinta Roriz, Touriga Nacional, Tinta Nacional and Tinta Barroca. However, there have been plantings of French varieties such as Cabernet Sauvignon, Sauvignon Blanc and even the Gewürztraminer. The best red wines are rich and fruity with balancing tannin and acidity but many other wines can still be harsh and dried-out. The whites, especially those from high altitude vineyards, can show fresh fruit and crisp acidity.

Dão

This vineyard area lies south of the Douro, about 80 kilometres inland. It takes its name from a tributary of the river Mondego and the best vineyards are at an altitude of between 200 and 500 m. They are protected on all sides by mountains and are generally planted with low, bush-trained vines on south-facing slopes. The soil is predominantly granitic. Because of its protected position, the climate is mild, without extremes in either winter or summer. Rainfall is slightly less than in Vinho Verde. The climate and method of training combine to induce ripe grapes which have a higher sugar level than is normally found in Vinho Verde.

Ninety per cent of production in the Dão is red wine. By law, a minimum of 20% of the red Dão blend must be Touriga Nacional. Historically, prolonged maturation in cask gave dry wines, combining vegetal and often dried-out fruit with high tannin, which took an exceptionally long time to show at their best. Local pre-EC laws also laid down that the wine had to be made either by the growers, or the co-operative cellars, which meant that changes were slow. Now, however, controlled vinifications by the major merchants mean that earlier maturing more commercial wines are becoming more commonplace.

For the white wine, Encruzado is the best grape. It tends to have a high lemony acidity when young but softens out with age.

Bairrada

Although the surface area of Bairrada is smaller than that of Dão, the region has a greater acreage of land under vine. The vineyards lie between those of Dão and the sea, on the plain to the north of the University city of Coimbra. The name Bairrada is derived from the Portuguese word for clay, *bairro,* and, not surprisingly, the soils have a mainly clay base, sometimes mixed with limestone. Close to the path of the river Mondego, they can be sandy.

The traditional wine of the region is a rich, full-flavoured red made from the Baga grape. Any red Bairrada must have at least 50% of this grape in the blend, although it is usually about 80%. The Baga is trained low and produces wines with medium to high tannin and acidity which age well. Fruity rather than vegetal in character, these are easier to drink than most Dão reds. In a relatively recent development, more white wine is now being produced, with the Maria Gomes as the predominant variety.

Other DOCs

Around the city of Lisbon, there are two light wine DOC areas, each with limited production. Bucelas lies to the north of the city on the west bank of the Tagus river. The soil is a limestone/clay mix. There are only 500 ha under vine, and, until recently, there has only been one major producer. Considerable investment has been made in the area, however, and the wine, always white, is becoming more popular. Traditionally, the wine has been sold old and is rich and full-bodied but lighter styles are now made; it is a blend of which a minimum of 75% must come from the main grape grown in Bucelas, Arinto.

Colares is something of an anachronism in the world of wine. The vineyards are planted on windswept sand-dunes overlooking the Atlantic Ocean. The vines are not grafted, as phylloxera has never arrived, and sprawl along the ground as a protection from the wind, though windbreaks are also erected. Colares must be one of the last vineyard regions where propagation of the vine is still carried out by layering, rather than by planting new stock. This is the long-established process of creating new plants by burying the branches of living vines and allowing them to form roots. This all makes for high labour costs. All the wine is made in one co-operative cellar and then sold to one of three merchants for the minimum two years' ageing in vat, though in practice, it is generally aged for much longer. Most of the wine is red and made from the Ramisco grape. When young, it is totally undrinkable because of its tannin and acidity; when mature, it is a magnificent, rich, heavy wine. The size of the vineyard area is being reduced as the vines are replaced by holiday and residential developments; because the best vineyards are those nearest the sea, where land for development is in most demand, the region is not only shrinking in size but is also retrenching on to the less good sites.

The hot, dry Alentejo region in eastern Portugal, south of the Tejo, has five DOCs, all of which have been promoted from IPR status. The two most important are Borba and Reguengos, both of which produce inexpensive wines from a number of grape varieties including Aragonez and Castelão Frances.

Indicação de Proveniencia Regulamentada (IPR)
Key wines:
Arrabida
Arruda
Palmela

IPRs can be broadly split into six regions; the names in brackets are those IPR wines which are likely to be of most interest.

1. Tras os Montes (Chaves, Valpaços) – This is in the extreme north-east of Portugal, up against the Spanish border.

2. Beira (Encostas de Nave, Castelo Rodrigo, Pinhel and Cova de Beira) – This region lies between the Dão region and Spain.

3. Oeste (Arruda, Torres Vedras, Alenquer) – This is the most productive wine region of Portugal, along the coast between Lisbon and Coimbra. Here vines grow on a sub-soil of limestone covered by a limestone-clay topsoil. A co-operative produces the red wines of Arruda, almost all of which are sold through a major UK supermarket and represent very good value for money.

4. Ribatejo – The fertile plain of the Tagus valley.

5. Arrabida Peninsula (Palmela, Arrabida) – Traditionally known for its liqueur wines from Setúbal, this area is also becoming noteworthy for light wine production by innovative winemakers using modern techniques.

6. Alentejo (Evora) – Lying to the east beyond the Tagus, it is here that much of the experimental work in Portuguese viticulture is being carried out. The climate is hotter and drier than in most other parts of the country. In part as a result, the red wines tend to be full and sometimes "jammy"; they lie towards the inexpensive end of the price spectrum.

Vinho de Mesa Rosé
There is still a very significant production in Portugal of light, slightly sparkling, medium dry rosé wines. These are all classified as *Vinho de Mesa*, and sold under brand names; the best known for many years in the British market is Mateus. Most are exported, and although UK imports have fallen away in recent years, other markets have taken up any slack. They are made to very high standards in some of the most technically advanced wineries in Portugal.

PORTUGUESE LABELLING TERMS

Adega	winery
Adega cooperativa	co-op winery
Bruto	dry sparkling wine
Casta	grape variety
Colheita	vintage, particularly used on Date of Harvest Ports (see Chapter 18)
Doce	sweet
Garrafa	bottle
Quinta	estate or vineyard
Seco	dry
Tinto	red
Verde	literally green, used on a wine it indicates youth
Vinho	wine

CHAPTER 14

CENTRAL AND SOUTH EASTERN EUROPE

The dominant feature of central Europe is the river Danube and whilst it does not flow through all the countries that will be dealt with in this chapter, it was the lynchpin of the Austro-Hungarian Empire, itself the heartland of wine production in this part of Europe.

Vines have been planted in the valley of the Danube since the times of the Celts in the fourth century BC, and as it has been one of the great military highways of Europe, it has seen a succession of conquerors. There have not always been vineyards along its banks, however; from the fall of the Western Roman Empire until the influx of German settlers in the 10th century, wine production had largely fallen into abeyance. As on most

The Danube is a major trading route in eastern Europe and acts as a common link for many of the countries covered in this chapter.

well-travelled routes in the Middle Ages, much of the overnight lodging and refreshment was supplied by monasteries. In Hungary, for example, it was the Benedictines who planted the vineyards of Eger and Somló; whilst the religious/military orders of the Teutonic Knights and the Knights of Malta planted vineyards in Austria and Switzerland.

Since the Second World War, there has been a broad diversity in the directions taken by the various wine industries. The collapse of Communist eastern Europe has posed severe problems for many economies; Greece, on the other hand, has benefitted from its entry into the European Community with grants for agricultural and viticultural improvement. Despite this diversity it is possible to identify some common factors, particularly with regard to two key influences on wine style, climate and grape variety.

CLIMATE

Across the countries dealt with in this chapter there are five distinct climatic zones which influence the very different styles of wine produced. Starting in the foothills of the Alps and then moving east and south to the Adriatic and Aegean seas, the types of climate and their zones are:

Central European Climate

Switzerland, Austria, Slovakia, Hungary, Slovenia, northern Croatia, northern Serbia and western Romania share a central European climate with short, cold winters and long warm summers. Autumns are late, making noble rot possible if there is sufficient humidity. There is less variation in annual weather patterns than in northern Europe. Much of the wine produced here is white, with medium alcohol (11–12.5% vol.), crisp acidity and good primary fruit aromas which are reflected on the palate.

Eastern Continental Climate

Western Bulgaria, central Romania and southern Serbia experience an Eastern continental climate. This is somewhat similar to the central European climate but warmer overall, with milder winters and warmer summers. Much of the wine produced in these areas is red with medium to high alcohol (12–13% vol.), medium acidity, a tendency towards soft tannin and good fruit character on nose and palate.

Black Sea Climate

Eastern Bulgaria, eastern Romania, south-east Moldova, the Crimea and other coastal parts of Ukraine share a Black Sea climate with mild winters and hot summers. As the name implies the principal influence here is the Black Sea which tempers what would otherwise be a harsher continental climate. Both red and white wines are found, which in style are not unlike those produced in the central European climate.

Steppe Climate
Moving inland within Ukraine, the influence of the Black Sea gives way to that of the Steppes. The Steppe climate is the harshest under consideration with long bitter winters and short hot summers. Unsuitable for the production of delicate wines, it is ideal for the sweeter styles of liqueur wine.

Mediterranean Climate
The final zone includes Cyprus in the eastern Mediterranean, Greece and its islands as well as the coastline and islands of Croatia. Here, the early Mediterranean spring comes after a mild winter, then quickly gives way to an often extreme summer. Rainfall is largely limited to autumn and spring with a little precipitation in winter, but summers are dry. Both red and white wines are found. These normally have high alcohol (12% vol. or more) whilst their acidity is often low; they frequently lack an aromatic nose.

GRAPE VARIETIES
Two main styles of wine are found in central and south east Europe. First, are those wines made from indigenous grape varieties, or varieties cultivated for so long that they can be thought of as indigenous. Second, are those wines made from grape varieties that are of western European origin which, for the most part, have been introduced since World War II. With one exception from the first group, the second style is now the more significant commercially as the western varieties steadily become pre-eminent.

Welschriesling/Laski Rizling/Olasz Rizling
That exception is the Welschriesling, a variety best known in the UK for medium dry white wines. These remain very successful commercially in the United Kingdom, although they are declining slowly in popularity.

The Welschriesling should not be confused with the Rhine Riesling: it is an entirely different variety, and a number of eastern European countries like Bulgaria grow both. European Community regulations state that the varietal description "Riesling" is reserved for the Rhine Riesling only. Welschriesling must, therefore, be described on labels, price lists, advertisements and the like under its full name or one of its principal local synonyms:

Welschriesling in Austria, Hungary and Bulgaria,

Laski Rizling in Slovenia, Croatia and Serbia, or

Olasz Rizling in Hungary.

Thought to have originated in France, though some say it has its origins in either Romania or north-east Italy, Welschriesling has been grown in the area for many centuries. Compared to the Rhine Riesling, it is an easier vine to cultivate, and it produces a less delicate wine with lower acidity. Mostly, it suffers from being overcropped, but in a few regions, particularly southern Austria, it is regarded as a top quality variety. Climatically, it does best in the central European and eastern continental zones.

SWITZERLAND

In many ways the wine industry of Switzerland is a special case. The demands of its domestic market far outstrip the production of the local vineyards. As a result, there is little incentive for growers to seek export markets. Furthermore, Swiss wine is expensive to produce; this, together with adverse exchange rates, means that by the time the wines reach the United Kingdom consumer, they tend to cost more than their intrinsic worth. This is a shame, for there are many local wines of interest.

With arable land at a premium, vineyards are often planted on steep slopes and everything is done to maximise production; chaptalisation is generally permitted and yields are often high.

Perhaps not surprisingly given the situation of Switzerland and its ethnic make-up, many of its products reflect the varying styles of wines found in neighbouring countries.

Regions and Wines
Key regions:
Vaud
Valais
Ticino
Neuchâtel
Thurgau

The main areas of production include the north shore of Lake Geneva (the region of Vaud, with the sub-regions of La Côte, Lavaux and Chablais). Here mainly white wines are made from the Chasselas grape,

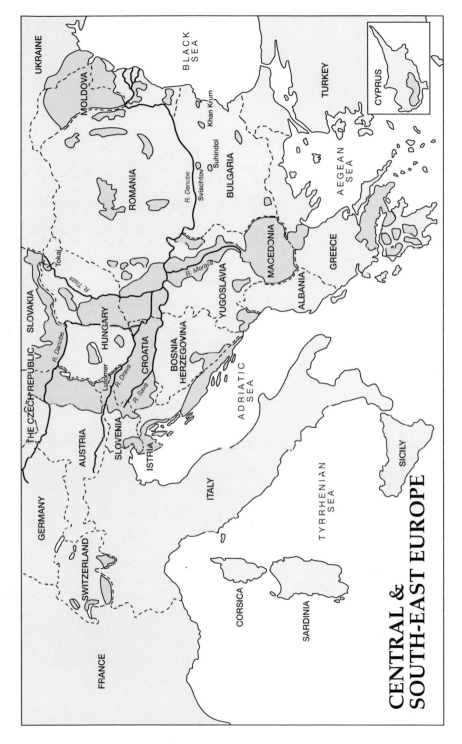

CENTRAL &
SOUTH-EAST EUROPE

known locally as Dorin (except around Geneva, where it is the Perlan), though there are also red and rosé wines made from Gamay.

The Valais is the upper valley of the Rhône. Here the main grape is again Chasselas, appearing under the name of Fendant. Dôle is a red wine made from Pinot Noir and Gamay. There are also a number of local varietals such as Amigne, Arvine and Humagne. The red and white wines of both Valais and Vaud are similar in style to those of the French Alps.

Ticino lies in the southern area of the Italian-speaking part of Switzerland. Red wines are the speciality with the best produced from Merlot in a style akin to that of north-east Italy.

Neuchâtel is a relatively large producer of very light white wine from the Chasselas and red wines from Pinot Noir. These latter are similar to those of the Jura across the border in France.

Finally, the region of Thurgau lies partly on the southern shore of Lake Constance and partly across the Rhine from the southern part of Baden. It produces wines similar to those of southern Germany: reds mainly from Pinot Noir and white wines, often with a hint of sweetness, from German grape varieties.

AUSTRIA

As a country, Austria dates only from the end of the First World War, but was of course the seat of the Austro-Hungarian Empire which encompassed several of the countries in this chapter for some centuries. The wines themselves have a much longer history, being drunk in England, for example, as early as the 11th century.

Wine Law

Austria's wine legislation is based on the same principles as German wine law but with more emphasis on yield restrictions, set at 75 hl/ha for red wines and 60 hl/ha for whites. The terms used (*Tafelwein, Landwein, Qualitätswein* and *Prädikatswein*) are similar to those for German wines, though the minimum must-weight for each category of Prädikatswein tends to be higher in Austria than Germany, and the term *Kabinett* in Austria is of *Qualitätswein* rather than *Prädikatswein* status.

There are two other terms used which are specifically Austrian; *Ausbruch*, which is a classification between *Beerenauslese* and *Trockenbeerenauslese* and *Strohwein*, where the bunches of grapes are laid out in the growers' lofts on beds of straw during the winter, to take on extra sweetness. For comparison, minimum must-weights in grams per litre of sugar are:

	Sugar (g/l)
Kabinettwein	170
Spätlese	190
Auslese	210
Strohwein	250
Eiswein	250
Beerenauslese	250
Ausbruch	270
Trockenbeerenauslese	320

Despite the similarity in wine law between Austria and Germany, the wines themselves are different in style. In particular, because of the central European climate, Austrian wines tend to have more alcohol and body than their German counterparts.

Grape Varieties

In all there are just under 57,000 ha of vines in Austria, of which five-sixths are planted with white varieties. Just over a third of the total is Grüner Veltliner, a grape which is capable of giving a variety of flavours: spicy, grassy, herby or oily. It is at its best drunk young, without cask-ageing and when dry or just off-dry. Wines made from Grüner Veltliner and Pinot Blanc are those most often found in the UK. The next most popular varieties making up 9% and 8.5% of the total planting, respectively, are Müller-Thurgau and Welschriesling (the latter capable of giving excellent late-picked wines). Other native Austrian white grapes are Neuburger (excellent fragrant and nutty dry wines) and Bouvier (a variety low in acidity, often affected by noble rot).

Red wine production is dominated by three varieties: Blauer Portugieser, which gives large yields of generally drab wine, Zweigelt, which when pruned back produces an agreeably fruity, cherry-flavoured wine and Blaufränkisch, similar in many ways to Gamay. Less widely planted is Saint Laurent which bears a resemblance to Pinot Noir, though it is particularly susceptible to coulure.

Regions and Wines

Key regions:
Vienna
Niederösterreich
Burgenland
Styria

Under the new legislation, Austria is split into four regions (*Weinbauregion*), which may, in their turn, be split into sub-regions

(*Weinbaugebiete*) and districts (*Grosslage*). These are all situated in the east of the country, the Alps of western Austria being unsuitable for viticulture.

1. Vienna (Wien) (704 ha vines)
The vineyards lie in the suburbs of Austria's capital city and much of the production is drunk in the growers' wine-bars specialising in the sale of young wine (*Heurige*). The best wines are probably those made from Riesling and Chardonnay.

2. Lower Austria (Niederösterreich) (33,648 ha)
This is the largest of the regions and the front-runner in both total production and exports to the United Kingdom. The majority of the vineyards lie in the valley of the Danube and further north towards the Slovak border. There are seven sub-regions: Wachau, Kamptal, Kremstal, Donauland, Weinviertel, Traisental and Thermenregion. The country's finest dry white wines come from the steeply sloping vineyards of the Wachau and Kamptal to the west of Vienna.

3. Burgenland (20,986 ha)
This region lies in the east of Austria, along the border with Hungary, and produces some top quality sweet wines. The dominant feature is the vast shallow lake in the north of the province, the Neusiedlersee, whose autumnal mists are ideal for the development of noble rot which only fails to form in very unusual years. The vineyards, for the most part, are on the plain and yields are relatively high. For this reason, and because production of botrytised wines is largely guaranteed each year, prices tend to be lower than those of equivalent wines from France or Germany. *Beerenauslese* and *Trockenbeerenauslese* wines are normally sold in half bottles. There are four sub-regions: Neusiedlersee, Neusiedlersee-Hügelland which includes the well-known village of Rust, Mittelburgenland and Südburgenland.

4. Styria (Steiermark) (2,844 ha)
Styria is south of Burgenland, in the south-east of the country towards the border with Slovenia. The principal grape variety is the Welschriesling. Whilst the best wines probably come from the sub-region of Süd-Oststeiermark, the best-known wine, Schilcher, comes from Südsteiermark. This is an aggressively dry rosé wine made from the Blauer Wildbacher grape. The third sub-region in Styria is the viticulturally unimportant Weststeiermark. The wines of Steiermark are seldom seen in the United Kingdom.

SLOVAKIA

In terms of wine production and exports to the UK, the Slovak Republic is the most significant element of the erstwhile Czechoslovak Federation. Recent improvements in vinification and bottling have led to exports of cheap and cheerful white wines from western varieties like Pinot Blanc, as well as wines from the more interesting local varieties: soft easy-drinking reds from the Frankovka grape and whites from Irsay Oliver, which is a Muscat cross.

HUNGARY

As in many East European countries, the collapse of Communism has had a dramatic effect on the wine industry in Hungary. Under the old régime, although more than half the vineyards were cultivated by small growers on land leased from the state, nearly all the wine was vinified in state wineries or heavily subsidised co-operatives. With the coming of the free market economy, the major cellars have been found to be bankrupt and foreign investment has been hard to find. This will be essential if the industry is to recover its full potential.

Wine Law

Hungary has a wine law based on the French AC system whereby geographical origin determines quality status. All wine is classified under one of three headings:

Asztali Bor (Table Wine) – Note that this term would not be permitted on labels if the wine were to be exported to the EC.

Minőségi Bor (Quality Wine) – A category equivalent to QWPSR in the EC.

Special-Quality Wine – These wines are made from nobly rotted grapes, and must bear the state wine seal.

Grape Varieties

Most wine seen on the British market is sold under the name of a grape variety, often with the name of the region it comes from before it. (An "i" at the end of a name means "of" or "from". Thus, a Soproni Kékfrankos is a wine made from the Kékfrankos grape grown in Sopron.) The majority are inexpensive varietals from west European grapes, some of which have local synonyms, such as Médoc for Merlot and Oporto for Portugieser. As well as these, there can be found the native Kadarka and Kékfrankos (Blaufränkisch) black grapes and the Ezerjó, Furmint, Hárslevelü and Juhfark white grapes. Olasz Riesling (Welschriesling) is also widely grown.

Regions and Wines

Hungary's terrain is more homogeneous than that of Austria. Its tallest mountains are just over 1000 m and it is generally much flatter. The River Danube divides the country east–west into two almost equal parts. Taken clockwise from the capital Budapest in the north, the relevant topographical features are:

the Northern Massif along the border with Slovakia to the north-east of the Danube

the Great Plain, a very flat sandy area to the east of the Danube

the hilly area west of the Danube particularly near the town of Pécs in the south and north of Lake Balaton

Within these three broad areas, there are sixteen wine regions, but only about half of them are of importance in export markets.

The Northern Massif

Key regions:
Tokaj Hegyalja
Eger

The best-known of all Hungary's regions is Tokaj Hegyalja in the foothills of the Northern Massif against the Slovakian border and alongside the Bodrog and Tisza rivers. Tokaji wine takes its name from a village in the area and is often anglicized to Tokay. The wines can be divided into two distinct groups, the Quality Wines, bottled into 75 cl bottles and the Special-Quality Wines, bottled into the traditional 50 cl dump bottles. These latter rank among the world's best sweet white wines and are strongly affected by noble rot. It is the mist from the tributaries of the Tisza river, including the Bodrog, which creates the ideal conditions for noble rot which is widespread in the vineyards of the area.

The one wine in the Quality (*Minőségi Bor*) group of note is Tokaji Furmint. It is made entirely from the Furmint variety, unaffected by noble rot, and is dry or medium dry.

The Special-Quality Wines are made from the Furmint and Hárslevelü grapes which represent 66% and 33% of the plantings respectively. They come in three styles:

Tokaji Szamorodni

Tokaji Aszú

Tokaji Aszú Essencia

The word *Szamorodni* literally means "as it comes" and this describes the vinification process whereby the wine is produced by putting together all the grapes as harvested, with no separation of healthy and botrytic berries. As a result the wine may be dry (*száraz*) or sweet (*édes*) depending upon the proportion of noble rot that is present, but even the dry style will show noble rot character. The wine is aged in a traditional cask called a *Gönc*. The *Göncs* for the dry *Szamorodni* are not completely filled to enable a flor-like yeast to form naturally on the wine. As a result the wine develops a fruit character similar to fino Sherry.

The word *Aszú* means nobly rotted grapes. In the production of Tokaji Aszú, healthy and noble rot grapes are separated in the vineyard after which the healthy grapes are made into dry white wine whilst the noble rot grapes are stored. These can be so rich in sugar that they hardly ferment. The *Aszú* grapes are then pounded into a paste before being added to the dry wine to produce the sweetness required which is dependent upon the amount of paste used.

In accordance with tradition the paste is measured in *puttonyos*. Originally *Aszú* grapes were collected at the vintage in a 20 kg hod or *puttony*. Now the measurement refers to the residual sugar content in the finished wine, and it is this latter which qualifies the wine for its designation. On a label you may see a wine classified as containing between 3 and 6 *puttonyos* which have the following residual sugar levels:

3 puttonyos:	60 g/l
4 puttonyos:	90 g/l
5 puttonyos:	120 g/l
6 puttonyos:	150 g/l

The wine is matured for between three and six years in casks. Producers are divided over the question of whether or not to allow oxidation during maturation.

Aszú Essencia is made in the same way as Aszú but only in the best years and only from the best vineyards. The sugar content is over six *puttonyos*, approximately 200 g/l, a degree of concentration that ensures the wine can age for over a century without losing its intense flavours. Tokaji Aszú Essencia is expensive as befits one of the world's greatest sweet wines, on a par with Château d'Yquem or a top German *Trockenbeerenauslese* in quality.

All the Aszú wines mentioned have an actual alcohol content of between 14 and 14.5%.

South-west of Tokaj along the line of the Northern Massif running towards Budapest, lie the vineyards of Eger and Mátra. The full-bodied red wine Egri Bikaver, or Bull's Blood, is produced in Eger. It is made from the Kékfrankos, Kadarka, Cabernet (which is not specified), Oporto and Médoc grapes and aged in large oak casks in miles of cellars which lie under the city of Eger itself.

The Great Plain
The majority of Hungary's wine is produced on the Great Plain. Here the soil is chalky sand, free from phylloxera, and the climate is one of extremes. Basic quality reds and whites are made but seldom seen in the UK. Of the white varieties, Olasz Rizling is dominant.

West of the Danube
Key regions:
Balaton
Somló
Sopron
Mór
Etyek
Villány
Pécs

Lake Balaton is protected from the dominant northerly winds by a range of hills. This creates an ideal microclimate for the production of wine; the soil, which ranges from volcanic to iron-rich, also contributes. Here there is a broad range of varieties planted.

To the north of the lake lie four quality wine regions:

Somló, historically known for a Tokaj-like wine;

Sopron, on the Austrian border producing high-quality red wines;

Mór, where the white Ezerjo grape reigns supreme;

Etyek, south-west of Budapest, particularly known for its Chardonnays.

To the south of the lake towards the border with Croatia lie two other areas worthy of mention Villány and Pécs. All six supply the United Kingdom with inexpensive varietals from western grapes. Their best wines tend to be those from aromatic white grapes such as Muscat and Gewürztraminer.

THE SOUTHERN SLAV COUNTRIES
In the current fluid political climate, it is perhaps best to deal separately with each of the republics of the former Yugoslavia. It is not clear how the wine laws, or indeed the labelling, will develop, but the most recent wine laws of the former Yugoslavia defined four different categories of wine. Of these, only the two highest have found their way to the UK. They are

Kvalitetno Vino (Premium wine), and *Čuveno Vino* or *Vrhunsko Vino* (Select Wine); both are equivalent to QWPSR.

Slovenia
Key regions:
Lutomer estate
Podrava
Primorski

Whilst the most northerly state of Slovenia only accounted for a tenth of the production in the old Yugoslavia, it was the most important region for shipments to the UK. Indeed, one of the top-selling white wine brands in Britain is the northern estate of Lutomer's easy-to-drink, fruity Laski Rizling (Welschriesling). Lutomer also produce wines from Chardonnay, Pinot Blanc and Gewürztraminer. All are inexpensive, simple versions of these grape varieties, and should be drunk fresh because they can lose their fruit after eighteen months or so in bottle.

Another good source of Laski Rizling is Podrava on the banks of the river Drava, around the town of Maribor. Rather more full-bodied is the sweetish Lutomer Radgona (Tiger's Milk): Ranina is the Bouvier grape of Austria.

The Primorski region, in the west of Solvenia, has a climate influenced by the Adriatic Sea and is the only region in the country to produce a substantial volume of red wine. Inexpensive varietals are exported to the UK.

Croatia
Key regions:
Istria
Kontinentalna Hrvatska

Perhaps the most individual wines come from the vineyards of the south Croat coast. Here, on mainly sandy soil, the sugar-rich Plavać Mali is grown, a red variety capable of high alcohol levels. Western varieties such as Pinot Noir, Merlot and Cabernet Sauvignon are more common on the Istrian Peninsula. Inland in northern Croatia Laski Rizling is grown in the region of Kontinentalna Hrvatska near the Hungarian border.

Bosnia-Herzegovina
This is the least important republic in wine-producing terms. The one wine of note is an outstanding dry white produced from the local Žilavka grape grown on limestone soils around the city of Mostar, just inland from the Adriatic.

Serbia
Key regions:
Fruška Gora
Vranje

In terms of both surface area and wine production, Serbia is the largest of the republics. Before United Nations sanctions were imposed in 1992 it supplied the United Kingdom with inexpensive red and white wines. Its finest white wines come from the Fruška Gora hills to the north-west of Belgrade, south of the Danube. Here, the cooler climate enables such classic varietals as Sauvignon Blanc, Sémillon and Gewürtztraminer to be grown successfully. South of Belgrade, on the river Morava, are the vineyards of Velika Morava, which produces Laski Rizling and Vranje, known for red wines from western varieties. To the east of Belgrade Oplenac is noted for its Cabernet Sauvignon. Kosovo, against the Albanian border, is best known for its red wines from Burgundec (Pinot Noir), Gamay and Cabernet Franc. A quality white wine is made from the local Smederevka.

Montenegro and Makedonija
These southern republics again produce mainly red wines from the Prokupac and Vranac grapes.

ROMANIA

Whilst Romania lies on the same latitude as central France, its largely continental climate is more extreme both in winter and summer. The two moderating factors, that enable quality wine to be made, are the Black Sea and the Carpathian mountains, which with their backwards "L" shape divide the country in two. Romania has the highest wine production of all the Balkan countries but, with high domestic consumption, most Romanian wine has always been sold locally. In recent years the need for hard currency has led to the larger cellars increasing export sales, and investing a proportion of foreign earnings in new winery equipment.

Regions and Wines

Key regions:
Cotnari
Murfatlar
Dealul Mare
Tarnave

The region with the finest reputation is Cotnari in the north east, renowned for botrytis-affected sweet white wines from the local Grasa, Francusa, Feteasca Alba, and highly scented Tamaîoasa grapes. Elsewhere, wines destined for export tend to be produced from international varieties such as Chardonnay, Sauvignon Blanc, Pinot Gris, Italian Riesling (Welschriesling), Cabernet Sauvignon, and Pinot Noir.

Closely behind Cotnari in reputation come the red wines of Dealul Mare, the white wines of Tarnave, and the red, white, and late-harvest wines of Murfatlar. Dealul Mare lies to the south of the Carpathians. Its vineyards enjoy a south-eastern aspect and are terraced above the banks of streams. Tarnave is situated within the inside angle of the Carpathian "L", on the Transylvanian plateau at an altitude that gives a cool microclimate. Murfatlar is in the south-east where the microclimate is influenced by the Black Sea. Although a range of red and white wines is produced at Murfatlar, the region's speciality is late harvest wines from grape varieties which include Muscat and Chardonnay.

Romania's largest vineyard area, however, is that of Focsani, to the east of the Carpathians. Here, red, white and traditional method sparkling wines are produced, mostly for domestic consumption.

THE FORMER SOVIET REPUBLICS

Wines from some of the former Soviet Republics are now being found on the UK market. These include dry sparkling wine produced at Odessa in Ukraine and an interesting red wine with great ageing potential, Negru de Purkar, a blend of Cabernet Sauvignon and the local Saperavi, from Moldova. Historically, the finest Soviet wines came from the Crimean peninsula in the Ukraine.

BULGARIA

Of all the East European wine-producing countries, there is no doubt that it is Bulgaria that has managed to be the most successful commercially. In 1980, it exported very little light wine to the United Kingdom; by 1988 it had become the country's fifth largest supplier. In the same period it grew to be the second largest exporter of bottled wine in the world, selling just under 90% of its total production beyond its borders.

The reasons for this success are firmly based on central planning of viticulture and vinification. Since 1970, plantings have been on a high cordon system, to facilitate mechanisation in the vineyards. In theory, this enables one worker to cultivate as much as nine hectares of vines. The planners' foresight has also meant that there have been major plantings of such acceptable varieties as Cabernet Sauvignon, Merlot, Riesling and Chardonnay. However, lack of working capital has had a severely restrictive effect on production, for instance, in the lack of

Many Bulgarian vineyards are trained high and widely spaced to permit mechanisation. Here the oenologist is checking the ripeness of the grapes in such a vineyard prior to harvesting.

machinery with which to take advantage of the high cordon planting scheme.

Whilst there has been much planting of French and German grape varieties, local varieties are also widely found. They include the black varieties Gamza, Mavrud and Melnik, and the white Misket and Dimiat. Rkatsiteli, a white grape originating in Georgia, is also common.

Wine Laws
Since 1978, sophisticated wine laws have been developed. These divide all wines into three categories: Standard Wines, High Quality Wines and Special Wines. The second of these categories, High Quality Wines, is particularly important and has a number of sub-divisions.

Standard Wines – Basic level still light wines, not exported to the UK.

Special Wines – This all-embracing group includes sparkling, liqueur and fruit wines.

High Quality Wines – Without geographical origin. These are wines without declared geographical origin, usually sold under a brand-name.

Declared Geographical Origin (DGO) – These wines state their geographical origin on the label. The grape variety or varieties used will commonly be stated, too. The words Declared Geographical Origin or their abbreviation, however, are not used on labels. An example would be "Russe Welschriesling," Russe being a town in the north of the country.

Controliran – This category is the equivalent of AC in France. The wines come from a specified grape variety grown in specified vineyards; the label must state both variety and region, and the wine has to be approved by a tasting panel before gaining *Controliran* status. The word "*Controliran*" will appear on the label.

Although *Controliran* is a step up in quality from DGO, and will come from different vineyards, both may share the same geographical name, which is a possible source of confusion between the two. Thus it is possible to find wines labelled not only Assenovgrad Mavrud Controliran, but also simply Assenovgrad Mavrud, the latter having the lesser DGO status.

There are a number of other terms which may be seen on the labels of Bulgarian wines:

Reserve – Since 1985, DGO and *Controliran* wines can qualify additionally as *Reserve* if they have been aged for a minimum period in oak. Many of the oak vats used are both large and old, and do not therefore impart much wood character to the wines, but rather mellow them. The minimum requirements are:

DGO white wines:	two years
DGO red wines:	three years
Controliran white wines:	three years
Controliran red wines:	four years

Special Reserve – These are wines from the DGO category. The ageing requirements are the same as for *Reserve* status, but these wines are from the best cuvées, and some of the ageing may have been in new oak. Although *Special Reserve* is not a legal term, and technically is below *Controliran* in rank, in terms of actual quality the range is often superior.

Country Wine – These are made from a blend of two grape varieties, which are stated on the label. In style the wines are made to be consumed whilst youthful and fresh. An example is Sliven Merlot & Pinot Noir.

Regions and Wines

There are vineyards in all parts of Bulgaria, except around the capital city of Sofia. For administrative reasons the vineyards have been grouped officially into five viticultural regions.

As the Bulgarian language uses Cyrillic script, spellings of the anglicised versions of wine names do vary from source to source.

Eastern Region

Key DGO areas
Shumen
Khan Krum
Novi Pazar
Varna

The Eastern region includes all the country's coastline on the Black Sea and stretches up to the river Danube. Its climate is affected by the Black Sea. In terms of production this is the second most important area, with the accent being placed on white wines, particularly Chardonnay, as far as exports are concerned. The best wines are produced in the hilly region of Shumen, which includes the areas of Novi Pazar and Khan Krum. The former has *Controliran* status for Chardonnay, the latter, unusually, for Gewürztraminer, though it is much better known for its *Special Reserve*

The sign on this winery at Shumen reads "Vinprom". The Bulgarian language uses the Cyrillic alphabet, which often leads to a number of alternative spellings of Bulgarian wine names when translated for the western European market.

Chardonnays. Good unoaked *Controliran* Chardonnays are also produced near Varna, on the coast. Inland, where the mountains cut off the maritime influence, red wines are more important.

Northern Region

Key DGO areas:	*Key Controliran wines:*
Svischtov	Svischtov Cabernet Sauvignon
Suhindol	Suhindol Gamza
Russe	
Pavlikeni	

The Northern region consists of the northern slopes of the Balkan Mountains down to the river Danube. Perhaps the best-known wines of this region are the Cabernet Sauvignons from Svischtov, a river port on the Danube. Both DGO and *Controliran* wines are available. Other good examples of Cabernet Sauvignon are found south of Svischtov in Suhindol, where Bulgaria's first co-operative cellar was established in 1909. Other important centres are Russe, another river-port on the Danube, and Pavlikeni. In all of these except Russe, it is red wines that dominate.

Southern Region

Key DGO areas:	*Key Controliran wines:*
Oriachovitza	Assenovgrad Mavrud
Plovdiv	Sakar Merlot
Sakar	Stambolovo Merlot
Stambolovo	
Assenovgrad	
Korten	

The majority of the vineyards of the Southern region lie in the valley of the Maritsa river. Quantitively, this is the most important of the regions, with the best known of the *Controliran* names being Stambolovo and Sakar for Merlot wines and Assenovgrad for Mavrud. There are also important plantings of Cabernet Sauvignon near Plovdiv, the country's second city; Korten and Oriachovitza are also known for their Cabernet Sauvignon *Reserve* wines.

Sub-Balkan Region

As far as western export markets are concerned the Sub-Balkan region is of minimal importance. The dominant grape varieties are Misket and Rkatsiteli and most of the wine goes for distillation or vermouth production.

South-Western Region

Key DGO areas:
Melnik
Harsovo
Petrich Damianitza

Key Controliran wines:
Harsovo Melnik

The South-Western region is centred around the town of Melnik, which is a DGO area, but which has also given its name to the grape variety grown there. The town of Harsovo has *Controliran* status for the Melnik variety, producing full-bodied, tannic wines that age well. The other wine exported from the region, is a light fruity, supple Cabernet Sauvignon.

GREECE

As Greece is such a mountainous country, vineyard space is at a premium. Even then, only half of the grape production is used for wine, with the remainder used for table grapes or raisins. Because of the latitude (most of the country is south of 40°N) and the proximity of the sea, the climate is one of mild winters but hot summers. The soil is generally very poor, and consists largely of limestone on the mainland and volcanic rock on the islands.

Until its arrival in the European Community, the wine industry of Greece had been largely inward looking. Now, with easier access to several million new customers, there has been a certain amount of consolidation and many of the larger companies have begun to make wines with a more international appeal. Many of the better wines sold on export markets come under the brand names of these major producers. In smaller companies catering for more local markets, however, wineries and winemaking practice can still be primitive.

Many Greek wines remain very traditional in style. One example of this is the classic Retsina, a wine flavoured with pine resin, of which mention was made by writers as early as the third century BC.

Wine laws have been harmonised with the European Community regime. Two QWPSR terms are found:

Appellation d'Origine Contrôlée (AOC) used for liqueur wines, and

Appellation d'Origine de Qualité Supérieure (AOQS) used for light wines.

Additionally, the term *Traditional Appellation* (TA) is used as a designation for Retsina in Greek wine law and is recognised by the European Community law, although it defines a production technique rather than a geographical zone. There is also an equivalent category to the French Vin de Pays.

In terms of production there is little QWPSR and some country wine; the vast majority of the production being table wine.

The majority of the vines planted are local varieties such as Savatiano, Rhoditis and Assyrtiko for white wines; Xynomavro, Agiorgitiko and Mandilaria for red wines and Mavrodaphne and Liatiko for high-strength wines. However, there are now small plantings of imported varieties such as Cabernet Sauvignon.

Five areas of Greece are significant in terms of wine production.

Peloponnese
Key wines:
Muscat of Patras AOC
Mavrodaphne of Patras AOC
Mantineia AOQS
Nemea AOQS

Much of the country's wine is produced in the Peloponnese, which is phylloxera-free. The region contains a third of the Greek vineyards, but many of the vines are grown for table grapes or raisins. The amount of wine produced is approximately one million hectolitres per annum. The best-known sweet liqueur wines are the white Muscat of Patras and the red Mavrodaphne of Patras, which enjoys pre-eminence among all Mavrodaphnes.

Two notable light wines are Mantineia, a dry white wine from mountainous vineyards in the centre of the region, and Nemea, a full-bodied, smooth red wine made from the Agiorgitiko grape near Corinth.

Macedonia
Key wines:
Naoussa AOQS
Côtes de Meliton AOQS

Much of the country's best wine is produced in the northern region of Macedonia which enjoys a very good climate. Its vineyards are planted on hills and thus benefit not only from a cooler latitude compared with the rest of Greece, but also from altitude.

The wines most often seen in the United Kingdom are Naoussa and Côtes de Meliton. The former is a rich heavy red wine produced from the Xynomavro grape. Côtes de Meliton from the next peninsula along from Mount Athos produces red, white and rosé wines from a mixture of native and French varieties. The main estate whose wines are seen in the UK is Château Carras.

Attica
Key wine:
Retsina TA

Otherwise known as Central Greece, Attica produces more wine than any other region. All is from local grape varieties, mostly white, and much is made into Retsina. The majority of the nation's production of Retsina occurs in Attica, possibly because of the plentiful number of pine trees in the area.

Although a rosé exists, true Retsina is a white wine. It is made by adding pine resin, obtained by cutting the bark of local pine trees. The resin is removed at the first racking but by then the wine has acquired its distinctive character.

Epirus
This region is worthy of mention for one wine only: Zitsa, a delicate often sweet white wine made from the local Debina grape.

The Greek Islands
Key wines:
Santorini AOQS
Muscat of Samos AOC

Most of the islands and particularly Crete produce wine. In terms of QWPSR, Crete has four, though it is better known for its country wines. Two other islands should be mentioned: Santorini produces a fine white wine, and Samos enjoys an international reputation for its sweet dessert Muscat which sells well in France amongst other places.

CYPRUS

Together with Chile, Cyprus claims to be the only wine-producing country that is totally phylloxera-free. Whilst this might have some benefits, there is no doubt that it has led to a form of mild xenophobia about the introduction of more noble varieties than the local black Mavron (or Mavro) and white Xynisteri grapes. These two account for just under 90% of the acreage and a pretty drab couple they are. Such vines that are brought to the island enter under strict Customs control and are put into quarantine before being cleared for use.

Most vineyards are to be found in the southern part of the island. Few are to be found north of the Green Line which has bisected the island, sadly, since the Turkish invasion of 1974. For the most part, the vineyards are on the southern slopes of the Troodos mountains, some as high as 1500 m

Many vineyards in Cyprus are planted high in the Troodos mountains and benefit from the cooler temperatures. The Mavron vines are usually bush trained.

above sea-level. The Troodos form the backbone of the island, and their altitude gives a degree of protection from the climate which, not unexpectedly for a latitude of 35 °N, is very hot and dry. Vines are trained in bush form.

As the growers have little choice but to sell their grapes to one of four big cellars, there is little incentive to grow quality fruit. Furthermore, the wineries are near the coast and the grapes have to be trucked many miles along winding roads often in antiquated lorries; road signs warning of "Slippery Road – Grape Juice" are not unknown. The fruit can suffer severe oxidation in the process, and may have begun to ferment by the time the load arrives at the winery.

Most of the Cyprus wine-grapes are sadly, but for the present perhaps deservedly, absorbed at the bottom end of the market as grape concentrate for British wines, as "Cyprus Sherry", as brandy or as basic wine for export to eastern Europe. Happily, the government appears to have realised the potential problems. There is now a distinct move towards the production of quality light wines and encouraging signs can be detected of small, independent wineries seeking to make more interesting wines of quality. Varietals such as Grenache and Carignan are slowly coming on to the local market.

Commandaria

Meanwhile, one wine with a great historical reputation lives on. Commandaria takes its name from the Grande Commanderie established by the Knights Templar who are credited with popularising it at the time of the Crusades. Once rated as one of the great dessert wines of the world, Commandaria was, in January 1993, the first Cypriot wine to be given the same legal status as a QWPSR in the European Community. It is made from sun-dried bunches of grapes. The sweet fermented wine has spirit added to it and then is aged in a solera system.

CHAPTER 15

THE NEW WORLD

By New World wines, we mean those of Australia, New Zealand, the Americas, north and south, and South Africa. Whilst it is only in the past few years that these have met with considerable success on the British market, we often forget that wines have been produced in these countries from their earliest colonial days.

Wines from Australia and South Africa were regularly shown with some success at International Exhibitions in Europe during the second half of the 19th century. However, it was the introduction of Imperial Preference in 1905, that led to their first ready acceptance on the British market. The demand was largely for liqueur wines – and this remained so until recent times.

Today, the demand for New World wines is growing rapidly. Across the international market place they have made the greatest strides in the United Kingdom where they are playing an important role in making the consumer more wine conscious. In part this is being achieved by the quality of their products but also, and perhaps more significantly, by breaking down artificial barriers and making their wine more approachable by skilful marketing and original presentation. The best instance of this, of course, is the New World emphasis on varietal labelling. They have not been so successful, to date, in making appreciable inroads into the markets of European winemaking countries. However, in the fields of viticulture and vinification, perhaps, much of the innovative and interesting developments now taking place in the Old World can be traced to the influence of the English-speaking countries of the New.

What do the winemakers of the New World have in common? Their main advantages are threefold. First, land, generally, is not as expensive as it is in the more crowded Europe. Secondly, the winemakers have not been bound by long-standing tradition, which in the Old World, at times, can be translated into unduly restrictive regulation. They are, therefore, better placed to build upon the best of old practice whilst rejecting the more stultifying, and can more easily start their enterprise using the latest techniques in viticulture and vinification. They also enjoy much more flexibility to experiment with the styles of wines they wish to produce and in the matching of vines to soil and climate. Less encumbered by bureaucracy, they can respond more quickly to market forces. Thirdly, they do not have the marginal climate for grape-growing so often found in Europe; with, for the most part, very long ripening seasons for the grapes and little fear of rain. Irrigation, which is forbidden in most parts of Europe, is often the dominant factor in their ability to produce good wines at low prices.

To give a broad perspective before each country is looked at individually, the following table shows details of the world ranking of the principal countries under consideration in terms of production:

Country	World ranking	Production in 1994 (hl)
Argentina	4th	18,173,000
USA	5th	16,175,000
South Africa	8th	8,664,000
Australia	7th	5,874,000
Chile	13th	3,598,000
Brazil	15th	3,020,000
New Zealand	24th	500,000

Note that in the USA, California accounts for 96% of the total, and could therefore be ranked 5th in the world in its own right.

In terms of imports into the United Kingdom, the picture is different. Australia is the most important country, followed by South Africa and the USA. The wines of Chile and New Zealand come next, followed by the rapidly growing Argentina, whose sales are small but rising.

AUSTRALIA

The potential for winemaking was recognised by the first Governor of the penal colony in New South Wales, Captain Arthur Philip, on his arrival in 1788. From the resultant first small plantings in New South Wales, vineyards have now spread to every state, even to the Northern Territory. This expansion and the rapidly growing reputation of Australian wines is the product of a technology second to none, made possible by heavy financial investment.

Wine Laws and Labels

The wine laws in Australia still accept, for the domestic markets, terms such as Burgundy, Claret, Chablis and Hock, and the industry is still some way from having a tightly organised appellation system. However, if a wine label bears a grape name on it, that grape must account for 80%

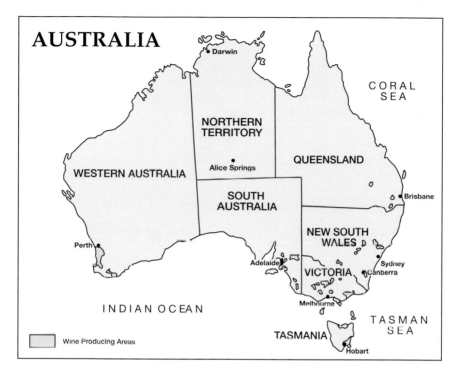

of the wine; if it bears a vintage, 95% of the wine must come from that year. Recently, an "Authentication of Origin" scheme has been established, by which if a geographical origin is mentioned, at least 80% of the wine must come from that source. This minimum figure rises to 85% in the case of wine exported to the United Kingdom and other countries of the European Community.

Climate, Topography and Soil

Climatically, the north and centre of the Australian land mass are least suited to the growing of vines. These areas, especially the heartland epitomised by Ayers Rock, are far too hot and dry. For this reason vineyards are principally found in the southern coastal areas. More specifically, the majority of the production is concentrated in the south-east of the country, with over half the total production coming from South Australia. Since the mid-1980s when the wines were first marketed seriously in the United Kingdom, imports of Australian wine have grown steadily and now head the "New World" league table.

Owing to its position in the southern hemisphere, the vintage in Australia takes place around February and March. In such a large country, vineyards and wineries can be widely separated and nothing is thought of trucking grapes 1600 kilometres or more. Whilst there are vineyard areas with distinctive reputations, many of the wines are made from grapes from several different sources. Quite often, a label may bear an origin as broad as "South-East Australia".

In such a vast country and across such widely scattered vine-growing areas, many different soils are found. Over the years, and in many cases as the result of experimentation, sometimes harshly enforced by Nature, growers have become increasingly adept in the matching of grape varieties to both soil and microclimate.

Grape Varieties

Most European varieties are found. Those most widely planted are shown below in approximate descending order by area:

White	*Black*
Chardonnay	Shiraz (Syrah)
Semillon	Cabernet Sauvignon
Rhine Riesling	Pinot Noir
Colombard	Ruby Cabernet
Chenin Blanc	Merlot

For the white wines there has been a distinct move recently towards wood-matured wines from Chardonnay and Sauvignon Blanc. In red wine production, the dominant grapes are Shiraz (with more than one third of the area under black varieties) and Cabernet Sauvignon.

South Australia

Key districts:

Adelaide Hills	Keppoch
Barossa Valley	McLaren Vale
Coonawarra	Padthaway
Clare	Riverland

Producing 50% of Australia's total, South Australia is a phylloxera-free state, largely due to strict quarantine regulations for plant material. The vineyards are concentrated in the extreme south-east of the state, for the most part north and south-east of the city of Adelaide. The Barossa Valley, some 60 kilometres to the north of the city, is the largest quality vineyard area in Australia. Situated close by is the famous Roseworthy Viticultural College which has played a significant part, through its graduate winemakers, in raising the status of the Australian wine trade. The valley was originally planted in the middle of the last century by German settlers who must have found the hot arid climate particularly challenging. The valley bottom, with soils of ironstone and limestone is now planted mainly with black varieties, such as Cabernet Sauvignon,

In contrast to most European vineyards, many in the New World, like these in Eden Ridge, Australia, are planted in the valley floor to collect precious rainfall.

Grenache and Shiraz. Recent plantings in the bordering hills have given delicious white wines, particularly from Rhine Riesling. This grape is also successful in Clare, which is further to the north.

Close to the coastal city of Adelaide are the Adelaide Hills, which have recently been replanted, and McLaren Vale where the proximity of the sea gives a cooler climate imparting more finesse to the wine.

Coonawarra lies almost 400 kilometres further south, close to the border with Victoria. Its vines are planted along a narrow strip of shallow soil on a limestone base. The dark red Terra Rossa, as this topsoil is called, has exceptional moisture retaining qualities. The combination of this soil and a fresher climate, give wines from Cabernet, Chardonnay and Shiraz which tend to be more French in style than many. Just to the north of Coonawarra and closer to the sea, Padthaway and Keppoch produce wines similar in style.

A third of all the wine-grapes grown in Australia come from the Riverland irrigated vineyards of the Murray Valley. The bulk wine that is produced here forms the backbone of all the major brands. Once of low quality, investment in better vinification methods has led to great improvement in the freshness and character of the wines.

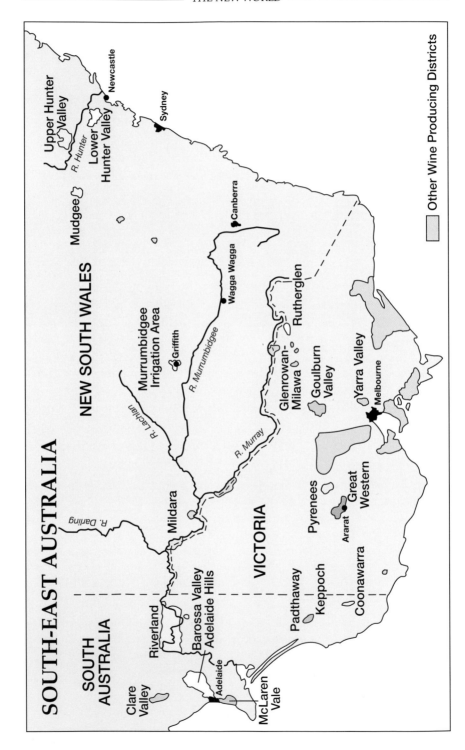

SOUTH-EAST AUSTRALIA

SOUTH AUSTRALIA

NEW SOUTH WALES

VICTORIA

Upper Hunter Valley

Newcastle

R. Hunter

Lower Hunter Valley

Sydney

Mudgee

Canberra

Wagga Wagga

Murrumbidgee Irrigation Area

Griffith

R. Murrumbidgee

R. Lachlan

R. Murray

Glenrowan-Milawa

Rutherglen

Goulburn Valley

Yarra Valley

Melbourne

R. Darling

Mildara

Pyrenees

Great Western

Ararat

Barossa Valley

Adelaide Hills

Riverland

Padthaway

Keppoch

Coonawarra

Clare Valley

Adelaide

McLaren Vale

Other Wine Producing Districts

New South Wales
Key districts:
Hunter Valley (Lower and Upper)
Mudgee
Riverina (Murrumbidgee Irrigation Area)

To the Sydneysider, the only wine in the world comes from the Hunter Valley, some 160 kilometres to the north of the city, inland from the port of Newcastle. The valley is in fact split into two parts with differing environments. In the Lower Hunter Valley, phylloxera and rain at vintage time are two of the hazards. The dominant grapes are Sémillon for white wines and Shiraz for reds. In the Upper Hunter Valley, where Chardonnay is successful, the climate is much drier and drip-irrigation is needed.

Good Chardonnays and Merlots are the specialities of the cooler climate vineyards of Mudgee which lie in the foothills of the Great Dividing Range. Shiraz, Trebbiano and Sémillon dominate in Riverina, or the Murrumbidgee Irrigation Area (MIA). Mechanisation and the use of refrigeration have turned the region from the production of liqueur wines to quality light wines. Sauvignon Blanc, Rhine Riesling, Cabernet Sauvignon and Malbec are also grown. Canberra, where vine-growing died out in the early 1900s because the climate was not considered warm enough, has recently been replanted.

With 26% of output, New South Wales is Australia's second largest producer.

Victoria
Key districts:

Glenrowan/Milawa	Pyrenees
Goulburn Valley	Rutherglen
Great Western	Yarra Valley
Mildara	

With 22% of Australia's total production, Victoria ranks as the third most important state, although its output in global terms is not large; as an example, the Beaujolais district produces twice as much wine. The vineyards are widely spread but, unlike those of South Australia, are planted with grafted vines to counter the threat of phylloxera, which was first found in 1875 in Geelong, across the bay from Melbourne.

In the north-east is Rutherglen, an old gold-mining region, where some of the finest dessert wines of Australia are produced from the Muscat grape. The climate is very hot and the soil is a dusty red loam. In the neighbouring regions of Glenrowan and Milawa, there is a contrast with the former giving heavy red wines and the latter cool-climate styles from vineyards planted high in the hills.

The central vineyards of the Goulburn Valley have a continental climate with hot summers and cold winters. The white Marsanne grape is a local speciality.

Melbourne's local vineyards are those of the Yarra Valley, where Pinot Noir, Cabernet Sauvignon and Chardonnay are particularly successful.

To the west of the state, the Great Western region is best known for its sparkling wines and Avoca, or the Pyrenees as it is sometimes known, has a growing reputation for its still light wines.

In the north, on the Murray river, the vineyards of Mildara are mainly for table grapes and dried fruit – the rich irrigated soil is amongst the most fertile in the country. However, a great deal of bulk wine is also made in the region.

Western Australia
Historically, the main area of production here has been the Swan River which flows north from Perth. Here the soil is alluvial, the climate mediterranean and the alcoholic strength of the wines often high. More recently there have been plantings by a number of smaller wineries in the cool-climate region of Margaret River, some 250 kilometres to the south, where the wines are respected for their concentrated flavours.

Other States
Modern viticulture started on the island of Tasmania in the 1950s when a hardy Frenchman finally established a vineyard in the Hobart area. He succeeded where the previous attempts of others had been thwarted by the cool, damp climate. This latter is now perceived as ideal for producing grapes for sparkling wines, but, as yet, total production is minute.

Once producing only liqueur wines, Queensland now has a number of quality light wines. These are produced in the Granite Belt region which is situated in the extreme south of the state, but even so at a latitude of 27 °S.

The Northern Territory is largely dry, hot and thinly populated, and not really suited for viticulture at all. Nevertheless, there are a few hectares under vine, the majority producing table-grapes, and against the odds, in Alice Springs itself, one irrigated estate producing wine.

NEW ZEALAND

It is all too easy for the British to think of New Zealand and Australia in the same breath and to make false comparisons. In so many ways, the two countries are different and this is especially true in the context of making wine, where the differences in geography and climate are very significant.

Location and Climate

The two countries are separated by more than 1600 kilometres and the Tasman Sea. Whilst Australia is a large land mass, comprising mostly hot desert or semi-desert, New Zealand comprises two relatively narrow islands with a maritime climate strongly influenced by the surrounding seas.

North Island, where most vineyards are found, extends slightly further south than the south-east of Australia; its most northern vineyards are on about the same latitude as those in Victoria (36 °S). South Island stretches even further towards the Antarctic; the latitude of its northern vineyards approximates to that of the Tasmanian grape-growing areas (42 °S).

The altogether cooler climate of New Zealand is much better suited to the growing of white rather than black grapes, and the damp maritime climate can cause severe problems, particularly with fungal diseases. Modern chemical sprays have been successful in combating these.

Early Winemaking
One point in common with Australia lies in New Zealand's history. In 1833, an early pioneer of Australian winemaking, James Busby, left for New Zealand to carry on his work there. Subsequently, towards the latter part of the 19th century, further vines were planted by the early settlers, mainly from Dalmatia, working in the gum forests to the north of Auckland. They produced mostly liqueur wines.

It was not until later in this century that light wine came to be widely made in New Zealand. Müller-Thurgau was the dominant wine variety, producing totally undistinguished, slightly sweet white wines.

Modern Grape Varieties and Wine Styles
The first plantings of quality varietals like Cabernet Sauvignon and Chardonnay were made as recently as the late 1960s. Since then, there has been a revolution, particularly in the field of white wines, with Sauvignon Blanc giving wines as good as any in the world from that variety. Chardonnay has now overtaken Müller-Thurgau as the top grape variety in terms of area under vine. Most of the quality European varieties are now grown: in addition to those already mentioned there are Sémillon, Chenin Blanc, Rhine Riesling and Gewürztraminer.

Red wines are gaining ground in New Zealand, as better sites continue to be found for planting, and as existing vines mature. Red wine production is much smaller, and it is Cabernet Sauvignon that dominates, sometimes blended with Merlot or Pinotage, but Pinot Noir is showing increasing promise, and seems well suited to the climate.

Far-sighted financial investment, technological enhancement and innovative winemakers have contributed to New Zealand's rapid strides. The existing experience of working with stainless steel in the dairy industry has no doubt also contributed greatly to its immediate acceptance in the wine industry. Although cold fermentation and the use of stainless steel have become almost synonymous with New Zealand winemaking, this is not to say that oak-ageing is not practised. Barrels are being imported from the traditional areas of France – Nevers, Tronçais,

Limousin – and from America. Initially concentrated exclusively in the north of the country, planting has moved south, particularly to Marlborough, in the north of South Island, where cultivation on a large scale has permitted a degree of mechanisation unknown until recently. Today's New Zealand whites are characterised by their very clean, pure aromas of the variety from which they were produced.

All of this has been exploited to the full by a good assertive marketing strategy. Now ranking 24th in the world league, New Zealand's most important market is the United Kingdom. Mostly white wines are being imported here but more red wines are becoming available and New Zealand's sparkling wines feature more prominently both in the shops and the columns of the wine-writers (see Chapter 16).

Regions and Wines
Key regions:

North Island	*South Island*
Auckland	Marlborough
Gisborne	Nelson
Hawkes Bay	Canterbury
Martinborough	

The Auckland region extends north of the city of the same name, producing mainly red wines from grapes grown on heavy clay soil. Auckland and the more northerly Northland are the warmest of New Zealand's vine-growing areas.

On the east coast, around Poverty Bay, is the region of Gisborne, best known for producing Müller-Thurgau based white wines from vineyards planted on very fertile soils. Further south on the east coast is Hawkes Bay, an area of lighter soils where, again, Müller-Thurgau is grown but here is joined by Cabernet Sauvignon.

Close to Wellington is the newly planted area of Martinborough where Chardonnay and Pinot Noir have been planted; the latter, in particular, is showing considerable promise.

On the north-east corner of South Island, around the town of Blenheim, is the fastest growing region in New Zealand, Marlborough. Here, on stony soil Sauvignon Blanc and Chardonnay have proved very successful. The climate is cool and the area is sheltered from the moist westerly winds, resulting in low rainfall so irrigation is necessary.

To the west of Marlborough is the smaller region of Nelson. Because of the topography, this is one of the sunniest parts of the country, although the climate is cool. Both white and black grapes are grown, with the long autumns permitting the production of some late-harvest dessert wines.

The famous Cloudy Bay vineyards are situated at Marlborough, in the north of New Zealand's South Island.

Further south still is the region of Canterbury, around the city of Christchurch. German varieties have proved successful here as has Pinot Noir. Vineyards have also been planted at Otago, north-west of Dunedin. These are the most southerly of any in the world.

NORTH AMERICA

If the Norsemen arrived in North America as many believe, they must have marvelled at the profusion of vines growing wild there to such an extent that they called the newly discovered land Vinland. Much later, successive waves of British, Dutch and French immigrants tried to plant vineyards on the eastern seaboard, but met with little success. (The endemic phylloxera louse had yet to be identified.) It was not until the end of the first half of the 19th century that vineyards in Ohio, planted with native, phylloxera-resistant, American vines, first met with commercial success.

It is only recently that the consumption of wine in the United States has overtaken that of spirits. Nevertheless, there are now wineries in a host of states including Hawaii, Texas and Virginia. Production, however, is concentrated in California, the Pacific North-West (Oregon, Idaho and Washington states) and New York State.

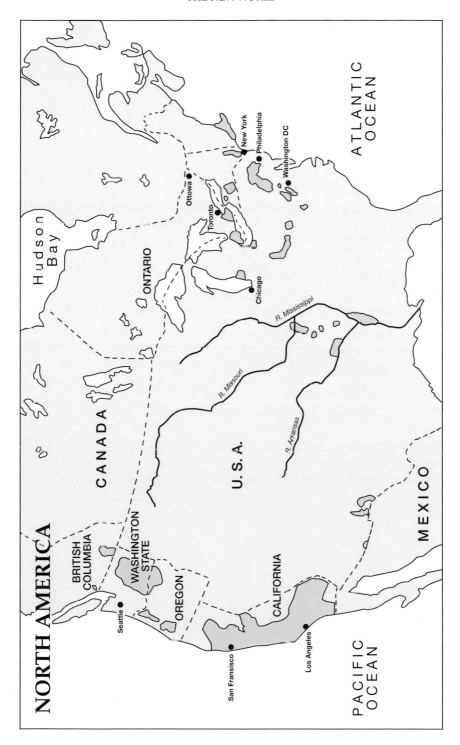

NORTH AMERICA

ATLANTIC OCEAN

Hudson Bay

New York
Philadelphia
Washington DC

Ottowa

Toronto

ONTARIO

Chicago

R. Mississippi

R. Missouri

R. Arransas

CANADA

U.S.A.

BRITISH COLUMBIA

WASHINGTON STATE

OREGON

CALIFORNIA

MEXICO

Seattle

San Fransisco

Los Angeles

PACIFIC OCEAN

Canada also produces wine some of which is slowly coming to be known in the United Kingdom. The leading Canadian wine regions are in the Provinces of Ontario and British Columbia.

Wine Laws
The controlling body for the drinks industry in the United States is the Bureau of Alcohol, Tobacco and Firearms (BATF). In 1978 the BATF introduced a system of American Viticultural Areas (AVAs) to supplement an existing appellation system and the combined scheme is still evolving. Under local law, to be labelled as a varietal, the wine must contain a minimum 75% of the grape concerned. Exceptionally, this figure is accepted by the EC rather than their more normal derogation to 85%. Similarly, if a geographical source is named, 75% of the wine must come from there. Wines coming from a specific vintage, or named property, must have 95% of that wine in the bottle. Outside the EC, American wines, like their Australian counterparts, are often labelled in generic terms: thus California Chablis or California Claret might be seen.

In Canada, the Provincial Liquor Boards perform a similar function.

California
Sometimes, it is difficult to realise just how young California is and this is particularly true of the wine industry which now accounts for 96% of the USA's total production.

The early twin influences of Spain and Catholicism, epitomised by the frequency among place names of the Spanish *San* or *Saint*, can still be seen in California and countries in South America. The first vineyards in the state were planted at the San Diego Mission in 1697 by Jesuit priests who had moved northwards from what is now Mexico. It is thought that the variety concerned was the imported *V. vinifera*, Mission, which is still grown largely for blending and liqueur wines. Wine was not, however, produced commercially until 1833. It was the Gold Rush of 1849 that led to a boom in the California wine industry, although the boom in both gold and wine was short-lived.

At about this period, a Hungarian, Agoston Haraszthy, introduced a number of grape varieties from his native Europe. After a futher visit to Europe, he returned in 1861 with no less than 100,000 cuttings from over 300 varieties. Sadly, these could have been barely established when, in 1870, phylloxera arrived from the eastern United States causing extensive damage, with Napa, Sonoma and Sacramento being especially badly hit.

Further disaster was to strike fifty years later when those wineries that had been re-established were almost totally destroyed by nation-wide Prohibition, introduced under the Volstead Act of 1920. From then until repeal in 1933, wines were only allowed to be produced and consumed

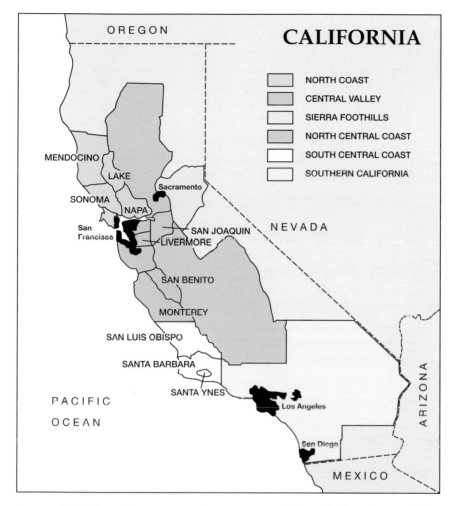

for medicinal and sacramental purposes, although the demand for table-grapes to make "grape juice" in the home was so great that the period turned out initially to be a boon for grape growers. From repeal until the mid 1960s, winemaking was concentrated in the Central (San Joaquin) Valley and was mainly liqueur or basic "jug" wines.

Since the 1960s, the area under vines has almost trebled and there has been a proliferation of small "boutique" wineries mostly making varietal wines. It was these producers and their marketing advisors who introduced into common usage the term and concept of "varietal" wines.

The diversity both of California's climate and the grape varieties planted combine to permit the making of all styles of wine, which, in turn, have contributed so significantly to modern attitudes to wine and winemaking.

Climate

Within the state of California, which measures some 1100 kilometres from north to south, there are very wide climatic differences. One feature common to the vineyard areas across the state is that rain rarely falls during the summer. Irrigation by sprinkler or drip-feed, therefore, is commonly practised in order to alleviate stress among the vines.

During research into the matching of vines to microclimate, the wide climatic variation led the University of California at Davis, a leading faculty in oenological studies, to create a climatic classification system based upon "Degree Days". In this, regional climates are ranged on a scale of one (I) to five (V) with one being the coolest and five the hottest. Using the system, all potential vineyard areas in California have been classified into one of these five zones and the grape varieties most suited to each zone have now been identified. Zones I to III are considered to be the most suitable for premium wine production. The system may be applied, of course, anywhere in the world (see Chapter 1).

The cool Pacific Ocean has a large role to play in the climate, for it creates mists and fogs which periodically roll inland and create much cooler growing conditions for the vines, resulting in greater finesse in the wines of these coastal regions. The mists are caused by the meeting, offshore, of the warm North Pacific Drift and the cold California Current and are particularly prevalent during late May and early summer as the land mass warms and creates breezes which bring the fogs in off the sea. Inland, away from this influence, daytime temperatures can rise above 40 °C.

Grape varieties

You can be sure that somewhere in California there will be someone growing almost any wine-grape that you have ever heard mentioned! For cheaper blends, French Colombard, Chenin Blanc, Carignan and Barbera are the major constituents. Zinfandel, California's "own" grape is also widely planted for blends, for varietal wines and for the faintly pink, or "blush", white Zinfandel. It is now the top selling single varietal in the United States. For a long time, the origins of Zinfandel were disputed, but it now seems to be generally accepted as the Italian Primitivo.

For quality wines, Cabernet Sauvignon and Chardonnay are the most common, but Merlot, Pinot Noir and Sauvignon Blanc, sometimes known locally as Fumé Blanc, are also widely grown.

In some regions, the soil is highly fertile, and exceptionally high yields are commonplace. As a result, a common criticism of many cheaper wines is that they lack concentration of fruit. In the main, though, the common perception of Californian wines, especially the reds, is that they abound in fruity flavours.

Main viticultural areas
The principal vineyards are grouped into six regions, three of which, by virtue of their more northern coastal position are important for the production of premium wines, and contain the majority of the well known districts and counties.

Key regions and areas:

North Coast region	South Central Coast region
Napa Valley	Santa Ynez Valley
Sonoma Valley	Santa Barbara County
Mendocino County	San Luis Obispo County
North Central Coast region	
Livermore Valley	
Monterey County	

The North Coast comprises the vineyards to the north of San Francisco Bay. Perhaps the best-known area of all is the Napa Valley. This has the most expensive vineyard land and some of the most prestigious wineries of California. Morning mist ensures the climate is milder to the south, which is in Davis's Zone I. Further up the valley, the climate is almost mediterranean, and the northern end is in Zone III. Frosts can be a danger in the valley bottom. The soil is basically volcanic. At the foot of Napa County and overlapping into Sonoma County, lies Carneros. This cool-climate (Zone I) region specialises in Chardonnays and Pinot Noirs which are often used for sparkling wine production. Sonoma County also produces fine wines in the areas of Sonoma Valley, Russian River and the Alexander Valley. Further north still come Lake and Mendocino Counties.

In the North Central Coast there is a broad variety of soils and climates varying from the richly fertile soils of the Salinas Valley to the cool climate of the Santa Cruz Mountains. The latter is in Zone I, most of the rest of this region is Zone III. To the east of the San Francisco Bay is Livermore Valley, where excellent white wines come from the gravelly soils. Further south lie San Benito and Monterey County which produce some pleasing white wines especially from Chardonnay.

The South Central Coast is an area north of Santa Barbara where, following climatic studies by the University of California, many of the Napa Valley wineries have gone in search of cheaper land on which to grow white grapes. Here the ocean again has a major effect upon the climate, creating Zone I and II areas close to the coast, with the inland areas reaching Zone III. The best known sub-regions are probably Edna Valley, Santa Ynez Valley and San Luis Obispo County.

California's other three regions are Southern California, Central Valley and the Sierra Foothills.

In Southern California the vineyards have largely disappeared as Los Angeles and San Diego inexorably stretch out towards each other. As they traditionally produced mainly dessert wines, their role as far as the consumer is concerned has also diminished. At Temecula, the potentially hot climate is cooled by a passage of air from the Pacific. This means that white wines are now made with success. This is an exception to the general climate, which is classified as Zones IV and V.

The Central Valley stretches for some 600 kilometres south from Sacramento and is the "bread basket" of the Californian wine industry. For the most part the climate is hot (Zone V) the soil rich and the yields high. This region accounts for four-fifths of California's production and because of the climate, the University of California has developed a number of new varieties to meet the circumstances. Amongst the more successful are Carnelian, Centurion, Ruby Cabernet and Emerald Riesling. Over the years different outlets have had to be found for the production – liqueur wines, fruit-flavoured "pop" wines, wine-coolers and, recently, what are euphemistically described as "premium" varietals. In the north of the region, in the delta of the Sacramento river, where the climate is cooler (Zone III and IV) wine of better quality is made.

Finally, the Sierra Foothills lie at the feet of the Rockies and contain the vineyards that were originally planted at the time of the Gold Rush; one can still find some vines more than a hundred years old. The foothills have hot days and cool nights, putting the region in Zones III and IV. The most successful varieties are Zinfandel and Barbera.

Future developments
It is perhaps as well that California has learned to triumph over adversity, as experiences with phylloxera, prohibition and the Depression have demonstrated, for the troubles do not appear to be entirely over. State legislators are insisting on more stringent labelling with regard to sulphur content, for instance, and on the home market, labels must also now carry health warnings. More immediately worrying, though, is the return of phylloxera. A combination of factors – too heavy reliance on just two common rootstocks, a new strain of the insect termed Biotype B, and complacency in some quarters – has led to significant destruction in the Californian vineyards. A big replanting programme is underway, funded in part by long term government loans.

The Pacific North-West
The vineyards of the north-west, from the three states of Oregon,

Washington and Idaho fall into two groups; those with an oceanic climate and those with a continental one. In Washington both groups are found, in Oregon only the former whilst the vineyards of land-locked Idaho all experience a continental climate. Washington State is the third largest US producer and is phylloxera-free.

Within the Pacific North-West, a system of controlled appellations has been created to reflect the character of the wines of each area. Benefiting from the warm currents of the North Pacific Drift, vineyards influenced by the ocean climate include four of these appellations:

in Washington State: the Puget Sound around Seattle and

in Oregon: the Willamette, Umpqua and Rogue River Valleys

The best wines come from cool-climate grapes like Pinot Noir, Pinot Blanc, Chardonnay and Riesling.

The continental climate vineyards are almost two hundred kilometres inland, with the appellations of Columbia Valley, Yakima Valley and Walla Walla Valley in the state of Washington. There are further groups of vineyards around Spokane in Washington and also in western Idaho. Here, where the land is very arid and irrigation is necessary, Cabernet Sauvignon, Merlot and Sémillon have all been successful.

Throughout these three states, the vineyards tend to be small in size. The extended daylight hours compensate for nights which are much cooler than those further south in California.

New York State

Rather sadly, the reputation of New York State wines has largely been controlled by the climate and the market they have traditionally supplied – urban New York. For long it was thought that the extreme continental climate, with exceptionally severe winters, would only permit the planting of native *Vitis labrusca* vines. These give wines with, according to Jancis Robinson, in "Vines, Grapes and Wines", "the musky smell of a wet and rather cheap fur coat which wine tasters have agreed to call 'foxy'." For many years, this could be satisfactorily disguised in sweet dessert wines or inferior sparkling wines for native New Yorkers. Many of the grapes were also processed into Grape Jelly. Permissive local legislation also allowed the admixture of high percentages of "imported" wine and water, to neutralise the special taste.

It was at the beginning of the 1970s that a Frenchman, Charles Fournier, and a Russian, Konstantin Frank, began to produce serious wines from *Vitis vinifera* vines. Plantings are now split three ways between:

hybrids of "native" varieties the most important of which are Catawba, Concord, Niagara and Noah;

other hybrids, mainly French, such as Seyval Blanc, Baco Noir and Marechal Foch; and

noble varieties such as Chardonnay and Riesling.

Eighty-five per cent of the production comes from the Finger Lakes region where the glacier age lakes have individual microclimates. The soil is predominantly shale.

The Hudson Valley, to the north of New York city, is one of the oldest wine growing regions in the United States. The climate is affected by the Atlantic and it has a long growing season. Mainly French-American hybrids are planted.

Finally, the Long Island vineyards are planted solely in *Vitis vinifera* grapes. The climate is moderate, with the ocean on three sides.

Canada
The most important quality wine production in Canada is in the Niagara peninsula on the south shores of Lake Ontario. Here, there is a mild climate because of the large body of water to the north, and the Niagara escarpment to the west and south. Recently, a quality label, the Vintners' Quality Alliance (VQA), has been established for the better wines made from *V. vinifera* and premium hybrid varieties. *V. Labrusca* wines, which until recently have accounted for the majority of production, are ineligible for the label. A blind tasting before an independent panel has to be undergone before approval.

The second most important vineyard area is in British Columbia, in the Okanagan and Similkameen Valleys, around the town of Kelowna. Here, the local wine production is increased by the importation of grapes from California.

SOUTH AMERICA
The Spanish arrived in South America in the 16th century and planted vines almost immediately. However, because of fear of competition with those from Spain itself, the vineyards were restricted to the production of wine for the Missions. It was not until the decade of 1820–1830, with the secession of the colonies from the Spanish Empire, that a true local wine industry began to establish itself.

Chile
Key regions:
Central Valley   Maipo Valley
                          Aconcagua

The most prominent South American wines on the United Kingdom

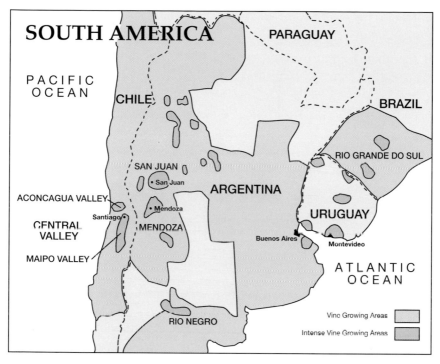

market currently come from Chile. The second largest producer in South America, ranked 13th in the world, Chile has many advantages for the making of good wine. The climate is near perfect, the prevailing winds blow onshore from the Pacific and there is a long ripening season. Any shortage of rainfall can be made up with the limitless water available for irrigation from the Andes. Together, the mountains and sandy desert to the north protect against phylloxera which has never arrived here.

On the other hand many of the wineries are primitive by any accepted standards; much of the wine is made from the high yield, low quality Pais grape and then aged in local *rauli* wood, which imparts a bizarre taste to the wine. Local taste seems to be for heavily oxidised wines and many wineries have to make two totally different styles, one for the domestic market and the other for export. Largely due to the rampant Pais, over-production can create problems.

Foreign investment in stainless steel vats and oak casks is now leading to rapid changes for the better. Most of the vineyards lie in the Central Valley between the coastal range of hills and the Andes. They stretch from about 60 kilometres north of the capital Santiago, to some 250 kilometres south. Many of the best vineyards are on Santiago's doorstep, in the Maipo and Aconcagua Valleys just to the south. Further south, the cooler climates in Curico and Talca give more finesse to white wines. At Casablanca, where the Pacific Ocean has a more important influence, a new vineyard area, west of Santiago, is considered to have great potential.

It appears to be the Bordeaux grape varieties that have the most success: Cabernet Sauvignon, Merlot and Malbec for the red wines, Sémillon and Sauvignon for the whites. The Burgundian Chardonnay is now widely planted to satisfy demands from the wider wine-drinking world and the Rhine Riesling is also grown.

In the arid north of the country grapes are grown for distillation into *pisco*, the widely appreciated local brandy.

Wine legislation is flexible with the only laws appearing to be about terms for age. A *"Special"* wine must be two years old, a *"Reserve"* four years and a *"Gran Vino"* six years old.

Argentina
Key regions:
Mendoza
San Juan

The largest producer of wine in South America, Argentina is the fourth largest in the world. Over 90% of its wines are produced in the Cuyo region, which comprises the two provinces of Mendoza and San Juan, just to the north of Santiago but on the other side of the Andes. Other wine-producing areas include the Rio Negro and the Northern Vineyards. The vineyards, which were largely planted by Italian immigrants towards the end of the last century, only came into their own when the railway arrived in 1880. The home market is important as the country is, *per capita*, the fourth largest consumer of wine. There has, therefore, been little incentive to export the wines, a situation exacerbated by the fact that there is a tax on all exports. Notwithstanding this, in the late 1970s Argentinian wines were becoming known on the United Kingdom market. The Falklands War disrupted this pattern until the late 1980s, since when the wines have been increasing in popularity once more.

The vineyard area is by nature desert but, as in Chile, water is readily available from the Andes for irrigation. Indeed, without this benefit there would be no vineyards. Most of the holdings are quite small, but the grapes are delivered to a number of large bodegas and co-operative cellars for vinification. Yields are regularly well in excess of 100 hl/ha, giving all the problems inherent in over-production. For this reason, and because of a general lack of understanding in winemaking, much of the wine is of medium to low quality, often being drunk watered down as a thirst quencher.

Almost as much rosé wine is made as red and for this the Criolla grape (the Pais of Chile and the most widely planted in the country) is grown. The main grapes for red wines show, perhaps, the diverse origins of those in the local wine trade: Malbec from Bordeaux, Bonarda from Piedmont, Tempranillo from Spain, followed by the Italian Barbera and Lambrusco and French Cabernet Sauvignon and Syrah (known locally as Balsamina). White wines have been taken less seriously as can be shown by the fact that by far the most widely planted variety is Pedro Ximénez – followed by Chenin Blanc and Sémillon; an up and coming white variety is seen to be Galician Torrontes.

Domestically wines are often labelled with European regional names and the situation is made even more confusing by the fact that one wine-producing region is called La Rioja.

Some sparkling wine is also produced in Argentina.

Brazil and Other Countries
Both Brazil, the 2nd largest producer in South America and 15th in the world, and Uruguay have wine industries. Once again, these have been largely established by Italian immigrants. Until recently, little of their wine has been seen on export markets. Interestingly enough, the best vineyards in both countries are probably found up against their common border.

In Brazil, more than 75% of the grapes grown for wine making are either *V. Labrusca* or hybrid. The climate is generally too hot for viticulture. However, considerable investment from the United States and Japan in *V. vinifera* vineyards in Rio Grande do Sul, which is situated in the most southern part of the country abutting Uruguay, is leading to the production of quality wine. The main grapes found here are:

White – Chardonnay, Rhine Riesling and Sémillon;

Red – Cabernet Sauvignon, Merlot, Pinot Noir and some Barbera and Bonarda.

In Central America, Mexico has, over the past few years, developed vineyards for the production of wines rather than, as previously, for distillation or the growing of table-grapes. The move now is for quality wine production from the best-known European varieties with Sonora and Baja California being the most important producing regions.

SOUTH AFRICA

The first serious plantings of vines in the New World were in the Dutch colony of the Cape which was subsequently incorporated into South Africa. This was an essential re-victualling point for the Dutch East India Company ships on their way to Java, and as early as 1654, the Governor

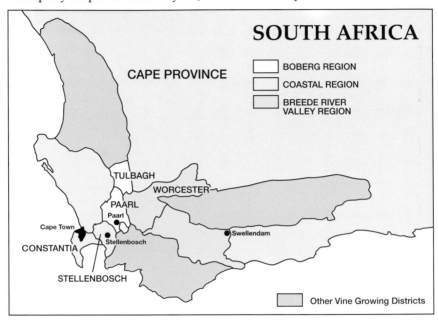

Jan Van Riebeck planted vines for wine production. In 1689, at about the time that a later Governor, Simon van der Stel, was settling in Stellenbosch and planting his own vineyard at his estate called Constantia in the shadow of Table Mountain, Huguenot refugee vine-growers came from France to establish the vineyards on a more permanent basis. Historically, South Africa has not been a light wine country, and much of today's production still goes for brandy and liqueur wine.

Wine Laws

It is perhaps fitting that the New World country with the longest tradition of producing quality wine (for the wine of Constantia came to be accepted as one of the great wines of the world more than a century and a half ago) should have, in theory at least, the best organised wine legislation. The Wine of Origin system dates from 1973 and ensures that quality wines bear a certification seal which is only awarded after tasting by an independent panel. The seal, usually on the capsule, guarantees the information on the label adheres to the rules laid down in the Wine of Origin scheme. To qualify for a vintage a minimum of 75% of the grapes

Irrigation is forbidden in European vineyards, but is common in many New World vineyards, as here at Franschhoek in South Africa.

must be from the stated year. If a variety, often locally called a cultivar, is stated it must form 75 percent of the total. Unlike American exports, South African wines exported to the EU must contain at least 85 percent of the variety. In the past the seal carried colour-coded bands, it has now been simplified and just carries the approval number.

The country has been divided into fourteen wine districts, some of which are grouped into one or other of the three regions, with the main vineyards being to the east of Cape Town, and the most important centres being Stellenbosch and Paarl in Cape Province.

Four-fifths of the total production is through co-operative cellars and the trade is controlled by a master co-operative the KWV. Founded in 1918, the role of the KWV is to stabilise an industry with a history of chronic over-production and, to achieve this, it has statutory regulatory powers over the whole wine industry in the country. Under its aegis in its heyday during the 1950s, South Africa led the way for a time in quality wine production, particularly of sparkling wine. Also during this period she pioneered night-time harvesting.

Climate and Grape Varieties

Overall, the climate is favourable to grape growing, though irrigation is frequently necessary. Recently, there has been a move by some growers to more cool-climate zones close to the sea, south-east of Cape Town.

The most widely planted black grape variety is Cinsaut (here spelt without an "l") and this has been crossed with Pinot Noir to create the indigenous Pinotage. For quality wines, there have been extensive recent plantings of Cabernet Sauvignon.

The dominant white grape is Chenin Blanc, locally known as Steen. This is very versatile and, as in the Loire, can make either sweet or dry wines. Chardonnay was a comparative latecomer, but is now widely planted, as are Sauvignon Blanc and Rhine (or Weisser) Riesling. Hanepoot is the local name for Muscat of Alexandria, which is the most widely grown variety for dessert wines.

Regions and Wines

Key regions and districts:
Coastal region
Constantia
Stellenbosch
Boberg region
Paarl
Tulbagh
Breede River Valley region
Worcester

South Africa's Cape Province is divided into a number of districts, some of which are grouped into one or other of the three vine-growing regions: Coastal region, Boberg, and Breede River Valley.

The Coastal Region is at the heart of South African winemaking. Constantia, the oldest district, and Durbanville face Table Bay and have a cool maritime climate. Stellenbosch lies slightly inland on granite and sandstone soils; the second oldest district, it houses the internationally famous Oenological Viticultural Research Institute. This region also houses the district of Swartland producing well-made inexpensive light wine.

The region of Boberg includes the town and district of Paarl, home to KWV's main winery and office. Paarl has light fertile soils and production is dominated by a small number of major producers. The district of Paarl includes the ward of Franschhoek which was the area first settled by The French Hugenots. The area has retained its French character which is also reflected in the wines. Further inland is Tulbagh which has variable soils, and is known for its white wines. The appellation Boberg is only used for liqueur wines.

Several producers in the Breede River Valley Region are now beginning to vie for recognition of their good quality still light wines from the district of Worcester (home of the KWV Brandy cellar), Robertson and Swellendam, although very little wine is yet exported from the latter.

Although not included in the three regions of South Africa, the district of Overberg has the most southerly vineyards of the country. Much of the area is not devoted to wine production, but near the town of Hermanus in Walker Bay, some excellent Pinot Noirs and Chardonnays are being produced.

CHAPTER 16

CHAMPAGNE AND OTHER SPARKLING WINES

There are a number of places in Europe that lay claim to having produced the first sparkling wines, Navarra and Limoux amongst others, but it was not until the very end of the 17th century that the most famous wine of them all, Champagne, came to be produced.

Indeed, it was not even in France that sparkling Champagne was first produced, but rather in London, where, from about 1665 onwards, there was a strong fashionable demand for "brisk and sparkling" wines. This demand for sparkling wines coincided with the wines of Champagne being in vogue at the English court, largely due to the efforts of the refugee Marquis de Saint Evremond. At that time the two necessities for the sale of such wine – solid glass bottles and cork stoppers – were only available in London. These did not arrive in France for another twenty-five years or so.

The success of the "new-look" Champagne once established in France was also rapid, due largely to its instant popularity at the court of Louis XV, where it was promoted by his "senior" mistress Madame de Mailly. The high reputation of Champagne was the first step in the creation of a market for sparkling wine which has continued to grow and develop to its current very significant size. In the UK, for instance, the annual sale of sparkling wine is something in excess of 36 million bottles.

Part of this development has been the introduction of newer methods of production, designed either to refine the original method or to achieve acceptable results at a lower cost. Today there are three basic ways of producing bubbles in a wine: a second fermentation in bottle, a second fermentation in tank, and carbonation.

The first is the classic method of producing Champagne and the finest sparkling wines, and there are two variations. In the full version, the wine remains in the original bottle throughout, from before the second, bubble-creating, fermentation to its eventual sale and consumption. This is the principle of the Champagne method. Often non-Champagnes made in this way have been described as *méthode champenoise*, but from 1994, under European Community rules, the use of this term was restricted to wines produced in the Champagne district. Wines from elsewhere made in the same way may be described as *méthode traditionelle*. A variation of this method does not involve keeping the wine in its original bottle throughout, and is appropriately known as the transfer method.

All three methods and their variations are described more fully in this chapter; Champagne is described in the section on the traditional method.

With the bubbles being induced in a separate process, almost any wine can be made to sparkle. Indeed, during the 19th century, you could find such products as Clos de Vougeot Mousseux – and this tradition is still carried on to a certain extent in some of the best German vineyards. Now, however, most sparkling wines are made from grapes grown specially for the purpose, in order to have the lightness and high acidity that give the best results. This usually means either cool growing conditions, or early picking. Most are white; there are a number of sparkling rosé wines, and even a small handful of reds.

THE TRADITIONAL METHOD

Champagne
Champagne existed long before the end of the seventeenth century, but until then it was a still wine. Both red and white Champagne wines were made in the 15th century when, it is thought, Pinot Noir was introduced. For a period Champagne sought to compete with Burgundy and achieved some initial success with its light elegant red.

The man who is often credited with the "creation" of Champagne as we know it, is Dom Pérignon, a monk from the Abbey of Hautvillers in the Marne valley, who was its cellar-master from 1668 until his death in 1715. He certainly knew which of his wines would re-ferment once put in a bottle and sealed with a cork, but he was also the first man to appreciate that Champagne was a better wine if it was created by blending together a number of constituents. Ironically, not only did he prefer to use his knowledge of wine to avoid the presence of bubbles in his wine, he also, reputedly, never drank.

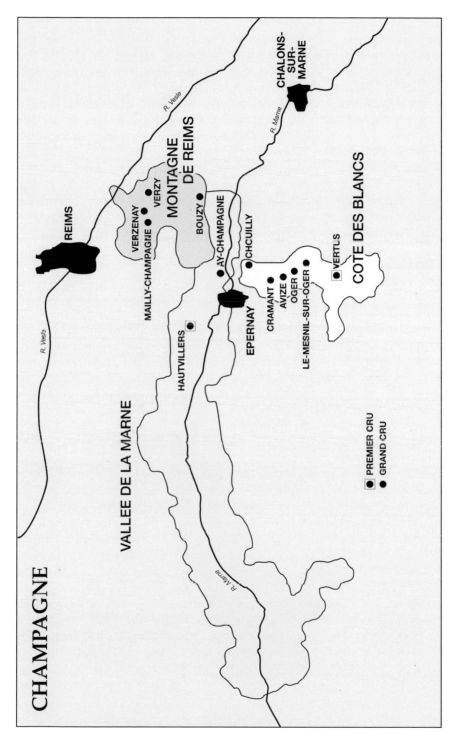

CHAMPAGNE

VALLEE DE LA MARNE

MONTAGNE DE REIMS

COTE DES BLANCS

REIMS

CHALONS-SUR-MARNE

R. Vesle

R. Marne

VERZY

VERZENAY

MAILLY-CHAMPAGNE

BOUZY

AY-CHAMPAGNE

CHCUILLY

VERTUS

CRAMANT

AVIZE

OGER

LE-MESNIL-SUR-OGER

EPERNAY

HAUTVILLERS

R. Vesle

R. Marne

R. Marne

PREMIER CRU

GRAND CRU

The Champagne Region

The most northern vineyard area in France, the Champagne region lies north-east of Paris; its heart is in the form of a double fish-hook, with the shank being the valley of the river Marne. The three main vineyard concentrations are firstly the Vallée de la Marne itself, where many of the most important companies are based in the town of Epernay. To the north is the Montagne de Reims, overlooking the cathedral city of that name, the other important centre for the Champagne trade, and to the south is the Côte des Blancs. These vineyards areas are in the Marne *département*. Some 90 kilometres south of the Côte des Blancs, but still part of the Appellation, are three detached vineyard areas round Sézanne, in the Marne, and Bar sur Seine and Bar sur Aube in the Aube *département*. More recently, in order to cater for increased demand, there has been an extension into the more northerly département of the Aisne.

Grape Varieties

Three grape varieties are used in the making of Champagne: Chardonnay, Pinot Noir and the rather more humble Pinot Meunier. (In theory, three other varieties, Petit Meslier, Arbanne and Pinot Blanc Vrai, are permitted but, in practice, rarely grown.) Chardonnay is most common on the Côte des Blancs, whilst the Montagne de Reims is largely planted in the black varieties, Pinot Noir and Pinot Meunier. In the Marne valley, all three varieties can be found, although Pinot Meunier is favoured. A late budding and early ripening variety, this latter is better suited to the climate than its more noble peers, being less prone both to frost initially and, later in the season, to rot.

Climate and Soils

Because these are amongst the most northerly vineyards in Europe, it is by no means easy to make a wine that is better than drinkable. The winters are cold and the summers warm rather than hot; the average temperature during the growing season is around 10 °C, the temperature at which the vine begins to grow. As a result, in an average year, grapes only just ripen; in some years they do not ripen sufficiently. The typical product therefore is a light crisp wine, high in acidity and low in alcohol. It is ideal as a base for sparkling wine, the high acidity, especially, playing a very important part in ensuring the final product is properly balanced. A very little wine is sold in its still form; it may not be called Champagne, however, but carries the separate Appellation Coteaux Champenois. In commercial terms, it is not particularly significant.

The sub-soil in the Champagne region is mainly chalk. Two types are found: *Belemnita quadrata* on the hillside and *Micraster* in the valleys. Clay, sand and lignite form the main topsoils which have little depth. The vineyards are to be found only on these chalk sub-soils which, because of the shallow nature of the topsoil, retain their heat overnight and in so doing mitigate, to some extent, the effects of the relatively cool summers which inhibit grape ripening.

Brands and Blends
The fact that the climate is marginal encourages the production of non-vintage blends to even out the differences between wines made in different years. Born out of pragmatism, but refined over the years, this practice now permits the winemaker to create, and thereafter to maintain consistently, the individual "house" style. In Champagne, therefore, it is the brand, or *marque*, that is king. The refinements to the blending system concern the other three variable elements beside the year of production: grape variety, vineyard rating and quality of juice.

Each of the three grape varieties will contribute something to the style of an individual Champagne. Chardonnay (26% of the plantings) here gives a much lighter wine than in Burgundy and is relied upon to impart elegance and finesse. Also of Burgundian origin, Pinot Noir (36%) produces wines of great structure and provides the backbone in a blend. Pinot Meunier (38%) gives an easy to drink fruitiness.

The soil characteristics of the different villages also have something to contribute to the characteristics of the fruit they grow. Each vineyard village in Champagne is therefore rated for quality on a percentage basis under a system known as the *Echelle des Crus*. Seventeen villages have the top rating, 100%, and are known as *Grands Crus*, with about forty villages, the *Premiers Crus*, rated between 90 and 99%. The lowest rating of all is 80% – and this is just for some villages outside the Marne *département*. Until 1990, it was on this basis that the growers were paid for their grapes, receiving for each kilo of grapes the percentage of a centrally agreed full price that their village rating indicated. Recently, there has been more freedom in the fixing of prices, so whilst the percentage rating may have a legal status, and is still largely the *de facto* basis for grape contracts, its relevance has diminished. Individual contracts between growers and houses now have to be signed, with the price payable the subject of negotiation between them. This has led to many hundreds of separate contracts and an inevitable proliferation of paperwork.

The final variable in a Champagne blend is the quality of juice obtained during the pressing of the grapes. This is covered in detail in the description of the Champagne method.

The Champagne Trade
Despite the fact that the process of making Champagne requires special equipment, space and time, therefore money, a small but significant

number of growers make their own Champagne, particularly those in the most highly rated villages. As their fruit is likely to come from one locality only, the terms "*Grand Cru*" and "*Premier Cru*" are generally seen only on the labels of these individual growers' Champagnes.

The majority of growers, though, sell their grapes either to one of the Champagne producing houses or to a co-operative. Indeed, few of the major names can satisfy more than a minor proportion of their requirements from their own vineyard holdings, and instead concentrate largely on the vinification and blending parts of the process.

Within the ranks of the Champagne houses, there is an inner group called the Syndicat des Grandes Marques de Champagne. A wine may only be described as being a Grande Marque if the house is a member of the group. Membership is granted on the vote of existing members.

Viticulture
Vineyards are laid out with the rows a maximum of 1.5 metres apart and the vines planted every 0.9 to 1.5 metres. There are a number of pruning methods permitted, though the finest vineyards must be either in the Taille Chablis or Cordon de Royat system. In both of these systems, the vines are trained low on wires and spur pruned. In the Cordon Royat, the spurs are all located along the length of one horizontal arm of old wood (the cordon); in the Chablis system, which is widely used for Chardonnay, the spurs are found each at the tip of between three and five branches of older wood.

Vinification: The Champagne Method/Traditional Method
Grapes for Champagne are picked manually because it is considered that machine picking would damage the grapes too much. This is especially so in the case of black grapes which when damaged make the production of white wine more difficult. Immediately after picking the grapes are taken to the press-house and weighed. They are then pressed quickly in order to avoid any danger of oxidation, or the juice from the black grapes being tinted by their skins. (It may appear strange that whilst most Champagne is white, it is mainly made from black grapes.) To ensure that the pressing is carried out rapidly, each village generally has at least one press-house.

Pressing
The quality of a Champagne is often judged on its finesse, and this in its turn depends on the pressing. The harder the grapes are pressed the more undesirable attributes, such as harsh tannins, are likely to be found in the wine, whereas the first, gentle, pressings are rich in both sugars and desirable acids. Dom Pérignon was the first to record this. He went on to design a large diameter vertical press specifically for making white wine

The traditional Champagne vertical press holds four tonnes of grapes, which will yield 2,550 litres of juice. The shallow press reduces the damage to the grapes.

from black grapes. This type of press, holding a 4 tonne charge of grapes known as a *marc*, is still in common use, although it is gradually being replaced by larger horizontal, usually pneumatic, machines which apply more gentle and controlled pressure.

Whichever press is used, the amount of juice that can be extracted is strictly controlled. The law states that to get 100 l (1 hl) of must entitled to the Appellation Champagne, 160 kg of grapes are needed. As the fruit is pressed, the juice is separated into two grades, *cuvée* and *taille*. Of the 100 litres just mentioned, the first 80 l would be *cuvée* and the last 20 l *taille*. Only the *cuvée* is used for the finest Champagnes. Any juice extracted beyond the maximum for the AC is known as *vin de rebèche*, and must be sent for distillation.

First fermentation

The must is then fermented at the producer's cellars. At this stage, *cuvée* and *taille* juice from each grape variety and each village are fermented separately. Nowadays, this is generally carried out in stainless steel tanks, though there remains a handful of traditional houses that still ferment either totally or partially in old oak casks. The winemaker's aim at this stage, it should be remembered, is to produce a still wine, with crisp to high acidity and moderate alcohol. Some wines will be allowed to undergo a malo-lactic fermentation, while in others this will have been prevented, depending on the final style of wine required.

Blending
Key Champagne styles:
Non-vintage
Vintage
Prestige Cuvée
Rosé
Blanc de Blancs

It is now time for the blender to practise the arcane art of *assemblage*. For a house's standard non-vintage wine, the aim is to produce, consistently over the years, a wine of chosen quality to a defined house style. The blender will select those wines, and the proportions of each, that are needed to construct that style, using his stocks of wines from different vintages, pressings, grapes and villages. Given that in one vintage alone the number of wines available to the blender can run into three figures, it is easy to see that the number of permutations possible can be astronomical. Laboratory analysis of the wines is of some assistance, but the blend is created largely by tasting. The blender is like an artist, selecting from his palette the different shades and hints that he needs to create the whole.

It is at this stage that the other principal styles of Champagne are created. Whilst it has often been said that the ideal wine from Champagne is non-vintage, occasionally, after an exceptional summer, it is felt that the wines of that year have enough character to stand on their own merits, and they will be blended and sold as a vintage wine. In that event, in order to protect stocks of reserve wines for non-vintage blends, only 80% of the year's crop may be sold as vintage. Overall, for these reasons, vintage Champagne remains the exception rather than the rule. In style, vintage Champagnes are fuller in body and have greater intensity of fruit than non-vintage wines.

Most houses like to produce a prestige wine, or *cuvée de prestige*. Most, though not all, are vintage wines; all are produced from the highest quality base wines – the top villages, *cuvée* quality juice – and are blended with great care.

For rosé wine, some traditional houses still make their base wine by the *saignée* method. Most produce their wine by blending together red and white base wines, which is permitted at any stage of the process up to, and including, the addition of *liqueur d'expedition*, described below. Within Europe, pink Champagne is the only rosé Quality Wine that may be made by blending red and white wines.

Other terms that may be found on a Champagne label include Blanc de Blancs, a wine made just from Chardonnay, or occasionally Blanc de Noirs, a white Champagne made just from black grapes. The term

Crémant is applied to wines with a little less than full sparkling wine pressure, and hence a more "creamy" mousse. From 1994 this term can no longer be applied to Champagne, as it will be reserved solely for Crémant AC wines from elsewhere in France (see Other traditional method wines, below).

Second fermentation
When the blend has been decided upon and created in the blending tanks, and before, or as, the wine is bottled, a small proportion of *liqueur de tirage* is added. This is a mixture of wine, sugar and yeast – and it is this that will set off a further fermentation in the bottle and create the sparkle.

The bottle is then sealed with a temporary seal. This is usually a crown cork with a plastic cup inserted to collect dead yeast cells. The bottles are then laid to rest horizontally in stacks in the producers' cellars. These cellars are dug out of the chalk and many of them stretch for miles under Epernay and Reims. In the latter city, there are even some that began their careers as chalk pits in Roman times. The advantage they all have is that of a constant, cool temperature of around 10–12 °C, ideal for the next stage of the process.

When the yeasts get to work on the sugar, causing a second fermentation, they create three things: alcohol, CO_2 gas and, when they die having completed their work, a deposit on the side of the bottle. As the wine slowly ferments, the gas, being unable to escape, dissolves into the wine.

Maturation
The dead yeast cells eventually break down, and their enzymes interact with the wine. The process is known as yeast autolysis and it adds a particular, and sought after, flavour to the wine. Thus the time that the wine spends on its lees contributes much towards its final quality. For non-vintage Champagne, it has to be a minimum of fifteen months and for vintage Champagne at least three, with the time being counted from the January following the vintage. Both these minimum periods are normally exceeded in practice.

Removal of sediment
The next two stages in the Champagne process are first to work all the sediment lying in the side of the stored bottle into its neck, a process called *remuage*. This is followed by *dégorgement*; the removal of the sediment.

Remuage is achieved, over a period of time, by altering the position of the bottle, from the horizontal plane, on which it has lain for some time, to the upside-down vertical. The result will be that the deposit slides gently

REMUAGE

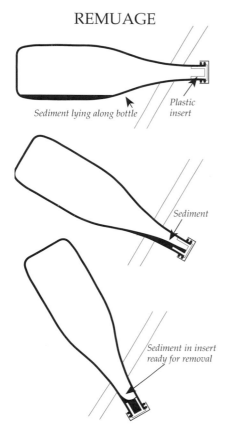

Sediment lying along bottle

Plastic insert

Sediment

Sediment in insert ready for removal

Champagne bottles in the traditional pupitres, which hold sixty bottles.

down from the side to the neck and finally into the plastic cup in the neck of the bottle.

The traditional method of achieving this is by riddling. This was developed at the beginning of the 19th century by the widow "Veuve" Clicquot herself. The neck of the bottle is put in an angled hole in a rack known as a *pupitre*. A *pupitre* is made up of two hinged boards each of which holds 60 bottles by the neck at any angle from horizontal to vertical. The bottle starts off horizontal, then each day it is given a gentle shake and a twist and inclined slightly more towards the inverted vertical. The work is done by hand; a skilled *remueur* can manipulate something in the region of 30,000 bottles in a day. Gradually the more solid yeast particles move down towards the neck pushing the lighter ones ahead of them. Ultimately, the bottle will be taken away to be binned with the crown cap downwards. This is a very labour intensive and, therefore, expensive method.

Accordingly, over the years, a number of mechanical and semi-mechanical systems have been developed so that this work can be carried out in bulk. Not only is there a considerable saving in labour but also in time. Perhaps the most effective is the gyropalette, which is a cage holding 504 bottles on a hydraulic arm, totally controlled by computer to rotate and incline, thus simulating the manual movements of the *remueur*.

Gyropalettes are far more efficient for remuage but represent a considerable investment on the part of the producer.

Most houses are now using these, though they tend to keep a number of the *pupitres* for the tourists to admire.

Whichever method is used, bottles which have completed the process and are being stored vertically upside down are referred to as being *sur pointes*. The wine may receive a further period of ageing *sur pointe* depending upon house style before *dégorgement*.

As the sediment is now lying on the inside of the crown cork, it will be driven out by the pressure inside the bottle once it is opened. To make this easier, the neck of the bottle is frozen in a brine solution. When the bottles are then moved into the upright position and placed on a conveyor belt the ice holds the now solid sediment in place, so keeping the wine clear. The crown cap is next removed and the plug of ice is ejected under pressure, sediment and all, together with its retaining plastic

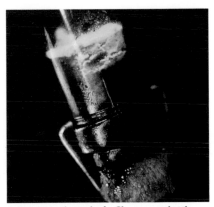

Sediment in the neck of a Champagne bottle prior to dégorgement. This bottle is sealed with a cork and staple; most houses use crown-corks.

cup. The whole process from here to inserting the final cork is automated and takes a very short time so as to avoid pressure loss.

Certain vintage Champagnes are described as R.D. (*récemment dégorgé*). These are old wines that have been disgorged just prior to shipment, and have therefore matured for longer than usual in contact with their lees.

Dosage

Inevitably during *dégorgement* a small amount of wine is lost. The bottle is therefore topped up to the correct level with a mixture of wine and cane sugar solution, known as the *liqueur d'expedition*. The amount of the sugar used will depend on the ultimate sweetness that is required for the wine. This part of the Champagne making process is known as *dosage*.

An important feature of each Champagne house's own style is the sweetness, or probably more accurately today, dryness of the wine. This element of house style is determined by the composition of the *dosage* which will vary from company to company. Champagne is naturally very dry. Nevertheless, as in any wine, even the driest will contain a very little unfermented, or residual, sugar. The figures that follow describe the total sugar content of the finished wine, rather than the quantity added as *dosage*. These are the terms widely used to describe the sweetness (or dryness) of Champagnes.

Ultra Brut, Extra Brut, Brut Zéro or Brut Sauvage – These terms are used to describe wines with no sugar at all in the *dosage*. They may however, by law, have up to a maximum of 6 g/l residual sugar.

Brut – Very dry, 0–15 g/l.

Extra sec – Dry, 12–20 g/l.

Sec – Off-dry, 17–35 g/l.

Demi-sec – Sweet, 33–50 g/l.

Doux – Luscious, 50+ g/l.

It will be noted that the grades overlap. As a result the winemakers (or marketing directors perhaps) have some flexibility in how they choose to describe their product. The Brut of one house, for instance, may be the Extra Sec of another.

Finishing

In order to maintain a perfect seal, a Champagne cork has to be compressed considerably before it is inserted into the neck of the bottle. In its original shape it takes the form of a cylinder with an area about three times that of the neck of the bottle; the familiar mushroom shape is only acquired after corking. Even with this degree of compression, a wire muzzle is added for complete security. The cork is made up of two sections, the combination of which has been shown to produce the most effective seal. The end that will be in contact with the wine consists of two or three horizontal slices of whole cork, and the balance is made up of composition cork.

By law the word Champagne must be branded on that part of the cork which enters the bottle. Champagne is also the only AC wine in France which does not have to have the words Appellation Contrôlée on the label.

Finally, before despatch to the customer, the bottle will be dressed, a process known as *habillage*. If you have ever wondered why there is a very deep foil around the neck of the Champagne and other sparkling wine bottles, it is because in olden days, when the wines were not topped up again after *dégorgement*, the foil was used to disguise the large gap between the wine and the cork!

Other Traditional Method Sparkling Wines

Whilst the climate and soil of Champagne provide a unique parentage for the wine, there are many other regions in the world that have adopted the method of secondary fermentation and maturation in the bottle to produce sparkling wine. Indeed, the Champagne houses themselves have not been slow to set up wineries in places as diverse as the Loire Valley, Brazil, India, Australia, New Zealand, California and Korea. The reasons for this are twofold: first, because of the geographically constrained vineyards, production of Champagne is limited and, particularly in boom years, the price can rise rapidly. Secondly, the whole image of Champagne is that of a luxury product (on a major brand, more than 10% of the cost is accounted for by the promotional spend). As a result of this, there are many governments that strictly limit its importation, particularly if there is a local wine industry to protect.

France
Key traditional method wines:
Crémant d'Alsace AC
Crémant de Bourgogne AC
Crémant de Limoux AC
Crémant de Loire AC
Saumur Mousseux AC
Vouvray Mousseux AC

Not surprisingly, there are a number of other French sparkling wines made by what must now be referred to as the traditional method. One important group of these is the Crémant wines. This is an upgraded status for a small number of long-standing AC fully sparkling wines. For example, AC Bourgogne Mousseux may still be sold under that name, but from 1975, if it has been made under tighter controls, for example, the proportion of the various grape varieties, the yields of juice and the time spent in bottle on the lees, it has had the right to call itself AC Crémant de Bourgogne. The other wines in this group are: Crémant d'Alsace, Crémant de Bordeaux, Crémant de Limoux, Crémant de Loire and, outside France but considered here for convenience, Crémant de Luxembourg. Whilst, in each case, the traditional local grape varieties are used, the other quality controls are at the same level.

Generally speaking each of the above wines will be made from the grapes used for making the best still white wines of the region. For example, Crémant de Bordeaux will be produced from Sémillon and Sauvignon; Loire, Chenin Blanc; Bourgogne, Chardonnay and Luxembourg, Müller-Thurgau and Riesling. However, a proportion of lesser varieties such as Aligoté in Burgundy, is also allowed. Crémant d'Alsace, however, forbids the use of such aromatic varieties as Gewurztraminer and Muscat, and relies mainly on Pinot Blanc and Riesling. In Limoux, the base variety is Mauzac (here called Blanquette); Crémant de Limoux allows more Chenin Blanc and Chardonnay in the blend than the traditional AC, Blanquette de Limoux, which still exists.

There are also a further number of traditional method AC sparkling wines in France. These include the Chenin Blanc based wines of Saumur and Vouvray in the Loire and the lesser, in quantity at least, wines of Clairette de Die and St Péray from the Rhône. Clairette de Die AC is a dry sparkling wine made from the Muscat and Clairette grapes by the traditional method. A second AC exists, for a sweeter wine produced by what is known as the *méthode rurale*, a controlled first fermentation in the bottle: confusingly, but with some justification, it is called Clairette de Die Tradition AC.

Spain
Key wine:
Cava DO

The second major European producer of traditional method sparkling wine is Spain, where it is known as Cava. The term Cava is itself a DO, and in this context, covers both the method and area of production. Whilst the majority of this wine is produced in the Catalan vineyards of Penedés, it is important to realise that it may be made in a number of DO regions in Spain. For example, there are Cavas made also in Rioja and Navarra. The wines must be made by the full traditional method and must spend a minimum of nine months in bottle before *dégorgement*. A Cava can be recognised by a four pointed star on the bottom of the cork.

In Penedés, the main grape varieties used are the those traditionally grown locally for white wine, Xarel-lo, Parellada and Macabeo (the Viura of Rioja). More producers are now also using Chardonnay. The trade centres round the town of San Sadurni de Noya, where the cellars rival those of Champagne. Labels sometimes show the Catalan spelling of the town, Sant Sadurni d'Anoia.

Most Cava is dry, with good yeast autolysis and a fuller flavour than Champagne. The traditional grapes give a rubbery/burnt toast character on the nose. Cava made from Chardonnay alone is fuller than Blanc de Blancs Champagne but lighter than traditional Cava.

Other countries
The market for bubbles in Italy is huge, and ranges from those wines which have just a gentle sparkle, *frizzante*, to the fully sparkling, or spumante, wines. Just as the production of still wines has become more sophisticated and quality conscious in Italy, so too has that of sparkling wines. This has led to an increase in the production of dry, traditional method (*metodo tradizionale*) wines. Some small producers now specialise in this type of wine; many of the large companies have added one to their range. There are few DOCs specifically for sparkling wine, but a surprising number of still DOC wines may be made in a spumante version, although not necessarily by the traditional method.

It is principally to the countries of the New World that a number of Champagne houses have turned in order to diversify, given the finite production levels of the Appellation Champagne region itself. In a series of solo and joint ventures, some fine quality sparkling wines are being produced using not only the traditional method, but also the long experience of Champagne industry specialists, in places as far apart as California and Australia.

That is not to say that there are no other excellent traditional method sparkling wines being made in the New World. There are, and they have been there for some time. In many areas one can find specialist sparkling wine producers, or companies for whom sparkling wines form a large part of the range. In their style, these New World sparkling wines are similar to their still counterparts in the fruitiness of their aromas and flavours. The ability to source grapes from, in some cases, very wide areas, up-to-date production methods and automation mean that these wines can offer excellent value for money.

THE TRANSFER METHOD

This method attempts to gain the advantages of a second fermentation in bottle without the disadvantages and expense of the complicated process of sediment removal required by the full traditional method. Up to the stage of *remuage*, the process is exactly the same as in the traditional method. In particular, as with that method, yeast autolysis occurs during maturation in the bottle as long as the wine is matured for sufficient time. In this case, though, the entire contents of the bottle are disgorged without *remuage* into a tank under pressure, filtered in bulk and re-bottled into a fresh bottle.

This can give good sparkling wine at a cheaper price than the Champagne method. It is accepted, though, that the process does reduce the quality of the bubble slightly compared with the traditional method. A distinction can be drawn between the two types of production on the label; one using this method might say something like "bottle-fermented" and another, using the traditional method, "fermented in this bottle".

Because it is a relatively technical process, the transfer method is used mainly in the New World. Although it is certainly not unknown in Europe, no one area makes a speciality of it.

THE TANK METHOD

Key wines:
Asti DOCG
Sekt

Perhaps most sparkling wine that is drunk in the world is produced by tank fermentation. This process in French is called *cuve close* and is often known as the Charmat method after the Frenchman who developed it at the beginning of the of the 20th century. In this method, the second fermentation takes place in a sealed tank (*cuve close*) rather than in a bottle. Dry base wine is placed, together with sugar and yeast, in the sealed tank and following the second fermentation the resulting sediment is removed by filtration under pressure before the wine is bottled.

The chief advantage of the tank method is its much lower cost. It does, however, tend to produce larger, more random bubbles that do not last as long as those from bottle-fermented wines. "The Art and Science of Wine" by James Halliday and Hugh Johnson describes *cuve close* wines as being "no substitute for the méthode champenoise". Whilst this is generally true, it need not necessarily be the case. Raw materials and care in production still count for much: the better the base wine, the finer the product, for instance. It is also true that the majority of tank method wines show none of the subtlety of flavour due to yeast autolysis, because this does not normally occur; but even here, current work is demonstrating that some autolysis can be induced by, for example, using paddles to stir up the sediment and bring it into contact with more of the wine during the second fermentation.

Nevertheless, under French law, no *cuve close* wine can be of AC status, but those with an extra period of ageing in the bottle can have the classification Vin Mousseux de Qualité.

Sekt
One of the most famous sparkling wines in the world, Sekt from Germany, is virtually all tank fermented, though a few of the most expensive brands are fermented in bottle. There is a large market in Germany for sparkling wine (*Schaumwein*), and in fact the *per capita* consumption is the highest in the world. Most of this is Sekt.

In legal terms, Sekt is not necessarily a German wine, but rather a wine which has been made sparkling in Germany; indeed the base wines often come from France or Italy. On the other hand, Deutscher Sekt, in addition to being made sparkling in Germany, has also to be purely from German grapes – the best being Riesling, though the higher yielding Müller-Thurgau is often used. If all the grapes for the wine come from one of the thirteen *Anbaugebieten*, then the wine can bear the superior appellation of Deutscher Sekt bA.

Asti
The Asti method is often considered to be a variation of the tank method, but it is different in that the process does not involve the initial stage of making a still wine. In the Asti Method, the sweet juice from pressed grapes is fermented to about 6% vol. and then chilled and filtered to stop the fermentation. At this stage the partially fermented must is still, not sparkling. Sugar and selected yeasts are then added and the must is put into sealed tanks to continue its fermentation. When the required alcoholic content is achieved, the wine is chilled, membrane-filtered and bottled under pressure. This means that the live yeasts have been filtered out, leaving a sparkling wine, quite light in alcohol, typically only 7 – 7.5% vol., but with a high residual sugar content. For the Asti DOCG itself, the grape used is Moscato, with its distinctly grapey aroma and taste. Asti is best drunk very young and is usually, therefore, only fermented when required, the unfermented must being held under refrigeration in the meantime.

CARBONATION
The third basic way of making a wine sparkle is by carbonation. This is the one method that does not use the carbonic gas produced as part of an alcoholic fermentation, but takes it from a cylinder. It puts bubbles in, but does not otherwise alter the wine. This is the cheapest method of all, and it shows: the bubbles are large and disappear quickly. For these reasons, the method is not used for any wine with claims to quality. In France, wine made this way has to state on the label *vin gazéifié;* such wines seem

to find their natural market as prizes on fairgrounds. In the UK, the method is only really found in sparkling light British wine.

SERVING SPARKLING WINE

The production of a good sparkling wine is not a cheap operation. In addition to the wine, there is the time involved and also the fact that the bottle has to be of very solid glass to resist the pressure of the wine, and the cork much more substantial in order to be a perfect seal. Good sparkling wine cannot be cheap and it deserves good glasses. Ideally these should be a tall tulip shape to concentrate the bubbles, and to ensure that the wine remains as cool as possible. The traditional Champagne *coupe* (yes, it really was modelled on Marie Antoinette's breast) is about as bad a glass as you could seek, as its shape might have been specifically designed to dissipate the bubbles quickly, as was that other abomination, the swizzle stick.

Because of the pressure within, great care has also to be taken when opening the bottle. The one golden rule is that it should be well chilled beforehand. Pressure and temperature being directly related, the warmer the bottle, the higher the pressure inside, and the greater the risk of the contents foaming up and out of the bottle. Bottle and cork should be held with a cloth, to provide a firmer grip. The bottle should be held firmly at an angle of about 45 ° and pointing away from anybody else before the wire muzzle is loosened and, optionally, removed. The cork should then be grasped firmly and the bottle itself turned with the emphasis on a twisting motion. Once the seal between cork and glass is broken, the pressure will be felt, and the cork should then be allowed to ease gently out. The aim is a small hiss rather than a loud bang, and no liquid loss. Because of the initial heavy mousse, at first just a little should be poured into each glass.

When tasting, one indication of the quality of a wine is its bubbles. Generally speaking long, slow bottle fermentation produces the smallest, finest bubbles. Another good sign is the length of time that the bubbles continue in the glass. In the mouth the best mousse is gentle yet persistent. However, a great deal can depend on how the glass has been washed, for detergents can quickly destroy the bubbles of even the finest Champagne.

CHAPTER 17

SHERRY AND SIMILAR WINES

Two different techniques are used in the production of liqueur wines. Either the wines are fortified after fermentation, or during fermentation. Sherry, or to give the official title of the DO, Jerez-Xérès-Sherry, is the classic liqueur wine of the first group.

SHERRY

The wine takes its name from the town of Jerez, which lies in the south of Spain, in the province of Cádiz in Andalucia. There is some dispute as to the origin of the name; does it come from "the town of Xera, near the pillars of Hercules", mentioned by the Greek writer Theopompos, or the Roman city Ceritium? Neither of these has been placed satisfactorily, but that Jerez now stands upon the site of the Moorish town of Sherish is certain.

It is probable that wine has been produced in the region since the earliest times, and winemaking continued even during the period of Arab domination, which finished with their expulsion from Sherish in 1264. Indeed, in the following year there is evidence of the Vintners' Guild being asked to raise funds for the restoration of a church.

England was an important customer for the wines of the region from perhaps as early as the reign of Henry I. In 1530, an English merchant was sentenced to a heavy fine and six months in prison for seeking to compete with the local merchants. Certainly, by Tudor times, the wines were popular here; an inventory of the Mouth Tavern, Bishopsgate Without, in London, dated 1612, includes "One ranlett of Sherry Sacke contayning sixteen gallande . . . £1 12s 0d". In 1675, in the "English Housewife", Gervase Markham says that the best sacks are those coming from Jerez and that "Sack, if it be Jerez – (as it should be) you shall know by the mark of a cork burned on one side of the bung", a remark which also gives evidence of early efforts to protect the reputation of the wines of Jerez.

It is known that English merchants had established themselves in the town in the 18th century and their number increased rapidly in the first quarter of the 19th. By the 1850s, 40% of all wine imported into Britain was Sherry.

Whilst Sherry, like all liqueur wines, has lost some of its popularity here, the United Kingdom still remains a very important market. Nevertheless, world-wide demand for the wine has fallen considerably over the past few years partly as a result of the flooding of the market with low-quality wine in the 1970s and early 1980s which damaged the region's reputation. As a result, with the support of the European Community, a considerable area of vines has been uprooted recently in order better to balance supply and demand. There has also been a move to increase the production of white table wines, though for the most part these are undistinguished.

Further, in a bid to raise once again the image of Sherry, two other steps have been taken. The first is a decree restricting the amount of stock that any company may sell on to the market in a year (usually set between 25 and 30%). This is a bid to ensure that the wine is aged sufficiently before release. The second move, which was made by a voluntary agreement on the part of all the Sherry companies, was to forbid exportation in bulk. Now, with the exception of certain state monopolies, all Sherry is bottled in the region of production. The fact that this decision was freely taken, not imposed, is important: it does not as a result run contrary to European Community law.

The Sherry Trade
It is interesting that the Sherry trade in Britain is moving in two different directions. First, overall sales appear to be declining, which may be seen as part of the general world-wide pattern of a movement away from liqueur wines. On the other hand, sales of quality Sherries, particularly the lighter ones such as Finos and Manzanillas are on the increase. In volume terms the sales to the United Kingdom are approximately 16% Finos (and rising), 27% "Medium", 24% Pale Cream and 29% Cream (and falling); sales of dry Amontillados, Olorosos and Palo Cortado are minute.

The Sherry trade is dominated by brands. These are owned by the major Sherry "houses", many of which are themselves foreign owned. These companies have their bodegas, or warehouses, in Jerez and the smaller towns of Sanlucar de Barrameda and Puerto de Santa Maria. Whilst they might own vineyards, they will also buy grapes and must from the large number of smaller vineyard owners, many of whom have grouped themselves together into co-operative cellars. In addition, there is a small group of *almacenistas,* or independent stock holders, who specialise in comparatively small parcels of high quality wine.

Soils and Vineyards

The soils of the area are split into three distinct types *albariza, arena* and *barro. Albariza* is a very compact soil with a high chalk content which gives good drainage. Muddy and slippery when wet, it dries to a hard crust which inhibits evaporation. There are a number of sub-types of this soil recognised locally, depending on the proportion of limestone which may be as much as 80% or as little as 30%. In the sunshine, the vineyards on this soil are a dazzling white due to the strong reflections off the chalk. *Albariza* accounts for about 62% of the total vineyard area and is mainly found in the heartland of the Sherry region, in the rolling hills between

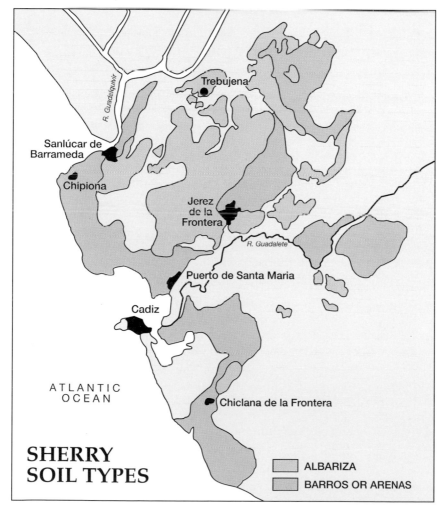

SHERRY SOIL TYPES

ALBARIZA
BARROS OR ARENAS

Contrasting brilliant white albariza soil in the background with browner soil in front.

Jerez and the Guadalquivir river. It is here that the finest wines are made, with of good acidity and high alcohol content.

Amongst the best vineyards, or *pagos*, in this region are Miraflores, towards the town of Sanlucar de Barrameda at the mouth of the Guadalquivir, Cuadrados and Balbaina on the road from Sanlucar to Jerez, and Macharnudo, Carrascal and Añina to the north and west of the latter city. Occasionally, these names can be found upon labels.

The second soil is *arena*, or sand. *Arena* contains a proportion of iron-oxide which gives it a russet brown colour, though its subsoil is often chalky. Productive and easy to work, its wines generally lack subtlety. The vineyards found on this soil are mainly to the north and east of Chipiona. The best *arenas pago* is Montealegre. The sand is compacted and accounts for 70% of the composition, with the limestone 10% or less.

The final soil is *barro*, or dark clay. This is the richest soil, lying on the lower land, mainly in the south-east of the region. It will give higher yields, its product having more body but less quality than that of *albariza*. As it is very fertile, weeds are a bigger problem and more ploughing is needed as the ground tends to crack in the summer heat.

Climate
The climate has been described as sub-tropical, with the average temperatures being 10.7 °C in the winter and 23.7 °C in the summer. The sun shines on almost three hundred days in any year.

The average rainfall is high for Spain, just under 650 mm, but most of this falls between October and May. Water, during the summer, therefore, is a precious commodity and must be carefully husbanded. For this purpose, collection troughs known as *serpias* may be dug between the rows of vines.

When all this is interpreted, it means that there is a very long ripening season for the grape, though drought can prove to be a problem.

Grape Varieties

At the beginning of the 19th century, it was reported that there were more than forty different grape varieties grown in the region. Nowadays, these have been reduced to just three.

The most important of these by far is Palomino (the Listan of southern France), which accounts for more than 90% of the total production. This is one of those varieties that appears to come into its own in just one wine – and that is Sherry. Elsewhere it seems incapable of giving a wine of distinction. The *albariza* soil of Jerez, where it is planted, must be its lifeblood, for here it is the base of almost every wine.

The grape is very thin-skinned and this can lead to the fruit splitting, causing rot in the period running up to the vintage. There is always a conflict as to when it should be picked: early so as to retain acidity, or late to give alcohol, and lessen the need for fortification spirit on which a high tax is payable. In either event it is picked by hand because of its delicate nature and susceptibility to damage, and the workers can be seen carefully placing their pickings in plastic boxes each containing just 15–17 kg of grapes. Clonal selection is widely used to improve quality and the Palomino Fino is now replacing the Palomino de Jerez.

The second grape is Pedro Ximénez, which is reputedly named after Peter Siemens, a soldier in the army of the Emperor Charles V, who is supposed to have introduced the variety to Andalucia from his native Germany. Some credence is given to this story, as the Pedro Ximénez, or PX as it is commonly called, bears a resemblance to the German Elbling grape. Perhaps sadly, the reality is less exciting; the variety probably arrived in Germany from its home in the Canary Islands, by way of Madeira and southern Spain.

This grape is normally planted in the lower lying vineyards on *arena* and *barro* soils and, after picking, the grapes are generally left to dry in the sun to concentrate the sugar content. The resultant wine is then used for sweetening purposes. In recent years, the area under PX has decreased considerably in the Sherry region, and the necessary grapes have been brought in from either Montilla or Málaga – which is permitted by the Sherry DO.

The third variety is Moscatel planted mainly on the poorer *barro* and *arena* soils, particularly near the coastal towns of Chipiona and Rota. Whilst important quantities of pure Moscatel Sherry are drunk in the local bars, overall it is of little comparative importance. Small quantities are also used as a sweetening wine.

Viticulture
Yields in Jerez, as elsewhere, vary considerably from vintage to vintage, but the average is around 65 hl/ha, with a maximum of 80 hl/ha being permitted in the finer vineyards and 100 hl/ha in the more peripheral regions. Soils are fertilised with manure every three to five years in order to maintain, but not increase, the yield level.

The traditional planting space in the vineyards was 1.5 m between the vines and 1.5 m between the rows. Now, in order to let the tractors pass more freely, the vines are planted 1 m apart with 2 m between the rows. The vines used to be free-standing with the producing branches supported by props. Now, wire training is becoming much more common.

The pruning technique used in Jerez is an adaptation of the single Guyot system. The vine is pruned so that the producing cane with eight or so buds is left, together with the spur for the following year which is cut back to a maximum of two buds. These are known, respectively, as the *espada* (sword) or *vara* (finger), and the *pulgar* (thumb). The productive life of a vine is perceived to be between thirty-five and forty years.

The main problems in the vineyards are rot and mildew due to early summer rains, and chlorosis due to the high limestone content of the soil.

Vinification
The vintage normally begins during the first week of September. When the grapes are picked, the Pedro Ximénez bunches are spread out in the sun to increase their sugar content. Plastic tunnels have largely replaced the traditional grass mats for this process. On the other hand, the Palomino grapes are pressed immediately. As the temperature at vintage time can be very high, there is a real danger of oxidation, so press-houses are often established out in the vineyards. Pressing is now generally carried out with horizontal (Vaslin or Willmes) presses. The first 70%, mainly free run, juice is used for Finos and the light Sherry styles; the next 20% or so up to the limit of 72.5 l per 100 kg of grapes for Olorosos and more coarse styles. The balance is sent for distillation.

Traditionally gypsum *(yeso)* was sprinkled on the grapes before they were pressed, partly as an antiseptic, partly to help with the precipitation of tartrates and partly to increase the acidity. This is one of the oldest winemaking practices in the world, having been recommended by such classical writers on the matter as Columella and Pliny. During the last century, the medical world split into two as to whether this was harmful or not, with the controversy lasting for many years, and the medical magazine, "The Lancet", sending a commission of enquiry to Jerez in 1898. This found that "it refines the wine and increases its power to develop those fragrant ethers which give to the wine its peculiarly pleasant characters in regard to bouquet, flavour and agreeable stimulating qualities". Notwithstanding this paean of praise, the practice of "plastering" as it was called has now largely disappeared. After pressing, acidification with tartaric acid is now commonplace.

The juice is held for 24 hours with SO_2 to clear. Normally, it is then pumped into stainless steel tanks where fermentation utilising specially cultured yeasts takes place. Occasionally, however, traditional 600 litre oak butts may still be used. The tanks are cooled to between 25 and 30 °C. These temperatures are higher than normal for the fermentation of white wines. Attempts have been made to reduce them, at cooler levels, however, it has not been possible to produce the aldehydes and other constituents that give Sherry its distinctive taste. It is important to realise that all Sherries are fermented dry. Any sweetness is added later.

Classification

There are two different basic styles of Sherry, Fino and Oloroso. The development of these owes as much to nature as to the winemaker. Whilst it is true that, for example, a Fino will generally be made from Palomino grapes grown on *albariza* soil, this is not necessarily the case.

The future of a wine can, however, be recognised when it is still very young. Soon after the first fermentation has finished, in December or

January following the vintage, each tank or cask is tasted and the wine in it classified.

The *capataz* or head cellarman will take samples in order to decide on each wine's future. If it is going to be a Fino, it will be marked with one stroke (una raya), /, if it is going to be an Oloroso, *dos rayas*, //. Even at this early stage, there will be growing on the surface of potential Finos, a yeast, known as flor. So as not to disturb this growing layer of flor the *capataz* collects his sample, in the case of butts, using the traditional and distinctive *venencia*.

Flor has an important effect on the wines that develop beneath its surface. To exist, it feeds on oxygen, alcohol and glycerine and in the process reduces the overall acidity in the wine. As it provides a protective blanket on the surface of the wine, it also prevents oxidation which, by contrast, is necessary for Oloroso Sherries. It also increases the level of acetaldehyde, which is responsible for the individual flavour of Fino Sherries. The optimum alcoholic level for flor to function is between 15 and 15.5%. Additionally, the heat of summer and cold of winter both inhibit the action of flor which works best at temperatures of between 15 and 20 °C. Therefore in Jerez it is most active in the spring and autumn. Its sensitivity to ambience is such that even microclimates of individual *bodegas* will influence the styles of the maturing Sherry. For optimum effect flor needs to be refreshed periodically and this is achieved by the periodic replenishment of maturing wine as part of the *solera* system described below.

Fortification

Once the selection of styles is made the wines are fortified with *mitad y mitad* – an equal mixture of spirit at 95.5% vol. and old wine at 12%, the latter used to reduce the "shock" to young wine. Until this fortification, both must and young wine are referred to as *mosta*. Finos are fortified to 15.5%, the optimum for the growth of flor, and Olorosos to 18% which prevents the yeast's growth.

Maturation

As Sherry is not sold as a vintage wine, but rather under a number of brand names, continuity of style and quality over the years is important. The way of achieving this consistency is by a form of fractional blending that was first developed in Jerez, known as the *solera* system.

Following their initial fortification, the wines are then racked from tank into clean butts until the latter are about 5/6ths full. Fino butts need to be inoculated with flor at this stage. All wines enter the preliminary stage of the *solera* system unblended, in what is known as the *añada* (the term is also used to describe the young wine before maturation and blending). After a further six months the Finos will then be split again into potential Finos and the more full-bodied Amontillados. These latter have a less thick flor. On the other hand the Olorosos are often stored outside so that the heat from the sun can increase the degree of oxidation.

Each style of wine will have its own *solera*, which is comprised of a number of different *criaderas*, or parcels of the same wine at a particular stage of ageing. The oldest *criadera* is known as the *solera* itself. When a quantity of a given wine is required for bottling, an equal amount is drawn out of each of the butts in the *solera*; this is replaced with an equal amount from each butt in the next oldest, and so on, with the youngest

THE SOLERA SYSTEM

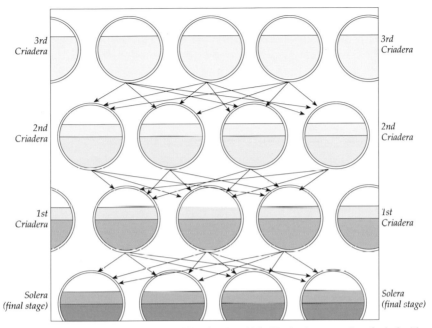

3rd Criadera — 3rd Criadera

2nd Criadera — 2nd Criadera

1st Criadera — 1st Criadera

Solera (final stage) — Solera (final stage)

The solera system is a method of fractional blending in which old wine is constantly refreshed with younger wine. To ensure consistency, wine is taken from each butt in one criadera to be blended in to each butt of the next.

Running the scales in a solera.

being topped up from the *añada*. This operation is called "running the scales" and is now usually mechanised except in the finest of *bodegas*. It can be complex and time consuming as care must be taken to blend horizontally as well as vertically. That is to say each butt being replenished with younger wine must receive wine from a number of "younger" butts. No more than a third can be drawn out of any one butt at any one time, and if as much as that is drawn out, the operation cannot take place more than three times in any one year. Usually less is drawn out, around 20% as a rule of thumb.

Effectively, this all means that in any one *solera*, there should remain an amount, albeit perpetually diminishing, of the original wine – and some *soleras*, in the older Sherry houses, were established more than a century and a half ago. Whilst no Sherries are vintage-dated, there are a number that might be *solera* dated.

Temperature control is important throughout the *solera* cycle. *Bodegas* are designed with high roofs to keep temperatures correct and to provide circulation. They are often watered to raise the humidity. Finos are normally to be found on the bottom tier of butts where the temperature is lowest.

Cathedral-like maturation bodegas help to maintain cool, even temperatures for the maturation of Sherry.

Finishing

Once the wine has finished ageing in the *solera*, five years for Finos, five to ten for the commercial styles such as Amontillados and Creams and up to 25 years or so for certain premium wines, it will undergo a variety of treatments to prepare it for bottling and sale.

The wine may be fortified again at this point, to standardize the strength and to meet a required style or character. As when first fortified, the tendency is for Finos to be more lightly fortified than the other styles. Also, the alcohol levels at which a wine is sold may well vary from country to country.

It is also at this stage that the wine may be sweetened or coloured by the addition of fortified sweetening wines and / or *vino de color* to produce the required style. The wine is sweetened by adding PX and Moscatel for the Creams and Palomino for the lighter types. These sweetening wines are either made from grapes which have been sunned to increase their sugar content before pressing and fortification or are concentrated grape juice. *Vino de color* is produced by boiling must to caramelise it and to reduce it in volume, this is then mixed with fresh must, fermented and matured.

After these blendings the alcohol level might require a final adjustment. The key point of the whole blending process which of course starts in the *solera* is to create the individual style required in the first place and thereafter to maintain consistency.

Sherry tends to have a naturally high tartrate content which might cause a crystalline deposit in the bottle in cold climates or when chilled. Before bottling, therefore, the bulk wine is chilled to –8 °C and kept at that temperature for 8 days in order to precipitate the tartrates. It is then normally fined and filtered to leave the wine star bright. The traditional fining agent is egg-white and this is still used for the finest wines. Usually, however, bentonite and gelatine are now employed. Kieselguhr is still used for filtration as are cellulose microfilters. Some fine wines are not filtered and therefore may throw a deposit in the bottle. Finally, the Sherry is cold sterile-bottled sometimes with screw caps and plastic seals under a blanket of inert nitrogen to ensure freshness.

Sherry Styles
Key styles:
Fino
Manzanilla
Amontillado
Pale Cream
Oloroso
Cream
Palo Cortado

Over the years, there has developed a broad range of different styles of Sherry available to the trade. These fall into three classes: Finos, Olorosos and the in-between Palo Cortado.

Fino – This is pale in colour and should be light, dry and clean on the palate. Fino is best when drunk young since it tends to lose its freshness progressively once bottled.

Manzanilla – This is a Fino which has been aged in *bodegas* in the seaside town of Sanlucar de Barrameda. Because of the cooler climate, the flor remains active throughout the year, rather than in the spring and autumn as with wines matured in Jerez, thereby imparting a different character. The wine has a delicate salty tang but this is not directly connected with any proximity to the sea!

Manzanilla Pasada – An older Manzanilla, which has lost some of its crispness, but has a more concentrated flavour.

Amontillado – An aged Fino from which the flor has died away. Somewhat higher in alcohol than a classic Fino, two styles exist. The first is naturally dry, the other sweetened to become medium or medium-dry. The latter style is more common in the United Kingdom. All should be browny-yellow in colour and have a full, nutty flavour. The name comes from the neighbouring vineyard area of Montilla. Literally, it suggests that the wine has been "Montilla-ised".

Pale cream – The latest addition to the Sherry family. It is a Fino that has been sweetened by the addition of concentrated must to give wines which are light in both colour and body.

Oloroso – A full-bodied, russet-coloured dry wine, rich and nutty, which ages well. It has been often adapted to the taste of individual markets to give such wines as:

Amoroso – A softly sweetened Oloroso. The term Bristol Milk has been used generically for such a wine.

Cream – An Oloroso which has been sweetened by the addition of PX or Moscatel wine.

Brown Sherry – This seems to have gone out of fashion. This is a cream Sherry to which *vino de color* has been added.

Moscatel – The dessert wine made from the grape of the same name.

Pedro Ximénez – The finest dessert wine of Jerez, made from sun-dried grapes. Very dark and sweet it can achieve a sugar content as high as 400 g/l and has a very concentrated, grapey flavour.

Palo Cortado – A rare style of wine that is clean on the nose like an Amontillado, but has the full body of a dry Oloroso.

Storage and Service
Fino Sherry, as previously intimated, needs to be sold soon after bottling and should be consumed soon after opening. Half-bottles as commonly

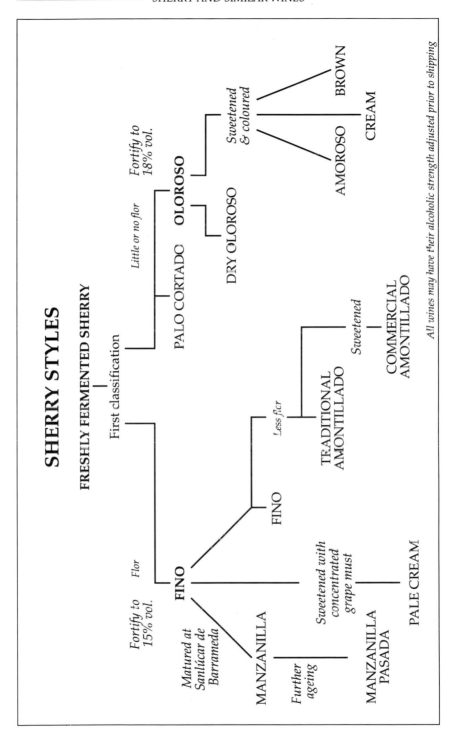

SHERRY STYLES

FRESHLY FERMENTED SHERRY

First classification

Fortify to 15% vol.   *Flor*

FINO

Matured at Sanlúcar de Barrameda

MANZANILLA

Further ageing

MANZANILLA PASADA

Sweetened with concentrated grape must

PALE CREAM

FINO

Less flor

TRADITIONAL AMONTILLADO

Sweetened

COMMERCIAL AMONTILLADO

Little or no flor   *Fortify to 18% vol.*

PALO CORTADO   **OLOROSO**

DRY OLOROSO

Sweetened & coloured

AMOROSO   BROWN

CREAM

All wines may have their alcoholic strength adjusted prior to shipping

COPITA

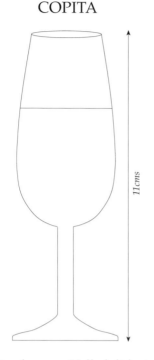

11cms

used in Spain are therefore ideal but not widely seen in the UK. Whilst freshness is not as critical for other styles of Sherry, even these will lose their finesse a week or so after opening. Finos should be served chilled, Amontillados and the sweeter styles should not. The best glasses are *copitas*, literally "little glass", which have a narrow top to concentrate aromas. The often seen Elgin style of glass is totally unsuitable.

OTHER SPANISH FORTIFIED AND SHERRY STYLE WINES

In Spain, liqueur wines are known as *vinos generosos* and a number are made in other regions apart from Jerez. These include the neighbouring Huelva, Gandia in Catalonia and Rueda near Valladolid. As far as international markets are concerned, however, the only one of any importance is Montilla.

Montilla

Officially known as Montilla-Moriles, the wines of this DO come from the province of Cordoba in southern Spain, to the north-east of the Sherry producing area. Indeed, Montilla for long formed part of the Sherry region and is still the main supplier of Pedro Ximénez wine for Sherry – as well as giving rise to the term Amontillado. One of the main differences from Sherry is that the wines achieve naturally high levels of alcohol to the extent that fortification is the exception rather than the rule. They are covered in this chapter because they are much closer in style to Sherry than to any light wine.

Commercially, Montilla has found its niche on the British supermarket shelves for the very simple reason that its wines can fall into a lower tax band than Sherry and so be cheaper. This is because the current relevant United Kingdom tax break point occurs at 15% volume of alcohol whilst the range of natural alcohol found in Montillas is 14% to 16%. Perhaps sadly therefore, because the majority of these wines imported are below 15% in alcohol, Montillas have come to be accepted as a cheap substitute for Sherry, when in fact there are some great distinctive wines produced.

All the same styles as for Sherry are found: Finos, Amontillados and Olorosos. However, the use of these terms is related by law to minimum alcohol content: 15% for Fino and 16% for Amontillado and Oloroso. The United Kingdom market, therefore, rarely sees these terms on Montilla labels but rather the more bland expressions dry, medium and cream.

The town of Montilla lies at the centre of the vineyard region and it is here that many of the larger *bodegas* are established. Being inland, the climate has rather more extremes than that of the Sherry region, with the temperature in the summer frequently topping 40 °C. The rainfall is also rather higher, falling in the winter.

The soils are of two types: there are the chalky *alberos*, similar to the *albarizas* of Jerez and the reddish, compact loam *ruedos*, which are found more to the centre and the west of the region.

More than 90% of the vineyard area is planted in Pedro Ximénez grapes, though the Lairen, Baladi, Moscatel and Torrontes are also permitted.

At the vintage, there are three qualities of juice: the free-run is put on one side for Finos, that from the first pressing is used for Olorosos and from the second for distillation. Fermentation generally takes place in the traditional concrete *tinajas*. Subsequently, flor occurs on some casks which will lead to Fino style wines being produced. Oloroso styles are kept in butts with no ullage in order to prevent the growth of flor. Ageing is carried out in butts in *bodegas* utilising the *solera* system.

OTHER SHERRY TYPE LIQUEUR WINES

Marsala
Marsala, which takes its name from the town found on the westernmost promontory of Sicily, is a liqueur wine that owes its creation to the British, in this case the Liverpool merchant John Woodhouse in 1773. Twenty years or so on, it came to the notice of Lord Nelson and in the process gained early wide fame. Nelson's victuallers bought it as an alternative to rum for his Mediterranean fleet before the Battle of the Nile in 1798.

It is made from fully fermented wine, the produce of Catarratto, Grillo and Inzolia grapes, fortified with grape spirit and sweetened, either with boiled down must (*mosto cotto*), or with grape juice whose fermentation has been stopped with spirit (*mistela*). The older wines are then aged in a form of the *solera* system.

For a long time, Marsala's reputation was debased by the permitted admixture of a number of flavourings, such as egg-yolks or coffee. The DOC has now been revised to exclude them; although they are still produced by a number of firms, they do not carry the name Marsala.

The DOC allows the following qualities:

Fine – 1 year's ageing.
Superiore – 2 years' ageing.
Superiore Riserva – 4 years' ageing.
Vergine or Solera – 5 years' ageing.
Vergine Stravecchio or Vergine Riserva – over 10 years' ageing.

Note that no sweetening may be added to Vergine wine.

Marsala is also classified by colour:

Ambra – Amber.
Oro – Gold – no *mosto cotto* allowed.
Rubino – Ruby – made from red grapes, new and still rare.

At its best it is a most agreeable complex wine – at the lower levels much goes for cooking.

The New World
In new vineyard areas, fortified wines have often dominated early production, largely because they are easier to preserve and also because it makes them better able to support shipment to foreign markets.

It is not surprising therefore that, such countries as Australia, New Zealand and South Africa have had wine industries that were for long dominated by the production of liqueur wines, in the style of both Sherry and Port. Generally speaking, the importance of such wines has been overtaken by the increasing demand for lower strength drinks, and as a result, light wines.

Often it was Palomino that was first planted for the production, but, generally speaking, it has never been as successful as in its home Sherry region. In South Africa, for example, the Chenin Blanc has proved to be more adaptable.

Where flor has not occurred naturally, for the making of Fino wines, it has been cultivated and injected into the wines.

British, Irish and Cyprus Fortified Wines
None of these wines may be described as simply "Sherry" which may only be used for the Spanish product. Until 31st December 1995 they were sold as British Sherry, Irish Sherry and Cyprus Sherry but from 1st January 1996 the British and Irish products will have to be labelled as Fortified British Wine, Fortified Irish Wine respectively, with the Cypriot version being sold as Cyprus Fortified Wine. The term "British Wine" cannot be split, so whist "Sweet Fortified British Wine" is permissible, "Fortified British Sweet Wine" is not.

British and Irish Sherries are fermented from imported concentrated must and then fortified. Currently, these products enjoy favourable tax advantages and sales outstrip those of genuine Sherry.

VERMOUTHS AND AROMATISED WINES

The history of vermouth is in many ways similar to that of many liqueurs. It dates back to medieval times when the goodness of wild herbs was preserved by steeping them in either wine, in the case of vermouth, or spirit in the case of liqueurs. Both were often prepared by monasteries for medicinal purposes.

Whilst there is no reason why vermouths should not be made anywhere where there is a plentiful supply of base white wine, the main centres of production have traditionally included Turin in Italy and Chambéry in the Savoie region of France.

Vermouth takes its name from the German word Wermut, which means wormwood, an essential ingredient. Each company will have its own formula for each of the qualities that it makes. These may include spices and fruits as well as herbs. These are macerated in the wine, which is then sweetened with sugar and fortified. If necessary, caramel is added to achieve the necessary colour.

For the best French vermouths, the wine may be aged for up to two years, with one year being spent outside in small casks, exposed to the sun.

Chambéry vermouth is generally more delicate in flavour than other French vermouths. Whilst the base wines can come from anywhere, the vermouth has to be produced in the town of Chambéry itself to be described as such.

CHAPTER 18

PORT AND SIMILAR WINES

The wines covered in this chapter are all in the second major category of liqueur wines: those where fortification is used to stop fermentation before it is complete, by raising the level of alcohol to a point at which the fermenting yeasts can no longer work. Wherever the wines are made, therefore, and from whatever grape variety, they will all have the presence of at least some residual sugar in common; some are very sweet indeed. Port is the classic wine of this group.

PORT

Port has been described as the archetypal wine of the British and the reason for this is not difficult to discover; it was created by the British for the British market.

As early as the middle of the fourteenth century, there were trading treaties between Lisbon and Oporto and London, and by the time of the reign of Henry VIII the English had established Factories, or merchants' associations, with legal status and certain diplomatic privileges, in the ports of Lisbon, Oporto and Viana. Portuguese wines were often traded for salt fish from Newfoundland or woollen goods from England.

For preference, the English have always tended to drink French wines, but in time of war with the French have often turned to the Portuguese for their supply. For eight years from 1678, the importation of French wines was prohibited and, in 1703, the Methuen Treaty was signed between Portugal and England, which greatly increased the possibilities of trade between the two countries.

There can be little doubt that at that time the red Portuguese wines on offer must have been highly astringent and acid. The answer to these two problems had been noted by two Englishmen on a wine-buying trip to Portugal as early as 1678. At the monastery of Lamego, some 90 kilometres up the Douro from Oporto, they had tasted a soft, slightly sweet red wine, which seemed to them infinitely preferable to anything that they had come across so far. The abbot told them that he added a small amount of brandy to the wine before it finished fermenting. Over half a century passed, however, before Port was "created" commercially.

As far as trade with Britain was concerned, the first priority was to ensure that the Portuguese wines were stable enough for shipment. In order to achieve this, brandy was added to the wine just before shipment, long after the fermentation had been completed. It was not until about 1730, that it became general practice to add the spirit during fermentation, to create the style of Ports that we know today. Indeed, the rival merits of the two styles of wine were discussed well into the 19th century.

Whilst Port is considered to be a typically British drink, in fact much more is now consumed in France, where it is normally taken as an aperitif, and where the preference is for much lighter styles than are consumed here. Port sales in the United Kingdom have declined from their heyday, but sales recently have been increasing and the better quality wines have always enjoyed a steady sale. Currently the UK takes nearly ten million bottles of Port each year, with the trend being towards the higher quality Ports (Vintage, LBV, premium Ruby and aged Tawny), and away from the cheaper ruby wines.

The Port Region
The region of Port production was the first in the world to be delimited, by the Marques of Pombal in 1756. It stretches up the valley of the river

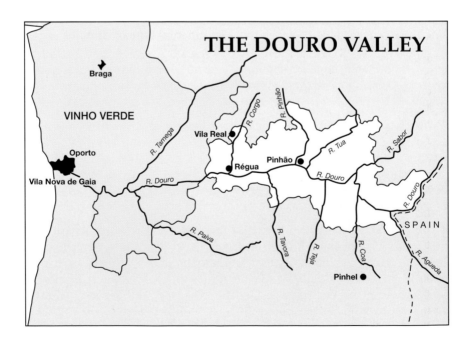

Douro and its tributaries, from just below the capital of the lower Douro, Peso da Régua (or simply Régua), to the Spanish frontier.

The trade in Port is centred upon Oporto, the main port and city in northern Portugal, second only to Lisbon in size. The nearest Port vineyards are approximately seventy kilometres away, as the crow flies, but rather further as the Douro flows. This physical separation has imposed its stamp upon the very nature of the Port trade since the trade began and has led to an ever-present underlying conflict between the merchants in the city and the growers up-country which periodically flares up into the open.

Whilst the vineyard region begins below Régua, which stands near where the Corgo flows into the Douro, the viticultural heart of the Port world lies some 20 kilometres further up river. The best wines are produced east of the point where the Douro is joined by the Pinhão tributary around the town of the same name, and it is from here on that the finest *quintas*, or vineyards, are encountered. Amongst the better known names, which might appear on labels are: Quinta do Noval, Quinta do Bomfim and Quinta da Foz.

Climate

Oporto has the distinction of being the second wettest city in Europe with an annual rainfall of 1200 mm. To the north the Vinho Verde area, it may be recalled, has a wet and warm climate strongly influenced by the Atlantic. In contrast the Douro demarcated area is hot and dry in summer and cold in the winter – a much more continental type of climate.

Rainfall and the other effects of the Atlantic diminish as one moves inland not only because of increasing distance from the ocean, but also because of the influence of the Serra do Marão. This mountain range stands to the north and west of the Douro and protects the region from the prevailing wet westerly winds. To illustrate, Régua has 900 mm of rain per annum, Pinhão 700 mm and Barca d'Alva on the Spanish frontier receives only 400 mm. Rain falls mainly in the spring and autumn, usually in very heavy and potentially damaging downpours; summer sees occasional storms.

Temperatures in the upper Douro in summer reach 40 °C and can remain as high as 30 °C into the harvest period. Frosts are widespread in winter but rarely, if ever, occur in the spring.

Grape Varieties

There can be few vineyard regions where there is such a host of grape varieties permitted. In all forty-eight are authorised though it is thought that at least twice as many as this are actually present. The traditional way of planting was to put in a selection of varieties, so in many older vineyards, and especially on small independent farms, even the growers themselves are often unsure as to what grapes they have! Larger growers, especially the shippers, are investing in block planting of single varieties taking into consideration individual microclimates and the characteristics of each variety. The final wine, though, is always a blend.

Six black varieties have assumed pre-eminence. These are:

1. *Tinta Roriz* – This is the Tempranillo of Spain, giving low yields of fruit that adds finesse to the blend. By Portuguese standards, it is something of a lightweight.

2. *Touriga Nacional* – The finest grape of the Douro, though with very low yields, perhaps a sixth of the average for the region. It gives very deep coloured, tannic juice, with a powerful aroma.

3. *Touriga Francesa* – Similar to the Nacional, but with a higher yield, and, if anything, a more powerful bouquet.

4. *Tinta Cão* – Producing very small bunches of tiny grapes, this had almost disappeared because of its resultant very low yield. Thanks to EC funded grants, however, it is now being replanted. It gives a complex wine with good tannin and colour, the products of its high skin-to-pulp ratio.

5. *Tinta Barroca* – In good years Tinta Barroca can give good yields with high sugar content, plenty of colour and a big, powerful nose. It is however an early ripener so, if not picked at the optimum time, can give a burnt flavour to the wine.

6. *Sousão* – Now perhaps more greatly appreciated for liqueur wine production in Australia and California than in the Douro. Peculiarly for a grape, it has a red flesh. This is good for colour but the wine tends to be coarse and rather low in acidity.

For the comparatively small amount of white Port that is made, six varieties are authorised of which three predominate:

Rabigato – This gives high yields of undistinguished wine with a high degree of alcohol.

Codega and Malvasia Fina – These are perhaps the best of the white grapes and consistently maintain a balanced acidity.

Topography, Soil and Viticulture
Over the centuries the River Douro has cut a deep steep-sided ravine through the largely granite rock formations. Even the more manageable slopes have gradients in excess of 60%. As Hugh Johnson, in his "World Atlas of Wine", has written, "Of all the places where men have planted

Different styles of terracing in the Alto Douro just west of Pinhão, with patamares on the left, socalcos on the right and uncultivated land below, with the vertical strata of schist exposed.

vineyards, the upper Douro is the most improbable. To begin with there was not even soil: only 60% slopes of slate and granite, flaking and unstable, baked in a 100 °F sun. It was a land of utter desolation."

Originally, the vines were planted on narrow terraces that were hewn out of schistous rock, and with the soil retained by dry-stone walling. Often these terraces, known as *socalcos*, have no more than two or three rows of vines, rarely more than a dozen. Fortunately, the schist frequently lies in vertical strata which permits the vines' roots to penetrate very deep to reach water and nourishment. Vineyard planting was more akin to quarrying than agriculture and must have been back-breaking. Now, bulldozers and even explosives create more viable, commercial, contoured vineyards (*patamares*) with erosion being minimised by earth embankments, and weed ground cover encouraged. Some vines are trained on wires up the hillside. On less steep slopes this method, known as *vinha ao alto*, has proved reasonably successful but on steeper gradients erosion, due to the topsoil being washed away, can be a problem.

Vineyard Classification
In order to try to maintain stability in the market, every year each vineyard is notified of the volume of Port that it is allowed to produce in that vintage. The allocation is based overall on an analysis of sales against stocks held, and distributed on a rating system for each vineyard which,

Cutting vineyard terraces in the Douro valley is more akin to quarry work than agriculture. Often dynamite is needed and the new patamares vineyards are cut by bulldozer.

in turn, is based on a number of different factors. In decreasing order of importance, these are:

Low yield
Altitude
Soil composition
Locality
Training of vines
Grape varieties planted
Degree of slope
Exposure to sun
Spacing of vines
Shelter from prevailing winds
Age of vines.

Evidently, the grower can control some of these factors, others not. The classification divides the vineyards into five ratings, from A to E; about 75% is rated either C or D. In addition to the production allowed, the price that is paid for the Port will also depend upon the vineyard's classification.

This allocation is only for production of Port; the grower still has the possibility of producing additional quantities of light wine with the DOC Douro, though the price that he can obtain is normally only about a third of that for Port.

Vinification

Maximum and speedy extraction of colour and tannin is of great importance at vintage time. The traditional method employed to achieve this is treading. Grapes, either crushed or uncrushed, are loaded into granite troughs or *lagares* and then trodden under foot by teams of workers, mainly male, over a period of up to twelve hours. The first two hours of a shift consist of regimented marching up and down, then follows a further two hour period of general dancing around. The treading often continues well into the night to the accompaniment of music. During the subsequent fermentation, the cap is kept submerged by manually pushing it down with paddles or by pumping over. The practice still takes place on some of the finest *quintas*, for the best quality Ports and for nearly all Ports destined to be declared Vintage, because although labour intensive, it is very effective.

Nevertheless only a small percentage of all Port is made this way. Now, tradition has generally been superseded by labour-saving, more cost-effective mechanisation. *Lagares* and human feet have been replaced by autovinifiers and by electric pumps. In the autovinification process the grapes are put in a sealed vat and the pressure of CO_2 is used to force the juice up through pipes to spray over the cap. About two-thirds of all Port is made in this way. The savings in labour costs are considerable. It has been estimated that treading by foot needs twenty man-hours per pipe of wine, whilst an autovinifier needs no more than half a man-hour per pipe. Another attraction of this method is that the autovinifiers do not need an outside power source and therefore may be used even in the most remote parts of the region.

The other modern method, which accounts for a little under one third of production, is pumping over, *remontagem*, the usual method of colour and tannin extraction in most other European vineyard areas. Only the wider installation of mains power is needed to make this more generally used. It has the advantage of using standard winery equipment.

Old style of concrete autovinifiers viewed from below, with modern stainless steel version being installed on right.

AUTOVINIFICATION

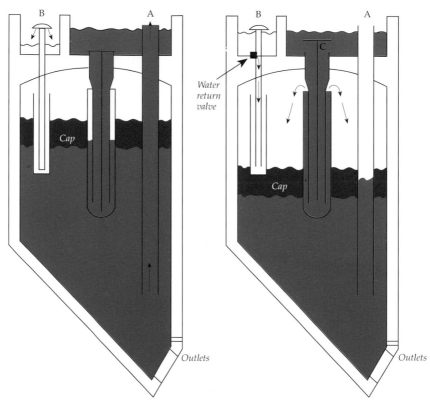

Grapes are crushed and loaded into the sealable, lower section of the autovinifier. As fermentation occurs, pressure builds up and forces must up column, A, into the open trough at the top. When a pre-determined pressure is reached the water valve, B, releases the gas pressure and the weight of the must forces it down the central column, C, and over the cap, submerging it and extracting both colour and tannin. The cycle is repeated every twenty minutes for the whole of the fermentation period, one and a half to two days.

Fortification

When the sugar in the must has been converted to between 6 and 9% vol., the must is run off and fortified. Spirit at 77% is added, in the proportion of one part spirit to four parts wine, which kills the yeasts and stops fermentation. Whilst the spirit must have a grape base, it can come from any country within the European Community and, usually, overspills from either the French or Italian wine lakes. The decision as to when to fortify depends upon the sweetness required in the final product. Maceration does not continue after fortification as alcohol is too powerful a solvent of harsh tannins.

Maturation and Wine styles
Key Port styles:
Ruby
Tawny
Tawny with Indicated Age
Vintage Character
Crusting
Late Bottled Vintage
Colheita
Vintage
Single Quinta Vintage

In the spring following fortification, the wine is transferred to the shippers' warehouses, known as lodges, in Vila Nova de Gaia. Here, on the south bank of the Douro opposite Oporto, the more temperate climate is better suited for maturation. Little wine is stored up the Douro, as the high summer temperatures are said to give it a peculiar burnt taste. It is aged in the lodges in traditional casks or pipes of either 550 or 534 litres capacity. The production or Douro pipe contains 550 litres and the shipping or Gaia pipe 534 l. Traditionally, the wines used to be brought down the river by special boats, the *barcos rabelos*, but since the river has been dammed for hydroelectric purposes, this is no longer feasible and the wines are transported by road tanker. A number of the boats are still maintained, however, for publicity purposes.

There are a number of different styles of wine on the market, depending

Vila Nova de Gaia is where most of the Port Houses have their maturation lodges, each with the shipper's name emblazoned on the roof. The flat bottomed barcos rabelos are now moored at Vila Nova de Gaia as a tourist attraction.

on the quality of the wine, whether it is the product of a single year or a blend of several, and how it has been aged. Maturation is either in wood or in bottle, and for a shorter or longer period of time. Starting with the three basic commercial Ports styles, they are:

White Ports – Made from white grapes, these are generally golden in colour and can be either almost fully dry or sweet. The label should say which. They are non-vintage, wood-matured and usually sold at two to three years old.

Ruby Ports – These are young, non-vintage, full-bodied wines. They are wood-matured and normally sold at three years old, though some better quality wines labelled "Reserve" will be aged for about six years. Traditionally, Ruby has been a popular Port style in the UK.

Tawny Ports – These fall into a variety of qualities. At its cheapest, a Tawny is a blend of ruby and white Ports. Such a wine can be recognised by having a pink rim. More expensive Tawnies develop only after extended ageing in cask. They are very soft and smooth and can be recognised by having a more russet, or tawny, rim. They are a blend of different years.

Tawny Ports with an Indication of Age – Under the regulations wines can be labelled only as 10, 20, 30 and over 40 years old. To qualify for such a label, the shipper must show that he has stock of sufficient wine of that age in his lodge and the wine must be of a character consistent with the age stated. The age stated may therefore, in effect, be an average rather than a minimum. The label must state the year of bottling and that the wine was aged in wood. These are the finest Tawny Ports; the best are amongst the finest wines of the region. They do not throw a sediment and therefore do not need to be decanted. After opening, they will last a few weeks.

Vintage Character Port – This is a blend of high quality wines from one or more vintages that is matured in wood for up to five years before bottling. It is full-bodied with rich fruit, and ready for drinking when bottled.

Crusted, or Crusting Port – This is a British speciality and not a recognised style in Portugal. It is a high quality ruby wine of more than one vintage that is bottled young and forms a sediment ("crusts") whilst it matures in bottle. It therefore needs decanting.

Late Bottled Vintage Port (LBV) – This a wine from a specific vintage, but not necessarily a "Declared Year" (see Vintage Port below), that has been aged in cask for between four and six years before bottling. The traditional style of LBV is bottled after four years and continues to improve in the bottle. This wine needs to be decanted; commercial production of this style is now limited. The modern style is matured in cask for six years and is bottled when ready for consumption; it need not be decanted and tends to be more full-bodied than its forebear. Until recently, LBV Ports had never been from the same year as a Vintage Port but now some companies will produce both wines with the same vintage. The label of an LBV wine must state the year of bottling as well as the vintage. Irrespective of style, all LBV Ports can be kept for a few weeks after opening.

Colheita Port – This is a wine of a single vintage that has been aged in cask until shortly before sale. The minimum period is eight years; in practice it is often aged for much longer. Effectively, it is a very fine old Tawny and therefore does not need decanting. As well as the vintage, the label must state that the wine has been aged in cask, and show when it was bottled. This style is very popular in Portugal and is only now coming on to the British market.

Vintage Port – This is one of the longest-lived wines produced. It is an exceptional product of one particular year, typically from the best vineyards only, that is bottled when it is only two years old. Very full, rich and tannic when young, Vintage Port matures slowly and is unlikely to reach its peak before it is twenty years old. It will throw a heavy deposit and should be decanted and then consumed within a few days. Each company can decide whether it wishes to "declare" a year as a vintage. There is not always agreement between the houses as to which is a vintage year. For example some companies declared both the 1982 and the 1983, some just the 1982 and others just the 1983. 1985, on the other hand, was almost unanimously declared.

Single Quinta Vintage Ports – These are full Vintage Ports that are the product of one single vineyard or *quinta*, often the flagship of a shipper's vineyard holdings. Like Vintage Port, they are not made every year. Being effectively the best vineyards of the region, the fruit they produce may be of high enough quality for a Vintage wine to be made, albeit in limited quantities, in years which do not warrant a full Vintage declaration. This is the option most shippers take; in the years when they do make a full Vintage declaration, the single *quinta's* wines join others in the shippers' Vintage Port. Single *quinta* wines are commonly held by the shippers for release when they are relatively mature.

The Port Wine Trade
Within the trade there are five official bodies which have a major role to play:

1. Instituto do Vinho do Porto (IVP) – This is a Government appointed body that oversees the trade generally and is based in Oporto. Its functions include research, PR and control of the market.

2. *Casa do Douro* – Based in Régua, the Casa do Douro represents the growers. Until recently it has had a monopoly on the supply and distribution of fortifying spirit. Controversially in 1990, it purchased a majority holding in a major Port company.

3. *Associação dos Exportadores do Vinho do Porto (the Port Wine Shippers' Association)* – This is a voluntary grouping of the exporting companies with lodges in Vila Nova de Gaia. It represents the merchants' interests.

4. *Associação dos Vinhos de Quinta (AVEPOD)* – Since 1986, growers have had the right to export their own wines directly, thus by-passing the merchants. This grouping represents the interests the growers taking advantage of this development.

5. *Comissão Interprofissional da Região Demarcada do Douro (CIRDD)* – A new group representing both traders and growers which has recently been formed to take over some of the regulatory functions of both the Casa do Douro and the IVP.

MADEIRA

The island of Madeira, a province of Portugal, and hence part of the European Community, lies in the North Atlantic Ocean, approximately 500 kilometres west of the Moroccan port of Casablanca and some 1100 from Lisbon. Its clement year-round climate is induced in part by the warm, moist trade winds on the path of which it sits. Apart from the few days in the summer when the Sirocco blows, and the temperature can reach 40 °C, it suffers no extremes of climate.

The product of ancient volcanic action, the island rises sheer out of the sea. There are no beaches and very little flat land; steep-sided ravines cut by rivers over the centuries lace the hinterland. Madeira measures approximately 23 kilometres from north to south and 60 east to west, and rises to nearly 2,000 m in the middle. It is extremely fertile, being covered with volcanic soil. Originally, it was densely forested, but in the 15th century all the trees were burnt to clear land for planting and grazing. The resulting high potash content is still considered to be a special factor in the soil.

As Madeira proved a useful revictualling point on voyages to the Americas, from as early as the middle of the 17th century its wines were shipped to the West Indies and North America. By the end of that century there were at least thirty companies established on the island specialising in the wine trade, with a third of them being English-owned.

The major British shippers now have an association, the Madeira Wine Company; the trade overall is controlled by the Instituto do Vinho da

Madeira. France is the most important export market for Madeira, though much of the wine shipped there is for culinary purposes.

The island has a very lush vegetation and is intensely cultivated. At sea-level, tropical and sub-tropical fruits are grown, whilst at the highest altitudes Douglas firs abound. In between, other fruits and crops vie for that land that is workable. Most vineyards are situated on hillside terraces and the vines generally trained on pergolas, to permit the growth of other crops underneath. Rain falls mainly on the high ground and is channelled down to farmers below by a system of aqueducts called *levadas*.

Grape Varieties and Wine Styles
Key Madeira styles:
Sercial
Verdelho
Bual
Malmsey

Following the ravages of phylloxera, the island was widely planted with American vine species and hybrids. Indeed, these still account for more than half the vineyard acreage, but since 1979 their grapes have been forbidden in the production of Madeira wine. They are still grown for local table wine production. As recently as 1982, two-thirds of the production of wine on the island was from such varieties. The EC has given grants to help with the uprooting of these vines and replanting costs.

By tradition, the wines of Madeira have been named after four local white grape varieties: Sercial, Verdelho, Bual and Malmsey (Malvasia). However, over the years these have come to be no more than styles, rather than any guarantee of the actual source of the wine. This practice too is being altered under EC regulations and now, if a specific grape name is shown on the label, the wine must contain at least 85% of that variety. Thus, many of the wines previously labelled as Sercial or Malmsey, and so on, but in fact made from other grapes, now appear under a brand or style name such as "Island Dry" or "Island Rich". One such name of long standing is "Rainwater", a name given to a style of off-dry Madeira.

The main grape varieties grown for the production of Madeira, are therefore these:

Sercial – Said by some to be related to Riesling, it produces the driest Madeira wines, not reaching their best until they are ten or more years old. Sercial is very rare and thrives best at higher altitudes.

Verdelho – Grows best on lower slopes and is used to make wine in a medium-dry style. It is an early ripener, and is now also planted in Australia.

Bual – Also seen labelled as "Boal", it is, like Sercial, rare. Strangely, it has hairy leaves and grows best in the higher vineyards. The wine made from it is rich and medium-sweet in style, but with a dryish finish.

Malmsey – This is the Malvasia, a grape that produces the sweetest of all Madeiras. It ripens late and crops best close to sea-level.

Tinta Negra Mole – It has been suggested that this black variety is the result of a cross between Pinot Noir and Grenache, though there seems to be little evidence for this. Among those varieties permitted for the production of Madeira, it is the most widely planted on the island. It gives wines high in alcohol and is capable of adding acidity tannin and colour, when needed. Indeed, some say that it can impart the individual characteristic of each of the four noble varieties described above, depending on the altitude at which it is planted. That said, Tinta Negra Mole is not used for high quality wines, for instance those classified as reserve or vintage.

Terrantez – This has now all but disappeared, though its name can still be found on very old bottles of Madeira.

Bastardo – Widely planted on the Portuguese mainland, this variety is also occasionally found in Madeira.

Given the vertiginous nature of the vineyards, it is not surprising that all the grapes are hand-picked. They are then taken to the wineries for processing, all of which are situated in the main town on the island, Funchal.

Vinification
Perhaps rather artificially, the traditional varietal descriptions have also been tied to the sweetness of the final wine, giving the following sugar contents:

Sercial	8–25 g/l
Verdelho	25–40 g/l
Bual	40–60 g/l
Malmsey	60–120 g/l

There is a great deal of individuality in the vinification of Madeira. Generally speaking, however, the two sweeter varieties, Bual and Malmsey, are fermented on their skins, whilst the others are not. Fermentation can take place either in cask, or in oak or concrete vats.

For the sweeter wines, the fermentation is stopped by the addition of spirit, as with Port, whilst, for the drier styles, the alcohol is added after fermentation has finished as happens with Sherry. In either case, the grape spirit used is the same as that used in the making of Port and is distributed locally by the Instituto do Vinho da Madeira.

Estufagem

The most individual part of the making of Madeiras, though, is the *estufagem*, or baking process, said to replicate the effects upon the wines of the voyages across the equator they used to make in the holds of trading ships in the 17th century. In this process, the wines spend a period of time under heat. For the finest wines, this might mean that they are stocked in cask for several years in those rooms in the lodges that are exposed to the sun; for the lesser qualities, they might spend the time in rooms centrally heated by steam (these are the actual *estufas*), or even in vats or tanks with hot water pipes in them. When the heating is artificial, the temperature might be anything between 40 and 50 °C. Even so, the wines will be required to spend the minimum three months in *estufagem*. The better the wine, though, the lower the temperature and the longer the process.

The effect of *estufagem* is, first, to caramelise the sugars in the wine. Secondly, it promotes a thorough oxidation in the wine: it is for this reason that another tasting term sometimes used instead of oxidation is "maderized." The overall results are not only the unique "burnt tang" of the wine on the palate, but also its virtual indestructibility. This is aided, not only by the high alcohol content, but also the acidity, which in all Madeiras, irrespective of style, is very high.

Ageing

Madeira may continue to be matured following *estufagem*. Individual casks may be aged and then blended, or the wine may be put through a *solera* system as used for Sherry. There are a number of statements relating to age that may be put on the label: they concern the age of the wine after the *estufagem* process is finished. The categories are:

Reserve – More than 5 years old

Special Reserve – More than 10 years old

Extra Reserve – More than 15 years old

Solera plus date – The date must be that of the original establishment of the *solera*, which must be at least five years old. It is important to distinguish between the date of a *solera* and that of a vintage.

Vintage – A wine so described must come entirely from the year stated, must be made entirely from one of the four noble varieties, and must have spent at least 20 years in cask and two in bottle before sale. This makes Vintage Madeira one of the very few wines which come of age too late to give to a godchild on his or her 21st birthday.

Any statement relating to quality, such as Finest, Choice or Extra Quality, cannot be used if the wine is not at least three years old.

OTHER PORT TYPE WINES

Portugal

One further Portuguese liqueur wine of note is Setúbal DOC. The vineyards lie across the mouth of the Tagus from Lisbon. Seventy per cent of the blend is Moscatel, and the wines are fortified in the same way as Port, with spirit being added to stop fermentation. Unusually, the skins are left with the wine for several months to extract the maximum Muscat taste. The wines are often aged for several years in cask before being sold.

Spain

Málaga is one of the classic liqueur wines of Spain, though its importance is now much less than it used to be. In 1769, at Christie's first sale dedicated to wine, Málaga was one of the wines to be offered and, in Victorian times, it was widely appreciated and known as "Mountain Wine".

There are four regions of production within the Province of Málaga, on the Mediterranean coast, though for the wine to have the appellation it has to be aged within the boundaries of the city of Málaga itself.

Two grape varieties are planted, Pedro Xímenez, known locally as the Pedro Ximen, and Moscatel. Whilst a few dry wines are made, the majority are very sweet, the grapes having been left out on mats after picking to concentrate the sugars.

The fermentation is stopped by the addition of alcohol, when the must has the required sugar level. The wines are commonly aged in a *solera* system.

The finest quality is called Lagrima, or "tear", because the juice comes from the weight of the grapes themselves, not from pressing. Next come wines named after the grape variety and then others described as *Dulce* (sweet) or *Seco* (dry).

France

Vins Doux Naturels (VDN) literally means "natural sweet wines", but is applied generically to a number of fortified sweet wines produced in the southern half of France often from the Muscat or Grenache grapes. They are all fortified before the sugar has completely fermented. In French this term is called *mutage* and the process is said to have been discovered as early as the 13th century by one Arnau de Vilanova. *Vins de Liqueur* (VdL) are wines made in a similar way but with much less stringent specifications as to grape variety, yield and minimum sugar content at harvest. All VDNs have AC status, most VdL do not.

Key wines:
VDN
Muscat de Beaumes de Venise AC
Muscat de Rivesaltes AC
Muscat de Frontignan AC
Banyuls AC
Banyuls Rancio AC
Rasteau AC
VdL
Pineau des Charentes AC

Banyuls is produced on very steep hillsides overlooking the Mediterranean, close to the Spanish frontier. Grenache is the main grape and yields are very low. For Banyuls, skins may be allowed to continue to macerate after *mutage*, to extract the maximum colour and tannin from a variety naturally low in both. The wine is aged either in demijohns or in oak casks. A Grand Cru wine must have been aged in wood for at least thirty months. If the containers are left outside in the sun, unsealed whenever possible, a slightly sour, strongly oxidised character develops. Banyuls made in this way qualifies for the additional description *rancio*. Maury is a much smaller appellation in the north of Roussillon, producing similar wines to Banyuls.

Rivesaltes is the largest VDN appellation, with vineyards split between Roussillon and Corbières. Four grapes are permitted: Grenache, Maccabéo, Malvoisie and Muscat, so the wine can be any colour from deep red to golden. Wine made solely from Muscat, labelled Muscat de Rivesaltes, is common, and may also be produced in Banyuls and Maury.

A number of other Muscat-based VDNs are produced in the Hérault *département*. Only the quality Muscat à Petits Grains may be used. The wines, varying in colour from golden to almost rosé, are fully sweet, and have a dried fruit flavour reminiscent of sultanas. They are: Muscat de Frontignan, Muscat de Mireval, Muscat de Lunel and Muscat de St Jean de Minervois.

In the Rhône Valley, two VDNs are produced, Rasteau from the Grenache grape, and the more common Muscat de Beaumes-de-Venise, again only from the Muscat à Petits Grains.

The most notable of the *Vins de Liqueur* is Pineau des Charentes AC, which is produced solely in the Cognac region from the same grape varieties used for Cognac, or the black grapes of nearby Bordeaux, Merlot and the two Cabernets. It is produced by adding young Cognac to grape juice that has not started fermenting. The result is most agreeable, with a sweetish attack and a clean, dry finish. It may be either red or white and is occasionally sold aged, or *vieux*.

A similar product made in the Armagnac region is known as Floc de Gascogne which also has AC status.

Other Countries

Historically, many of the world's best known wines were fortified and sweet; some have very long histories, and are still produced today, though in smaller quantities than once they were. Commanderia, the Cypriot wine from raisined grapes is one (see Chapter 14); Constantia, a Muscat-based wine from South Africa, is another. The latter had completely died out by the early years of this century, but is currently undergoing a limited revival.

Indeed, many of the New World countries we now know as producers of light wines began their wine histories with the production of Port-style wines. Whilst those that are still produced are little exported, one group of wines is establishing itself as a more modern classic: the lusciously sweet and highly concentrated Liqueur Muscats produced in Australia, in the north of the state of Victoria.

CHAPTER 19

SPIRITS AND LIQUEURS

Spirits are drinks which have been produced by concentrating the alcohol present in a fermented liquid by distillation. They are normally sold at between 37 and 43% vol., compared with around 12% vol. for most wines, and even less for most beers.

Distillation was used as early as 3500 BC in the manufacture of perfumes in Mesopotamia, but it was not until about 1100 AD that wine was first distilled to make spirit. The result was considered to have magical properties and was called *aqua vitae*, the water of life. In Gaelic, this translated to *uisge beatha*, or whisky as we know it today; in French to *eau-de-vie*.

THE PRINCIPLE OF DISTILLATION

The concentration of the alcohol is achieved by separating the various components or fractions that make up the fermented liquid, called the alcoholic wash. This separation is possible because each of the fractions that go to make up that liquid boil, turning to vapour, at different temperatures. It is possible, therefore, to heat the liquid to a particular temperature, collect the vapours, and turn them back to liquid by condensing them.

As far as spirits for human consumption are concerned, the relevant factor is that ethanol, or potable alcohol, boils at 78.5 °C and water at 100 °C. If the alcoholic base product is heated to around 78.5 °C the alcohol is boiled off leaving the other constituents, mostly water, behind. The broader the range of vapours that are condensed, the more flavour the spirit will have.

The Stills

There are two basic types of still, the pot still and the continuous still. A pot still looks like a large kettle made of copper and is heated by direct heat. The vapours collect in the head and are led off through a narrow tube at the top, called the swan's neck, from where they go to the condenser, a copper coil cooled by running water, to be liquefied. Such a still is not very heat-effective, but it gives spirits with plenty of character. Pot still distillation is a batch process, and the spirit will go through at least two distillations.

The most commonly used continuous still is the patent still, sometimes called a Coffey still, after Aeneas Coffey its inventor. This consists of two vertical columns, called the analyzer and the rectifier. Steam enters the bottom of the analyzer, rises and meets the wash, which has been heated in the rectifier, descending the column. The alcohol in the wash is

COFFEY STILL

Analyzer   Rectifier

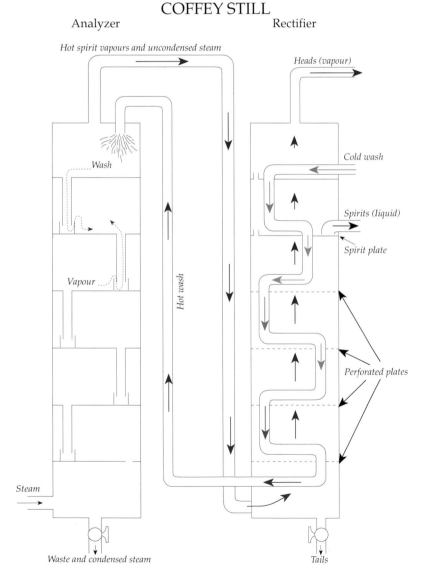

vaporised and is passed to the bottom of the rectifier. As the hot vapour rises it is cooled by the pipe carrying the cold wash and will condense. The distillation is a continuous process, with the various vapours being condensed and drawn off from the still at different alcoholic strengths, depending on where the spirit plate is positioned. The distillate has a high degree of purity and a high alcoholic content, so the continuous still spirit will only go through a single distillation. This tends to give a more neutral spirit than the pot still.

In all cases where a potable spirit is being made the distillate is separated into three: the heads, the most volatile compounds; the heart, or potable fraction; and the tails. The first and last of these will not be used in the final spirit as they contain toxic compounds.

All spirit when it comes off the still is colourless; any colour in the final drink is a result of the ageing process, or added colour.

Raw Materials
Any fermented raw material can be used as a base material for spirit, be it fruit, grain or other vegetable. Where sugar is present in the raw material, as in fruit or molasses, the fermentation can be started directly. With grain spirits, the initial fermentation may only take place after the starch that is naturally present has been converted into sugar. Some spirits can only be made from one particular material, brandy must be made from grapes, for example. Others, such as vodka, can be made from a range of raw materials, grain in western Europe, sugar-cane in the West Indies, and traditionally potatoes in eastern Europe.

The spirit produced from wine made from grapes is generically known as brandy and is produced widely in the world. The two most prestigious brandies are made in France, Cognac and Armagnac, both of which have AC status. Spirit can also be distilled from the *marc* or pomace or from the lees of wine.

Some spirits, such as gin, are flavoured, others both flavoured and sweetened, in which case they are called liqueurs. This chapter will look at some of the major spirits and their sources.

COGNAC

The Cognac region lies in the two *départements* of Charente and Charente-Maritime, just north of, and contiguous to, the vineyards of Bordeaux. Because of the proximity of the vineyards to the sea-ports, the wines of the Cognac region found keen customers in England and the Low Countries. Their lightness, however, made them poor travellers and they found a more ready market if they were distilled. The first mention of *eau de vie* in the region, dates back to 1549, though distillation did not

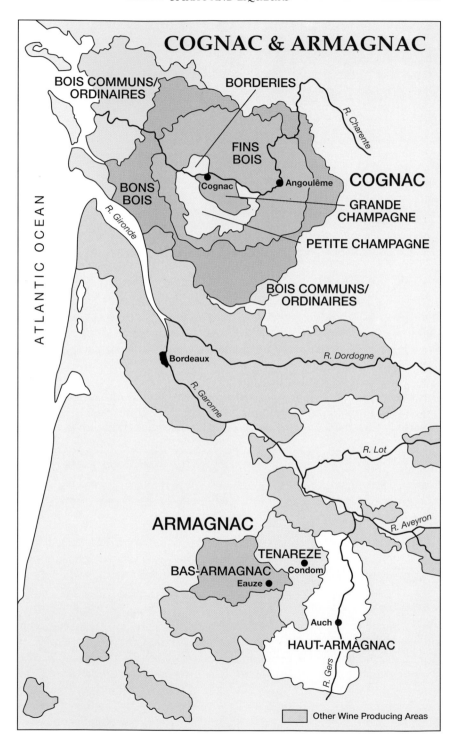

COGNAC & ARMAGNAC

BOIS COMMUNS/
ORDINAIRES

BORDERIES

FINS
BOIS

BONS
BOIS

Cognac

Angoulême

COGNAC

GRANDE
CHAMPAGNE

PETITE CHAMPAGNE

BOIS COMMUNS/
ORDINAIRES

ATLANTIC OCEAN

R. Gironde

R. Charente

Bordeaux

R. Dordogne

R. Garonne

R. Lot

ARMAGNAC

R. Aveyron

TENAREZE

BAS-ARMAGNAC

Condom

Eauze

Auch

HAUT-ARMAGNAC

R. Gers

Other Wine Producing Areas

become commonplace until the following century. It was during the 18th century that many foreign merchants came to the region to establish the companies that we know today. The Martells came from Jersey, the Hennessys and Hardys from Ireland, the Hines from Dorset and the Otards from Scotland.

Viticulture and Vinification

Cognac is the third largest vineyard area in France and the vines are cultivated by a number of small growers who sell their produce to the distilling firms. The ideal wine for distillation should be high in acidity, so the dominant grapes grown in the area tend to produce wines that, by themselves, would not be agreeable to drink. They are also low in alcohol, between 8 and 10% vol. Chaptalisation is not permitted for wines destined to be distilled. There are eight varieties permitted, but the three most important are Ugni Blanc, Folle Blanche (historically the most important) and Colombard. When phylloxera destroyed the Cognac vineyards, between 1872 and 1890, the Folle Blanche was found not to graft well so now Ugni Blanc, known locally as Saint Emilion, is considered the most suitable and accounts for over 90% of the total planting.

Districts and Soil

The region is divided into six districts:

Grande Champagne	Fins Bois
Petite Champagne	Bons Bois
Borderies	Bois Ordinaires/Bois Communs

The term Champagne here has nothing to do with the Champagne region but they both have the name for the same reason, namely the nature of the soil, which is high in chalk. The chalkier the soil, the more suitable the wine for brandy production. The two Champagne districts and Borderies lie around the town of Cognac and it is these three which produce the best spirits. The Fins Bois is the largest of the regions accounting for just over 40% of the production. The Bois Ordinaires are of minimal importance, with the vineyards mainly being on the sandy soil of the Atlantic coast.

Sometimes the area appears on the labels, in which case the Cognac will have been produced entirely from wine from that area. The term Fine Champagne is used for a blend from the two best areas, the Grande and Petite Champagnes, with Grande Champagne accounting for at least half of the blend.

The traditional Cognac pot still in use with the heart of the spirits being collected in the cask. Unusually, this still does not include a chauffe-vin.

Distillation

The distillation season in Cognac runs from the November following the vintage to the end of March of the following year. Cognac is a double distilled spirit, and the only still used is the copper Charentais pot still.

The still has a capacity of 30 hl, but is only filled to 25 hl to allow for expansion when boiling. The wine is heated to 80 °C by direct heat. Now, this is normally gas, though solid fuel used to be used. The vapours collect in the top of the still (the *chapeau)* and then pass through the Swan's Neck (*Col du Cygne*), by pipe through a vessel where it part warms the next batch of wine due for distillation (the *chauffe-vin*), into the condenser. The result of this first distillation, the *brouillis*, has a strength of between 26 and 30% vol. and will be about a third the volume of the original wine.

For the second distillation the *brouillis* from three first distillations are put together and redistilled to produce a spirit of up to 72% vol. On this occasion, the first vapours to come off, the heads, and the last, the tails, are removed. These have alcoholic strengths of about 80% and 60% respectively, and contain toxic substances such as methanol and fusel oils so cannot form part of the potable spirit. However, they still contain useable ethanol so are collected and returned to the still with the next batch of *brouillis* to be redistilled. The style and quality of the spirit are affected by the original wine, the shape of the still, in particular the head or *chapeau*, and the proportion of heart collected, as well as the subsequent maturation.

COGNAC POT STILL

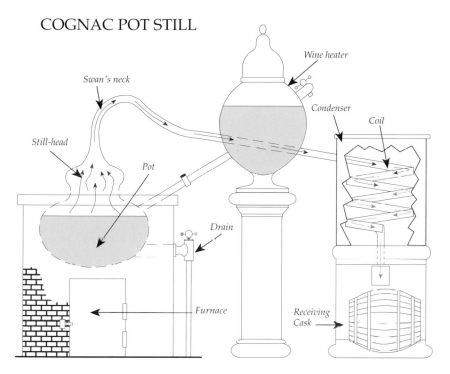

Maturation

The heart of the spirit is then aged for a minimum of two years, usually much longer, in casks made from either Tronçais or Limousin oak. During the ageing period the strength of the spirit will reduce naturally, often to about 60%vol. It will also mellow and soften, and take on colour and flavour from the wood. What evaporates is known as *la part des anges* (the angels' share) and leads to a black fungus growth on the buildings which gives them a smoked look.

During ageing the individual Cognacs are regularly blended together so as to achieve the continuity that is needed for the big brands. Prior to shipping a final blending to the house style will be carried out and the spirit will be broken down to 40% vol. with distilled water. The colour can be adjusted at this stage by the addition of a small amount of caramel.

The authorities guarantee the age of a Cognac only for the first six years of its life and the following definitions are backed by that guarantee, though in practice spirits labelled as such will generally be much older:

*** or VS	2 years old
VSOP	4 years old
XO	6 years old.

Within the Cognac industry there is system of certificates of age, known as *comptes* and each parcel of spirit must have the relevant documentation. The certificates are based on the length of time that the spirit has spent in oak. When the spirit comes off the still it is classified as *compte 00*, a classification it holds until the distilling season ends on 31st March in the year following the vintage. During the first full year in oak it is *compte 0*, changing on the 31st March when it becomes *compte 1*. At the end of the second year it becomes *compte 2*, third year *compte 3*, etc. Thus, *compte 6* Cognac can describe itself as XO.

Because the cellars in Cognac are often quite warm, the spirits often develop rapidly. For this reason Cognac is sometimes shipped to Britain when young and aged here in cold, damp cellars. Over the years this produces a much smoother spirit, known as early-landed Cognac. The label should state the date of shipment and of bottling, for it is the ageing in cask that is important.

At present vintage Cognac is forbidden in France, but again it may be shipped young in cask to Britain for ageing under Government supervision. In such circumstances, as long as it is the distillation of a single year, it may bear a vintage date.

ARMAGNAC

The second great AC grape spirit of France is Armagnac. This also is produced in the south-west of France, but to the south-east of Bordeaux, to the west of the river Gers. Being further inland the climate is less maritime than in Cognac, with warmer summers.

Armagnac claims a longer history than Cognac, probably first having been produced by Moors in the 12th Century. It remained, however, very much a locally consumed product until the middle of the last century, mainly because of the difficulty of distribution from an inland region.

Districts and Soil

This is an area of mixed agriculture, with vines providing only a small part of the local economy. The vineyards are split into three areas. The finest is the Bas Armagnac in the west of the region. Here there is a rich topsoil, known as *boulbène*, covering sand and clay subsoil. The wines from here, which are low in alcohol and high in acidity, give the best spirit and this is often bottled and sold under single domain names – and with a vintage. The area of Ténarèze has a mixture of *boulbène* and chalk, giving wines that make full-flavoured brandies. The final area, the Haut-Armagnac has chalky soil, but, in contrast to the Cognac region, this gives the poorest wines for distillation. Ironically, this is because the wines here are of better quality and can be sold as wine, rather than being distilled.

Grape Varieties

The grape varieties used are Ugni Blanc, Picpoule (Folle Blanche) Colombard, Blanquette and Baco Blanc 22A, a hybrid known locally as the Piquepouls de Pays. Baco 22A, which is a crossing of a *V. vinifera* and the American Noah, was introduced after the devastation caused by phylloxera as it is a direct producer, that is it does not need to be grafted on to American rootstock. This is the only hybrid permitted in the AC structure in France, though further plantings are forbidden.

Distillation

Distillation is on a more artisanal scale than in Cognac, and is generally carried out in the single-distillation Armagnac still, an early continuous still. In operation it is similar to the patent still, with the wine being heated by the steam in the condensing tube and then entering the top of a second column where it meets hot air rising from the furnace. The alcohol vaporises and passes into the condenser to be liquefied. Heads and tails are removed during the single distillation, heads coming off as

ARMAGNAC STILL

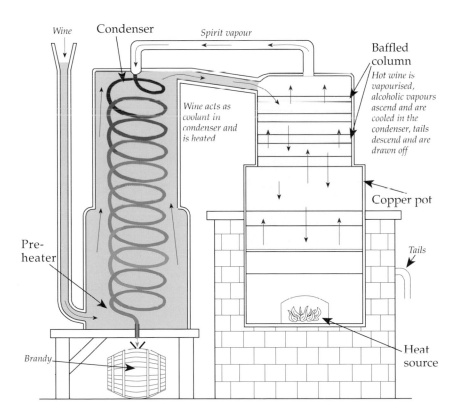

Wine
Condenser
Spirit vapour

Baffled column
Hot wine is vapourised, alcoholic vapours ascend and are cooled in the condenser, tails descend and are drawn off

Wine acts as coolant in condenser and is heated

Copper pot

Pre-heater

Tails

Brandy

Heat source

Armagnac is distilled in both pot stills as in Cognac and, as here, in the traditional Armagnac still, a continuous still consisting of two copper columns.

vapour, the tails as liquid residue. The spirit comes off the still at a lower strength than in a pot still (about 60% vol.) and has a higher proportion of flavouring congeners left in. Since 1972 the Cognac pot still has also been permitted, though this gives a less-pungent, stronger spirit.

Maturation

The other big factor in the style of Armagnac is the wood used for the casks. For the most part this is the locally sappy, "black" Monlezun oak, from forests in the Bas Armagnac, though Tronçais is now also permitted. As with Cognac, much of the colour of the final spirit comes from the oak although final adjustment with caramel is permitted to ensure a consistent product.

Armagnac has been described as a more rustic spirit than Cognac. Because of the nature of its distillation and the casks in which it is aged, it tends to be much more soft and round, particularly with age, and has a fuller flavour both on the nose and palate. The finest Cognac will always have an "edge" on the palate, but the higher qualities of Armagnac will seem more mellow.

Armagnac matures quite quickly and has lower age requirements than those for Cognac. They are:

***	1 year old
VSOP	4 years old
XO	5 years old.

Vintages are permitted in Armagnac, with the date of bottling being mentioned on the label.

OTHER GRAPE SPIRITS

France

French Grape Brandy is produced in a small number of government controlled distilleries situated around the country. The raw material does not always come from France and it is distilled in a patent still. Although it will often be labelled with terms similar to those used on Cognac or

Armagnac such as VSOP or Napoleon, these have little legal significance when applied to these non-AC products.

Marc, the residue of skins and stalks from the wine press, is distilled in a number of regions, particularly Champagne and Burgundy to produce *eau-de-vie-de-marc*. Similar spirits are produced in most wine-producing countries. *"Fine"* is the term used for high quality brandies distilled from wine within areas other than Cognac and Armagnac, often including wine lees. *Fine de la Marne* is the product obtained by distilling the lees-rich wine removed from Champagne bottles at the time of *dégorgement*.

Spain
There are two regions with DO controlled brandy production, Jerez and Penedés. The base wines come often from La Mancha. The control is over the distillation and ageing. In Jerez, the ageing is on the *solera* system. The expression *Gran Reserva* guarantees that the youngest spirit in the blend is three years old, though in practice it is more likely to be 10–15 years old.

Italy
Italy produces a great deal of brandy, often from the Trebbiano (Ugni Blanc) grape. It is generally lighter in style than Cognac and Armagnac, having been distilled at a higher strength using the patent still. Very little is seen on the UK market.

More famous is grappa, the local spirit made from *marc*. It is often drunk unaged. Small scale artisanal production is currently very fashionable in Italy.

South America
Pisco is widely produced. It is the pot still distillation of locally produced wine. Peru is reputed to produce the best, and this from the Quebranta grape. The world's biggest selling brandy brand, Presidente, is produced in Mexico.

CALVADOS
This is the best known of the world's apple spirits (generically described as applejack in North America). It comes from Normandy and Brittany in northern France, and forms part of the AC system. In all, there are eleven different regional Calvados appellations, but the best comes from the Vallée d'Auge, just east of Caen. This has the AC Calvados du Pays d'Auge and has to be distilled twice in copper pot stills and aged for at least two years. The lesser *eau-de-vie de Cidre de Normandie* can be made in patent stills and thus lacks the same flavour.

FRUIT EAU-DE-VIE

These are the result of the distillation of fermented fruit, which is then aged, generally in glass carboys. As a result they take on no colour and are usually served very cold to accentuate the pure fruit flavour.

Such spirits are made widely in Europe, with many examples, including Slivovitz from Bosnia, coming from the eastern countries. The finest are considered to come from Alsace and the Vosges Mountains in France, the Black Forest in Germany and the northern part of Switzerland. In Germany, the pure distilled spirit is described as *Wasser*, and *Geist* if some of the relevant fruit has then been macerated in it to give it extra flavour.

Amongst the most popular fruit are cherries (*eau-de-vie de kirsch*), pears (*Poire Williams*) raspberries (*eau-de-vie de framboise/Himbeergeist*), blue plums (*eau-de-vie de quetsch/Zwetschgen*) and yellow plums (*eau-de-vie de mirabelle*).

SCOTCH WHISKY

An essential stage in the production of any spirit is the fermentation of the raw material to form an alcoholic wash that can be distilled. For fruit spirits this is a simple process as fruit contains sugar. For grain spirits the starch in the grain must be converted into sugar before fermentation can take place.

By far the most important of the grain spirits is whisk(e)y, which was probably first distilled by monks in Ireland as early as the 15th century. There is one distillery, believed to be the oldest still operating, in Co. Antrim which received its grant in 1608. Even up until Victorian times, Irish whiskey was much more popular than Scotch.

The main difference between Scotch and other whiskies is that whilst the majority of whiskies are the product of a single distillery, since the middle of the last century, Scotch whisky has generally been the result of blending the product of a number of distilleries together. In addition, there are two distinct types of whisky used in that blend; malt whiskies, the result of a pot still distillation using malted barley as the raw material, and grain whisky, from patent stills using mainly maize. The former provides the flavour, and may account for less than half of the blend, with the latter being the "filling out". Each of these types is also available unblended.

Malt Whisky

Malt whisky is the original Scotch whisky, produced from barley and distilled in a pot still. The first stage of its production is the conversion of the starch in the barley to sugar. This is, in effect, a controlled germination. The barley grains are seeds which would, under the right

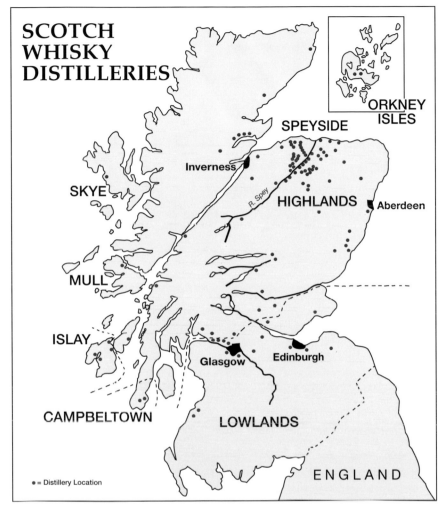

SCOTCH WHISKY DISTILLERIES

ORKNEY ISLES

SPEYSIDE

Inverness

SKYE

R. Spey

HIGHLANDS   Aberdeen

MULL

ISLAY

Glasgow   Edinburgh

CAMPBELTOWN   LOWLANDS

ENGLAND

● = Distillery Location

conditions, grow into new plants. The grain is first soaked in regularly changed water for forty-eight hours in the "steeps". This releases the enzymes, which convert the stored energy in the form of starch into sugar, which the seed needs in order to grow. The damp barley is then spread out on a malting floor and turned regularly, or put into rotating, temperature-controlled saladin boxes. Here germination starts and the barley becomes "*green-malt*". Once the conversion is started, but before leaves and roots are formed, the growth is arrested in peat-fired kilns. The heat of the kiln dries the grains and stops germination while the peat smoke, or "*reek*" adds an extra flavour to the barley, now called malt.

The malt is then ground in a mill to form *grist*, and mixed with hot water in a large vat with rotating paddles known as a mash-tun to complete the conversion and extract the sugar. The resultant sweet liquid is known as *wort*. This is drawn off into large fermenting vats, generally made of varnished pine, called wash-backs. It is here that the raw material for distillation, an ale-like liquid called the *"wash"*, is produced.

Distillation

All Scotch malt whisky is produced using the pot still, usually in a double distillation, but occasionally a distiller will distil three times. Two separate stills are used. The first, the wash-still, converts the *wash*, at about 12%, to *low-wines* (around 30% vol.). The *low-wines* are collected and redistilled in the smaller spirit still which produces raw whisky, known as *British Plain Spirits*, at about 70% vol. This is the middle part of the distillate; the heads, called *foreshots*, and tails,

A mash-tun in operation in the Glenfiddich distillery on Speyside. The grist and water are stirred mechanically to extract the sugar.

called *feints*, having been removed. As in Cognac these contain ethanol as well as toxic substances and so are added to the next batch of low-wines and redistilled.

Where the spirit leaves the second still, it passes through the spirit safe, under the control of the Customs & Excise. From this moment it remains under their control until it is exported, or duty is paid. The distiller therefore has to decide which portion must be rejected as foreshots or feints by experience and by controls, rather than by smell and, possibly, taste as in Cognac.

Scotch whisky stills are generally much larger than their equivalents in Cognac. These are the tops of the smaller spirit stills.

There are a number of factors which affect the style of the individual malt whisky. These include the barley (in particular the malting), the yeast, the water, the design and height of the head of the spirit-still and the maturation.

Maturation

The distillate cannot be described as Scotch whisky until it has been aged in oak cask for at least three years. Traditionally, the finest casks for the maturation of Scotch whisky have been freshly emptied sherry butts, but, as all bottling of Sherry now takes place in the region of production, they are no longer as cheap or as readily available as in the past. Bourbon barrels are also widely used, particularly for grain whisky.

Districts
There are four main types of malt whisky, dependent on the location of the distillery. They are:

1. *Highland* – The majority of the Scotch whisky distilleries are classed as Highland and are situated north of a line from Greenock to Dundee. They produce the most delicately flavoured malts. Within this group, the finest area is Speyside, with some of the best distilleries adding Glenlivet to their name. More individual are the malt whiskies from the islands, particularly those from Orkney.

2. *Islay* – The distilleries on this island off the west coast produce the most fully flavoured and most peaty malts, often with hints of iodine and tar. This reputedly comes from the local peat created from marine vegetable matter that is used in malting.

3. *Campbeltown* – Probably home to the first distilleries in Scotland but now only two distilleries remain. Traditionally smoky in style.

4. *Lowland* – South of the Greenock/Dundee line, they are the lightest of the malts, largely used in blends.

Grain Whisky
This is made in a patent rather than a pot still. The raw material used is mainly maize which is ground to form a flour and then cooked under steam pressure to release the starch. A small amount of malted barley added and the enzymes in the barley convert the starch to sugar. The wort produced from this is of a lower strength than for malt whiskies. Grain whisky is distilled to a high degree of purity. The resultant spirit is generally less-flavoured than from a pot still, and matures more rapidly.

Whisky Blends and Styles
Key styles:
Standard blend
Deluxe blend
Single malt
Vatted malt

Both malt and grain whiskies are available as "single" whiskies, that is, the product of one distillery only. Most whisky, however, is sold as blended whisky, a mixture of grain whisky with any number of different malt whiskies. Standard blends rarely state an age on the label.

Deluxe blended whisky
As with a standard blended whisky this is blend of both malt and grain whiskies, but with a higher percentage of more expensive, older malts. Deluxe blends are often sold as twelve year old whiskies, or even older.

Single malt
The product of one distillery, often aged for a considerable time before release. This whisky will be a blend of different casks and ages in order to maintain consistency, but all the whiskies will be from the same distillery. Each malt has its own distinctive flavour and style.

Vatted malt
A blend of the whiskies from a number of different malt whisky distilleries only. Own-label malts are usually vatted.

Single grain
The product of a grain distillery only. Very light in style and far more neutral than a malt.

If a Scotch whisky declares an age on the label this must refer to the youngest whisky in the blend.

Other Whiskeys
Traditionally, all Scotch whisky is spelt without an "e", and other countries include it, thus Irish whiskey, not whisky. Some Canadian whiskies are exceptions to this.

Irish Whiskey is traditionally pot stilled three times from a mixture of malted and unmalted barley, oats and wheat. Peat is not used in the malting and the heads and tails are removed on both second and third distillations, resulting in a very smooth, mellow spirit. There has recently been a considerable integration in the distilling of Irish whiskies, with most of the production being in one complex in County Cork.

Bourbon Whiskey takes its name from Bourbon County in Kentucky, where it was first produced, though it may now be distilled anywhere in the United States. By law it must be distilled at not more than 80% vol. from a mash containing not less than 51% maize and then stored in new charred oak containers, for a period of not less than two years. The charring of the barrels imparts a smoky character to the spirit. For the most part it is produced in patent stills, though there are some pot stills.

Rye Whiskey in the United States must be made with a mash of not less than 51% rye. This gives a whiskey with more body and one that needs longer ageing, even though it is generally distilled in a patent still. In Canada, there is no restriction as to the proportion of grains in the mash.

Whiskey is distilled in a number of other countries around the world, notably Japan, which has the world's largest malt distillery. So far these are of little importance to the UK retail market, but reduce the size of the export market for Scotch. Malt whisky from Scotland, however, is often exported in bulk for blending with local spirits to make Dutch, Japanese, Panamanian whisky etc.

OTHER UNFLAVOURED SPIRITS

Vodka

Vodka is a neutral spirit that originates from the Baltic countries. It can be distilled from a variety of raw materials including grain (often rye), molasses and potatoes, but for western markets it is almost invariably high-strength, neutral grain spirit. This is charcoal-filtered to remove any hint of colour, broken-down with distilled water and a little glycerine to give it body, and bottled. It is mainly consumed as an alcoholic vehicle for whatever it is mixed with. In Russia and Poland, however, vodkas flavoured with herbs and spices are popular.

Rum

Rum is one of the most widely distilled spirits in the world, for it is produced wherever the sugar-cane grows. As far as European consumption is concerned, this means the islands of the West Indies and Guyana, though there are other major centres of production in South America, South Africa, India, the Indian Ocean islands and Australia.

It can be made either from the fermented juice of the sugar-cane, or from fermented molasses, the residue left after sugar has been refined. If molasses is used, water is added to dissolve the remaining sugar to facilitate fermentation.

Both pot and patent stills are used; as a result there is a wide variety in the flavour of rums ranging from the neutral white rums of Puerto Rico and Cuba, to the full-bodied Wedderburn rums of Jamaica. The colour in dark navy rum comes from added caramel, that in lighter, golden rums either from caramel or from the casks used during maturation. With rum there is no minimum legal ageing requirement.

Tequila

This spirit is distilled from the sap of a variety of the *agave*, a cactus like plant which grows in five provinces in Mexico. Tequila itself is a town in that area. It can be sold oak-aged or non-aged and is generally used outside Mexico as a cocktail ingredient.

FLAVOURED SPIRITS

Gin

Gin differs from the previous spirits that we have dealt with in that it is a flavoured spirit. This means that a base neutral spirit, grain from the American market, or grain or molasses for Europe, is taken and then redistilled, in what is known as a carterhead pot still, with a number of flavouring agents known as botanicals.

The most important of these is juniper, *genever* in Dutch, from which the name gin is derived. Coriander is another regular ingredient, but each distillery will have its own ingredients including orris root, angelica, orange and lemon peel. An alternative method of making gin is by cold compounding, the blending together of the base spirit and a specially concentrated distillate of botanicals. No ageing is required, after distillation the spirit is broken-down to selling strength with distilled water and bottled.

Schnapps

This is the national drink of many north European countries. It might be distilled from grain or potatoes and is then flavoured with caraway or aniseed. Akvavit is the Scandinavian form of the drink.

LIQUEURS

A liqueur is a spirit that has been both sweetened and flavoured. Their origins are largely medicinal. In the Middle Ages the monastic orders were the centres of both learning and healing. Most monasteries had their own herb-garden in which they would grow what was needed for their specialist remedies, which were often in the form of infusions. It was possible to dry many of these herbs, but it was discovered that their merits were better preserved if they were steeped in alcohol. The treatment would then be readily available throughout the year.

Like many medicines, they were scarcely palatable and their wider appreciation did not come about until their flavour was improved by the addition of sugar. This first arrived in Europe at the time of the Crusaders, but remained a luxury product until the end of the 16th century, by which time it was widely grown in the West Indies. Even today, many of the finest liqueurs maintain their monastic origins (e.g. Chartreuse) or are produced in ports where the sugar and other exotic ingredients arrived (Bordeaux, Amsterdam).

Most liqueurs are intended for use in cocktails and will be based on neutral spirit. Those liqueurs that are more traditional, or are intended to be drunk neat, are usually based on specific spirits, for example Grand Marnier has a Cognac base, Drambuie a whisky base and sloe gin, gin.

The best liqueurs are simply made by infusing the flavouring ingredient or ingredients in the spirit and adding sugar. Cheaper liqueurs are made by simply mixing flavouring essences with the spirit and sugar, often with colouring added too.

It is important to distinguish between a liqueur such as cherry brandy and the distilled fruit spirit equivalent, kirsch. The former is sweeter, usually has a lower alcohol content, will probably be coloured, and is cheaper than the latter.

There are also some branded liqueurs that are simply a representative of a generic liqueur. A good example of this is Cointreau, just one triple-sec curaçao amongst many.

Cream has recently become an ingredient in a number of liqueurs as it is a good vehicle for softening the harshness of spirits whilst accentuating the flavour of the other ingredients.

There are four categories of flavourings into which liqueurs may be divided:

Fruit
Blackcurrant: Crème de Cassis
Sloe: Crème de Prunelle, Sloe Gin
Apricot: Apricot Brandy
Cherry: Cherry Brandy, Cherry Heering, Guignolet, Maraschino
Orange: Curaçao, Cointreau, Grand Marnier, Van der Hum, Mandarine Napoleon
Peach: Southern Comfort

Herb
Multi-herb: Galliano, Benedictine, Chartreuse, Drambuie, Glayva, Strega, Izarra
Seed: Aniseed: Anise/anisette, Genepi, Ouzo, Pastis

Mint: Crème de Menthe

Bean, kernel
Coffee: Tia Maria, Kahlua
Chocolate: Crème de Cacao
Nuts: Amaretto, Malibu, Frangelico

Dairy
Egg: Advocaat
Cream: Bailey's Irish Cream

Various other cream based liqueurs have been produced, often as new versions of existing liqueurs.

CHAPTER 20

PROFESSIONAL RESPONSIBILITY

Globally, the drinks business is changing. It is becoming more sophisticated, both in terms of the application of technology and in the way its products are marketed. It is becoming more international, not only in the popularisation of certain grape varieties, but also in the freer exchange of information and techniques between grape growers, winemakers and academics world-wide. It is also under pressure, principally from the anti-alcohol lobby.

The available evidence on the effects of alcohol is conflicting. Nobody would seek to deny that consumption to excess, whether in the short or in the long term, is at best a drain on a nation's health resources and at worst, when innocent third parties become involved, abhorrent. Recent medical evidence, however, also suggests that moderate consumption of alcohol can have a beneficial effect upon an individual's health and well-being. Public opinion, though, would seem to be increasingly less tolerant of those who over-indulge, and there are more instances of government controls over the promotion and sale of alcoholic beverages being tightened than relaxed.

The drinks industry world-wide is well aware, not only of what it understandably sees as a threat, but also of its responsibilities. In the UK, for instance, industry-sponsored organisations such as the Portman group are actively promoting the moderate, responsible approach to drinking through their publications and education programmes.

It is essential, though, that all those who work within the industry are aware of the controls that exist, and of their responsibility to abide by them. As far as the sale and promotion of alcoholic drinks in the United Kingdom is concerned, Higher Certificate students should be aware of the following points concerning drinks advertising and the Law regarding Licensing.

Advertising
The European Community defines advertising as the communication of an idea from one person to another; this might include circulars,

shelf-talkers or even sales-talk. There is always a narrow line to be drawn as to what is, and what is not permitted. Codes of practice drawn up between the Advertising Standards Authority and the drinks and advertising industries give four key areas that any drinks advertisement should avoid:

1. It should not be aimed at young people or imply that drinking is a particularly adult or macho habit.

2. It should not imply that drinking could in any way make one more attractive, or improve performance in any direction.

Imply is the operative word; a successful complaint could be brought to the Advertising Standards Authority if an advert was shown to imply one of the above, even if it did not explicitly state either.

3. It should not encourage excess either in the individual or a group, or promote the concept of buying large rounds.

4. There should be no association between drinking and driving. It is permitted to make the association between drinking non-alcoholic or alcohol-free drinks and driving or operating machinery, but it is safest not to make such an association in the case of low-alcohol.

Licensing
The availability of alcoholic beverages by retail is controlled by the Licensing laws. These have quite a wide scope, including the suitability of premises and licensees, as well as the extent of opening hours, the types of alcoholic beverage that may be served and whether or not they may be consumed on the licensee's premises.

Particularly important for anyone responsible for the service of alcoholic drinks, though, are the following four specific prohibitions under Licensing law:

1. The sale of alcohol to anyone under the age of 18. An exception is that someone between 16 and 18, seated at a table or counter in a room set apart for the consumption of food, may purchase cider, perry or beer for consumption with a meal.

2. Permitting anyone under 18 to consume alcohol in a bar, knowingly or unknowingly.

3. The sale of alcohol to a drunken person.

4. Allowing drunkenness, quarrelsome, riotous or violent conduct on licensed premises.

No person under fourteen may enter a bar during opening hours, unless they are passing from one part of the building to another and there is no suitable alternative route or the premises has been granted a Children's Certificate. A bar is defined as a place exclusively or mainly used for the sale and consumption of intoxicating liquor. Restaurants are, therefore, not necessarily classed as bars so families may use them. Restaurateurs, however, should be careful to check the precise terms of the licence as certain parts of the premises may be classified as a bar.

Perhaps the last word on the subject of alcohol and society should go to Professor George Saintsbury, whose "Notes on a Cellar Book" was first published in 1920. Whilst his book is essentially a commentary on the wines he himself purchased and enjoyed, in an oft-quoted passage, he has this to say in his introduction:

". . . there is the unbroken testimony of all history that alcoholic liquors have been used by the strongest, wisest, handsomest, and in every way best races of all times. . ."

GLOSSARY

Abbreviations: F=French; G=German; I=Italian; P=Portuguese;
S=Spanish.

acetic acid	(CH_3COOH) The acid component of vinegar. The product of oxidation of ethanol by the action of acetobacter in the presence of oxygen. A volatile acid, (q.v.), present in small quantities in all wines, excessive amounts result in a vinegary nose and taste.
aerobic	Requiring oxygen to operate.
alcohol	Potable alcohol as contained in alcoholic drinks is ethanol, sometimes called ethyl alcohol, C_2H_5OH. **Actual Alcohol** is the amount of ethanol present in a wine, spirit, etc., measured as a percentage of the total volume at 20 °C and shown on the label. **Potential Alcohol** is amount of alcohol which would be produced by a complete fermentation of any residual sugar present. **Total Alcohol** is the sum of the actual and potential alcohols.
anaerobic	Able to operate without oxygen
analyzer	That part of a Coffey or patent still in which the alcohol present in the pre-heated wash (q.v.) is vaporized by steam.
anreicherung (G)	Must-enrichment (q.v.).
ascorbic acid	Vitamin C. Used in winemaking along with sulphur dioxide to prevent oxidation.
aspersion	Method of protection from spring frosts whereby the vines are sprayed with water which freezes, coating the buds with ice. The buds are not damaged because of the latent heat of the ice.

assemblage(F)	Blending of a number of different parcels of wine, especially in Champagne and Bordeaux.
barrique	Cask (q.v.) with a capacity of 225 litres. Traditional to Bordeaux but now used extensively in other regions throughout the world.
Baumé	French scale used in measurement of must-weight (q.v.).
bentonite	Clay like material used in fining (q.v.).
blackrot	Fungal disease of the vine prevalent in warm, wet weather, which causes black stains on the leaves.
blue fining	Removal of iron or copper casse (q.v.) from a wine by the addition of potassium ferrocyanide.
bonne chauffe (F)	Literally the "good heating". The second distillation used in Cognac to convert brouillis (q.v.) to *eau-de-vie*.
Bordeaux mixture	Solution of copper sulphate and calcium hydroxide (lime) in water, used to spray vines as protection from fungal diseases.
botanicals	Flavourings used in gin production.
botrytis cinerea	Fungus which attacks the grape berry. In certain circumstances it will form unwanted grey rot, in others, desirable noble rot. (See Chapter 3).
botte (I)	Traditional large barrels used in Italy of various sizes up to 160 hl (Plural botti).
brouillis (F)	The result of the first distillation in Cognac.
bush training	Training of vines as free-standing plants, not requiring the support of a trellis (q.v.).
butt	Traditional barrel used in Sherry production with a capacity of 600 litres, usually filled only to about 500 litres.
cane	Partially lignified one-year-old wood on a vine, pruned to between eight and fifteen buds. If pruned to two or three buds it is referred to as a spur (q.v.).

cane pruning	System of vine pruning in which one or more long canes of one-year-old wood, each with between eight and fifteen buds, remain to produce new shoots.
cap	Floating mass of grape skins, stalks, etc. on the surface of red must when fermenting.
carbonic maceration	Fermentation of whole bunches of black grapes with the berries initially intact. The intercellular fermentation results in well-coloured, fruity red wines with little tannin.
cask	Wooden barrel, usually made of oak, used for fermentation, maturation and storage of wines. Traditional sizes and names vary from region to region.
casse	Unwanted haze in wine caused by instability.
chaptalisation	Must-enrichment (q.v.) specifically using beet or cane sugar. The name derives from M. Chaptal, the French Agriculture minister who first wrote about the process.
charmat method	Sparkling wine production process in which the secondary fermentation producing the sparkle takes place in a sealed tank. Also called tank method or cuve close.
clonal selection	Selection of plants from a particular variety for specific, desirable features, (which may include early ripening, good fruit, high (or low) yields, disease resistance
clone	One of a population of plants that are the descendants of a single individual and have been propagated by vegetative means. Unlike descendants by sexual propagation, each clone will have features identical to the parent plant.
compte (F)	Age classification system used in Cognac, starting with compte 00 for freshly distilled spirit.

congeners	Organic compounds giving flavouring and aroma in alcoholic beverages. Products of the fermentation, distillation and maturation processes, they include such compounds as ketones, esters and aldehydes.
cordon	Horizontal extension of a vine trunk.
courbe de fermentation (F)	Record of temperature and density of a particular vat of must/wine during fermentation, plotted as a graph, used by the winemaker to monitor the wine's progress.
crossing	Breeding of new vine varieties by cross-pollination of two different varieties of the same species (q.v.). For wine production, this is usually two varieties of *V. vinifera*.
cuvée (F)	1. The juice resulting from the first pressing in Champagne, representing 75 litres from each 160 kilograms of grapes.
	2. A blend.
dégorgement (F)	Removal of the sediment from the bottle in traditional method sparkling wine production.
degree-day	A method of classifying climatic zones based on the sum of the average daily temperatures less 10 °C (the temperature at which the vine starts to grow) during the growing season.
density of planting	The number of vine plants per area of land, usually expressed as vines per hectare and will vary from 3,000 vines to 10,000 or more per hectare. Low plant density has the advantage of lower establishment costs but higher density will generally give higher quality wines, given a fixed yield per hectare. Factors such as mechanisation will affect the choice of plant density.
dosage (F)	Adjustment of the sugar level in Champagne by the addition of *liqueur d'expedition* (q.v.) after *dégorgement* (q.v.) to create the various styles available.

downy mildew	Fungus appearing as downy patches on the vine leaves, reducing photosynthesis. Also called peronospera.
eau-de-vie (F)	Spirit, literally "water of life".
estufagem (P)	"Cooking" process used in Madeira production to caramelise the sugars in the wines.
ethanol	See alcohol.
feints	The tails (q.v.) fraction of the second distillation of Scotch Whisky.
fermentation	The conversion, by the action of yeast enzymes, of sugar to alcohol.
fining	Removal of matter in suspension in a wine by the addition of a fining agent such as bentonite (q.v.) which acts as a coagulant.
fixed acidity	The acidity in wine detectable only on the palate [cf. volatile acidity (q.v.)], composed of tartaric, malic and lactic acids.
flor	Yeast which forms on the surface of fino and manzanilla Sherries giving them a distinctive taste and protecting them from oxidation.
foreshots	The heads (q.v.) fraction of the second distillation of Scotch Whisky.
fusel oils	Toxic by-products of distillation containing long chain hydro-carbons, removed as part of the tails (q.v.).
governo (I)	Vinification technique occasionally used in the production of Chianti in which a small quantity of semi-dried grapes, or concentrated must, is added to the wine after fermentation to induce a slight secondary fermentation, increasing the glycerine content of the wine.
graft	The union of a small piece of one plant, including a bud, [the scion (q.v.)] on to a supporting rootstock (q.v.). In viticulture the most important use is the grafting of a *V. vinifera* scion on to a rootstock having some American parentage, and therefore tolerant of *Phylloxera vastatrix*.

green-malt	Grains of barley which have been soaked and have started to germinate, converting the stored starch into sugar. When dried in a kiln, green-malt becomes malt (q.v.).
grey rot	Malevolent form of *Botrytis cinerea* (q.v.), affecting unripe berries or black grapes, causing off-flavours and lack of colour.
gyropalette	Hydraulically operated, computer controlled racks for mechanical *remuage* (q.v.)
heads	The first fraction to be vaporized during distillation; containing, in addition to ethanol, volatile and toxic compounds such as methanol.
hybrid	A vine variety resulting from the cross-pollination of two vines of different species, usually one *V. vinifera* and one of American origins to breed-in tolerance of phylloxera. Also called interspecific crossing.
irrigation	The supply of water to the vine by means of artificial canals, overhead sprays, or drip-irrigation systems on individual vines. Irrigation is forbidden in European Community countries except for young, unproductive vines and experimental vineyards, but is used widely in other countries.
lagar (P & S)	Stone trough used for treading grapes. Superseded in most regions by more modern methods but still in use in the Douro.
lees	The sediment of dead yeast cells which collects at the bottom of any fermentation vessel once fermentation is complete.
liqueur de tirage (F)	Mixture of wine, sugar and yeast added to still wine to promote a secondary fermentation in sparkling wine production.
liqueur d'expédition (F)	Final adjustment of the sweetness of sparkling wine prior to corking. Also called dosage.

low-wines	The water-white liquid with an alcoholic content of around 30% vol. that results from the first distillation in Scotch Whisky. cf. *brouillis* (q.v.).
maceration	Period of time when the skins are in contact with the fermenting must during red wine vinification.
malo-lactic fermentation	Conversion of harsh malic acid into softer lactic acid by the action of lactic bacteria.
malt	Barley which has undergone the malting process of soaking, germination and kilning to convert the starch present in the original grain into fermentable sugar.
marc (F)	1. The residue of skins, pips and stalks left in a press after the extraction of juice or wine, sometimes distilled to produce *eau-de-vie de marc*.
	2. The name give to one charge of a traditional press, especially in Champagne.
must	Unfermented grape juice destined to become wine.
must enrichment	The addition of sugar or rectified concentrated must to grape juice prior to fermentation to increase the final alcoholic content of the wine. Strict controls govern its use (see also Chaptalisation).
must-weight	Density, or specific gravity, of grape juice prior to fermentation. Measurement of the must-weight enables the winemaker to estimate the final alcoholic content of the wine.
noble rot	Benevolent form of *Botrytis cinerea* (q.v.) which concentrates the sugars of ripe grapes facilitating the production of the finest sweet wines.
Oechsle	German scale for measuring must-weight (q.v.).
photosynthesis	The conversion of carbon dioxide and water to usable organic compounds, especially carbohydrates, by plants; using light energy absorbed by the green chlorophyll in their leaves.

Phylloxera vastatrix The most important insect pest of the vine. It feeds on the roots of the vine and, in the case of the European *V. vinifera*, will kill it. There is no known way of eradicating the louse but its effect can be stopped by grafting the *V. vinifera* scion (q.v.) on to American rootstock.

pipe (P) Traditional cask (q.v.) used in the Douro for Port production. There are two sizes recognized, the production, or Douro, pipe of 550 l and the shipping pipe of 534 l.

powdery mildew Fungus which attacks the vine, initially appearing as floury white dust on the leaves and grapes, eventually causing the berries to split open. Also called *Oidium tuckerii*.

pruning Removal of unwanted parts of the vine, mostly wood that is one-year-old or less, in order to regulate the yield and control the vine's shape. The main pruning, usually carried out by hand, is during the vine's dormant period in the winter.

pupitre Rack consisting of two hinged boards through which holes have been bored to hold the necks of sparkling wine bottles during *remuage* (q.v.).

racking Drawing off clear wine from a cask or vat and moving it to another, leaving any sediment behind.

rectifier The second column of a Coffey or patent still, in which the alcohol rich vapour from the analyzer (q.v.) is condensed to form spirit whilst heating the cold wash. Heads and tails are removed here.

refractometer Hand-held instrument consisting of a prism and a series of lenses used for gauging the must-weight (q.v.) of grape juice to assess their ripeness.

remuage (F) "Riddling." Moving the sediment to the neck of the bottle prior to *dégorgement* (q.v.) in traditional method of sparkling wine production.

residual sugar	Unfermented sugar remaining in the wine after bottling. Even dry wines will contain a very small amount.
rootstock	Phylloxera resistant or tolerant vine with some American parentage on to which a *V. vinifera* scion (q.v.) is grafted.
scion	Section of *V. vinifera* vine grafted on to American rootstock (q.v.).
solera	System of fractional blending used in the production of Sherry and some Madeira wherein older wine is refreshed by the addition of younger wine.
spur	A short cane (q.v.) of one-year-old wood with two or three buds.
sulphur dioxide (SO$_2$)	Highly reactive and pungent gas which is used in winemaking as an anti-oxidant and antiseptic. May be added to wines and musts as gas, in the form of metabisulphite (solid) or produced in an empty cask by burning a sulphur candle (additive E 220).
süssreserve (G)	Unfermented, sterile grape must added to dry wine prior to bottling to increase sweetness and balance excess acidity. Not to be confused with must enrichment (q.v.).
systemic fungicides	Chemicals used to combat fungal diseases of the vine by being absorbed into its tissues rather than remaining on the surface.
taille (F)	The juice resulting from the second pressing of grapes in Champagne, yielding 25 litres from each 100 kilograms of grapes.
tails	The third fraction collected during distillation, containing ethanol and a number of less volatile compounds, many of which are toxic.
tannin	Chemical compound present in the skins of grapes which is extracted during red wine vinification. Tannin is a preservative in red wine, giving a drying sensation on the gums when present.

tartaric acid	The acid responsible for most of a wine's acidity. Detectable only on the palate. May be added to wines lacking acidity in warm vineyard regions.
trellis	Any man-made system of support for the vine, usually consisting of posts and wires.
vin de rebèche (F)	Any juice remaining in the grapes after the extraction of the tailles (q.v.) in Champagne. It must be distilled and cannot be made into wine.
vine/grape variety	One of a number of recognisable members of a particular vine species. They may result from natural mutation or deliberate crossing (q.v.).
vine species	Any of the members of the genus *Vitis*. Most wine is made from the European species, *Vitis vinifera*, but using American rootstocks from the species *V. rupestris* or *V. riparia*.
vinification	Winemaking.
viticulture	Grape growing.
volatile acidity	Acetic acid in a wine. A small amount exists in all wines and is an important part of the aroma or bouquet, excessive amounts indicate a faulty wine.
wash	Any alcoholic liquid resulting from fermentation which is destined to be distilled.
wort	The sweet liquid resulting from the extraction of sugar from malt which is fermented to form wash (q.v.) in whisky production.
yeast autolysis	Breakdown of dead yeast cells after the secondary fermentation in sparkling wine production, giving the wines a yeasty or biscuity nose.
yeast	Generic term for a number of single-celled micro-organisms which produce zymase, the enzyme responsible for converting sugar to alcohol. The most important wine yeast is *Saccharomyces cerevisiae*.

BIBLIOGRAPHY

Adams, L. D., *Wines of America* (3rd Edition, McGraw Hill, New York, 1985)

Anderson, B., *The Wine Atlas of Italy* (Mitchell Beazley, London, 1990)

Anderson, B., *The Wines of Italy* (Mitchell Beazley, London, 1992)

Anderson, B., *Wines of Italy* (ICE, London, 1992)

Arlott, J. and Fielden, C., *Burgundy, Vines and Wines* (Davis-Poynter, London, 1976)

Barrier, C. *et al.*, *Wines and Vineyards of France* (English Edition, Ebury Press, London, 1990)

Baxevanis, J., *The Wine Regions of America* (Vinifore Winegrowers Journal, Strasbourg, 1992)

Belfrage, N., *Life Beyond Lambrusco* (Sidgwick & Jackson, London, 1985)

Bonal, F., *Champagne* (Editions du Grand Pont, Lausanne, 1984)

Broadbent, M., *Wine Tasting* (Mitchell Beazley, London, 1992)

Burroughs, D. and Bezzant, N., *Wine Regions of the World* (2nd Edition, Butterworth Heinemann, London, 1992)

Cirana, J., *los Vinos Catalanes* (General de Catalunya, Barcelona, 1980)

Chancrin, E. and Long, J., *Viticulture Moderne* (Hatchette, Paris, 1966)

Clavel, J. and Baillaud, R., *Histoire et Avenir des Vins en Languedoc* (Privat, Toulouse, 1985)

Croft-Cooke, R., *Madeira* (Putnam, London, 1961)

da Fonseca, A. *et al.*, *Port Wine* (Instituto do Vinho do Porto, Porto, 1981)

Duijker, H., *The Loire, Alsace and Champagne* (Mitchell Beazley, London, 1983)

Duijker, H., *The Wines of Rioja* (Mitchell Beazley, London, 1987)

Duijker, H., *The Wine Atlas of Spain* (Mitchell Beazley, London, 1992)

Evans, L., *Australia and New Zealand, the Complete Book of Wine* (Hamlyn, Sydney, 1973)

Faith, N., *The Wine Masters* (Hamish Hamilton, London, 1978)

Faith, N., *Cognac and Other Brandies* (Mitchell Beazley, London, 1987)

Féret, C., *Bordeaux et Ses Vins* (13th Edition, Féret, Bordeaux, 1982)

Fridjhon, M., *The Penguin Book of South African Wine* (Penguin, London, 1992)

Galet, P., *Precis d'Ampelographie Pratique* (4th Edition, Paul Déhan, Montpellier, 1976)

Garner, M. and Merritt P., *Barolo* (Century, London, 1990)

George, R., *Chablis* (Sotheby's, London, 1984)

George, R., *French Country Wines* (Faber, London, 1990)

George, R., *Chianti* (Sotheby's, London, 1990)

González Gordon, M. K.B.E., *Sherry* (Cassell, London, 1972)

Fielden, C., *White Burgundy* (Christopher Helm, London, 1988)

Fisher, M., *Liqueurs* (Maurice Meyer, London, 1951)

Forbes, P., *Champagne* (Gollancz, London, 1977)

Haliday, J., *The Australian Wine Compendium* (Angus & Robertson, North Ryde, 1985)

Haliday, J. and Johnson, H., *Art and Science of Wine* (Mitchell Beazley, London, 1992)

Hanson, A., *Burgundy* (Faber, London, 1982)

Hardy, T., *Pictorial Atlas of Australian Wines* (Published by the author, undated)

Hidalgo, L. (ed.), *La Viticultura Americana y sus Raices* (Ministerio de Agricultra, Madrid, 1992)

Howkins, B., *Rich, Rare and Red* (Heinemann, London, 1982)

Jackson, M., *The World Guide to Whisky* (Dorling Kindersley, London, 1987)

Jamieson, I., *German Wines* (Faber, London, 1991)

Jeffs, J., *Sherry* (3rd Edition, Faber, London, 1982)

Johnson, H., *World Wine Atlas* (3rd Edition, Mitchell Beazley, London, 1985)

Johnson, H., *The Story of Wine* (Mitchell Beazley, London, 1989)

Johnson, H., *The Wine Companion* (3rd Edition, Mitchell Beazley, London, 1991)

Jung, H. (ed), *German Wine Academy Notes* (GWA, Mainz, 1992)

Katona, J., *A Guide to Hungarian Wine* (Corvina, Budapest, 1987)

Leglise, M., *Principes de Vinification* (C.I.V.B., Beaune, 1974)

Lichine, A., *Encyclopedia of Wines and Spirits* (6th Edition, Cassell, London, 1985)

Livingstone-Learmonth, J. and Master, M., *The Wines of the Rhône* (Faber, London, 1983)

MacDonough, G., *Wine and Food of Austria* (Mitchell Beazley, London, 1992)

Mayson, R., *Portugal's Wines and Wine Makers* (Ebury Press, London, 1992)

Metcalfe, C. and McWhirter, K., *Wines of Spain and Portugal* (Salamander, London, 1988)

Ordish, G., *The Great Wine Blight* (Sidgwick & Jackson, London, 1972)

Parker, R., *Bordeaux* (Dorling Kindersley, London, 1987)

Parker, R., *The Wines of the Rhône Valley and Provence* (Dorling Kindersley, London, 1987)

Pearkes, G., *Vinegrowing in Britain* (J.M. Dent, London, 1982)

Peñin, J., *Vinos y Bodegas de España* (Peñin y Reeder SA, Madrid, 1990)

Penning-Rowsell, E., *The Wines of Bordeaux* (5th Edition, Penguin, 1985)

Peppercorn, D., *Bordeaux* (Faber, London, 1982)

Peynaud, E., *Knowing and Making Wine*, translated Spencer, A. (New York, 1981)

Philpott, D., *Wine and Food of Bulgaria* (Mitchell Beazley, London, 1989)

Pitipot, S. and Poupon, P., *Atlas des Grands Vignobles de Bourgogne* (Jacques Legrand, Paris, 1985)

Platter, J., *South African Wine Guide* (John and Erica Platter, Somerset West, 1992)

Poupon, P. and Forgeot, P., *The Wines of Burgundy*, translated by Ott, E. and M. (5th Edition, Presses Universitaires de France, Paris, 1974)

Prisnea, C., *Bacchus en Roumanie* (Méridiens Editions, Bucharest, 1962)

Quittanson, C., *Aide-memoire sur les Appellations d'Origine* (manuscript)

Ray, C., *Cognac* (Peter Davies, London, 1973)

Robertson, G., *Port* (Faber, London, 1987)

Robinson, J., *Vines, Grapes and Wines* (Mitchell Beazley, London, 1986)

Roncarati, B., *Viva Vino 200+* (Wine & Spirit Publications, London, 1971)

Spurrier, S., *French Country Wines* (Collins, London, 1984)

Spurrier, S., *Guide to French Wines* (Mitchell Beazley, London, 1991)

Stevenson, T. *Champagne* (Sotheby's, London, 1986)

Stevenson, T. *World Wine Encyclopedia* (Sotheby's, London, 1988)

Sutcliffe, S., *A Celebration of Champagne* (Mitchell Beazley, London, 1988)

Sutcliffe, S., *The Wines of Burgundy* (Mitchell Beazley, London, 1992)

Todd, W., *Port* (Jonathan Cape, London, 1927)

Vandyke-Price, P., *The Penguin Book of Spirits and Liqueurs* (Penguin, London, 1979)

Vandyke-Price, P. *Alsace* (Sotheby's, London, 1984)

Vasserot Fuentes, A., *Málaga Wines* (Grupo de Ordenacion Comercial Exterior, Málaga, 1978)

Winkler, A.J. *et al.*, *General Viticulture* (University of California Press, London, 1974)

Young, A., *Making Sense of Wine Tasting* (Greenhouse, Richmond, 1986)

The Drink Pocket Book (NTC, Henley-on-Thames, 1993)

The Times Atlas (Times Publications, London)

Vins de Pays of France (ANIVIT, Paris, 1991)

World Drink Trends (NTC, Henley-on-Thames, 1993)

Décrets et Arrêtés des Vins et Eaux-de-Vie d'Appellation d'Origine (INAO, Paris, 1991)

Periodicals:
Wine & Spirit International
Wine Magazine
Decanter
Italian Wines and Spirits
Harpers Wine & Spirit Gazette
The Grape Press

INDEX

abboccato, 185
Abouriou, 101
Abruzzi, 203
Abymes, 129
acetic acid, 359, 368
acetobacter, 31–32, 45, 359
acidification, 5, **34**, 65, 168, 305
Aconcagua, 272–273
actual alcohol, 35, 41, 163, 239, 359
Adelaide Hills, 256–257
Adriatic, 187, 230
advertising, 355–356
Advertising Standards Authority, 356
Aegean, 230
aerated sparkling wine, 69
aerobic, 31, 45, 359
age (of wines and spirits), 39, **42**, 52, 55,
   56, 200, 209, 213, 225, 239, 326, 331–332,
   341–342, 344, 349–350
Agiorgitiko, 249
Aglianico del Vulture, 205
Agoston Haraszthy, 266
Ahr, 170
Airén, 217, 219
akvavit, 352
Albana di Romagna, 184, 196–197
Albariño, 217
albariza, 301–302, 303
alberello, 189
albumen, 43
alcohol, 5, 29–32, 33, **35**, 39, 56–57, 63–64,
   66, 71, 83, 161, 163, 168–169, 186, 239, 306,
   324, 330–332, 335–337, 340, 343, 346, 351,
   355–357, **359**
alcohol free, 64, 356
Alenquer, 226
Alentejo, 226
Alexander Valley, 269
Algarve, 225
Alicante, 217
Alice Springs, 260
Aligoté, **23**, 109, 111, 116, 129, 150, 294
allier, 111, 131, 189

almacenistas, 301
Almansa, 217
Aloxe-Corton, 115–116
Alsace, 5, 10, 18, 55, **121–129**, 142,
   293–294, 346
Alsace Grand Cru, 127
Altesse, 129
altitude, **7**, 187, 199, 207, 216, 224, 243,
   249, 251, 322, 329–330
Alto Adige, 193–194
Alvarinho, 217, 223
amabile, 185, 197
amarone, 195–196
America, 4, 5, 15–16, 253, 254, **264–275**,
   276, 345, 351
amertume, 45
Amigne, 234
amontillado, 300, 306, **308–310**, 312, 313
amoroso, 310
Amtliche Prüfungsnummer, 169
anaerobic, 31, 359
analyzer, 336, 359, 366
Anbaugebiet, 161, 164, 170, 193, 297
animals, 9, 16
Añina, 302
Anjou-Saumur, 131, **135–138**
Anreicherung, 168–169
anthracnose, 18
appearance, 45, 49, **52–53**
Appellation Contrôlée, 65, 70, 77, **79**, 87,
   88, 103, 105, 127, 131–133, 232, 293
Appennines, 187, 199
Approved Viticultural Areas (AVA), 266
Apremont, 129
Aragon, 214
Aramon, 152–153
Arbanne, 284
Ardèche, 26, 131
arena, 301–303
Argentina, 15, 24, 28, 254, **274–275**
Arinto, 225
Armagnac, 101–102, 334, 337, **342–345**
aromatised wine, 62, 315

Bold page numbers indicate the main reference.